HOW TO DO
just about
ANYTHING ON THE
INTERNET

READER'S DIGEST

HOW TO
ANYTHING

DO *just about*
ON THE
INTERNET

Published by The Reader's Digest Association Limited
LONDON • NEW YORK • SYDNEY • MONTREAL

Contents

MAKING WEB SITES

How to use this book

Discover how to **make the most of the Internet**

How to do Just About Anything on the Internet will make the Internet more accessible to all. With easy-to-follow, clearly illustrated step-by-step procedures, we guide you through the basics of using the Internet, giving information of the benefits (and drawbacks) you will encounter along the way. On virtually every page, there are helpful tips on how to save time and solve problems, plus useful information to help you to get the most out of the Internet. We reveal exactly what will be shown on the screen as you use the Internet, so that you can check your progress at every stage of your journey around the Web.

Finding your way around

The book is arranged in three main sections. They do not need to be read in order, but you will probably get more out of the Internet if you read the introductions to getting on-line and using e-mail, before starting out. If you are looking for something specific, try the index on page 344.

Getting started

Here we explain how to send e-mail and guide you through the first steps of browsing the Internet. This section will address any areas of concern there might be, so that you and your family can use the Internet safely and without worry.

Explore the Web

This is your tour guide to the best Web sites on a variety of subjects from grocery shopping to organising a wedding. It shows how to use the Internet to make your life easier and more enjoyable, and how to browse to best advantage.

Making Web sites

Use this section if you want to know how to design and set up your own Web site, then enhance it by adding extra features such as sounds, videos and pictures.

Directory

Find all the sites mentioned in the book and hundreds more in this A-Z reference guide.

HOW THE PAGES WORK

Signposts, steps and other features are designed to make the book clear and easy to use.

CD-ROM
The CD-ROM supplied with this book contains a wealth of items you can use to make your own Web site, links to sites with useful software and a directory of links to all the sites mentioned in the book. You will also find all the software needed to get on-line.

Where you are
This indicates which section of the book you are reading.

The best Web sites
The names and addresses of Web sites relating to the topic in question, as well as a brief description of why they are worth visiting. Web addresses are given in **bold type** so that you can identify them easily. You will also find many snapshots of what the Web sites look like.

Additional information
Other useful information relating to the subject, such as 'case studies' explaining how people have succeeded in using the Internet to find what they want.

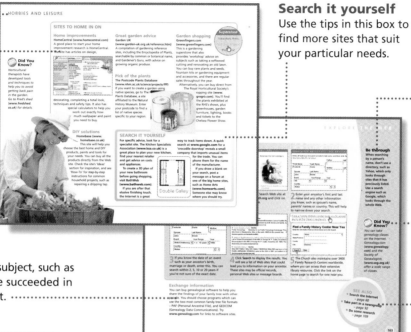

Search it yourself
Use the tips in this box to find more sites that suit your particular needs.

Extra help
Often a summary of the key information on the page, a list of DOs and DON'Ts, or important points to remember.

Hints and tips
There are seven types of tip, each clearly marked with its own icon: Did You Know?, Time Saver!, Watch Out!, Problem Solver!, Money Saver! Jargon Buster and iMac. These will help explain different aspects of Internet browsing.

See also
Other pages of the book that deal with related subjects.

What you need
This book assumes that readers are operating PCs that run Windows Millennium (Me), but users of Windows 98 will be able to use the book without problems. Users of iMacs will also be able to follow the book – the screen shots will look different, but the principles are largely the same. Significant differences are pointed out as appropriate.

The browser shown in all the screen snapshots is Internet Explorer 5 and the e-mail software is Outlook Express 5. Users of other programs will be able to follow all the principles shown.

To see whether you have all the hardware necessary for accessing the Internet, see *Are You Net Ready?*, page 14.

'How-to' step-by-steps
A brief introduction introduces each operation and provides key information.

Screen snapshots
Every step is illustrated with a snapshot or 'grab' of exactly how the screen will look as you proceed. Intermediate stages are illustrated with smaller inset images.

Clear instructions
Each step is fully explained and **bold type** is used to indicate each time you have to click on something with your mouse.

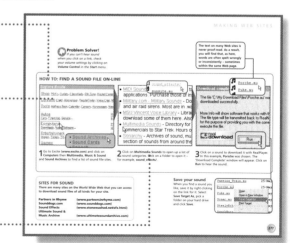

1 Getting started

Use your computer to access the Internet and send e-mail. Then discover the range of information available on the Web, and how you can find and use it.

What is the Internet?

Discover the **uses and potential of the Web**

The word 'Internet' is a contraction of the words *inter*national and *net*work. It is a vast worldwide network of powerful computer servers that are constantly connected to each other via high-speed communication cables. All the information that is on the Internet is stored on one of these servers. When you connect to the Internet, you connect to just one of these computers, but it is able to give you access to all the files stored on the other servers. Internet connection is also called going on-line or dialling up.

How it works

Imagine you had two computers in your house that were connected to each other with a cable. You could write a message on one and send it to the other over the cable. You could also use one computer to open a file on the other one. This is exactly how the Internet began way back in the late 1960s.

Today's Internet works in the same way except that there are now millions of powerful computers called servers connected together via a dedicated communication network.

As an individual computer user, you connect to one of these server computers, then use it as your gateway to the rest of the Internet.

THE USES OF THE NET

There are two main uses of the Internet – transferring electronic mail (e-mail) from computer to computer, and digital publishing on the World Wide Web (WWW or Web for short). Because the World Wide Web is the part of the Internet that you can see on your screen, people often use the terms 'Web' and 'Internet' interchangeably. But in fact the Web is only part of what the Internet has to offer.

The World Wide Web

Search   Favorites   History

This is a unique service offered by the Internet. It is a huge collection of 'pages' containing text, graphics and other media, which you can view via your computer's Web browser. Anyone with an Internet-connected computer can view Web pages – no matter where the pages originate from or where the viewer is in the world.

Web pages are also connected by 'links'. These are electronic connections between pages on the same or different Web sites, usually on similar or related subjects. This makes information on the Web more accessible.

Electronic mail

More commonly known as e-mail, electronic mail is the primary means of communicating over the Internet. E-mail can be text-only, or can include attached files – such as sounds or images. It is extremely fast, transferring information almost instantaneously (see *What is e-mail?*, page 26).

Newsgroups

Areas on the Net where people can read others' messages and leave their own, newsgroups are another useful aspect of the Internet. Many thousands of newsgroups can be found on every subject imaginable. In fact, newsgroups existed before the Web in a system called Usenet. They are a good example of a way in which the Internet unites people with shared interests (see *Take part in a newsgroup*, page 92).

THE HISTORY OF THE NET

The Internet has its origins in a US Department of Defense (DOD) project dating from the 1960s. Called ARPANET (Advanced Research Projects Agency Network), this linked various DOD computers, and was designed to protect key data from nuclear attack.

Simultaneously, the US university sector started to link remote computers together as a means of sharing research papers between distant campuses. The network grew quickly and, in the early 1970s, spread to Europe, with England and Norway coming on board first.

In the mid 1980s, the National Science Foundation linked five supercomputers to form NSnet.

Other institutions took advantage of the power these provided, and this spurred more international growth.

But the Internet as we know it was still far from formed. It wasn't until 1989 that Tim Berners-Lee, a British physicist, devised a network in which data from any source could be accessed in a simple way using the same program, on any type of computer. This laid the foundations for what we know today as the World Wide Web.

Jargon Buster!

Web page
A document that is published on the Internet and can be viewed on a computer screen (see What is a Web site, *page 246).*

Money Saver!

The Internet is growing and changing all the time. One of the newer services is Internet telephony (see Other ways to communicate, *page 88). You can use this to make international phone calls at a fraction of their usual cost.*

Did You Know?

There are many different indexing services for the Web. Called 'search engines', they index Web sites on your behalf, and can be searched by using keywords. For more on this, see Search the Internet, page 60.

Money Saver!

Sometimes goods are offered for sale on the Internet for a cheaper price than in stores. This is often because on-line stores have fewer overheads and they pass savings on to the customer.

PROS AND CONS OF THE INTERNET

The Internet has assets that set it apart from other sources of information and forms of communication. But it is by no means perfect and cannot fully replace other forms of media.

Speed

The Internet provides an amazingly quick way to access information and send messages – taking just seconds to send data around the world. On the other hand, the speed of the Internet depends on how many people are using it, and the speed of your telephone connection. The Internet can be maddeningly slow – especially when a phonecall might provide all the information you need.

Economy

Except for the connection charges incurred while you are on-line, the Internet is free. You can access information and then print it out or save it to your own computer to look at later. The Internet cannot replace books, newspapers and magazines, but it lets you access much of the same information – and much more – in a different way.

Accessibility

All this is available if you have a computer and a phoneline. Internet cafés and on-line services in public places such as libraries mean that you don't need to be at your own computer to access the Internet. However, the Internet can be impersonal, and sometimes it is easier to phone a person, rather than spend time searching on-line.

Breadth of information

The Internet contains detailed information on almost every subject you could possibly think of, and can offer specialised information that you might be unable to find elsewhere.

Quality

A lot of the information on the Web is inaccurate or out-of-date, so you need to exercise your own critical judgements and common sense when on-line. Fortunately, search engines and the Web's link-based structure make it easy for you to move from one site to another to compare and check information.

The Internet also makes it easy to publish pornography or other offensive material. However, there are steps you can take to ensure that you don't encounter any of it (see *Filter out unsavoury sites*, page 52). It is also easy to publish libellous material on-line, although courts in most countries treat on-line libel as seriously as printed libel.

Multimedia

You can download pictures, text, video, sounds, software and many other things to enhance both your computer and the time you spend on and off it.

WHO OWNS IT ALL?

No single organisation owns the Internet. Its technical infrastructure is maintained by a mix of commercial, government and academic institutions. Some of the information and services on the Internet are provided by and for commercial companies, some by clubs and organisations. Other material comes from or is used by schools, charities, and government bodies. Still more is produced by individuals – themselves also Internet users. Literally anyone can be a part of the Internet, but nobody can claim to control it.

Despite the huge revenues it generates for some companies, the Internet itself runs on a non profit-making basis. Several organisations are involved. The Internet Society (**www.isoc.org**) ratifies technical standards, and the World Wide Web Consortium (**www.w3.org**) considers the Web's future.

WHAT TO DO ON-LINE

Go shopping

You can buy things on-line that are unavailable in shops in your own country. These items can often be delivered to your door within hours. From fresh food to a car, you can buy it on the Internet (see *Do your weekly shop*, page 192).

Find information

A range of Web sites and reference sources mean that you can find out almost anything on the Internet – and usually very quickly. From academic or scientific information to news and weather, entertaining trivia, or information about your computer, the Internet can provide information updates faster than any newspaper or book.

Have a chat

Internet chatrooms make it easy for you to exchange views and information with other Internet users from all around the world, and to communicate with people you would never otherwise have been able to find (see *Use a chatroom*, page 98).

Send an e-mail

E-mail allows you to send and receive text, pictures and other media almost instantaneously around the world (see *Send and receive e-mail*, page 34).

Run a business

The Internet makes it easier than ever before to set up a business – provided you have something worth while to offer. Whether selling a product or a service, you can investigate the Internet as a possible way of generating income (see *Set up a business site*, page 298).

Follow the news

News Web sites provide as-it-happens updates. Follow a story as it evolves, rather than waiting for intermittent bulletins on TV or radio. You can also install an on-screen device to relay news updates on your computer whilst you work off-line (see *Get the latest news on-line*, page 112).

Listen to music

You can download music of all kinds from the Internet. You can also send and receive music files via e-mail. The law regarding on-line music is currently under review and you may find that in future you have to pay for previously free downloads.

Have fun

All kinds of computer games can be played on-line or downloaded to your PC. Play against an opponent on the other side of the planet, or even against a 'virtual' opponent (see *Play games on-line*, page 186).

Learn something new

It is hard to rival the Internet as an extensive reference tool (see *Search the Internet*, page 60). You can trace a family member, look up a historical event, or follow technological discoveries (see *Learn something new*, page 106).

Help others

Charity Web sites make donating money (or your time) easy and fun. Many have a 'click-to-give' feature which allows you to help a cause simply by clicking your mouse. You can also find out how to join a charity or how to help in other ways (see *Support a charity*, page 206).

Publish your point of view

In other forms of media, such as television, books and newspapers, the power to publish is in the hands of a few people. The Internet is different because anyone can have their own Web site, dealing with any subject (see *Making Web sites*, page 244). This means that the Internet is an exciting publishing and social phenomenon, but it also means that the quality of its content varies wildly.

Did You Know?

Estimates suggest there are more than 450 million Internet users around the world. At the end of 2000, over 135 million of these lived in the USA, and 27 million in Japan.

SEE ALSO
- Are you Net ready? – page 14
- What is e-mail? – page 26
- Security on the Internet – page 48
- Search the Internet – page 60

Are you Net ready?

Discover what **hardware** and **software** you need to start **surfing the Web**

Most computers bought in the past five years will be equipped to access the Internet. Certainly any home PC bought in the past two years will have sufficient memory, a modem, and all the necessary software – and it will probably all be set up for you. But there are a few checks you should make to be sure (see right).

BASIC HARDWARE

When you buy a new computer, the hardware necessary to access the Internet should all be provided.

Computer
The ability of your computer to access the Internet depends on how quick its central processing unit (CPU) is and how much memory (RAM) it has.

The CPU is your computer's brain. Every time you ask your computer to do anything, you are issuing thousands or even millions of instructions. The speed of your CPU depends on how quickly it processes these instructions. This is given as the number of 'clock ticks' in each second (every instruction can take one or more clock ticks). A 400MHz chip is capable of 400,000,000 clock ticks each second – enough to keep up with most Internet software.

Your computer's memory is the amount of space it has for storing and using software. All software, whether the Windows operating system or programs, is loaded into the computer's memory from the hard disk when you open it. Memory, like hard disk space, is measured in terms of 'bits' and 'bytes'.

A bit is the smallest unit of computer storage. A combination of eight bits makes up a byte. A kilobyte (Kb) is 1024 bytes; a megabyte (Mb) is 1024Kb; and a gigabyte (Gb) is 1024Mb. A typical home PC has up to 128Mb of memory. You only need 32Mb to use the Internet.

Modem
A modem is a device which connects your computer to the Internet. It allows digital data to be sent through telephone lines. Most computers come with the modem built in. If your computer does not have a modem you can buy an external modem and connect it yourself (see *Set up your modem*, page 18).

Modems operate at different speeds. The fastest transfer data at a rate of 56 kilobits a second (56K), but a speed of 33.6K is sufficient for accessing the Internet.

Sound card and speakers
Web sites can incorporate sounds, but you won't hear them unless you have a sound card to process the information and speakers to play it on. Most new computers are supplied with these features as standard.

If your PC plays a tune when you turn it on, then it has a sound card and speakers. If not, although you don't need separate speakers to access the Net, you may wish to contact your local supplier to get them fitted.

Monitor
A 17 inch monitor (measured diagonally across the screen) is more than good enough for browsing the Net. But the bigger your monitor, the more of each Web page you can view on-screen at a time.

THE BASIC SOFTWARE

To begin using the Internet you need two pieces of software: a Web browser and an e-mail program. Both are likely to have come pre-installed on your computer.

Web browser

This is the software your computer uses to display Web sites. Internet Explorer and Netscape Navigator are the best-known browsers. They are usually included with your computer or provided by your ISP. There are important differences between them, but Internet Explorer is by far the most widely used, so sites are more likely to display correctly through this software. For more information on using browsers, see *Start browsing*, page 22.

Internet Explorer   Outlook Express

E-mail software

You'll need an e-mail program, such as Outlook Express to send and receive mail using your computer. Again, this should be pre-installed on your computer. If it is not, you can download a free version (**www.microsoft.com/windows/oe**). For more information on using e-mail software, see *What is e-mail?*, page 26.

News reader

There are e-mail-based discussion forums on the Web, called newsgroups, that are free to join. To access them you need a news reader program. To start with, you can use Outlook Express as a news reader. For other programs, see *Software on the Web*, page 80. However, you can do without news reader software for most surfing purposes.

Check your software

To see the software on your PC, go to the **Start** menu and click **Programs**. Check the list that comes up for programs such as Outlook Express and Internet Explorer or Netscape Navigator.

INTERNET ACCOUNTS

If you have all the hardware and software that you require to access the Internet, the next step is to set up an account with an Internet Service Provider (ISP). An ISP is a company that provides you with access to the Internet. They do this by giving you a telephone number, which your modem uses to connect to a large computer owned by the ISP each time you want to go on-line. Once you are connected to this computer, you can access the rest of the Internet.

There are now many hundreds of ISPs to choose from, each offering slightly different services with different costs and payment methods. Some, for example, charge for each minute you spend on-line. Others charge a flat rate monthly fee. Your choice of ISP is one of the most important decisions to make when first accessing the Internet. To find out more information, see *Choose an ISP?*, page 16.

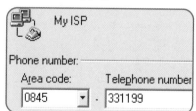

Extra software

As you become more proficient as an Internet user, you may find that you need additional software. This may include FTP software, which you can use to upload your own Web pages onto the Internet, Macromedia Flash, which allows you to view animations and RealPlayer, which allows you to listen to Internet radio and other sound files. Most additional software can be acquired for free over the Internet (see *Software on the Web*, page 80).

 **Did You Know?**

You do not have to connect to the Internet via a modem. For other connection types, such as cable, see Other ways to connect, page 84.

SEE ALSO
● **Make the connection** – *page 20*
● **Download from the Web** – *page 82*
● **Take part in a newsgroup** – *page 92*

Choose an ISP

Find out which **provider** is best for you

An Internet Service Provider (ISP) is a company which provides you with access to the Internet. With many ISPs to choose from, it is important to select the best one for you. ISPs vary in a range of respects, in order to cater for a wide variety of different needs – business, leisure or personal.

Before you choose an ISP you need to work out what your needs are, then do some research to see which ISPs meet them. It is quite usual for people to try out a few ISPs before they find the service that matches their requirements.

HOW ISPS DIFFER

There are three main ways in which ISPs differ from each other – content, which is the selection of services it offers, reliability and the amount and method of payment.

Content

Two of the most popular ISPs, AOL (**www.aol.com**) and CompuServe (**www.compuserve.co.uk**), provide exclusive benefits for their members. This is known as 'content'. AOL, for example, offers common interest sections, instant messaging, seven free e-mail addresses, and a calendar function. You can also quickly access the latest news and movie listings.

Reliability

The reliability of an ISP is also important – can you connect to the Internet first time, or is the line often busy? How quickly can you access Web pages once you are on-line? Unless you are willing to try out a number of ISPs, the only way to judge this is to read magazine or Web site reviews of the services on offer – see opposite.

Payment

Some ISPs, such as CompuServe, charge a monthly subscription fee (of about £5 to £15). Others are available for free. Free ISPs, such as Netscape, make their money by taking a percentage of the local telephone call price you pay when you're on-line. They also create revenue through advertising and by charging for technical support.

Subscription and free ISPs vary in quality but, in general, free ISPs do not offer the same level of content as subscription-based services, and have more expensive support services. However, you do save around £100 a year in subscription fees. If you don't use the Internet very much, a free ISP is probably the better option.

Some subscription ISPs offer 'unmetered' access to the Internet. This involves paying a flat monthly fee for unlimited Web access.

WORTH A LOOK

● **ISP Review (www.ispreview.co.uk)**
Advice and articles on a range of ISPs to help you make a selection.
● **Demon (www.demon.net)**
A well-known ISP with excellent support. It offers a 30-day trial, a booklet for beginners and has one of the quickest Internet connections.
● **Netscape (www.netscape.com)**
One of the best free ISPs with great installation and support.

● **Tiscali (www.tiscali.co.uk)**
Choice of services offered to suit different browsing needs. Lots of e-mail and Web space available.
● **CompuServe (www.compuserve.co.uk)**
High-quality content and well priced for a subscription service.

CHOOSING AN ISP

Questions and answers

Do you require a lot of assistance with the Internet?
Some ISPs, such as Demon, provide free technical support on 0800 phone numbers. Others charge by the minute, or use other premium-rated phone numbers for technical support.

How much time will you spend on-line?
A number of ISPs, such as AOL, offer flat-rate Internet access, with no additional phone charges. Work out roughly how many hours you expect to spend on-line a month, and how much that works out at the local phone call rate. Then see if a flat-rate provider can provide what you need for less money.

Will you use the Internet outside normal office hours?
If so, you may need technical support to be available off peak and/or at weekends.

9,700 **Internet Service Providers and Growing!**

How fast should your connection be?
Standard modem connections operate at a speed of 56Kbps. Other options, which can be faster, and which require special subscriptions, include ADSL (Asymmetrical Digital Subscriber Line) and cable from your cable TV provider. 56Kbps is fast enough for most people's needs.

How do you get help setting up an ISP on your computer?
Choose an ISP, such as CompuServe, that provides a CD which completes the set-up automatically.

How many e-mail addresses will you get?
If several family members want to share the same computer, they each might like to have their own separate e-mail addresses. Some ISPs, such as AOL, provide you with seven e-mail accounts free of charge. However, it is worth remembering that you cannot keep the same e-mail address if you change your ISP. The only way to do this is to sign up with a non-ISP e-mail address such as Hotmail (**www.hotmail.com**).

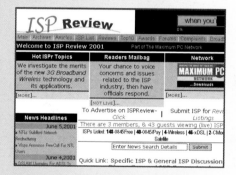

Will you want to run your own Web site?
Most ISPs will provide some free Web space for the publication of your site. Note that in some cases, you will be obliged to carry their advertising on your pages.

FURTHER RESEARCH

As well as the checklist above, there are also several other methods you can use to evaluate an ISP:

- **Computer magazines regularly research ISPs, saving you time and effort.**
- **It is well worth asking friends for recommendations, and learning from their experiences.**
- **If you are already on-line, check sites such as Internet Magazine Resource (www.internet-magazine.com/resource/isp), Net4Nowt (www.net4nowt.com) and ISP Review (www.ispreview.com) for further information.**

 Did You Know?

For a guide to all the Internet Service Providers available, go to The List (http://thelist. internet.com).

Jargon Buster!

Broadband A collective term for technologies that allow Internet connections which are faster than modems. ADSL and cable access, are both broadband types.

SEE ALSO
- **Are you Net ready?** – page 14
- **Set up your modem** – page 18
- **Other ways to connect** – page 84

Set up your modem

Your modem **links** your computer to the Internet – it needs to be set up correctly for maximum **speed** and **efficiency**

A modem is the device that connects your PC to the Internet. It translates the digital data that your computer understands into a signal that can pass through the telephone network. It also works in reverse, converting the signal received through the telephone line back to a digital format that your PC can display on screen. Most new computers come either with a modem built in, or supplied as an external device. For older machines, you may need to buy and install the modem yourself.

CHOOSE A MODEM

The most important factor in choosing a modem is its speed. The faster your modem, the faster you can download Web pages, send e-mail and surf on the Internet. The fastest standard modems currently available are rated at 56K (kilobits of electronic data transferred a second). To use the Internet you need at least a 33.6K modem.

Internal or external
Hardware modems come in two types, internal and external. Internal modems are cheaper to buy, but more fiddly to fit and move between computers than external modems. For fitting either type of modem, see opposite.

Hardware or software
Some newer PCs use software to perform all the tasks of a modem without the need for extra hardware. These 'software modems' are inexpensive and easy to upgrade.

However, they use your computer's central processor to a greater extent than hardware modems, and so can slow it down. The PC also needs to have a telephone socket.

Extra features
Many modems include extra features, such as the facility to fax directly to and from your PC, or use it as a telephone answering machine. If you're interested in any of these capabilities, ask your local computer dealer.

Modems for portable PCs
There are special modems available for portable PCs. They are called PCMCIA (Personal Computer Memory Card International Association) PC Cards. These credit-card sized devices fit in special slots on portable PCs. They are small and light, but drain battery power when used for long periods, limiting their usefulness for Internet browsing on the move.

Upgrading your modem
The process for upgrading your modem is almost identical to installing a new one. Simply remove the old device and insert or connect the new one. When you then turn your PC on, it will recognise that a new modem has been installed and ask you to insert the CD-ROM that came with it.

Alternative connections
You do not need to have a modem to connect to the Internet. In fact you can get a speedier connection by paying for services such as ADSL (Asymmetrical Digital Subscriber Line), or cable modems. These are fitted by your cable TV or telephone company and use different technologies (see *Other ways to connect*, page 84).

 Swann External Modem Installation
Contents

▶ Software Installation

FITTING & STARTING UP

If you've opted for an internal modem, install it as shown on the right. Installing an external modem is more straightforward and is explained below.

EXTERNAL MODEMS

To fit an external modem, shut down your PC and disconnect it from the mains socket. Then use the cables provided with your modem to plug it into your PC, the phone socket and the mains. When you turn your PC on again, it will see that you have attached a new device and ask you to insert the disk containing software that came with the modem. Do this, following the on-screen instructions to complete the software installation.

Instructions vary, but you should only have to agree with suggestions the software itself makes, as it will automatically identify the files you need and where they should be stored on your hard drive.

INTERNAL MODEMS

1 Turn off the mains power. Remove the hard external case of your PC (refer to your PC manual for the correct way to do this).

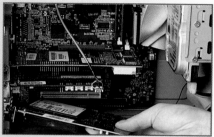

2 Locate a free slot and remove the thin metal back plate by unscrewing it. Gently push the modem into place and secure it with the supplied screw.

3 Replace the case. You need to plug the telephone cable into the modem card. Turn your PC on.

4 When the PC prompts you, insert the software installation CD into your CD-ROM drive. Follow the on-screen instructions to install the software.

Now configure your PC
Your PC needs to know how to use the new modem you have fitted.

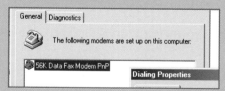

1 Go to **Settings**, select **Control Panel** and open **Modems**. Highlight your modem, then click **Dialing Properties**. Set your location, region and area code.

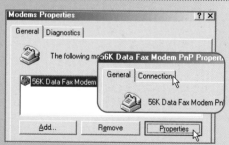

2 Click **OK** to save your settings and go back to the **Modems Properties** window. Now click on **Properties** and choose the **Connection** tab.

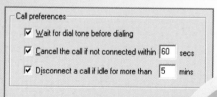

3 Under 'Call preferences', choose the options which suit you. Then click on **OK** and finally **OK** again.

Did You Know?

The speed rating of a modem is only its potential top speed. Factors such as the number of people on-line and the amount of static on your phone line can slow your modem down.

Watch Out!

Make sure you disable 'call waiting' if you use it (there is usually a button on your phone to do this). If someone calls you while you are on-line, the 'call waiting' signal will break your Web connection.

SEE ALSO
● **Choose an ISP**
– *page 16*
● **Make the connection**
– *page 20*
● **Start browsing** – *page 22*
● **Other ways to connect** – *page 84*

Make the connection

How to set up your computer to **access the Internet**

When you have chosen an Internet Service Provider, and are sure you have a modem installed (see page 18), you are ready to set up your computer to connect to the Internet for the first time. This is often referred to as 'configuring your ISP account' because it involves giving your computer the details of your ISP.

There are two ways to do this. Some ISPs provide you with a CD-ROM, which automatically sets up your computer (asking you for some personal details as it does so). Other ISPs give you information with which to set up your computer manually.

USE A CD-ROM TO SET UP AN ACCOUNT

This process will almost certainly involve going on-line so make sure your modem is connected to the phone line and then insert the

rdplus.net

Welcome to Online Signup

installation CD-ROM. You will now be presented with a set of easy on-screen instructions. All you have to do is fill in your personal details as you go. When you have finished, you can then access the Internet (see *Testing your new connection*, opposite).

Before you insert the CD-ROM, it is a good idea to gather together all the information you are likely to need. The things you need to know are:

Your modem type and connection speed

This information can usually be found on the packaging that came with the modem or on the modem itself.

The details are also stored on your computer. To find them, go to the **Start** menu and click on **Settings** and **Control Panel**. Then click on the **Modems** icon. This opens a dialogue box which shows you what type of modem you have and the speed of its connection.

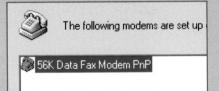

A username

As part of the installation process, your ISP will give you an e-mail address. To do this, it first asks you for a username, which will form the first part of the address. This can be your name, a nickname, a company name – whatever you like. It is worth having a couple of choices ready because many names will already have been taken by other users of your ISP.

○ laura.hesleton@rdplus.n
◉ l.hesleton@rdplus.net
○ laura.h@rdplus.net

One trick is to combine your name and house number (for example, susan34). This is unlikely to have been taken and is easy to remember.

Your User Name	l.hesleto
Your Email Address	l.hesleto

A password

Some ISPs require their users to enter a password every time they connect to the Web – to ensure that no one else can use your ISP account. A few ISPs generate a random password for you but many ask you to choose your own.

Be sure to read the ISP's guidelines on choosing a password. Some set a minimum and maximum length, or ask you not to use symbols such as '?' or '*'.

Try to think of something that only you can know and that would be hard to guess – such as your grandfather's middle name. You should also choose something easy to remember or – if you absolutely have to – write down the password and keep it somewhere safe.

SET UP YOUR INTERNET CONNECTION MANUALLY

If your ISP does not provide you with an installation CD-ROM, you will instead receive various details that you need to enter into your computer.

The essentials are the telephone number you call to connect to your ISP, and your username and password. A few ISPs may also supply two DNS addresses. DNS stands for Domain Name Server. This is the computer that translates text addresses – such as **www.yahoo.com** – into a numerical address.

DNS addresses are made up of four sets of numbers (each up to three figures long) divided by full stops, such as 192.168.52.4.

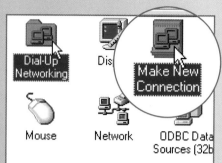

1 Go to the **Start** menu and select **Settings**. Click on **Control Panel**, then double-click on **Dial-Up Networking**. Now double-click on **Make New Connection**.

2 First give the connection a name (this can be anything but here we have entered the name of the ISP). Your modem details will already appear under 'Select a device'. Click **Next**.

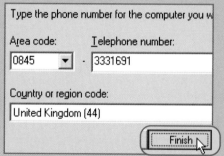

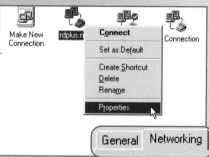

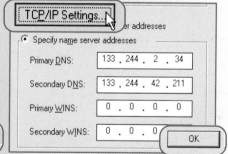

3 Now type in the area code and telephone number of your ISP and select a country or region code, then click **Next**. To save the new connection click **Finish** in the final confirmation box.

4 An icon for your new connection will appear next to 'Make New Connection'. If your ISP supplies DNS addresses, right-click this icon and choose **Properties**. Then click the **Networking** tab.

5 Now click on the **TCP/IP Settings** button. Click next to 'Specify name server addresses' and enter the two DNS numbers. Click **OK**, and then click **OK** again to complete the process.

Testing your new connection

Double-click on your browser icon. A 'Connect To' dialogue box appears asking whether you want to use your new settings. Type in your username and password and click **Connect**.

Your modem now begins to dial up to the Internet and various on-screen messages relay its progress. When the connection has been made, the messages will disappear and a Web page will appear.

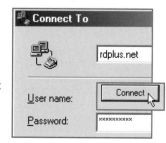

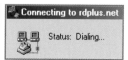

 Problem Solver!

If your modem details do not appear in Step 2, check that you have a modem installed and that it is switched on.

 Did you Know?

If you have trouble setting up your computer, you can call your ISP. They will talk you through the process. Some ISP helplines are free, others are charged at a premium rate.

SEE ALSO
● **Choose an ISP** – page 16
● **Set up your modem** – page 18
● **Start browsing** – page 22
● **Set up Outlook Express** – page 30

Start browsing

Find out how to **move around** the **Internet**

Browsing simply means exploring the World Wide Web. It is also called 'surfing' – although surfing might better be defined as 'browsing without a specific purpose'. To move around the Web you need a piece of software called a browser. A browser is your window on the Web – it is the program that displays pages on your screen and takes you from one Web site to the next. The most widely used browser is Internet Explorer, produced by Microsoft, but there are others that you may want to try.

Internet Explorer and Netscape Navigator

When choosing a browser you need to consider how you use the Web. If your primary interests lie in e-mailing, finding information and downloading files, then Netscape Navigator is easier and quicker to use. For example, Netscape's search tool gives you access to many search engines while Explorer provides only one.

However, if you want an easy way to keep track of your favourite sites or value the ability to customise your browser to suit you, then Internet Explorer is your best bet.

Internet Explorer often comes pre-installed on your computer, while Netscape Navigator can be downloaded from the Internet (**www.netscape.com**). Alternatively, check your ISP software to see which browser they provide.

Other browsers

There are other options – such as NeoPlanet (**www.neoplanet.com**), Opera (**www.opera.com**) and MSN Explorer (**http://explorer.msn.co.uk**). They are all free to use, so you can try them out at your leisure.

BROWSING COMMANDS

When you open your browser you will see icons at the top of the screen. This is the toolbar. Each icon represents a function of the browser – which will come in useful as you explore the Web.

Back returns you to the page that you visited last. Clicking on the downward arrow to the right of this will drop down a list of the last several pages you visited.

Stop prevents a page from loading up. You might want to use this if a page is taking a particularly long time to load, or if you have typed in the wrong address by mistake.

Home takes you to your homepage – generally your favourite page or the one you wish to begin on.

Favorites opens up a list of Web sites which you have stored there previously so that you can revisit them more easily.

Mail drops down a list of e-mail options: **Read Mail** opens your e-mail software. **New Message** opens a new e-mail for you to send. **Send a Link** opens a new mail containing the address of the page you're viewing (if you want to send it to someone). **Send Page** e-mails the whole page. **Read News** opens up your newsgroup software.

Address Box displays the address of the site you are viewing or loading. This is where you type the address of any site you wish to view – click **Go** when you want to go to it.

Forward takes you on to pages you visited after the one you are now viewing. This is particularly useful if you have clicked back several pages and now wish to return to where you were.

Refresh reloads the page you are currently viewing. If the page has been updated since you first loaded it (for instance, a news page), this ensures that you are viewing the most recent version.

Search splits the screen into two parts to let you search for a particular term without losing the page you are viewing.

History opens up a list of sites you've used recently on the left-hand side of the screen, so that you can look through them and return to them more quickly.

Print sends a copy of the page you are viewing to your printer.

 iMac

Internet Explorer looks different on an iMac. For example, the buttons for 'Search', 'Favorites' and 'History' all appear down the left side of the browser window. But the program still works in much the same way.

Progress Box displays how much of the page has been loaded, indicated by the amount of blue showing. Messages also pop up to the left of this area to indicate what your browser is doing.

HOW TO: START BROWSING

When you double-click on your browser icon to open the program, you are asked whether you want to connect to the Internet. Click **Connect** or **OK**. Your modem will then be activated and an Internet connection will be made.

You can then begin to browse. Here's how you can access the site of a known address. (If you don't have a Web site address, you could try searching under the subject area – see *Search the Internet*, page 60).

Say you read in a magazine about a music site called The Blues Archive (**www.bluesarchive.com**). Here's how to bring the site up on-screen, move around it and move on to other Web sites with similar themes.

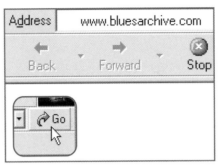

1 First, click in the Address Box and delete the text inside it. Then type in the Web address of the Blues Archive site (**www.bluesarchive.com**) and click **Go**.

2 Most Web sites consist of a number of pages. You can move between them by clicking on a 'link', which is often an underlined piece of text. Click on one to open up that part of the site.

3 As the new page opens you can see the address change in the address box. After viewing this page, click on the **Back** button to go to the previous page or click another link to continue.

4 Most Web sites also have links that take you to other Web sites. Look for a section called 'Links' and click on it. Then click on one of the links provided to move to a different site.

Watch Out!

Some parts of a Web address are case-sensitive. This means you need to type them with upper and lower case letters in the right place to access a site – www.hq.nasa.gov/ office/pao/History for example.

WEB ADDRESSES

A Web address can be any combination of letters, numbers and symbols, which refer to the location of a Web site. Your Web browser uses these details to find the Web site's 'real' address, which actually consists of a series of numbers.

Web addresses are generally kept as simple as possible so that it is easier for people to remember them. They follow the same conventions for suffixes as e-mail, which help to indicate the type of organisation behind the Web site, and its location – for example, .com, .org and .co.uk. See *Send and receive e-mail*, page 34, for a list of these.

How to stop browsing

Close your browser window. Your computer should then ask if you want to disconnect from the Internet. Click **Disconnect Now**. If your computer does not ask you, double-click on the icon with two computers on it in the bottom right-hand corner of your screen. Then click **Disconnect**.

To ensure that your computer does ask you, right-click on your browser icon and select **Properties**. Click on the **Connections** tab, then **Settings** and **Properties**. Finally click on the **Dialing** tab and click next to 'Disconnect when connection may not be needed'.

HOW TO: SET YOUR HOMEPAGE

Every time you start up your browser, it begins at the same page, which was pre-set by the browser's manufacturer. This is called your homepage. You can change this to any Web site you want, allowing you to begin browsing at a Web page that is useful for you – for example, your favourite search engine.

To select a new homepage, identify the site you want to use (see below) and type its address into your brower to open it up.

1 Go to the **Tools** menu at the top of the screen, then select **Internet Options** from the drop-down list.

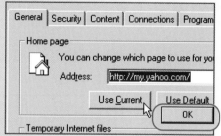

2 A new window will appear. In the 'Home page' section, click on the **Use Current** button and the address of the page you are currently viewing appears in the address box. Click **OK**.

CHOOSING A HOMEPAGE

You should first consider whether there is a site that you often go on-line specifically to see. It may be worth making this your home page to save you the bother of having to enter its address every time.

Many people choose a charity site as their homepage, where just clicking a button means that the site's corporate sponsors will make a small donation to the cause. This can be a good way to make a regular contribution. Sites such as The Hunger Site (**www.thehungersite.com**) are popular choices.

Or you might like to start browsing at a page that shows the latest news. In this case it would be best to choose a site that you can set up to show the type of news and other features that you want to see. Sites such as My Yahoo! (**http://my.yahoo.com**) allow you to customise a homepage

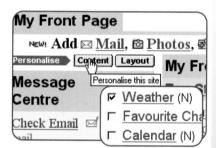

to show TV listings, weather forecasts, and headlines in subjects such as politics and sport.

Go to My Yahoo! (**http://my.yahoo. com**) and register for free with the site. Then click on **Continue to My Yahoo!**. Click on the **Content** button at the top left of the screen. The next page lists the items that you can add or remove from your page. Sections called '**Layout**' and '**Colors**' allow you to alter the appearance of the page as well. Make your choices and click **Finish**.

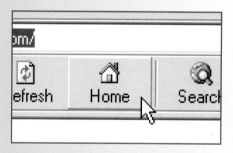

3 Now, whenever you click the **Home** button or open Internet Explorer you will be taken directly to that Web site.

Did You Know?

Watch the cursor as you move it around a Web page. If it changes into the shape of a hand, the object you are hovering over is a link, and clicking on it will take you to another Web page.

SEE ALSO
● Security on the Internet – *page 48*
● Search the Internet – *page 60*
● Solve browsing problems – *page 78*

What is e-mail?

Find out **about e-mail** and **how to use it**

Electronic mail (e-mail for short) is the system that allows you to send a message from one computer to another over the Internet. For many people e-mail is the most important aspect of the Internet. You can use it to transmit a message to any computer in a matter of seconds, for the cost of a local telephone call. You need only be connected to the Internet for as long as it takes to send and receive your messages. So the amount of time and money you spend on the phone line is kept to a minimum.

Software

To start using e-mail, you need two things: some software and an e-mail account. Your computer should come supplied with e-mail software already on it – usually a program called Outlook Express. There is more information on this and other e-mail programs overleaf.

E-mail accounts

You will get an e-mail account as part of your contract with an Internet Service Provider (ISP) – the company that gives you a connection to the Internet. They will give you an e-mail address (or let you choose one) and either set up your e-mail program or explain what details are needed so that you can do it yourself. To set up an e-mail account, see page 30.

Your e-mail address is, in effect, a mailbox kept by your ISP. When someone sends you an e-mail message, it is stored by your ISP until you connect to the Internet to check for mail.

HOW E-MAIL WORKS

The process
There are five major steps involved in sending an e-mail. Imagine that there are two friends, Bob in Liverpool, England and Emma in Sydney, Australia.

Message written and sent
In Liverpool, Bob opens up his e-mail program and – before he goes on-line – composes a message to Emma. He enters Emma's e-mail address at the top of the message and clicks the **Send** button.

Connection to the Net
Bob's e-mail program then connects to the Internet and transfers the message over the telephone line (via a modem) to the 'server' computer owned by his Internet Service Provider (ISP).

Address checked
The ISP's computer looks at the address on the message. This address shows whereabouts on the Internet one of the server computers owned by Emma's ISP is. It also specifies which of the ISP's customers the message is for. The message is then sent there.

> To: emma.bradley@revolution.co.au

Recipient connects
Emma decides to check for e-mail messages. She uses her e-mail program to connect to the Internet. The program then asks the ISP's computer if Emma has any messages.

Message received
The ISP's computer then sends the message to Emma's computer via her modem where it appears in the Inbox of her e-mail program.

> To: emma.bradley@revolution.co.au
> Cc:
> Subject: Bob's E-mail Address
> Arial ▾ 10 ▾ 🖹 B I U
> Dear Emma,

WHAT MAKES IT SO QUICK?

When you send an e-mail, your modem takes the electronic file and converts it into a form that can be sent over the telephone line. The message is also split into smaller packets of information because each part can travel more quickly over the Web via different routes than the whole message would via one route.

The parts are then reassembled at the other end before being deposited in your recipient's in-box. Each part of the message is passed from one 'router' computer to another according to an automatic routing system. Each stage of the journey is the equivalent of a telephone call that is instantly answered, understood and passed on.

This makes the whole process only marginally slower than talking to your recipient over the phone – but the difference is that you can say as much as you like in just a couple of seconds.

Where it all began
The first e-mail was sent in 1971 by Ray Tomlinson, a computer engineer, working for the company hired by the United States Defense Department in 1968 to build ARPANET (Advanced Research Projects Agency Network) – the precursor to the Internet. The message was sent between two computers placed next to each other. The program was designed to allow programmers and researchers working in different parts of the Defense Department to leave messages for each other.

Did You Know?
In the year 2000, an average of ten billion e-mails were sent every day. It is estimated that by 2005, this figure will have risen to 35 billion.

SEE ALSO
● **Different e-mail programs** – *page 28*
● **Set up Outlook Express** – *page 30*
● **Send and receive e-mail** – *page 34*

Different e-mail programs

Select **the right software** to send your messages

Most computers come with some e-mail software – probably Outlook Express – already installed. But there are many other e-mail programs on the market, such as Netscape Messenger, Eudora and Pegasus, one of which may suit your needs better. It doesn't matter which one you choose – all the programs perform the basic e-mail functions equally well and you can use any one of them alongside any browser. It is largely a matter for personal choice – perhaps based on the look of the program or a particular feature that it offers.

Outlook Express

Outlook Express is the e-mail program that is used in this book. It is made by Microsoft, the company that also devised Internet Explorer, Windows and Word. The design of Outlook Express is similar to other Microsoft products, so if you are familiar with programs such as Word and Excel, you will find it easier to use.

Because Outlook Express comes free with Internet Explorer (which is distributed with most new PCs), it is by far the most popular and widely used e-mail package. That means it's easy to find helpful tips on using the program in magazines, books and Web sites.

Outlook Express integrates seamlessly with Internet Explorer, and automatically opens when you click on e-mail links in Web sites.

If you do not have Outlook Express on your computer, you can download it from the Microsoft Web site (**www.microsoft.com**).

OTHER PROGRAMS

If you do not want to use Outlook Express, or would like to sample some alternatives, you can download and use other e-mail programs for free from the Web sites of their manufacturers.

Netscape Messenger
(www.netscape.com)
Designed to work with the popular Web browser Netscape Navigator, Netscape Messenger works with any browser. One advantage of Messenger is that as soon as you install it, you are given a free

Netscape e-mail address. You can access this address from any Internet-connected computer, so you do not need to be limited to your own machine.

Eudora
(www.eudora.com)
This program looks different because it often uses icons in place of words. Unlike some other programs, it can be set up to leave e-mail on the server, even after you have read it. That's useful if you are

accessing e-mail from a computer other than your own. Eudora also lets you view the last few links to Web pages that you received via e-mail. You can view any sites mentioned in e-mails – even if you can't recall who sent them to you.

Pegasus
(www.pmail.com)
Unlike the other programs mentioned here, Pegasus does not have a Mac version, but it has a number of excellent features, such as the option to download message headers before you download the whole message. This means you can look through the headers to choose which messages you most urgently wish to download – a useful time-saver if you are often sent large files.

Another advantage of Pegasus is that it takes up comparatively little of your computer's memory. Like some other programs, it also allows you to use multiple e-mail addresses. This is useful if, for example, several family members use the same computer to access their e-mail.

WEB-BASED E-MAIL

Providers such as MSN Hotmail, Yahoo and Excite offer free e-mail accounts that you can access from any computer worldwide with an Internet connection – particularly useful if you are on holiday.

You do have to be on-line to compose, read and send messages, which means connect time charges can mount up. Despite being stored on-line, your messages are private and secure – you are required to enter a password to view message folders.

The first part of the e-mail address can be personalised, making it easy for you and others to remember.

Providers such as Nameplanet (**www.nameplanet.com**) even let you use your name as an e-mail address. Popular addresses such as 'david@jones.net' are likely to be taken, but by adding a middle name or a number, you can still create a good personalised address.

 iMac

Eudora, Netscape Messenger and Outlook Express are all available on the Mac. Each may look different to its PC equivalent but the functions remain the same.

 Did You Know?

If you have a WAP phone, you can use it to access your e-mail messages.

SEE ALSO
● **Make the connection** – *page 20*
● **What is e-mail?** – *page 26*
● **Set up Outlook Express** – *page 30*

Set up Outlook Express

Let your **e-mail program** know your e-mail address

Before you can send and receive messages, you need to have an e-mail address. You are provided with an address when you register for an account with an Internet Service Provider during the registration process. Your e-mail program will probably be set up to use this address automatically. But if not, you will be required to enter your address and other account details yourself.

Testing your program

First check whether your e-mail program has been set up for you. To do this, go to the Start menu and select Programs and then Outlook Express. When the program has opened, click on the button marked Send/Recv. A dialogue box will appear asking if you want to connect to the Internet. Click Connect.

If your program has been set up automatically, your modem should now dial up to the Internet and check to see if there are any messages for you. Normally, there is one from your ISP, welcoming you to their service. This will appear in the Outlook Express 'Inbox'. You can click on the message icon to open it.

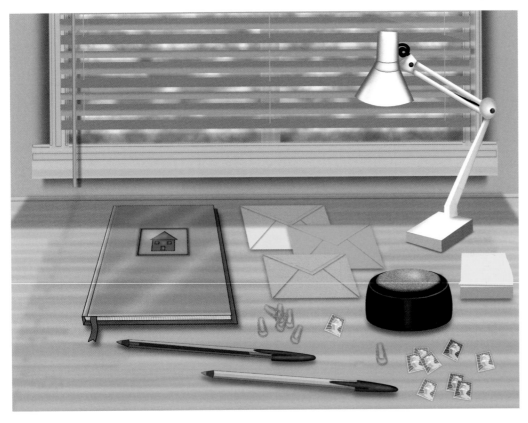

Do-it-yourself

If this process fails, you need to set up Outlook Express manually. To do this, you will need some information from your ISP, which should have been sent to you in the post. The set-up process is described opposite.

HOW TO: SET UP YOUR PROGRAM MANUALLY

The process for setting up Outlook Express is similar to the one you used to set up Internet Explorer (see *Make the connection*, page 20). In fact, Outlook Express uses the same Internet connection as your Web browser. All you need to do is to let Outlook Express know what e-mail address to check and where to check it. To do this, you need to have some information to hand – see *The information you need* below.

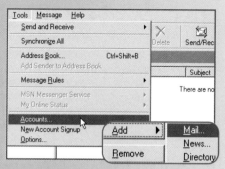

1 First go to the **Tools** menu and select **Accounts**. Then click on **Add** and then **Mail**.

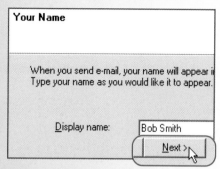

2 This opens the Internet Connection Wizard, which first asks you to give your account a name. Enter your own name, then click **Next**.

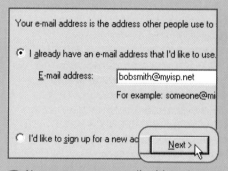

3 Now enter your e-mail address in the box under 'I already have an e-mail address that I'd like to use'. Then click **Next**.

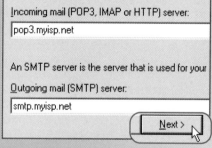

4 On the next page of the Wizard, enter the addresses for your incoming and outgoing mail servers (see below). Then click **Next**.

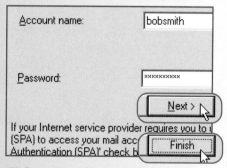

5 Enter your ISP account name and password and click **Next**. Click **Finish** to save your settings. Repeat the process shown opposite in *Testing your program* to check that your account is working.

 Jargon Buster!

Mail server *A large computer owned by an ISP which handles e-mail for the ISP's clients. An outgoing mail server handles messages sent by a client. An incoming mail server stores messages sent to the clients.*

 Did You Know?

Some people like to have more than one ISP and e-mail address (for example, to separate personal and business mail). You can use the process shown here to add new e-mail accounts, without affecting your original one.

The information you need

To set up your e-mail program manually, you need your e-mail address, an address for your 'incoming mail server', often referred to as a POP3 (Post Office Protocol) server, and another for your 'outgoing mail server' – often known as an SMTP (Simple Mail Transfer Protocol) server. These addresses should have been sent to you by your ISP. You also need your ISP account name and password. If you are in doubt about any of these details, call the ISP's support line.

SEE ALSO
- **What is e-mail?** – page 26
- **Explore Outlook Express** – page 32
- **Manage your e-mail** – page 38

Explore Outlook Express

Open your **e-mail program** and see how it works

Outlook Express is an electronic postman, delivering all the messages you want to send and bringing in all the mail sent to you. It is also an efficient filing clerk, automatically storing all the messages you have sent or received, filing any documents enclosed with the messages, and keeping a record of all your e-mail contacts. All you need to do is give it a few simple commands.

Giving orders

Outlook Express works in a similar way to other Microsoft programs such as Word, Excel and Internet Explorer. You can enter commands by clicking on a drop-down menu and selecting an option, or you can click on an icon on the program's toolbar.

The toolbar contains the functions you are likely to need most regularly, such as creating a new message, sending and receiving mail and opening your list of contacts. But all these functions can be found in the drop-down menus too.

Opening Outlook Express

To open the program, go to the **Start** menu and select **Programs**, then **Outlook Express**. Alternatively, click on the icon for the program on your desktop, or the Windows taskbar. When the program has opened, you may be asked if you want to connect to the Internet. For the moment, click **Cancel**. You can explore the program without going on-line.

TOOLBAR ICONS

The quickest way to get things done in Outlook Express is to use the icons provided on the program's toolbar. All the most commonly used functions can be accessed here.

Click on this to open up a blank message window, which you can use to compose a new e-mail. Click on the arrow next to 'New Mail' to see a list of e-mail 'stationery'. These are colourful patterns which you can use as backgrounds to your message. Click on the one you want to open a blank message window with the background in place.

These are the folders already set up in Outlook Express for storing your incoming and outgoing e-mail messages.

When you have read an incoming message, click this button to open up a pre-addressed message window ready for you to compose a reply.

 If a message was sent to several people including you, click **Reply All** to open a new message addressed to the sender and the other recipients.

 If you want someone else to read an e-mail you have been sent, click on **Forward**. This opens a new message window with the text already inserted, ready for you to send on to your intended recipient. You just add the address.

 To obtain a paper copy of an e-mail message, click **Print**.

 To erase an unwanted message, click on it and click **Delete**. This moves it into the 'Deleted Items' folder, which Outlook Express empties at intervals of your choice.

 Click here to connect to the Internet, to send any mail you have composed and to receive any waiting for you.

 Click here to search for a particular e-mail message using criteria such as name of sender or the time it was sent.

OTHER BUTTONS

When you click on New Mail to compose a new message, the toolbar will contain four more useful buttons.

 Allows you to enclose a separate file with an outgoing message.

 Lets your recipient know the message is urgent or important.

 Checks the spelling in your message.

 Puts your message in the 'Outbox', ready to be delivered.

 To find an e-mail address, or to add a new address to your list of contacts, click on this icon.

Send and receive e-mail

With **Outlook Express** it is easy to start e-mailing, using just a few simple commands

The two most basic functions of your e-mail program are sending messages and receiving them. Once you master these processes, you will know most of what you need to understand about e-mail. From beginning to end, sending a message should take as long as it takes to type your message and click on a couple of buttons.

E-MAIL ADDRESSES

Before you can send an e-mail to anyone, you will need their e-mail address. E-mail addresses usually take the form shown below, or a variation on this theme. The '@' symbol – read as 'at' – tells you that this is an e-mail address. Everything after the '@' symbol is known as the 'domain name'.

E-Mail Address
al.o'connor@ucl.ac.uk
anajonston@facemakersplc.co.uk
BJPrentice@aol.com
caradavies@devolution.org.uk
cjmasters@peoplefirst.co.uk

The person's first name, account name or Web site name

The domain name: this is usually the company or organisation where the person works, or their ISP address

The type of site suffix (co = corporation; org = organisation) – see below for more examples

firstname.surname@companyname.co.uk

The dot is a programming code which separates different parts of an address. This can also be an underscore or omitted altogether

The country code for the physical location of the company or ISP – see below for more examples

UNDERSTANDING ADDRESSES

The domain name and country code in an e-mail address can often tell you what sort of organisation your correspondent works for or has an e-mail account with, and where in the world they live. Addresses which do not specify a country code are probably based in the USA (where the country code – us – is rarely used).

Domain types:

ac	Academic (UK) (universities, etc.)
com	US or international company
co	Company/commercial organisation (UK)
edu	Educational institution (USA)
net	Network (a major Internet server site)
org	Non-profit organisation (i.e. a charity, pressure group or school)

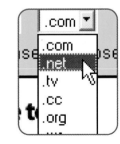

Country codes:

au	Australia	de	Germany	jp	Japan
ca	Canada	fr	France	uk	United Kingdom

HOW TO: SEND E-MAIL

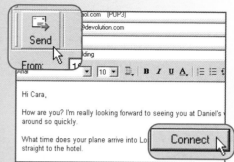

1 Double-click the Outlook Express icon on your desktop. A box will ask if you want to connect to the Internet. Click **Cancel**. It's cheaper to connect only when you're ready to send your e-mail.

2 Click on **New Mail**. A message window opens up. Type the address of your recipient in the 'To:' section, a subject in the 'Subject:' section, and then write your message in the main window.

3 To send your message, click **Send**. A dialogue box appears asking if you want to connect to the Internet. Click **Connect**. Your modem will then dial up to the Internet and send your message.

Finding an e-mail address

- **Ask the person for it**, but be sure to copy it down correctly: the slightest misspelling and your e-mail will be returned to you.
- **Check the address on an e-mail** from the person or ask them to send you one. The address will be included in their e-mail.
- **Look up their address on-line** with an e-mail finder service such as Yahoo! (**http://dir.yahoo.com**), Excite (**www.excite.com**) and My Email Address Is (**http://my.email.address.is**) and MSN (**www.msn.co.uk**).
- **Have a guess** (name.surname@company.co.uk). If there's no such account, your e-mail program will tell you the next time you log on.
- **Search on the usenet address server** (**http://usenet-addresses.mit.edu**) by name or organisation.

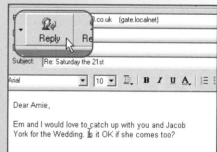

4 To check to see if you have any messages, click on the **Send/Recv** button. Your PC will connect to the Internet and place any new messages into your in-box. To read a message, click on it.

5 To reply, click on **Reply**. A new window opens with your recipient's e-mail address entered and a suggested title. You may change the title if you wish. Type your reply and repeat step 3 to send it.

Sent or not?

When you send a message, Outlook Express first places it in its 'Outbox'. Once it has been sent successfully, the message is moved into the 'Sent Items' folder. Click on the icon for either folder to see its contents.

Time Saver!

You can write as many messages as you want at a time, then send and receive all your e-mail in one go.

SEE ALSO
- **What is e-mail?** – page 26
- **Manage your e-mail** – page 38
- **Send e-mail attachments** – page 42

Build an address book

Use your e-mail **address book** to keep track of friends, family and contacts around the world

As soon as you get an e-mail address of your own, you'll find that you quickly start collecting other people's. A dedicated e-mail address book will make it easy to handle these details. It also makes it quicker to send out e-mail messages because there is no need to keep entering those awkward long addresses every time. You can do this using Outlook Express, which allows you to store all sorts of useful information about your contacts and friends.

ADD A CONTACT

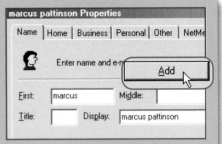

1 Open Outlook Express, then click on the **Addresses** button on the toolbar. Next click **New** and then select **New Contact**.

2 Type in the details in the form provided and click **Add** and then **OK**. Repeat this process for as many contacts as you have.

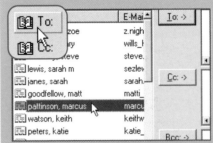

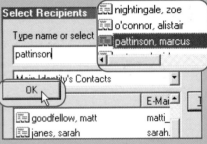

3 To send a message to one of your contacts, open a new message and click on the 'To:' button. Next, double-click on the person you wish to e-mail. Their address will appear in the 'To:' box. Click **OK** to confirm.

4 If you have several contacts, you can quickly find a particular one by typing part of their name in the search box. Outlook will guess the rest, based on what you've typed. Double-click on the correct contact to select it. Click **OK**.

AUTOMATIC ENTRY

You can set up Outlook Express to add an e-mail address to your address book whenever you reply to an incoming e-mail. Click on the **Tools** menu and choose **Options**. Click on the **Send** tab, and then put a tick next to 'Automatically put people I reply to in my Address Book'. Then click **OK**.

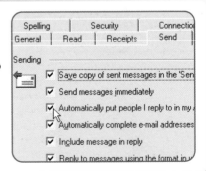

HOW TO: SET UP GROUP E-MAILS

It's easy to set up groups of contacts in your Outlook Express address book. If you are sending out similar information to several people it's a quick and easy way to communicate this information. By entering the name of the group in the 'To:' dialogue box, you can make sure that you include all its members.

1 Click on **Addresses** in the toolbar, click on the **New** button, and choose **New Group** from the list.

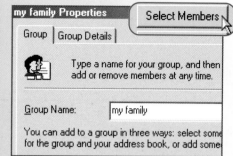

2 Enter a name for your Group – such as 'My Family' or 'Club Members' and click on the **Select Members** button.

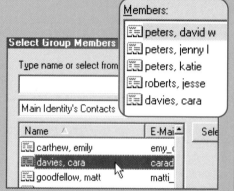

3 Double-click all the entries in the list on the left that you want to be part of your group. These names will then appear in the 'Members:' box to the right of your screen.

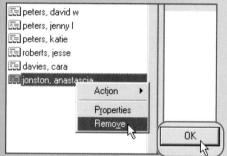

4 If you make a mistake, right-click the offending entry in the list on the right and choose **Remove**. When you have put everyone on the list, click the **OK** button twice.

5 To send a message to your new Group, open a new e-mail message, click the 'To:' button, and choose your Group from the list you've made.

Did You Know?
You can print out your entire address book. Go to the File menu and select Print.

Time Saver!
To delete a contact, open the address book, click on the name and then click the Delete button on the toolbar. Click Yes to confirm.

Utilise your address book

You can store more than e-mail addresses in your address book. By clicking on the **Address** button, selecting a **Contact** and then **Properties** you can add home, business, personal and conferencing details.

You can use your address book in other Windows applications, import contact details from Outlook Express into Excel and use the names and addresses for a Mail Merge in Word.

SEE ALSO
● Send and receive e-mail – *page 34*
● Manage your e-mail – *page 38*
● Multiple e-mail users – *page 46*

Manage your e-mail

Organise your e-mail inbox

Once you have an e-mail address, you'll be surprised how quickly your inbox begins to fill up. Outlook Express is designed to make it easy for you to deal with your messages. It is a good idea to keep your inbox tidy, because the more messages it contains, the longer it takes for Outlook Express to open. File the ones you need but try to weed out old messages.

Good housekeeping

Outlook Express can help to manage your e-mail in lots of different ways. You can forward messages to people at the press of a button, so there is no need for cutting and pasting. You can view your inbox and outbox and see which messages you have sent and received. You can also arrange e-mails by date, name, subject or sender, and create folders to file, say, work or personal e-mail in different places.

Automatic response

You can set up Outlook Express to sort your messages into folders before you read them, or to send an automatic reply to incoming messages if you are away on holiday or unable to respond.

Deleting a message

An important part of mail management is deleting messages that you no longer need. When you delete a message in Outlook Express, it is first moved to the 'Deleted Items' folder within Outlook Express.

To make sure you don't delete any messages by mistake, Outlook Express will not empty the 'Deleted Items' folder until you tell it to.

HOW TO: FORWARD MESSAGES

You will often receive messages that you want other people to see, such as an e-mail from a family member on holiday, a business message from a client, or just a good joke. Outlook Express makes it easy to pass on the message to lots of people, for example if you're spreading good news, or if the original sender does not know a third party's e-mail address, and wants you to pass a message on to them.

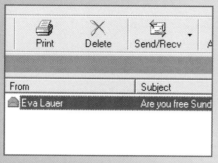

1 In your Outlook Express inbox, click once on the message that you want to forward.

2 Now click the **Forward** button on the toolbar. A new message window will open, with the text and title of the first message already in place. Only the address section needs filling in.

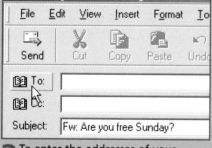

3 To enter the addresses of your intended recipients, type in the address or click on the **To:** button and choose entries from your contacts list.

4 You can also add some words of your own at the top of the message, explaining why you are forwarding it. You simply type in text as you would for a normal message.

5 Finally click the **Send** button to despatch your message.

On-line petitions

Many petitions are circulated via e-mail in support of charities and aid organisations. These rely on the recipients forwarding the petition on, and they are a way to promote awareness for specific causes. However, they can also be annoying if they are unsolicited or worded unsympathetically.

 Watch Out!

Only respond to petitions and chain letters from reliable sources. Many are not genuine – often intended to clog up the Internet rather than help a cause.

HOW TO: CREATE FOLDERS

Outlook Express comes with all the folders you will need to get started, including an inbox folder, an outbox folder, a sent items folder, a deleted items folder and a drafts folder. However, it is possible to add as many new folders as you like to help you to organise your mail. You might like to try creating a folder for work-related mail, or one for mail from your friends.

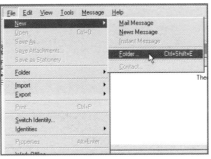

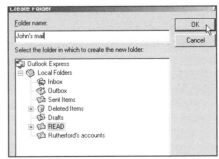

1 To create a new folder, go to the **File** menu, select **New** and then **Folder**.

2 Your new folder can stand alongside the other folders in the list, or it can be a sub-folder within any of them. Select where you want the new folder to be created and enter a name. Click **OK**.

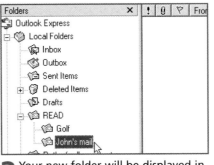

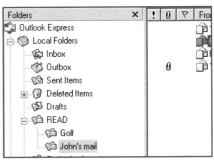

3 Your new folder will be displayed in the 'Folder' list on the left of the Outlook Express window. If you created it inside another folder, you will see it indented beneath that folder.

4 To see the messages in your folder, click the folder icon. The messages are in the main Outlook Express window. To file a message in your new folder, drag it over the folder icon.

DELETING MESSAGES

There are a number of ways to delete e-mail messages:

- Click on the message to be removed and press the **Delete** key on your keyboard.
- Drag the message to the 'Deleted Items' folder which you can find under **Folders** in the main Outlook Express window.
- Right-click on the message and choose **Delete** from the pop-up menu.
- Select the e-mail and click the **Delete** button on the toolbar.

All these methods place the messages in the 'Deleted items' folder in Outlook Express. To delete the items for good, right-click on the **Deleted items** folder and select **Empty folder** from the pop-up menu.

HOW TO: SET UP AN AUTOMATIC REPLY

You can set up Outlook Express to perform many tasks automatically such as sending a reply to any messages you receive while you are on holiday.

However in order to do this, you will have to leave your computer on. For this reason, some people prefer to use this function only for short breaks or days away from the office rather than longer holidays.

You also need to set up your computer to check for incoming messages automatically (see below). But beware – an unforeseen glitch could mean that your computer stays on-line for hours or even days.

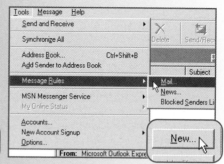

1 Go to **New Mail** and type your message in the box. There is no need to fill out the 'To' or 'CC' boxes. Go to **File** and **Save As**. Name your file and click **Save**. Close the message box.

2 Go to the **Tools** menu and select **Message Rules** and then **Mail**. Click on **New** to create a new mail rule – a pre-set course of action for dealing with the mail you receive.

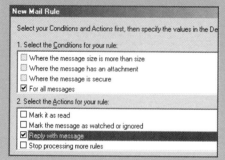

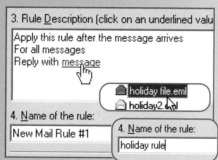

3 A new window with four sections will open. In the first section, click in the box next to 'For all messages'. In the second section, click on the box next to 'Reply with message'.

4 In the third section, click on **message**, locate your saved message and double-click on it. Next, give your new rule a name and click **OK**.

5 Your rule will now be applied to Mail messages. Click **OK**. If you want to delete or modify your message go to the Message Rules box as instructed in step 2, and click on **Remove** or **Modify**.

Checking for messages

To set up your computer to check for messages automatically, go to the **Tools** menu and then **Options**. Next to 'Check for new messages every' enter how often you want the computer to check. Then click on '**Connect even when working offline**'. Click **OK**.

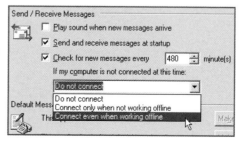

CHECKLIST
- Deal with your incoming mail immediately
- Delete all unwanted messages
- Create a clear filing system
- Empty the Deleted Items folder regularly

Did You Know?

To empty the 'Deleted Items' folder every time you close Outlook Express, go to Tools and select Options. Click Maintenance and tick next to 'Empty messages from the Deleted Items folder on exit'.

SEE ALSO
- What is e-mail? – page 26
- Different e-mail programs – page 28
- Build an address book – page 36

Send e-mail attachments

Use Outlook Express to send documents with your e-mail messages

Y ou can enclose pictures, spreadsheets and lengthy documents with your e-mail messages. To do this, you attach them to a standard e-mail message, much like enclosing photographs or a cassette in a package along with a letter. Any file included with an e-mail is called an 'attachment'. Adding an attachment to an e-mail is simple, and – provided you follow a few rules – the recipient will also find it easy to open.

HOW TO: ATTACH A FILE TO A MESSAGE

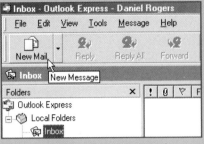

1 Make a note of the name and location of the file you want to attach to your e-mail message. Open Outlook Express and click on **New Mail**.

2 Draft your message in the normal way. When you are ready to attach the file, click on **Attach** or go to the **Insert** menu and click **File Attachment**.

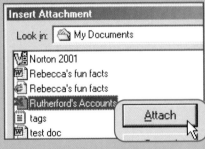

3 The 'Insert Attachment' window will open. Locate your file on your hard drive and click **Attach**.

4 The attached file will now be displayed next to 'Attach' in the message window. Click **Send** to place your message in the Outbox.

SENDING ATTACHMENTS

Before sending attachments, always bear the following points in mind:
- **Explain in your message what the attachment is and why you are sending it.**
- **Use a virus-scanner to check that your attachment isn't infected with a virus.**

- **Don't send very large files – even if they have been compressed – without prior agreement.**
- **Make sure your correspondent can read your attachment. Don't send it unless they have the appropriate compression package, graphics or application software to decompress and open your file.**

HOW TO: COMPRESS AN ATTACHMENT

If an attached file takes up a lot of space on your hard drive, it will take longer to send by e-mail. It will also be slower to download onto the recipient's computer. An attached Word document would take only seconds to send, whereas a minute-long home movie clip might take over an hour.

It is a good idea to reduce the size of large files by using compression software such as WinZip. For details of how to download the program, see *Download from the Web*, page 82.

1 Open the compression program WinZip Classic, and click on the **New** icon to create a new Zip archive – a file to contain the file or files you want to compress.

2 Next, type in a name for your Zip archive and click **OK**.

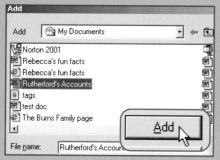

3 The 'Add' window will now appear on your screen. Select the file you want to compress and click **Add**. The file will be automatically compressed and added to the Zip file archive.

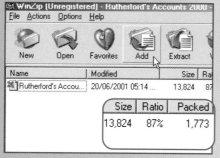

4 The contents of the Zip file are displayed. The 'Ratio' column shows how much space has been saved. You can add as many files as you wish to a single Zip file. Just click on the **Add** icon.

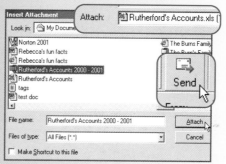

5 Close WinZip and return to Outlook Express. Attach your Zip file to your e-mail message and click **Send** to place it in the Outbox.

E-etiquette

If you are forwarding a message you have received with an attachment, you should always check it is what it says it is, and that it is virus-free. You should also only send on attachments you know will be appreciated by the recipient. Be particularly careful if their e-mail address is at their place of work.

 Watch Out!

Compression software works better with some file formats than others. It is more effective on large Excel files, for example (reducing them by half), than on pictures.

 Did You Know?

You can check the size of a file by right-clicking on it and selecting **Properties**. *You should compress any file over 500Kb (kilobytes) before sending.*

SEE ALSO
● **Receive e-mail attachments** – page 44
● **Spam and viruses** – page 56
● **Download from the Web** – page 82

Receive e-mail attachments

Check whether a file has been enclosed with an **e-mail** message before opening it

L earning how to recognise and open e-mail attachments is very useful as it means you can be sent – and make use of – pictures, videos and spreadsheets. You will need specialist software in order to open some attachments. Others may be unwanted viruses that you need to recognise and then delete.

DEALING WITH ATTACHMENTS

How do I know if I have received an e-mail attachment?

You will be able to recognise whether a message has an attachment or not by the presence of the paperclip icon on your message. This signifies that something extra has been included along with the e-mail.

Ⓤ	From
Ⓤ	✉ Telephony Team
Ⓤ	✉ Stephen.Ng@int

Should I open the attachment?

When you open the message, you'll see an icon for the attached file between the subject and body of the message. If the file extension is one which your PC is set up to recognise (for instance, a .doc Microsoft Word file), then the application's document icon will be displayed.

Subject:	Letter
Attach:	📄 Treasurer (25.1 KB)

Hi John

Here's a copy of the letter I sent to th

It is tempting to just double-click on the icon to open the attached file in the application, but you shouldn't do this immediately.

If the sender is not known to you and the message is unsolicited and general (for example, with a name such as 'you must see this!'), then you should delete the message and attachment immediately. It could well contain a virus (see *Avoid computer viruses*, page 54).

How do I open the attachment?

Take a moment to check that this attachment is from a trusted source, and that you know what it is likely to contain. Then right-click on the icon and select **Save As** and save the file to a folder on your hard drive.

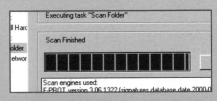

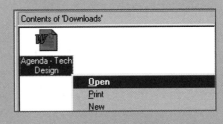

You should now run your anti-virus software to check that the file is not infected with a virus. It could still have been accidentally contaminated even if you trust the source (see *Spam and viruses*, page 56).

Once you are sure that the file is virus-free, you can double-click on it to open it and view the contents.

WHAT IF YOU CAN'T OPEN AN ATTACHMENT?

If it is not immediately obvious what a file contains, or what application it should be opened with, read the accompanying message to see if the sender has provided any information to help you out. The file may not open because it has been compressed using software different to that on your computer, or the sender may have forgotten to add the appropriate extension to the file name.

File extensions

The file extension is the two or three letter appendix to the file name that identifies the application required to open the file. For instance, agenda.doc is a document called 'Agenda' that should be opened using Microsoft Word (.doc).

If the file has an unfamiliar extension, you can check the index at the Extsearch Web site (**http://extsearch.com**). Type

ExtSearch

Add File Extension | Advertise | Link Books

arch engine lets you query 1,801 file
date of database: June 14, 2001

ch - File Extension Search Engine

the file extension into the search box and the appropriate program will then be identified from the site's database.

Common application extensions are:

doc	Word document
xls	Excel spreadsheet
txt	Notepad text file
bmp	image file
gif	image file
jpg	image file
tif	image file
mov	video file
avi	video file
mpg	video file

Decompression packages

If the document has been compressed, the file extension will refer to the compression program used.

Attachments with file extensions such as arj, lha, .arc, .sit or .uue are compressed files. In order to open these files, you will need to use decompression software.

Some decompression applications, such as Stuffit Expander, can decompress

files from many different compression programs. But the most popular compression used is the .zip format used by WinZip. For more information on downloading and using WinZip, see *Download from the Web*, page 82.

FILE YOUR ATTACHMENTS

You may want to detach and file an attachment separately from the message it is attached to. There are two ways to do this. In Outlook Express, open the e-mail message, then double-click on the icon for the attachment. This will open the attached document. Then go to the **File** menu, select **Save As** and choose a folder to save it in.

Alternatively, you can separate the attachment before you open it. When you have opened your e-mail, click on the attachment icon

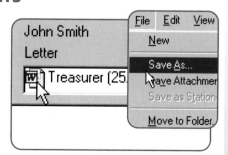

and hold the mouse button down. Then move the mouse to 'drag' the attachment on to your desktop or straight into a waiting folder.

Time Saver!

It is good practice to have a 'Downloads' folder set aside for new files you have received over the Internet. Get into the habit of saving any attachments to this folder for virus-scanning prior to opening.

Problem Solver!

You can download Stuffit Expander from Aladdin Systems, Inc. (www.aladdinsys. com). This free decompression utility works with most compressed files.

SEE ALSO
- Manage your e-mail – page 38
- Software on the Web – page 80
- Other ways to communicate – page 88

Multiple e-mail users

Set up Outlook Express to manage your e-mail for you, create separate e-mail identities and **protect the privacy** of your messages

Outlook Express has a useful feature that allows you to set up a user name and password for every member of the family. These separate 'identities' – as they are known – function like individual letterboxes: each person's mail arrives in his or her own inbox, so there is no chance of getting someone else's post by mistake. This is a very handy feature if several people are using the same computer to collect their messages.

HOW TO: CHANGE THE MAIN IDENTITY

Unless it is told otherwise, Outlook Express assumes that only one person is using the program and assigns that person a pre-programmed identity. This is called the 'main identity'. However, your computer does not assign the main identity a specific username or password. Before you begin creating new identities for everyone in the family, it is a good idea to give this pre-set identity a name and password to suit the main user of your computer.

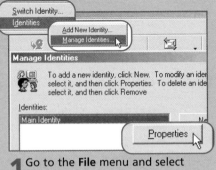

1 Go to the **File** menu and select **Identities**, then **Manage Identities**. Highlight 'Main Identity', then click on **Properties**.

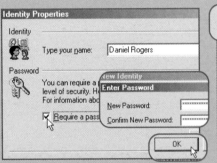

2 Next, change the name in the 'Type your name' box and tick 'Require a password'. Enter a password and confirm it. Click **OK**.

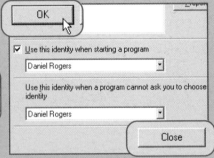

3 Click **OK** again, then make sure that the box next to 'Use this identity when starting a program' is ticked. Finally, click **Close**.

RETAINING PRIVACY

Creating individual identities means that each person using the computer has their own mailbox, contacts and newsgroups – protected by a password. Although this prevents anyone else accidentally receiving or reading your mail, it offers little protection against a determined snooper.

Outlook Express stores all your e-mail messages on your computer's hard drive, so these are accessible to anyone with enough computer know-how to understand how Outlook works. If you are seriously concerned about e-mail confidentiality, think carefully before allowing anyone else to use your computer, ever.

HOW TO: ADD A NEW IDENTITY

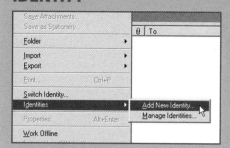

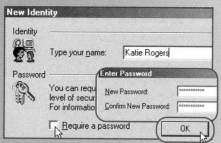

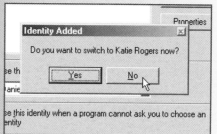

1 To add the first new identity, go to the **File** menu, select **Identities** and then **Add New Identity**.

2 When the 'New Identity' window opens, ask the new user to choose a username and a private password. When they have finished, click **OK**.

3 Outlook Express will now ask if you want to switch to the new identity. Click **No**.

HOW TO: SWITCH BETWEEN IDENTITIES

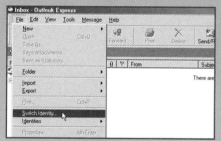

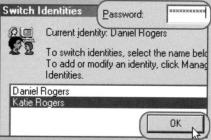

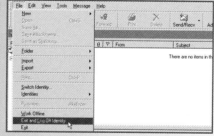

1 Open Outlook Express and go to the **File** menu and click **Switch Identity**.

2 Select the new identity you require, enter your password and click **OK**. The Internet Connection Wizard starts up, so you can type in details of the new identity's e-mail account (see page 30).

3 When you have finished with your e-mail and wish to reactivate your password protection, go to the **File** menu and click **Exit and Log Off Identity**.

Switching identities

You don't have to make a new Dial-Up Networking connection for each new e-mail account. If you're all on the same ISP, you can switch identities without disconnecting. If the new user has a completely different ISP and account, you can tell Outlook Express to disconnect and reconnect to the new ISP automatically when switching identities.

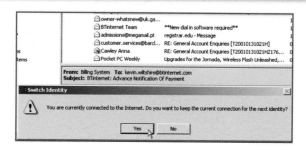

Problem Solver!

For many people privacy is not an issue, but they still want e-mail for different family members to be filed in different folders as it arrives. You can get Outlook Express to do this by setting a mail rule. For the principles involved in this process, see Manage your e-mail, *page 38.*

SEE ALSO
• **What is e-mail?** – page 26
• **Send and receive e-mail** – page 34
• **Manage your e-mail** – page 38

Security on the Internet

Take your **first steps** towards **browsing the Web safely**

Stories abound about the dangers of the Internet: hackers getting into your system, viruses bringing down companies, people having their credit card details stolen and, most commonly, unsuitable material that children could access. There are people who use the Internet for unsavoury ends. But, by taking a few precautions, and by avoiding trouble, you and your children can use the Internet perfectly safely.

The facts

You are extremely unlikely to fall victim to a hacker, or to be a victim of credit card fraud on the Internet. Such instances are statistically rare, and criminal hackers tend to concentrate on big businesses, rather than individual users.

Safety measures

It doesn't hurt to protect yourself and be aware. Basic precautions you can take when using the Internet – from setting up your browser to avoid certain sites, to only using secure shopping sites – are discussed in the following pages.

Filtering software

You can also use protective software (see page 52). Some programs filter the sites you visit, to ensure you encounter only those you would like to view. You can also install anti-virus software, to protect your computer from damage.

HOW TO: SET UP YOUR BROWSER'S DEFENCES

Internet Explorer's filtering system allows you to choose the levels of language, nudity, sex and violence you think are acceptable. Each time you try to access a site, your browser will check it first and decide whether to show it. You can change these settings at any time – provided you use your password.

Internet Explorer's filtering system only works on sites whose authors have added a special rating file describing their site's contents. This means that any sites without these files are also blocked – even if their content is harmless. Other filtering programs may be more practical (see page 52).

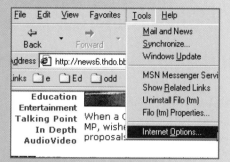

1 Open Internet Explorer. Go to the **Tools** menu and then select **Internet Options** from the drop-down menu.

2 In the dialogue box that appears, click on the tab marked **Content**. In the top half of this is a section marked Content Advisor. Click on **Enable**.

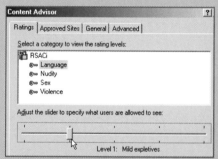

3 Set the levels of language, nudity, sex and violence you want to allow. Click on each category and adjust the slider from, in 'Language', for example, Mild expletives to Explicit or crude language.

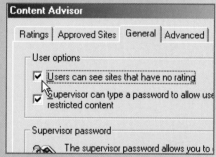

4 To allow Web sites that don't have a rating file, click on the **General** tab and tick the box next to 'Users can see sites that have no rating'. Note that many unsavoury sites will still slip through.

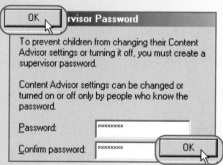

5 Once you're happy with your settings, click **OK**. You will be asked to choose and confirm a password, then click **OK**. No one else will be able to change your settings, if you keep the password secret.

Even greater protection

You can also set your browser to block any site you have not vetted personally. To do this, follow the procedure above but miss out step 4. This means that if a site has no rating (because you have not yet vetted it), your browser will not show it. As a consequence, you won't be able to visit any site you haven't already visited.

Jargon Buster!

Hacker A person who uses a computer to gain unauthorised access to data on another computer.

iMac

*To access Internet Explorer's filtering system, go to the **Edit** menu, select **Preferences** and then **Ratings**.*

SEE ALSO
● Shop safely on the Web – page 50
● Avoid computer viruses – page 54
● Spam and viruses – page 56

Shop safely on the Web

Learn how to **go shopping** with **confidence** on the Internet

Many people worry about buying goods on the Internet, but the rules for shopping safely on-line are no different from those you would use when shopping on the high street or via mail order. You can protect yourself by using a reputable company, keeping your credit card details safe, and checking a shop's customer service policy. Shopping over the Internet is at least as safe as, say, giving your credit card details over the telephone.

Secure sites
The most common concern with shopping over the Internet is that your credit card details might fall into the wrong hands. Reputable sites have worked to counter this fear by setting up a system that encrypts all the details that a shopper sends to them. These are known as 'secure' sites and can be used with confidence.

Encryption
When data is encrypted, it is translated into code that can only be deciphered by the recipient with the key to it – in this case, the shop you are buying from. This makes it almost impossible for a hacker to gain access to your credit card details or any other information you have supplied.

What to look for
Use the guidelines opposite to ensure that you are using a reputable, secure site. The first time you deal with a new company, it is also a good idea always to look for a real-life address (not a PO box), along with a telephone number. If they don't provide this, it is going to be harder for them to be successfully prosecuted if things go awry.

HOW TO: SHOP SAFELY

When shopping on the Net, be sure you know who you are doing business with. Ask around – if someone else has had a good experience using a certain shop, the chances are that you will too.

Look for official approval
Reputable on-line businesses submit the security systems on their sites to be tested by impartial monitors, in the hope that they will gain an accreditation and so increase consumer confidence in their site.

Look for the logo of a monitor such as Which? Web Trader (**www.which.net/webtrader**), TRUSTe (**www.truste.com**), or Clicksure (**www.clicksure.com**).

The logo normally acts as a link to the monitor's own Web site.

Check terms and conditions
A reputable shopping site should have a clearly marked section devoted to its terms and conditions and customer service policy. This should tell you how secure the site is and its refund and billing policy. It may also list frequently asked questions (FAQs) and allow you to monitor the progress of your order.

If you can't find this section, or are not satisfied with what it says, either contact the company or quit the site without buying. If you do decide to go ahead with your purchase, print out these terms and hold onto them. This can help if a site changes its terms after you have placed an order.

Look for the padlock
Once you've picked your 'shop', you should check that your credit card details are safe. You can do this by looking at the purchasing process.

When you are asked to submit your payment details, there should be a small padlock icon at the bottom of your browser window. The padlock shows that you are in a secure site. Depending on the way your browser is set up, a small box might also appear on screen, saying 'You are about to view pages over a secure connection'. This is also telling you that your credit card details will be safe. If the padlock does not appear, then you are not in a secure area. Contact the site to ask why.

Know your rights
If the site has a padlock and service policy, yet refuses to address problems with payment or delivery, then you can

Trading Standards
—— CENTRAL

get in touch with the trading standards authority (**www.tradingstandards.gov. uk**). Inform the site that this is what you are doing. Just the threat of action may prompt them to reconsider.

Use common sense
Above all, use your common sense. If you see a deal that seems too good to be true, then it probably is.

CHECKLIST
- Ask friends to recommend reliable sites
- Check for a physical address
- Look for an accreditation
- Read the terms and conditions
- Look for the padlock sign
- Keep written details of all transactions
- Use your common sense
- If in doubt, don't proceed

Watch Out!

Never give out your credit card details via e-mail or in a chatroom. These are not secure areas.

Guard against fraud
All credit card companies offer protection against traditional types of fraud, but it is worth checking the exact terms of your bank or card supplier's policy on Internet shopping.

If you suspect that you have been the victim of Internet credit card fraud, contact your card company immediately and give them as many details of your transactions as you can. It's a good idea to keep a written note of these.

SEE ALSO
- Do your weekly shop
  – page 192
- Buy a book, CD or video
  – page 201
- Buy and sell at auction
  – page 208

Filter out unsavoury sites

Use **filtering software** to control the sites **your family** can see

Filtering software is designed to help people who are worried about material they or their children will stumble across on the Internet. Also known as net nannies or censorware, filtering programs view and assess all the sites you wish to access. They judge the sites on criteria that you control, which means that you can choose which Web sites you and your children can or cannot view on the Internet.

FILTERING SOFTWARE

What it does

As well as blocking access to undesirable sites, filtering software lets you monitor any personal information being given out by you (or other users of your computer), and allows you to track on-line activity.

You can customise settings for different users, control the use of particular words and phrases, and prevent use of your browser at certain times of the day or night.

The drawbacks

Filtering software does have certain limitations. For instance, programs that block any site containing the word 'sex' might stop you viewing gardening sites that deal with the pollination of flowers.

Likewise, some filtering programs rely heavily on regularly updated lists

of offensive sites. Although you can get frequent software updates containing these lists, it is impossible to keep a list of every offensive site on the Internet, when new ones are continually being created.

What software is available?

A number of filtering programs are available to buy or download from the Internet. They include Net Nanny

(www.netnanny.com), Cyber Patrol (www.cyberpatrol. com), and CYBERsitter (www.solidoak.com).

Cyber Patrol has daily updates, called 'HotNOTS', listing inappropriate and approved sites, while CYBERsitter and Net Nanny have no recurring subscription fees.

At some of these sites, such as Net Nanny, you can submit your own suggestions for unsuitable sites.

Most filtering software can also prevent children from divulging personal information over the Internet. This will help to protect them from giving out addresses, phone numbers or other contact details that might put them at risk.

Choosing your software

It is well worth downloading free trial versions of the software, and using them for a few days. You can then attempt to access a selection of sites, in order to see how well the software is working. The software that you find most effective and easiest to use – and the best value for money – should be the one you continue to use.

HOW TO: BUY AND SET UP FILTERING SOFTWARE

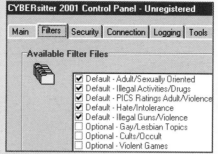

1 To download CYBERsitter, go to **www.solidoak.com**. Click on **Download Now!** and then the icon for its trial version. An installation program will download on to your computer.

2 Now double-click on the icon that appears on your desktop, and follow the on-screen instructions. Then double-click on the new icon that appears in the corner of your screen.

3 A control panel for CYBERsitter now opens. Click on the tabs and adjust the program settings. For instance, 'Filters' allows you to filter out sites by category from 'sexual' to 'horoscopes'.

Safety guidelines

- Try educating your children to use the Internet safely in the first place.
- The best method of monitoring Internet use is through supervision.
- Encourage children to search using search engines such as Yahooligans! (**www.yahooligans.com**), which list only sites suitable for young users.
- Teach children to search using categories, such as 'Science & Nature' or 'Sports & Recreation', not keywords. Sites found within categories will have already been approved by the search engine.
- If you cannot provide supervision, use a program, such as Internet Watcher (**www.internetwatcher. com**), which keeps a log file listing every Web site and page that has been visited by your computer, so you can find out exactly which Web pages have been viewed.

- Remember: you cannot put all your trust in filtering software. Criteria used by programmers to sift Internet content may differ from your own, and may pass sites you would still consider harmful or block data you would actually wish to receive.

4 Once you have finished, click on **Done**. Now, if you attempt to access any sites deemed unsuitable according to your criteria, you will be told that the page is not available.

 Watch Out!

Place the computer in a room used by all the family (not, for example, a bedroom), so that you or another adult can keep an eye on any sites that flash up on screen.

SEE ALSO
- **Security on the Internet** – *page 48*
- **Search the Internet** – *page 60*
- **Improve your browsing** – *page 72*

Avoid computer viruses

Protect your **computer** by **understanding** what viruses are, how they work and by installing **anti-virus software**

A virus is a computer program or piece of code designed to copy itself on as many computers as possible. Some are harmless, but others are designed to destroy programs or documents. While there are many viruses in existence, you can – with good practice, protective software and common sense – prevent your computer from being infected. The most important method of defence is to buy and use anti-virus software.

VIRUS QUESTIONS

Where do computer viruses come from?

Viruses are created, either accidentally or intentionally, by humans. Viruses can come from anywhere in the world, and are often designed by malicious programmers attempting to annoy other computer users.

The huge number of people using e-mail has made it easy for viruses attached to e-mail messages to be sent around the world at a remarkable speed.

How can you catch a virus?

One of the most common ways of 'catching' a virus is by opening an e-mail attachment that contains a virus. Other viruses can be transmitted when you load a floppy disk onto your computer or, much more rarely, through using a CD-ROM.

How likely are you to catch a virus?

This will depend on how often you use your computer, what you use it for, and what precautions you take.

If you never use e-mail or borrow floppy disks, it is highly unlikely that your computer will contract a virus.

What will a virus do to your PC?

The most common viruses send e-mails with the virus attached to everyone in your PC's address book. Other types of virus infect programs instead of e-mails, causing PCs to crash unexpectedly. The more harmless viruses will simply cause a message to be displayed on your monitor.

About 75 percent of viruses are known as 'macro' viruses. These are incorporated into pictures or documents such as Word files. Every time you open the 'infected' document, you will activate another copy of the virus, and so slowly infect your computer even further.

What can you do?

In most cases, you can find the source of the virus and search the Internet for a disinfecting program (a specific piece of anti-virus software), to solve the problem. Software manufacturers are constantly creating cures for the latest viruses. The best place to look for this software is at the Symantec site (www.symantec.com), one of the world leaders in anti-virus products. Click on **Symantec AntiVirus Research Center** for definitions of almost every virus and tools for dealing with them.

tools and downloads

Symantec Security Check   Try Our Sof

Subscription Services Assistance   Upgrade Y

Download Virus Removal Tools   Get Produc

HOW TO: SET UP VIRUS PROTECTION

Anti-virus software works by looking at all potentially vulnerable files. Once these are identified, they are searched for particular 'signatures' (the recognisable markings of known viruses). The software contains details of more than 40,000 virus signatures. If it matches a signature with one in a suspect file, it will alert you, giving you the option of erasing the file, or restoring the original file from a back-up disk.

New viruses appear all the time, so it is important to update your software's list of signatures. Most software manufacturers offer a subscription to an update service. For a small cost, you can ensure that your software receives automatic updates on all the latest viruses. To do this, visit your software manufacturer's Web site.

A trial version of the Norton 2001 anti-virus software, shown here, is available to download without charge at Symantec (**www.symantec.com**). It is suitable for users of Windows 95, 98 and Millennium Edition. Note that the download process may take more than two hours.

1 Go to **www.symantec.com** and click on **downloads**. Scroll down the page and click on **Consumer Product Trialware**. Then click the link to the next page.

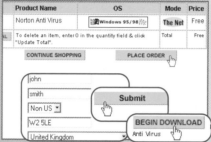

3 On the next page, click **PLACE ORDER**. You will then need to submit some contact details. Click **Submit**. On the next page, click **BEGIN DOWNLOAD**.

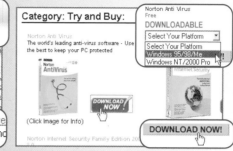

2 Choose **Norton AntiVirus** and click **DOWNLOAD NOW!**. From the 'Select Your Platform' box, choose **Windows 95/98/Me** and click **DOWNLOAD NOW!**.

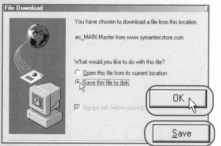

4 Click against 'Save this program to disk' then click **OK**. Choose **Desktop** as the location to save the program, then click **Save** to begin the download.

5 Once it has downloaded, double-click on the program icon to install the software.

RESCUE DISK

When your PC restarts after you've downloaded Norton AntiVirus 2001, you have the option of creating a 'rescue disk' to help get your system back on track if it is damaged by a virus. To create a disk, click **Create** and follow the on-screen instructions.

Once you have created your rescue disk, click **OK**. The program will scan your computer and give you a virus

report – this may take up to 30 minutes. Follow the instructions, then click **Close**. The program will now scan any incoming e-mails for viruses.

To change the settings on Norton, double-click on the icon and select **Options**. You can change which e-mail programs it scans, whether it starts immediately and whether you want it to make a start-up noise.

 iMac

There is an iMac version of Norton AntiVirus. You cannot download a free trial version of this, but you can buy it from the Symantec site.

 Problem Solver!

To keep up-to-date with the latest virus-related news and software, go to V-Buster (www. v-buster.com/faqs/ faqs.shtml).

SEE ALSO
● **Receive e-mail attachments** – *page 44*
● **Spam and viruses** – *page 56*
● **Download from the Web** – *page 82*

Spam and viruses

Avoid **junk e-mail** and malicious messages

Anyone who uses e-mail needs to be aware of two common problems: spam and viruses. Spam is the term used for unsolicited e-mail messages – the Internet equivalent of junk mail. Often they take the form of 'too good to be true' offers. Like paper junk mail, they aren't harmful – just annoying. Viruses, on the other hand, can be damaging, and the worst, most virulent viruses wreak havoc with computer users around the world. There are some simple steps that you can take to keep your computer safe.

How viruses work

An e-mail virus is a small program that is transmitted via e-mail usually as an attachment (see *Avoid computer viruses,* page 54). Viruses sent as attachments are activated once the e-mail attachment program is opened, not when you open the e-mail message itself. So you can usually 'defuse' a virus by deleting it without opening it. This may cause you some inconvenience if you accidentally erase an important message but it is better than infecting your PC.

Some viruses have an immediate effect; others are like time bombs which can go off days or weeks later.

Junk e-mailers

Unsolicited e-mail can come from a number of sources, some of which are perfectly reputable. But other junk mailers, such as pornographic sites, will send messages with personal-looking but often false e-mail addresses. These addresses serve the purpose of both preventing messages from looking like junk mail, and stopping the recipient from replying directly to the company.

DEALING WITH VIRUSES

Is there an attachment?
When an e-mail arrives, you should first look to see whether it has been sent with an attachment. Usually this is signalled by a paperclip symbol or

something similar. If you were expecting the attached file and know what it is, there is no need to worry. But if you were not, the next step is to check who the sender is.

Who sent it?
If you do not recognise the sender, always treat the attachment with suspicion. And even if you *do* recognise the sender, you should always remain alert.

Some viruses send themselves on automatically from an infected computer. It is therefore possible for a virus to arrive from a personal friend or contact.

Read the cover message
Next you should read the cover message (remember: few viruses can be caught by opening and reading a basic e-mail message). The cover message should explain what the attachment is.

Most attachments are perfectly innocent – and if you are convinced of the sender's honesty, you should open it. But remember that the cover message with a virus is intended to encourage you to open the attachment. So do not be taken in by free offers.

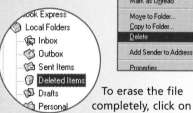

Ask the sender
If you are still in doubt, write back to the sender before opening the file and ask for clarification. It is perfectly safe to do this via e-mail.

Scan the file
Most viruses can be detected using anti-virus software. Follow the instructions on page 55 in order to scan the suspect file.

Don't take risks
If the file still appears to be dubious, the safest thing to do is get rid of it. You can always have it re-sent if necessary.

Delete it
First right-click on the suspect message and select **Delete** from the pop-up menu. This places the file in the 'Deleted Items' folder.

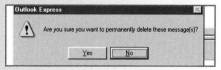

To erase the file completely, click on the **Deleted Items** folder icon. Then right-click on the suspect file again and click **Delete** again.

A window pops up asking you if you want to delete the file permanently. Click **Yes**. The file will now have been fully removed from your computer.

Hoaxes
You may receive messages alerting you to an e-mail with a name like 'Penpal Greetings'. Such warnings are usually hoax chain letters: there is no real virus.

These e-mails do no harm to your PC, but create a huge volume of mail when they are passed on, which slows the Web down.

Go to **http:// kumite.com/ myths** for more on hoaxes.

Jargon Buster!
Attachment Any document sent with an e-mail. It is just like putting a photograph or newspaper cutting into an envelope along with a letter.

HOW TO: SCAN YOUR E-MAILS FOR VIRUSES

Watch Out!

Make sure your e-mail software is not open before setting up a virus scan – otherwise the process will not work.

It is easy to set up a security program, such as Symantec's Norton AntiVirus 2001, to scan your incoming e-mails for any viruses. If a virus is located, an alert box will appear on screen informing you of what has been found. The alert box will also ask you what you want to do. You can repair an infected file, 'quarantine' a suspicious item, delete an infected file, or respond to any damaging activity that may have been caused by a virus and stop it.

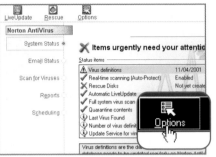

1 Open up Norton AntiVirus 2001 and click on **Options** towards the middle of the top of the window.

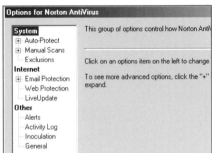

2 A new window will open. From the menu in the left-hand column, select **Internet** and then **Email Protection**.

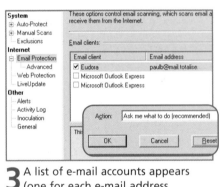

3 A list of e-mail accounts appears (one for each e-mail address accessed from this computer). Click in the box next to the accounts you wish to scan. Then click **OK**.

4 You should now be returned to the main Norton AntiVirus 2001 screen. Finally, to confirm that your e-mails are scanned for viruses, click on **Email Status**.

HOW TO: DELETE SPAM AUTOMATICALLY

Outlook Express allows you to specify what should happen to e-mail messages from certain sources. You can use this to delete spam automatically and prevent it from clogging up your inbox.

For example, you may receive an unwanted promotional e-mail from a marketing company. You may then want to delete any more messages that come from that source.

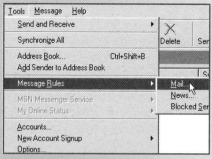

1 Open Outlook Express. Click on **Tools**, and select **Message Rules** and then **Mail**.

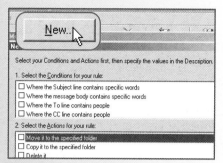

2 The 'New Mail Rule' window will open. (If the 'Message Rules' window appears, click on **New**.) This dialogue box presents a list of ways to filter your e-mail.

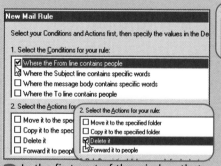

3 In the first part of the window that appears, click next to 'Where the From line contains people'. In the second part, click next to 'Delete it'.

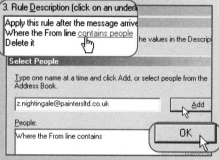

4 In the third part of the window click on **contains people** and type in the e-mail address of the source of spam you have received. Click **Add** after each one. Then click **OK**.

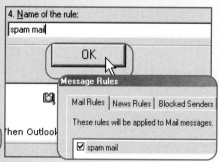

5 In the final part of the window give your message rule a name and click **OK**. It should now appear in your 'Message Rules' window. Click **OK**.

Problem Solver!

If you are registering with mailing lists, you can set up an alternative e-mail address using a Web-based service such as Hotmail. Many such services also offer filters that will stop junk mail reaching you.

Avoiding spam

To avoid receiving spam, remember to be careful about who you give your e-mail address to. Look out for privacy agreements on any sites where you supply your details, and for boxes you can tick to state that you do not wish your e-mail address to be sold or used for advertising.

If you have subscribed to a mailing list, keep the e-mail which explains how to cancel the subscription.

SEE ALSO
- Send and receive e-mail – page 34
- Send e-mail attachments – page 42
- Avoid computer viruses – page 54

Search the Internet

Find what you're **looking for** on the **Web**

Finding what you want on the Internet is not always easy. But there are free tools to help you to seek out the particular piece of information you are looking for. These are known collectively as 'search engines', although a search engine is in fact only one type of search tool. To make searching quicker and more profitable it is worth taking time to learn how different search tools work.

Search options

There are three main types of search tool on the Internet – search engines, search directories and search agents. You tell them to search for something by entering 'keywords' or 'search words' and they then check your words against a database of Web sites and list the results. The difference between the three is the way in which they compile their databases.

Engines

Search engines use programs to scan the Web and retrieve information on the content of as many sites as they can find. This means they can provide a thorough, regularly updated, database of sites.

Directories

Search directories employ people to pick the best sites on the Web and then file them under categories and sub-categories, which you can search through. They include fewer Web sites, because people cannot sort information as quickly – but they generally list better-quality ones.

Agents

Search agents look through other databases rather than creating their own – and they can search several databases at once.

TYPES OF SEARCH TOOL

Most search tools fall into one of three main categories:

Search engines

Strictly speaking, the term 'search engine' applies to only one kind of service. These are engines which automatically produce indexes of Web sites using software that does no more than index the words on the site's homepage.

You enter some information about what you want the engine to find. It then searches its index for matches to your search terms. In a matter of seconds it returns a list of matches and you can select which sites to visit. Search engines are fast and efficient, but because they are generated 'blindly' they can turn up hundreds or even thousands of answers to a general enquiry.

Some search engines, such as Google (**www.google.com**), for example, have a

very simple look, while other more specific search engines, such as AltaVista (**www.altavista.com**), are more complex in appearance and structure.

Search directories

These services generally use people to research Web sites, and to organise sites into topic groups. You can click on topics and further sub-headings until you find sites suited to your specific interest. Alternatively, you can enter a keyword and search the directory for

Using search tools

Search engines and search directories produce different results when carrying out the same search. If you enter 'vegetables' into the Google search engine and the Yahoo! search directory, Google will come up with approximately 1,910,000 sites and Yahoo! with 612 relevant sites.

suitable sites. Examples include Yahoo! (**www.yahoo.com**) and Looksmart (**www.looksmart.com**).

Search agents

When you enter a keyword into a search agent, it employs several ordinary search engines at once to look for it. One such site, which gives you information on, and lets you choose which engines to search, is Surfsearcher (**www.surfsearcher.co.uk**).

There are also comparison agents, which can search sites for much more detailed information. At 1stHeadlines (**www.1stheadlines.com**), for example, you can search for news stories on selected topics and from particular newspapers from all around the world, while ShopSmart (**www.shopsmart.com**) will compare prices from a range of on-line shops.

 **iMac**

*There is a search agent built in to many iMacs. Go to the **File** menu and select **Search Internet**. Enter your search term and click the magnifying glass to begin searching.*

Did You Know?

Search engines can index millions and millions of Web sites in advance, so you should never have to wait more than a few seconds for a search to be completed.

CHOOSE A SEARCH ENGINE

Selecting which search tool to use for any given search can be difficult. Some people try to get to know a large number of search tools, but this is not the most effective tactic.

A better option might be to try out some search tools and find a small number you really like and which are the most relevant to what you are doing. Learn how they work and how to make the best of them by reading their 'help' pages and practising with them. Using this method, you can build a small library of search tools in your 'Favorites' list that you can turn to for any

eventuality. Here are some suggestions for different kinds of search tool you might want to examine as a way of starting your Favorites list:

● An engine with country-specific site options, for example Yahoo!, which allows you to click on a country name to limit your search to sites from that nation. These are useful as they can narrow the number of Web sites indexed in a database, ensuring that the results of a search are more specific. They also prevent you from searching for sites in countries which will obviously not include the data you require, if, for example, you are looking for a local shop selling designer hats.

Many search engines have a specific UK equivalent:

Yahoo!: http://uk.yahoo.com
AltaVista: http://uk.altavista.com

● An engine which allows combining of terms. Most search engines have rules that let you combine terms in very specific ways to get precise results (see overleaf). One example is AOL NetFind (**http://search.aol.com**).

● An engine that can find images and other specific kinds of media, for example, AltaVista (**www.altavista.com**).

● A search directory with listings within subject areas such as 'Health' or 'Recreation', such as AOL (**http://search.aol.com**), can help you to search under a topic even if you are not sure precisely what you are looking for.

● A search agent that can combine a search of several different engines at once, such as Ask Jeeves (**www.ask.com**), is suitable for those times when you need to get a general overview quickly, and simply want a list of sites to browse through. It is also a useful way to find more unusual sites.

Time Saver!

Put any search tools you find useful into the Favorites list in your Web browser. You can make a special folder for them. Then you will be able to return to them easily whenever they are needed.

MAJOR SEARCH ENGINES

● AltaVista (**www.altavista.com**)
An excellent search engine that also offers a directory and specialist image and video clip searches.
● Excite (**www.excite.com**)
Offers a search facility as part of its good wider content. Popularly used as a homepage.
● Google (**www.google.com**)
A simple-looking automated search engine with a vast database and quicker than average response time.
● HotBot (**www.hotbot.com**)
A well-designed search engine that offers simple ways to make your search more accurate.

● Looksmart (**www.looksmart.com**)
One of the best search directories around with top-quality sites and an exhaustive list of categories.
● Lycos (**www.lycos.com**)
Good search engine with a built-in directory. Also allows you to search more specifically within your first search results.
● WebCrawler (**www.webcrawler.com**)
Simply designed search engine with a directory provided by Looksmart.
● Yahoo! (**www.yahoo.com**)
Excellent search directory with great breadth and depth of coverage. Often used as a homepage.

HOW TO: SEARCH

Most search engines work in roughly the same way. On the homepage you need to enter the search terms you are interested in (see overleaf for more guidance on choosing search terms).

If you are searching for general information on a particular health condition, such as diabetes, use a search engine such as Lycos (**www.lycos.co.uk**) as you can click to decide whether to make a country specific or worldwide search. In this example it makes sense to perform a worldwide search because diabetics have similar concerns the world over.

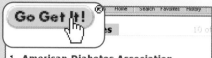

1 Go to **www.lycos.co.uk** and locate the 'search box'. Type in the subject of your search. We have chosen 'diabetes'. Then click on either 'UK' or 'Worldwide' to decide where you search.

2 Click **Go Get It!** to start the search. The search results will appear within a few seconds. The first few sites (the ones which best match your search terms) will be listed, and you can click to see more.

2. **children with DIABETES On-line Commu**
--0001ad2067c7a4e Content-type: text/htm
length: 32769 Last-modified: Mon, 04 Jun 2
21:19:22 GMT Content-Range: bytes 0-3276
on-line community for kids, families and add
diabetes. June 3,...
http://www.kwd.org/

3. **Juvenile Diabetes Research Foundation
International--The Diabetes Research..**
The Juvenile **Diabetes** Foundation Internati
mission is to find a cure for **diabetes** and it
complications through the support of researc
http://www.jdf.org/

3 Each site is listed with a short description and its address. If one of the sites listed is what you want, then click the link to go to it.

4 If there are too many sites listed, you can search again using more specific terms. Repeat your search using different combinations of terms until you find the sites you want.

5 You can open the site in a separate browser window, so that you can still view the listing easily and quickly in the original window. Right-click the link and choose **Open in New Window**.

Relevancy ratings

Some search tools indicate how closely their finds match your search criteria and list the best ones first. This rating is usually expressed as a percentage. It is judged on how many of your search terms are found in the document and whether they appear in the title, the address or just in the main text.

However, assessing the relevance of a site is a difficult qualitative task for a computer to perform, so don't be surprised if a highly rated result turns out to be of limited use, or vice versa.

 Watch Out!

Many search tools show the last time that each site it has found was updated. If a site has not been updated for months, it may be out of date and not worth visiting.

Did You Know?

Some search tools, such as Excite (www.excite.com) allow you to choose whether you want to see brief descriptions of each site. If you do not, there will be room for the engine to list more sites on-screen.

ENTERING THE CORRECT SEARCH TERMS

The more specific you are when using search terms, the more precise the results found will be. Search engines generally have a place for you to enter search terms on their main page, but you may also find a link to an 'Advanced Search' option, or to some search tips. If you find either of these, explore them.

Advanced searches may provide a form you can fill in to give precise information about what you want to find – such as words you'd like to include or exclude or the date when the site was created.

There are also symbols you can combine with your search terms to help you to achieve greater precision. There are several ways to do this:

● Use '+' before a word to indicate you want it to be in all the sites that the search engine finds. If it's not there, you don't want to see them.

Find This:

King Charles - Spaniel

● Use '–' before a word if you want it excluded: for example, 'King Charles – Spaniel'. This command tells the search engine to find sites about the historical figure but to ignore sites about dogs.

● Use '*' to search for sites that include a certain word regardless of its ending. For example, if you enter 'garden*' the search engine will return sites that include the words gardening, gardens and gardeners as well as garden.

garden*

1. Garden.com - **garden** Burpee **Garden** School online courses are d best out of their **gardens.** With our **Garden** http://www.garden.com/ [more from this site] Directory: Home and Real Estate > Gardening

2. National **Gardening** - The Name Gardeners landscaping, **gardens,** and horticulture Extensive resources for gardeners of all lev **gardening** with kids, events calendar, mess

marathon +battle

● To find an exact phrase, put it in quotation marks – for example, "hanging gardens of Babylon". This will bring up far fewer sites and most of them should be very closely related to your chosen topic.

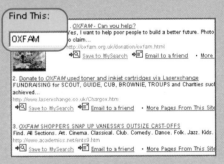

hanging gardens of Babylon"   Search

yellow pages   maps   horoscopes   ch   ...cient Babylon

Web Results for: "hanging gardens of Babylon" (25 of 150) - show summaries for these results.
- The Seven Wonders: The Hanging Gardens of Babylon
- The UnMuseum - Hanging Gardens of Babylon
- Hanging Gardens of Babylon
- Hanging Gardens of Babylon
- Hanging gardens
- Destination: The Seven Wonders of the Ancient World
- The Seven Wonders: The Hanging Gardens of Babylon

● Use upper-case letters only when you know you are looking for a proper noun. A lower-case search will find both upper and lower-case results, for example, OXFAM and oxfam.

Find This:

OXFAM

. OXFAM - Can you help? ...Yes, I want to help poor people to build a better future. Photo to claim... http://oxfam.org.uk/donation/oxfam.html ✚ Save to MySearch ✚ Email to a friend • More

2. Donate to OXFAM used toner and inkjet cartridges via Laserxchange FUNDRAISING for SCOUT, GUIDE, CUB, BROWNIE, TROUPS and Charities such achieved... http://www.laserxchange.co.uk/Chargox.htm ✚ Save to MySearch ✚ Email to a friend • More Pages From This Site

3. OXFAM SHOPPERS SNAP UP VANESSA'S OUTSIZE CAST-OFFS Find. All Sections. Art. Cinema. Classical. Club. Comedy. Dance. Folk. Jazz. Kids. http://www.academics.net/ents9.htm ✚ Save to MySearch ✚ Email to a friend • More Pages From This Site

Watch Out!

Different search engines have individual ways of listing search results and are therefore useful for different reasons. For example, Google prioritises results according to how close together your search terms appear – for instance, ten words apart – on a site.

SEARCH NATIONALLY

Some search engines, such as AltaVista (www.altavista.com) allow you to search for sites written in a specific language. This can be helpful if you want to narrow down the sites found to their country of origin, but it could also mean that you miss some really useful Web sites.

altavista
THE SEARCH COMPANY

Home | Advanced Search | Images | MP3/Audio | Video Clips | Search To

Find This: pasta   Italian ▾   Sear

Find Results: ○ UK ● Worldwide

rch Tools

COMBINE SEARCH TERMS

You can determine how search terms combine to include and exclude each other in a search. You can use the terms 'AND', 'OR', 'NOT' and 'NEAR' to tell a search engine how to bring individual words together in a search. This is sometimes referred to as 'Boolean Logic'.

AND

This tells the search engine to show only sites that include both terms. Type in 'Cosmetics AND allergies' to find Web sites about allergies of this specific type.

OR

Typing 'OR' between search terms lets you look for two separate terms simultaneously and bring up results that feature either or both the terms included in the search. Type in 'Edna Everage OR Barry Humphries' and you will get a list of sites about the Australian celebrity and her less glamorous alter ego.

1. Dame-Edna.com
   An Online Healing Centre Press your afflicted bits on this gone remember to wipe your monitors off afterwards Possums!)
   http://www.dame-edna.com/ [more from this site]
   Directory: Entertainment > Fine Arts > Theater > Shows and Reviews > Shows >

2. Biography - Barry Humphries Wired - Barry Humphries is an Barry Humphries Wired, Welcome to Barry Humphries Wired t Australian entertainer and creator of such characters as Dame Barry H
   http://users.aol.com/ralegems/biography.htm [more from this site]

3. Dame Edna: The Royal Tour. Dame Edna Everage on Tour
   Home page of the official production web site for 'Dame Edna'

NOT

This lets you search for sites that include the first term but not the second. Type 'Python NOT Monty' into the search box to rule out references to the cult comedy series from your search for snakes.

NEAR

An extension of the AND search, this lets you specify that the terms must appear close to each other on the site.

For example, 'cooking near5 vegetarian' will find sites with the word cooking within five words of vegetarian.

Boolean combinations

Many search engines allow you to combine Boolean terms using brackets. For example, 'browser and (Microsoft or Netscape)' will find sites which contain either the word 'Microsoft' or the word 'Netscape' and the word 'browser'.

CASE STUDY

Erin had been told by a friend about a plant that had purple-coloured leaves, which were light-sensitive and folded at night into a sort of pyramid shape. As someone that had recently moved into a home with a garden she was keen to find out more about plants, and maybe buy this particular one. Her friend thought the plant might be called oxalis, or perhaps sorrel, and so Erin started an Internet search.

She began with a general search engine, Google (**www.google.co.uk**), where she entered the search term 'oxalis'. By doing this, Erin learned that while some species of oxalis are called sorrels, the genus is unrelated to the true sorrel. She also discovered that some oxalis species are edible and used in salads.

But this was all rather general botanical information, and finding it was relatively hard work as many of the sites Erin's search retrieved were for various companies called Oxalis.

Oxalis Kit
ITEM #: 24726
Includes one ba
instructions. (O
plant. Covered w
handsome foliag
shamrock-shape
Top Size Zone: 1

What Erin needed, she decided, was the exact name of her plant. This would help her search more precisely.

Erin visited AltaVista (**www.uk.altavista.com**) and chose to do an image search. As she had suspected, most of the oxalis plants had green leaves, but she found a few with purple ones. Clicking the links to go to their Web sites, she soon learned her plant's full name – *Oxalis triangularis*.

Erin then returned to Google, and searched under the plant's correct name. There were lots of Web sites mentioning it which she was then able to learn from and she even found places to buy the plant on-line.

Did You Know?

Many search engines have their own methods to help make your search more exact. Look for a link called 'Advanced Search' or similar which will provide this service.

Downloads

It is possible to download search agent programs onto your computer free of charge. Programs such as Surf Pilot operate on your PC's desktop and look through more than one hundred search engines at a time. Go to **www. surfpilot.net** for more details.

Did You Know?

Because search engines use their own individual databases, a search with one engine may reveal different results from a search with another.

USING A SEARCH AGENT

Search agents are able to send queries to a number of different search engines at once and retrieve the results in a single operation. They aren't good at very precise searches, but they are excellent for helping you to get a broad idea of what is available on a given subject. One search agent that works in this way is Quickbrowse (**www.qb search.com**). Here, you will get a

simple form that lets you enter a search term and choose which engines to search with.

Other search agents, such as ShopSmart (**www.shopsmart.com**), compare the contents of Web sites for practical purposes, in this case buying items on-line. You might want to use ShopSmart if you are considering making an on-line purchase and want to get a good deal.

1 First go to the ShopSmart Web site (**www.shopsmart.com**) and select the kind of product you are looking for. For example, **Books and Magazines**.

3 If there are several matches to your search term, you will need to choose the one that is most relevant from the list provided. Click on **Compare prices** to view the cost of the book.

2 On the next page, type in the information you want to search for in the search box. In this example, the name of the author Dick Francis was typed in. Click on **GO!**

4 Now you can see, and compare, the prices from various Web sites. From here you can either buy straightaway – by clicking on **Click here** – or go to the seller's site to learn more about them.

HOW TO: USE SEARCH DIRECTORIES

Directories organise their Web sites into subject areas. This means they are useful if you aren't sure what you want, or want to see what the Internet has to offer on a broad topic. Directories usually offer keyword searching in addition to browsing through their subject lists.

Lycos (**www.lycos.com**) and Excite (**www.excite.com**) are Web directories that have high-quality sites but the number included is very small. Yahoo! (**www.uk.yahoo.com**) is a much larger directory-listing Web site – worth using if you want to find as wide a range of Web sites as possible and don't mind spending some time browsing.

1 First, go to the Yahoo! homepage. This is the UK version of Yahoo! (**www.uk.yahoo.com**).

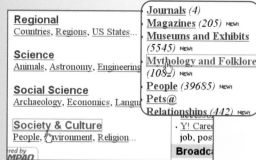

2 Choose the main subject heading you want to browse, then pick a topic from those listed. If your chosen subject is not obvious, enter it in the search box and then click **Search** to find it.

- **Art History**@
- **Books**@
- **Fabulous Creatures** *(258)*
- **Institutes** *(7)*
- **Labyrinths**@
- **Magazines** *(11)*

- **Legends & Myths in Cornwall** - ghost stories.
- **Mysterious Britain Webring** - brings together
- **North East Folklore Archive** - established for

3 You may be presented with more subject divisions, and Web sites will also be listed. Yahoo! UK and Ireland lists British and Irish Web sites before the rest, so it is easy to find local information.

YOUNGER INTERNET USERS

Many adults are concerned about protecting younger users from the less desirable areas of the Internet. So it is good to know that there are search engines which cater specifically for their needs.

Many popular search engines, such as AltaVista, have a 'family filter' which can be used to block the retrieval of some Web sites. Such filters tend to rely on special Internet filtering software which uses keywords and lists of blocked sites to prevent access to some information (see *Filter out unsavoury sites*, page 52). This is similar to the kinds of filtering software you might use at home, and is not always totally reliable.

Another option is to choose a search directory with contents selected to be appropriate for children. Such search directories use a database of Web sites chosen by people who check their content before including them – so you can be sure that nothing undesirable can creep in. Suitable directories include Yahooligans! (**www. yahooligans.com**), KidsClick! (**http://sunsite.berkeley. edu/kidsclick**), Ask Jeeves Kids (**www.ajkids.com**), and Kids AOL NetFind (**www.aol.co.uk/ channels/kids/netfind**).

SPECIALIST SEARCHES

Many search tools specialise in finding specific items on the Web, such as images, video and news stories.

Images

Some search engines, such as AltaVista (**www.altavista.com**) and specialist search engines, such as Diggit (**www.diggit.com**) will help you to find images on-line. If Diggit finds an image that meets your needs, you can simply click the **Similar** link and ask it to find more images like it.

Video clips

AltaVista (**www.altavista.com**) is also a good place to start searching for a video clip. Choose **Video Clips** on the homepage, then type in what you are looking for. If you need a special type of video format, make sure that you select it before you search.

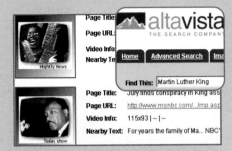

News and current affairs

There are several Web sites which gather news stories from around the world. One such service is 1stHeadlines (**www.1stheadlines.com**). This functions very much like a search engine: you can choose a subject of interest from a large list, or select a country of interest. There is also a search tool so you can look for something specific.

USENET is a collection of more than 30,000 discussion groups, each covering a different subject. Joining these groups is mostly free, and you don't have to be a member to read the information on offer. Visit **http://groups.google.com**, and you can search the USENET archive, and also join in with groups.

In most areas of interest there are Web sites that act as searchable databases – as you get more familiar with using the Internet, you will find those that suit your field of interest. For example, book-lovers might like to visit two search sites. Bibliofind (**www.bibliofind.com**) and JustBooks (**www.justbooks.co.uk**) are comprehensive

databases that collect the catalogues of a number of secondhand booksellers and allow them to be searched in one go.

Did You Know?

There is a search facility built into Internet Explorer. Click on the Search button to open a search box to the left of your browser window. Enter your text and start your search.

Time Saver!

If you find a Web site with useful links, remember to put it in your Favorites list for future reference.

SEARCHING THE WEB FOR A PERSON

The Internet can help you to track down an individual, and there are several tools to help you.

People Finder

To search for people in the UK, go to Info Space (**www.infospaceuk.com**) and choose **People Finder** from the subject listing. Then type the name and home town of the person you want to find, and the address and phone number will be searched for.

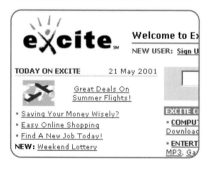

U.K. People Search
Last Name (required):   First Name:

Town:
                        Find People
▶ International People Search

BT

To find an individual's phone number in the UK, visit the BT site (**www.bt.com**) and choose **Directory Enquiries**. Type the name and area of the person or business you are looking for to start a search.

Postcodes online

Find any postcode

Royal Mail

You can find postcodes using the Royal Mail's postcode finder. Simply go to the Royal Mail (**www.royalmail.com**) Web site, click on **Quick Tools**, then **Postcodes online** to find any postcode in the United Kingdom. The United States Postal Service (**www.usps.gov/ncsc**) offers a similar service for finding zip codes. Click on **ZIP Code Look-Up & Address Information**.

Royal Mail

Phone directories

If you want to find the telephone number for a person or business in other countries, a good place to start is Teldir.com (**www.teldir.com**). This site links to telephone directories from all over the world.

E-mail address finders

Finding someone's e-mail address is a little more tricky. There is no single directory of e-mail addresses. Instead there are many sources which could prove useful (see *Send and receive e-mail*, page 34). You can start by trying WhoWhere? (**www.whowhere.lycos.com**). However, many of these directories rely on people submitting their own details to the listing.

WhoWhere?....the way to find people on the web
First Name: Last Name: Search Type:
                                    -Email- ▾

WEB PORTALS

A portal is a Web page that combines searching services and other information in one place. The idea behind Web portals is that you choose a site and set it as your homepage so that every time you start an Internet session your browser automatically goes there first. Then you are immediately presented with information you like to have handy.

Some major search engines offer portal services. Excite (**www.excite.co.uk**), for example, offers a range of information services at its homepage, including stock market

excite℠
Welcome to Ex
NEW USER: Sign U

TODAY ON EXCITE   21 May 2001
                Great Deals On
                Summer Flights!
▪ Saving Your Money Wisely?
▪ Easy Online Shopping   EXCITE C
▪ Find A New Job Today!   ▪ COMPUT
NEW: Weekend Lottery   Download
                                ▪ ENTERT
                                MP3, Ga

quotes, weather information, cinema and TV listings, daily news headlines, event reminders and horoscopes. To set the service, you need to register, then configure it to meet your needs.

Watch Out!

People-search tools are only as good as their databases, and there is no guarantee you will be able to locate a person using the Internet. Use a combination of these tools to increase your chances of success.

Did You Know?

The first thing most people do when they try using a search engine is enter their own name. It is fascinating to find out if you have made it onto the Web and whether you have any interesting namesakes around the world.

PROBLEM SOLVING

Sometimes you will find a Web site listed in a search engine and try to go to it, only to get a message saying that the site is not available. There are several reasons why this might be the case.

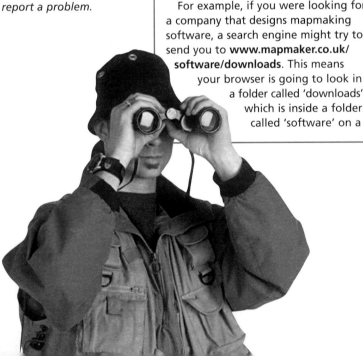

> ⓘ The page cannot be display
>
> The page you are looking for is currently unava site might be experiencing technical difficulties, to adjust your browser settings.

Out of date search engines

Web search engines regularly trawl the Internet to produce databases of sites. When you use a search engine, it is these databases – rather than the Web as it is at that instant – which are scanned. This means a search engine might not know that the site authors have changed the structure of their site, or removed it from the Web completely.

For example, if you were looking for a company that designs mapmaking software, a search engine might try to send you to **www.mapmaker.co.uk/ software/downloads**. This means your browser is going to look in a folder called 'downloads', which is inside a folder called 'software' on a

site called Mapmaker.co.uk. If the site's author has changed the way information is filed at the site since the search engine created its index, your browser will be unable to find what it wants, even though it may not be far away.

You can still find out if the Web site is running by trying to go to the homepage. This page is generally easy to find. Simply delete everything after and including the first '/' in the site address. For example, **www.mapmaker. co.uk/software/downloads** becomes **www.mapmaker.co.uk**. If you can get there, you can then look for the information you wanted which may be listed under a different heading.

Problems with a server

Another possible cause of being unable to get through to a particular Web page is that the server you need to connect to is temporarily unavailable. If you get an error message to this effect, try again at a later time.

The site has moved

Alternatively, the Web site you want might still be available, but may have moved – for example, to a new Internet Service Provider. If you think this might be the case, try another search engine and see if this comes up with a different site address.

Gremlins in the program

Sometimes when you click on one of the links provided by a search engine, the site doesn't appear and you don't even get a message. This may just be a glitch in your browser software. Try clicking on the **Stop** button to stop your browser's attempt to load the page, then click the link again. If it doesn't work a second time, there is more likely to be a problem with the Web page itself.

Keep looking

If all else fails, don't despair. There are millions of Web sites on the Internet, and if there are problems with the one that seems to cover the information you want, you can be sure that there will be many others that deal with similar material – and that do work.

HOW TO: PLAN YOUR SEARCH STRATEGY

Trying to find what you want on the Internet can seem like looking for a needle in a haystack. But if you learn about how search engines work, and plan a search in your mind before starting it, locating information can be remarkably straightforward.

Think before you start

Decide what it is that you want to find. It might be something very precise, such as the population of a city, next week's weather forecast in Rome, a place to buy German sausage, or a map of the Moon. Or, it could be something more general – basic data on a holiday destination, some tips on using your new digital camera, or a few Web sites for your Favorites list that cover a hobby. The important thing is to have an idea of what you want.

> **Web Page Matches** (1 - 20 of 8370)
>
> • <u>CNN.com - Weather - Rome</u>, <u>Italy</u>
> ad info, CNN.com, **weather** > world forecasts. **Rom**
> http://www.cnn.com/WEATHER/html/RomeItaly.html
>
> • <u>Yahoo! Weather - Rome IY Forecast</u>
> ... **Rome** IY **Forecast**. Tropical System Organizes i
> 1:42 PM). Unsettled **Weather** Invades the Ohio Vall
> http://weather.yahoo.com/forecast/Rome_IY_c.html
>
> • <u>Rome Weather Forecast - Rome</u> Museums a
> **Rome** Museums and Galleries. **Rome Weather Fo**
> for **Rome**, Italy **Weather Forecast** for **Rome** ...
> http://www.rome-galleries.com/weather.shtml

Be specific

Tell a search engine precisely what you are looking for. If you want cooking recipes that use chillies, ask for 'cooking with chillies' not simply for 'cooking'.

> 1. CHILLIES
> There`s so many recipes where the chilli is concerned
> my faves to begin the launch of my homepage. They
> tastebuds and also they`re not too...
> http://www.sped98.freeserve.co.uk/chilli%20page.htm
>
> 2. <u>Mridula Baljekar's Indian Kitchen: Recipes:Fried</u>
> Here is a quick recipe from my latest book, Real Fast
> Calcutta for which fatty pork is used. I have, however
> dill has a unique affinity...
> http://www.mridula.co.uk/friedpork.html
>
> 3. <u>Chillies with care - Very Lazy by English Provend</u>
> Very Lazy **chillies** are quick to prepare but very hot t
> 'Buyer beware, handle with care? The product, supplie

If a search engine doesn't locate what you're looking for, then try:

• A wider or narrower search

Perhaps you aren't being specific enough, or the words or phrase you are using are too precise such as 'cooking with bird's eye chillies'.

> Searched the web for **cooking** **with** **bird's eye** chillie
>
> <u>Bird's Eye</u> Chilli
> ... and has a 5mm diameter.We call **Bird's eye chillies**
> red ... lot of themn to do any **cooking**. We use them in r
> samcgees.com/webpost/d1/c3/html/89.htm?rnd=38 - 40k
>
> <u>Balinese Recipe - Basic Ingredients</u>
> ... mix green or unripe **bird's-eye** chilli together with the
> suggested. ... is widely used in Balinese **cooking**. Alway
> www.balifolder.com/feature/recipe/basic-ingredients2.sht

• Synonyms

Maybe there are other ways to describe what you want – use a dictionary or thesaurus to find similar words and try those, for example, 'chilli', 'chilli pepper', or 'chillies'. There are on-line dictionaries and thesauruses that can help you out. Try Merriam-Webster OnLine (**www.m-w.com**) and Thesaurus.com (**www.thesaurus.com**).

• Using the appropriate search tool

Try a search agent (see *Types of search tool*, page 61) if you want to get a broad range of Web sites related to a subject, and use a single search engine if you want to find something very precise. If you are having trouble with one search engine, go to a different one and try that.

Always remember:

Think laterally about your subject, considering every single possibility, and you stand a better chance of finding exactly what you are looking for.

Refining your search

After you have completed your first search, some search engines, such as Lycos (**www.lycos.co.uk**) allow you to conduct another search within those results. This can be a good way to narrow your search down, especially if you had not anticipated a problem with your first search. For example, an initial search for 'springbok' may bring up a lot of sites about the South African national rugby union side as well as about the species of antelope you were looking for. Searching within your initial results for 'antelope' should cut out most of the irrelevant sites.

Watch Out!

Search engines often use American wording, so for example, you may find 'coriander' under 'cilantro' or 'grilling' under 'broiling'.

SEE ALSO
• **Filter out unsavoury sites** – *page 52*
• **Improve your browsing** – *page 72*
• **Learn something new** – *page 106*

Improve your browsing

Get more out of **surfing the Web**

Once you have learnt the basic browsing commands, it only takes a few simple steps to build on this knowledge so that browsing on the Web becomes faster and more effective. Internet Explorer provides a variety of tools you can use to make the most of your time on the Net.

History
The History tool keeps a record of the sites you have visited – for a specified length of time. This is especially useful for those sites whose addresses you have forgotten, but would like to revisit.

Favorites
The Favorites function lets you create a list of the sites that you visit most often. These can then be accessed quickly, without having to type in the address again. Using this list to store addresses also means that you can often access pages off-line. This will save time and money spent connected to the Internet.

Time savers
There are other practices which can make your browsing time more efficient, such as opening several different Web sites at the same time or checking your e-mails while downloading from the Web.

HOW TO: USE HISTORY

Internet Explorer keeps a record of the sites you have visited most recently. This feature is known as History. You can use this to revisit a site when you have forgotten its address. You can also use History to keep an eye on what your children have been looking at on the Web – although this is by no means foolproof, as History is easy to edit.

1 Click on **History**. A window will open in the left-hand column entitled 'History'. There are various folders – for today, preceding days, and others for previous weeks.

2 If you recall when you saw a site, click on the folder for that day or week. A list of sites will drop down in alphabetical order. Click on the one you want to access.

SETTING YOUR HISTORY

You can change the length of time for which your browser will remember the Web sites you have visited and store them in your History – or clear out your History altogether.

Click on **Tools** at the top of the screen, then select **Internet Options** from the drop-down menu. A new window will open. Towards the bottom of this is a section named 'History'. To change the number of days you want to store details for, click on the number next to 'Days to keep pages in history:' and type a new one in. You can also empty your history, freeing up memory space, by clicking **Clear History**.

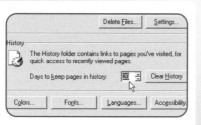

3 Another list of all the pages within that site that you visited will now drop down. Again, find the one you want, and click on it. It will then load up in the main browser window.

Using 'Search'

If you want to find a site quickly, and you know its name, click on **Search** and a box will appear enabling you to search through the whole History listing. Type what you are looking for into the 'Search for' box, then click **Search now**.

 Did You Know?

There are other ways of ordering site lists than by date. Click on **View** *and you will be given the choice of ordering sites by name, or by the number of times you have visited them.*

Favorites button

An alternative way to add a favourite and to access the 'favorites' list is to click on the **Favorites button** on the toolbar. This opens a panel on the left of the screen. A button allows you to add a site. Clicking on a site name takes you to it.

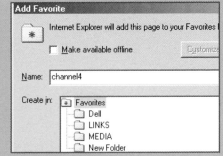

HOW TO: USE FAVORITES

Most browsers allow you to make a list of the sites that you visit most often. In Internet Explorer, this function is called 'Favorites'. By adding a site to your Favorites list, a link is created to it, which you can use to access the site more quickly. This is also a good way to ensure you don't forget a particularly useful Web site address.

1 When you find a useful site, go to the **Favorites** menu at the top of the screen, above the toolbar, then select **Add to Favorites** from the drop-down menu.

2 A new window will appear. In the 'Name' box at the top of the screen is the name of the page you wish to store. Beneath is a list of folders in which you can store the site.

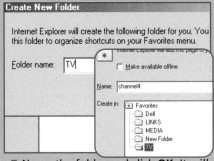

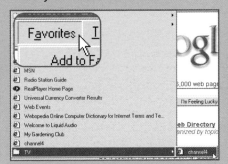

3 If you want to create a new folder, click on the button to the right marked **New Folder**.

4 Name the folder and click **OK**. It will then be displayed with the others in the lower box. To store the site in here, click **OK**.

5 Go to the **Favorites** menu again. A drop-down menu will appear. Click on the folder you've created. A list will appear with the site you've just added. Click on this, and it will begin to load up.

Creating shortcuts

To create a shortcut to your most visited favourites, click on **View**, and **Toolbars**, then select **Links**. A bar will now appear under your Address Box. To store a Web site on this, go to the site, wait until it is fully loaded, then click on the small Web page icon next to the site address in the Address Box, and drag it onto the Links toolbar. After a moment the name of the site will appear there. You can then click on it at any time to go straight to that Web site.

Time Saver!

*There is a quick way to add any Web page to your Favorites. Hold down **Ctrl + D** and the page will be stored. You may want to organise it into a folder later, however.*

HOW TO: BROWSE OFF-LINE

With Internet Explorer it is possible to make certain Web sites available to view off-line. This means that your computer stores the site on its hard drive so that you don't have to access the Internet to view it. This can be extremely useful when looking at huge documents which would take hours to read. Not only does it allow you to access the information later, but it will also save you time and money spent on-line.

1 Find the Web site you wish to make available off-line. Go to the **Favorites** menu, and select **Add to Favorites** from the drop-down list.

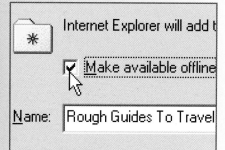

2 In the next window tick the box marked 'Make available offline'.

SAVING TO YOUR PC

An alternative way of storing a Web page to view when you are not on-line is by saving it to your computer. This is a similar process to saving any document.

Find the Web page you wish to store, go to the **File** menu, and select **Save As**. A new window will open enabling you to choose where on your computer you save the page, what name to give it, and what format you save it in. If you want to retain the whole Web page, select **Web Page, complete** in the box marked 'Save as type'.

If you do not want to save pictures – so making it a smaller file – select **Web Page, HTML only**. Then click **Save**.

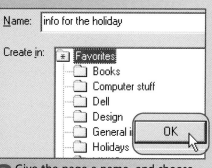

3 Give the page a name, and choose or create the folder you wish to store it in. Click **OK**. The page will now be stored.

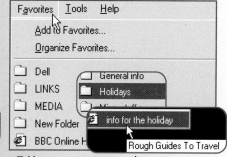

4 You can now access the page through your **Favorites** menu, and you may not even need to be connected to the Internet as many sites remain available off-line.

Links

You can make further pages available by clicking on **Customize** in the 'Add Favorite' dialog box. This shows pages linked to the one you are saving. You can then choose if you want to make any of these pages available off-line as well.

Did You Know?

You can copy text from a Web page into a Word document by highlighting the text, right-clicking on it and selecting **Copy***, then opening (or creating) a Word document and clicking* **Paste***.*

MAKE THE MOST OF YOUR TIME ON THE WEB

Spending time on-line means spending money, so it is a good idea to find ways of maximising your browsing efficiency.

Browse in separate windows

If you are going on-line to look at several different Web sites, why not have them all open at the same time? While you are viewing one site, your PC can load up another one or more in the background. To do this open your first Web site then go to the **File** menu and select **New**, then **Window**. Type in the address of the next site you want to see. You can then click back to the first window while the second site loads.

Check e-mail, browse and download at the same time

Whenever you are browsing the Internet, you can check your e-mail or download some files at the same time.

You can begin the download procedure and then open another browser window and continue browsing while you have to be on-line. To check your e-mail, open Outlook Express and click on **Send/Recv**, because you are already on-line, any new messages will appear in your in-box immediately.

Work off-line when possible

The cheapest way to surf the Web is to save a Web site to view off-line (see *How to browse off-line*, page 75). This way you can browse through the page

at your leisure. When you start up your browser, click **Work off-line** rather than **Connect** and then select the site from your favorites list. Most sites are available off-line but some may not be.

Add particular favourites to your toolbar

Rather than accessing a favourite site through menus, you can add it directly to your toolbar. Simply drag the address from the Address Box onto the Links bar underneath (or to the right), and a button will appear.

Turn off pictures or animated GIFs

Pictures and animations take longer to load, so if you don't want to spend the time waiting for them, click on **Tools**, then **Internet Options** and select the **Advanced** tab. Scroll down to the Multimedia section and untick the boxes next to 'Play animations' and/or 'Show pictures'. Click **OK**. If there are any pictures you do want to see, you can always right-click on the empty picture box and select **Show Picture**.

USING AUTOCOMPLETE

Save time filling out on-line registration forms by using the AutoComplete facility on Internet Explorer. You can turn this facility on by clicking on Tools, then Internet Options, and clicking on the Content tab.

The AutoComplete section is at the bottom of the window. Click on **AutoComplete** and place a tick next to 'forms', then click **OK**. You can also click beside 'user names and passwords on forms' to instruct your PC to remember your identity and password. The next time you

AutoComplete lists possible matches from typed before.

— Use AutoComplete for —

☑ Web addresses
☑ Forms
☑ User names and passwords on forms
☐ Prompt me to save passwords

have to complete a registration form, you will only need to begin typing in your name for the browser to anticipate what you are typing and offer to complete the entry for you.

SPECIAL BROWSING FEATURES FOR MACS

The Macintosh version of Internet Explorer varies from the PC version in a number of ways:

Internet scrapbook

This is a separate section of the browser where you can store copies of any pages, images or on-line documents that you may wish to refer to later. This is particularly useful for receipts for on-line shopping, or news articles that you might want to refer to after they have disappeared from the site. You can access this while looking at any Web page by clicking **Scrapbook** on the far left of the window.

Auction manager

Internet Explorer for Macs also offers the extra accessory of Auction manager. This feature enables you to keep track of any bids you might have with on-line auctions. As well as alerting you when someone has made a higher bid, it also allows you to set a maximum bid limit and instruct it to keep bidding in pre-set increments when necessary. Find this by clicking **Tools** then **Auction Manager**.

Page Holder

Another bonus for Apple Mac users, the Page Holder function enables the Internet browser to place its main page in a side window while any

links that are clicked on open in the main window. To take the full benefit of this, you need a large monitor and your screen set to a wide resolution.

Access this function by clicking **View** then **Explorer bar**, then clicking **Page Holder** on the far left of the window. To use the Page Holder function, copy the Web page whose links you want to browse to the Page Holder pane. Then, when you click a link on the page, you will see the link's destination page in the main window.

TRANSLATION

Because the Internet is a global phenomenon, there are sites in many different languages. But with the help of translation Web sites such as Babel Fish, you can transform them into English – opening up many more sites from around the world.

It is worth pointing out that Babel Fish offers only a limited range of languages and the translations are often highly inaccurate. Nevertheless it is a useful resource if, for example, you wanted to get an idea of what an auction item is on the German version of Ebay (**www. ebay.de**). To translate a Web site, go to Babel Fish (**http://babelfish. altavista.com**), type the Web address of the site you wish to translate into the appropriate box,

Translate with Babel Fish

Text Enter text for translation

Website Enter the Web Address of the p wish to translate.

http://

and select the languages you wish to translate from and to, from the 'Translate from:' drop-down menu. Click **Translate**. After a few moments, the translated page will appear. You can also use the facility for individual sections of text.

The Google search engine offers a similar service. When it lists a foreign language site as one of your search results, it also offers to translate the page for you. Again, the translations offered can be very flawed, and cannot be relied on.

 Problem Solver!

If you cannot see a button for Scrapbook to the left of your screen, go to the View menu and select Explorer bar. It will now appear.

Did You Know?

You can change the background colour of Internet Explorer to match your iMac. Click and hold on the toolbar and a menu will appear with the different colour schemes.

SEE ALSO
● **Download from the Web** – *page 82*
● **Do some research** – *page 109*
● **Buy and sell at auction** – *page 208*

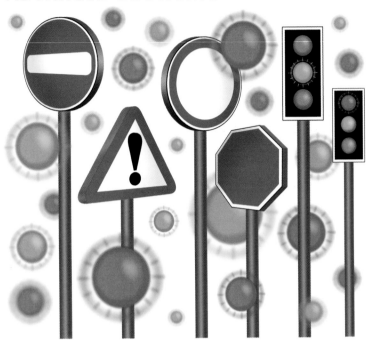

Solve browsing problems

Find **solutions** to make your time on the Internet trouble-free

Much of the time you spend surfing the Web will be completely trouble-free – your browser software is designed to view all standard Web pages without a problem. But sometimes you will come across a page that won't load, or a warning message that you haven't seen before.

This is perfectly normal and doesn't mean that there is anything wrong with your computer. Some Web pages include advanced features that your browser cannot see without some help. Other pages have programming errors or have simply been removed. In most cases, the problem is easy to resolve.

PLUG-IN PROGRAMS

Sometimes when accessing a Web page you will be told you need some extra software to view it properly. These pieces of software are known as 'plug-ins'. They are mini-programs that work alongside your browser to allow you to view special Web site features such as animations and film, or to participate in other interactive features such as games and virtual tours.

The most common plug-ins are Shockwave (**www.shockwave.com**), Flash (**www.flash.com**) and RealPlayer (**www.real.com**). For more on what these programs do, see *Software on the Web*, page 80.

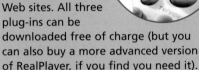

You can load plug-ins onto your computer directly from the manufacturer's Web sites. All three plug-ins can be downloaded free of charge (but you can also buy a more advanced version of RealPlayer, if you find you need it).

If you come across a page that needs any of these plug-ins, it is likely that you will be given a link to the manufacturer's Web site. There you can choose to download the plug-in, which can take anything from a few minutes to an hour depending on your modem speed (see *Download from the Web*, page 82). But if you want to be prepared, it is easy to visit the plug-in sites and download the software in advance.

USING COOKIES

You may receive a warning that 'Cookies need to be enabled'. Cookies are files issued by Web sites to identify you when you visit them. They are stored on your computer and contain details that the Web site can access. Users of a groceries site, for example, might be given a cookie that tells the site who they are so that their last shopping list can be displayed.

You can choose to enable all cookies automatically wherever they come from, disable all cookies or ask your computer to prompt you whenever a site offers you a cookie.

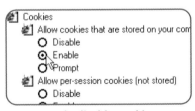

Some people disable cookies so that they can choose when to give out information. Others prefer the convenience of not having to type in their details on each visit to a site.

To make your choice, select **Tools**, then **Internet Options**. Click on the **Security** tab and the **Custom Level** button, then scroll down to the Cookies section.

OTHER PROBLEMS

The page won't load
The message that tells you that it won't load may give some clues. The most common error message is 'Error 404 File not found', meaning that the address does not exist. Often the problem is just that you have typed the address wrongly. All it takes is one full stop out of place or a space between letters. Check the Web address again, and make sure you have typed it accurately.

Other error messages include 'Host Unavailable' meaning that there is a problem with the server that stores the page, or '401 Unauthorized', which usually means you have entered an incorrect password.

Everything has stopped
Look at the far right of the taskbar at the bottom of your desktop screen for an icon showing two computers. Click on it to open a window showing the data flow through your modem. If the numbers are

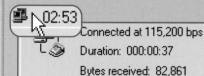

changing, the page is still loading. If they are not, the page has stopped loading. In that case, click **Stop**, then **Refresh**. If that doesn't work, try restarting your PC and trying again. This clears your computer's temporary memory, which may free it up to solve the problem. If this does not work, something is wrong with the page and there is nothing you can do.

My computer is frozen
If everything has stopped and your computer is not responding to your mouse clicks, press **Ctrl + Alt + Delete** together. In the window that appears, click on **End Task**. If this doesn't get your machine going again, switch your computer off and on again.

The wrong page has loaded
If you've accessed the page via a link, it may be that the link is wrongly set up. Try typing in the Web address directly or going via other pages or search engines.

I don't know the address
Have a guess. Try the site name preceded by 'www.' and ending with '.com'. If it is a specific page on a site,

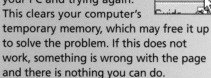

go to that site's homepage and click through to find it. If you've visited the site before, use 'History' to find it. Click on **History** and scroll through until you locate it. Finally, try a Web search.

I clicked a warning and was taken to another site
Some advertisements are designed like warning messages to entice you to click them. Look closely – if they are not in a separate window, they are not genuine.

I need to enable Java
You may get an on-screen message saying you need to have Java enabled to view a page. Java allows you to play interactive games. To enable Java, open up Internet Explorer, select **Tools**, then **Internet Options**. Click **Advanced** and scroll down to Microsoft VM. Three options are under this. Make sure there is a tick next to 'JIT compiler for virtual machine enabled'.

Plug-in demonstrations
The Web sites for most plug-ins also contain entertaining demonstrations of what their products can do. The Shockwave site, in particular, contains dozens of games, animations, videos, greetings cards and more. It is worth downloading the plug-in just to see them.

Too slow
Connection speed depends on the time of day you are on-line. If your connection is always slow, check if there is a problem on your telephone line. If that is fine, then contact your ISP to report the slow connection.

Time Saver!
To ensure the quickest Internet connection, close down all other programs so that you only have your Web browser open. This will mean that all available resources are used to browse the Web.

SEE ALSO
● Security on the Internet – page 48
● Search the Internet – page 60
● Improve your browsing – page 72

Software on the Web

Use the Internet to access different kinds of **software** for your PC

As you become a more proficient Internet user, you will find that you need more than a Web browser and some e-mail software to get things done. You may come across a site that requires special software to view its content. Or you may need a program to help you to tackle your tax return or listen to music on-line. There is often software available on-line that can help – some of which you can acquire for free.

Once you have located some software that you want, you can load it straight from the Web site onto your computer. This is called 'downloading'.

SOFTWARE ON-LINE

On-line software is classified according to the terms on which it is made available. Some is free, some comes with various kinds of strings attached.

What is freeware?

These are programs – usually produced by hobby programmers – that you can download free of charge. But they are protected by copyright laws, which means that you cannot sell or pass them on without the author's permission. If anyone else is interested in the program, direct them to the source you got it from.

What is shareware?

These are programs, or reduced versions of programs, that can be sampled for free – usually for just a limited period. Users are then supposed to purchase the program in its full version to continue to use it, which entitles you to assistance and updates. Some shareware stops working after its trial period to encourage you to buy the full version. Others continue to work but put you on your honour to pay if you continue to use it.

It is also possible to buy and download the full versions of many programs from the manufacturer's sites. Reduced versions of programs perhaps allow you to do everything but save your work, or offer the first couple of levels of a game. These omissions are deliberate inconveniences designed to encourage you to buy the full version of the software. Reduced versions of software are often called demos or sampleware.

What are updates?

These are mini-programs designed to add new features to existing software packages. They are also used to fix problems that have come to the attention of the manufacturer since the software was launched. When you run these mini-programs, they look for the existing program on your hard drive and make the required alterations. The next time you open your program, it will have all the extra features. You can then delete the update program.

WHAT SOFTWARE DO YOU NEED?

Your choice of what type of software to download often depends on what tasks you need to perform. The most common are listed here. But there are thousands of programs available, which perform functions you may never have thought of. It is often worth browsing through a general download site, such as the ones listed in the box below, for ideas.

Plug-in software

As you use the Web, you may be asked if you want to download a plug-in to add to your browser. Plug-ins are small programs that help your Web browser to perform different functions.

One example you may come across early is Macromedia Flash (**www. macromedia.com**), which is used to view animations. Another is RealPlayer (**www.real.com**), which allows you to listen to Internet radio and other sound files. If you need to download a plug-in to view a site, you will be told to do so by the site and offered a link to the software manufacturer's site. Otherwise, you do not need to download a plug-in until the need arises.

Compression software

If you often send or receive large files by e-mail, it is worth getting compression software. You can use this kind of program to reduce (or compress) the size of your files before you send them and to 'decompress' them whenever you receive one yourself. Common compression programs include WinZip, which you can download from Tucows (see below) and Stuffit Expander (**www.aladdinsys.com**), which can also be used on Macs.

Adobe Acrobat Reader

This is a program that reads PDF (Portable Document Format) files. PDF files make it easier to share documents on-line. Since the millions of Internet users worldwide

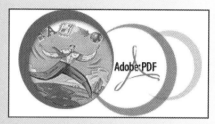

do not all have the same software, some people may not be able to view a file properly, with all the right formatting. PDF files, on the other hand, can be viewed by anyone with Acrobat Reader.

A PDF file is a read-only version of a document – effectively a snapshot that cannot be altered by the recipient. They can be greatly compressed, so they are much quicker to send over the Internet. Download a free version of Acrobat Reader from the Adobe Web site (**www.adobe.com/acrobat**). To create PDF files yourself, you will need the full version of the software.

FTP software

File Transfer Protocol (FTP) software is used to load Web pages onto the Internet. If you decide to set up your own site, you can use FTP software to upload your files. Popular FTP applications include CuteFTP (**www.globalscape.com**) and WS_FTP (**www.ipswitch.com**).

Time Saver!

Some software publishers and shareware libraries have mailing lists. If you want to get the latest news on software updates, it is a good idea to register for these.

RealPlayer 8 Pl
Now with GoldPass
Only RealPlayer Plus

▸ Your choice of 2500

▸ Amazing audio and

▸ Advanced picture co

DOWNLOAD SITES

Tucows (www.tucows.com)
More than 30,000 software titles – all available on a trial basis.

Cnet (http://download.cnet.com)
Large shareware library, with popular downloads clearly marked.

Jumbo (www.jumbo.com)
Offers range of downloads, but strong on entertainment software.

Microsoft (www.microsoft.com)
Software add-ons, upgrades and extras for most of its products.

ZDNet (www.zdnet.com/downloads)
Software for every aspect of using your computer and the Internet.

SEE ALSO
● Search the Internet
– *page 60*
● Play games on-line
– *page 186*
● File your tax return
– *page 196*

Download from the Web

Find out how to copy **computer files** from the Internet

Downloading is the process of getting software or other files from a Web site onto your own computer using a standard Internet connection. The availability of software, images, video clips and many other resources on the Internet is one of the reasons it has become so popular, and it is worth mastering the download procedure. The one main disadvantage of the process is that it can take a long time. Also, other software on your computer may slow down while downloading is in progress.

What do I need?
If you use Internet Explorer or Netscape Navigator as your Web browsers, downloading requires no additional software.

How long will it take?
Downloading files can take from a few seconds to several hours depending on the size of the file, the speed of your modem and the amount of activity on the Internet at the time you are connected.

Is there a risk of viruses?
It is unlikely that you will get a virus while downloading, but it depends on how reputable a source you are using. As a precaution, always run anti-virus software to check files when they are being downloaded and when they are being run.

How can I check the quality of downloaded software?
You can visit sites, such as Cnet (**http://download.cnet.com**), for a chart which shows how many times software has been downloaded (a good indication of its quality).

HOW TO: DOWNLOAD SOFTWARE

One of the first things it is worth downloading is some free compression software, such as WinZip. This is because many files on the Web are compressed to save space and you need this software to open them.

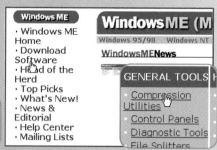

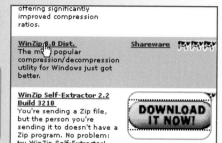

1 Go to **www.tucows.com**. Under 'Tucows Downloads', click **Windows ME**. Select a region and a provider close to your location.

2 A new page will open. Click on **Download Software**. Next, scroll down to 'General Tools' and click on **Compression Utilities**.

3 Under 'Windows ME – Compression', scroll right down to 'WinZip 8.0 Dist' and click on it. On the new page scroll down to click **DOWNLOAD IT NOW!**.

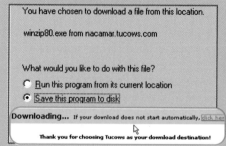

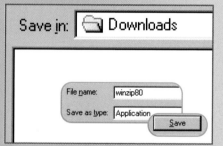

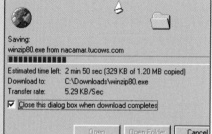

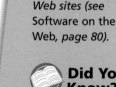

4 Your download software should start to run automatically. If it doesn't, then a downloading message will appear. Click on **click here**.

5 Use the dialogue box to indicate where you want the file to be saved. It is best to set up a 'Downloads' folder so that they are easy to find later.

6 Watch as the software downloads. You get a visual representation of how much has been downloaded, and an estimate of the remaining time.

COMPRESSION TOOLS

Many downloads are compressed so that they take the smallest amount of space possible on your hard drive. The most popular compression tool is WinZip – a piece of shareware. Some downloads need to be opened by WinZip, while others will decompress automatically. First, find the file and then double-click on it. If the file requires WinZip it will have a special icon and, if you have WinZip installed, your computer will find and use it when you double-click on the icon. If it does not need WinZip, the file will decompress automatically and you can follow the on-screen instructions.

winzip80.exe

7 When the download is complete, close your Internet connection. Double click on the software icon to set it up.

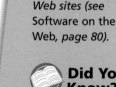

Watch Out!

Sometimes files are circulated illegally for downloading on the Internet. To ensure you download a legal copy, ensure you obtain them from widely recognised Web sites (see Software on the Web, page 80).

Did You Know?

If, for any reason, you want to stop the downloading process, you can click Cancel at any stage.

SEE ALSO
● Avoid computer viruses – *page 54*
● Software on the Web – *page 80*
● Solve computer problems – *page 129*

Other ways to connect

A standard **modem connection** is not the only way to go on-line

The most common way to access the Internet is to connect your home computer to a telephone line via a modem. While this method is good enough for most Internet users, there are quicker connections available for those who spend a lot of time on-line. There are also ways to access the Internet when you are away from home – either from publicly accessible computers or on your own mobile phone or laptop computer.

Connection speeds

A standard modem connection is the cheapest way to access the Internet, but also the slowest: you often have to spend time waiting for pages to download. Faster connections such as ISDN and ADSL (see right) can work out cheaper over time because they cut down on waiting.

Comparing costs

A BT ADSL line, for example, costs £39.99 a month, with a one-time connection fee of £150. If you spend a lot of time on-line at peak rate, ADSL may work out cheaper than paying by the minute for a standard modem connection.

Weighing it up

You must balance the saving offered by faster connections against the cost of installation and the subsequent monthly subscription costs. The average home user doesn't spend enough time on-line to make it worth while – but you might need a faster connection if you play on-line games, do large amounts of research, run a small business or download a lot of video and music files.

FASTER CONNECTIONS

ISDN

For many years, the main alternative to a modem has been ISDN (Integrated Services Digital Network) – a digital phone line that lets you send and receive data three times faster than the rate provided by today's fastest modems.

To use an ISDN connection, you need an adaptor for your current line. ISDN lines are available from British Telecom

and some cable companies – but you must live within a certain distance of the local telephone exchange. If you order an ISDN line from BT, they will first run a free check to see whether you live in a suitable location.

You will not need new cables to be installed, but your phone company will have to install an ISDN modem on your computer. You should also bear in mind that installing a new line can involve changing your telephone number or installing a new line dedicated to Internet use. You may also need to change your Internet Service Provider, because not all ISPs offer ISDN access.

Connection time

Examine your telephone bill to see how you use the Internet before choosing a new connection method. That way you'll find out how much time you spend on-line in a month and what it costs you. Sometimes an offer that looks good may turn out to be more expensive than you first think.

ADSL

A cheaper and much faster option than ISDN is ADSL (Asymmetric Digital Subscriber Line) – though still relatively expensive. This technology allows you to use conventional phone lines to send greater amounts of data than a modem can – and at faster speeds. To use ADSL, you need to get an ADSL modem installed. There is an initial set-up cost and then a flat monthly rate.

At the moment, ADSL is available only if you are within reach of a telephone exchange which has broadband technology. To find out whether this is

available in your area, access their Web site at **www.btopenworld.com/ broadband** or call BT on 0800 917 9189. As with ISDN, ADSL is not offered by all ISPs. Visit **www.adslguide.org.uk** to discover the latest news on ADSL in the UK and to compare hosting ISPs.

Cable

Many cable TV companies offer Internet access via a cable modem, using the same cables that deliver your TV signal. Most areas of the country now have access to cable. You do not need to be a cable TV subscriber in order to have a cable modem subscription, but the two services are often offered together at a discount. To find out how to get yourself connected, call your local cable TV provider.

Cable access can be extremely fast, but you need to check the charge rates, as these vary depending on how much information you need to send down the cable. Some cable providers also place a limit on the amount of data you can send and/or receive before they begin charging a premium rate. Check the precise terms of your cable provider to make sure that you are getting the best value package.

 Watch Out!

It may not always be possible to achieve the highest connection speeds with an ADSL line. Just as with a modem line, the rate at which data is transferred can slow down considerably at peak usage times.

ACCESS THE INTERNET ON A HANDHELD DEVICE

Computers and mobile phones

If you have a portable laptop or palmtop computer, it is possible to link it up to your mobile phone and access the Internet from anywhere, provided your mobile phone can get a good signal.

To do this, you need to slot in a GSM (Global System for Mobile Communications) internal modem (see *Set up your modem*, page 18).

Data transfer speeds for GSM modems are currently around 9600Kbps, which is slower than standard land-line services.

Faster technology, called General Packet Radio Service (GPRS) allows quicker data transfer, but is still slower than a land-line modem. The next wave of mobile technology, called 3G (Third Generation), will be much faster and will become available during 2002.

WAP

Wireless Application Protocol (WAP) is a way to access text from 'WAP-enabled' sites on the Internet on your mobile phone. WAP phones can only access Web sites that have been specially written in that format, so you will only be able to see a fraction of the sites that you can on your computer.

The most popular use for WAP phones is to access up-to-the-minute news and travel information, but they can also be used for reading e-mail and playing games. However, the images available are small and of poor quality.

To take advantage of this system, you'll need a WAP-capable phone, which you can buy at a mobile phone retailer.

Handheld communicators

These devices are palmtop computers combined with mobile phones in one unit. In addition to voice calls and other mobile services, you can send faxes or e-mail and access the Web, without having to buy any extra components.

Palmtop TV

Newer, faster mobile communications technologies will soon make it possible for you to watch live or recorded TV broadcasts on tiny palmtop computers.

METHODS OF ACCESS

Most Internet users spend the majority of their time on-line at home or at work. But there are other places you can go to get on-line:

Internet cafés

If you need access to the Internet while travelling, Internet cafés are ideal. They provide computers that you can use to access the Internet on the premises. They normally charge by the minute

from the time you log in to the Internet to the time you log out – so you should be wary of using a computer with a particularly slow connection. You are free to browse and send and receive e-mail, but you may have to pay extra to print out anything. You should also ask before downloading any files from the Internet, since

this could potentially leave the café open to a virus attack.

Enterprising retailers have set up Internet cafés in almost every part of

the world – facilities range from huge computer-filled halls to sandwich shops with an ancient PC in the corner. Such cafés are a great way to keep in touch when you or your family are away on holiday, and they are normally far cheaper than an international telephone call.

Internet kiosks

These kiosks are rather like phone boxes, but they provide access to the Internet. In the United Kingdom, BT has a range of kiosks called Multi-Phones in railway and tube stations, airports, motorway service stations and shopping centres. They provide a series of touch-screen links to popular sites and a keyboard to enter the address of any other site. You can

use them to browse the Web and to send and receive e-mail. Payment is made by swiping a credit card or a BT phonecard through the machine.

E-MAIL ON THE MOVE

To use an Internet café or kiosk for e-mail, it it best to first open an account with a Web-based e-mail service such as Hotmail, Excite or Yahoo! (see *Different e-mail programs*, page 28). With these free accounts you can access your e-mail from anywhere. Your e-mail will remain private, because you need to enter a password to access your account.

Satellite connections

It's already possible to use satellites to access the Internet, providing very fast connection speeds. You need a dish, and the technology is still at its early stages, but it is bound to become more common in the future.

SEE ALSO
● **What is the Internet?**
– *page 10*
● **Are you Net ready?**
– *page 14*
● **Security on the Internet** – *page 48*

Other ways to communicate

E-mail is **not the only way** to make contact on-line

With the addition of some software, you can communicate in several different ways on the Internet. You can use services such as instant messaging, which allows you to see when a friend is on-line and exchange messages with them instantaneously. And with the appropriate hardware, such as a microphone and Web-cam, you can use your computer to make inexpensive telephone calls and even see live moving images of your correspondent as you talk to them.

Live communication
The disadvantage of e-mail is that you cannot guarantee instantaneous communication. Although you can send an e-mail message across the world in seconds, it may be hours before your recipient goes on-line and picks it up. More immediate communication is now possible.

Instant messaging
This enables you to create a private chatroom with another person on the Net. You can pass written messages to and fro as easily as if you were sitting next to each other.

Internet telephony
Telephone communication across the Internet. This is similar to using a standard phone, except that calls are much cheaper and sound quality may be inferior.

Video telephony
Telephone communication with live pictures. Previously only available in expensive 'live satellite link-ups' seen on television, this is now a cheaper and increasingly popular form of communication.

INSTANT MESSAGING

Instant messaging applications monitor when your family, friends and contacts are on-line and allow you to conduct text-based conversations with them.

Virtual meetings

There are already more than 900 million instant messages sent every day and instant messaging is becoming popular with businesses as a way of conducting 'virtual' meetings.

You will also find instant messaging a useful and enjoyable way to keep in contact with friends and family who use the Internet. It's especially useful if they live abroad in different countries – provided you can find a mutually convenient time to chat.

Instant messaging can also be a good way to make new friends. Many services hold events for users to meet up on-line and allow you to search for users who are interested in a particular topic.

The software is free, so the only overhead is any connection charges from your ISP or telephone company.

Applications

There are a number of instant messaging applications available. These services include AOL Instant Messenger (www.aol.com/aim/homenew.adp) MSN

Messenger Service (**http://messenger. msn.com/download**), ICQ (**http:// web.icq.com**), and Yahoo! Messenger (**http://messenger.yahoo.com**).

A few of these services allow you to exchange messages with users of other services. AOL Instant Messenger lets anyone who subscribes to AOL, CompuServe 2000 and AOL Instant Messenger communicate using the Instant Messenger. Your choice of

Instant Message software may depend on what software your contacts already use. In this sense it is less flexible than choosing an e-mail application (which will receive mail from any other program).

Using instant messaging

To use instant messaging, you need to subscribe to a service, download and install the software, and register a username. The program operates in the background during the time you are on-line. It includes an address book of your friends and contacts, and notifies you whenever they are on-line at the same time as you.

PC FAXING

Internet fax services, such as eFax (**www.efax.com**) allow you to send or receive faxes via e-mail.

eFax provides you with a phone number that you should give to anyone wanting to fax you. Faxes will be forwarded to you as an e-mail attachment. This service is usually free (the sender of the fax pays a call charge, as they would anyway). You can also get an answering service that forwards voice messages to your e-mail account.

You can send a document from your PC direct to any fax machine using software such as WinFax Pro (available for download from

www.symantec.com), or check to see if basic fax software is included with your modem by looking on the modem installation CD-ROM. These programs are ideal if you only need to send a small number of faxes.

 Watch Out!

To get the most out of instant messaging, you need to be on-line regularly and for longer than just a few minutes. Consider what this will mean for your phone bill.

Time Saver!

Rather than wait for your friends to come on-line, send an e-mail well in advance to suggest a time that suits everyone. Then you can all chat together at the most economical rate.

MAKING PHONE CALLS ON THE NET

Internet Telephony uses your computer to transmit and receive voice signals so that you can talk on-line just as you would over a telephone. Your PC will need a sound card with speakers or headphones and a microphone. Recent computers will probably have these installed already. If both parties also install a Web-cam, you will be able to see each other as you talk.

Software
The software you need to get started is built into the latest versions of most

Instant Messaging text applications. There are also specialist telephony applications such as DialPad (**www. dialpad.com**) that you can use if you do not need an Instant Messaging account.

PC-to-PC conversations
You can use an on-line telephony service to talk to other PC users, as long as they have a microphone, headphones and an account with the same ISP. Because of this, you and your possible contacts should try to accommodate these needs in advance.

No matter where in the world you are calling, a PC-to-PC conversation will only cost as much as your local telephone connection to the Internet. You can also make PC-to-telephone calls. This will involve a charge, but it will generally cost less than a telephone-to-telephone call for a comparable length of time.

Limitations
Internet Telephony works by breaking conversations down into digital 'packets' for transmission on-line. These packets are then reconstructed at the listener's PC.

The sound quality of the call will be dependent on the quality of the Internet connection and on the amount of traffic between the two callers' connections. Therefore, sound quality may suffer during busier periods, and be subject to the occasional 'clipping' effect, similar to a poor mobile phone connection.

Additional hardware
Yahoo! Chat and PalTalk have links to sites where you can purchase Web-cams and microphones. Yahoo! Chat has a link to the Logitech site (www. logitech.com). Here you can buy various Web-cams, some of which have microphones installed.

At the PalTalk site, click on **No Microphone? Get one Here!** You are taken to another page on the PalTalk site where you can purchase microphones and Web-cams.

The Logitech Camera Family
Now it's a snap to produce professional video, send photos over the Internet and enjoy a

Most high-quality sound cards, such as the SoundBlaster AWE 64, which you can buy at Geek.com (**www. geek.com**), come with a microphone included.

It is also worth trying ZDnet (**http://computershopper.zdnet. com**) and CNET (**http://computers. cnet.com**) for a range of Web-cams and microphones.

Using a Web-cam
A Web-cam is a tiny, inexpensive camera connected to your computer that you can use to send live images of yourself. The most convenient place to put it is on top of your monitor, facing you. Web-cam images are not very detailed, but they do provide a unique opportunity to see a long-distance correspondent.

Problem Solver!

To avoid on-line echo during Internet voice calls, you – and the person you are speaking to – should listen using headphones, or keep your speaker volume turned as low as possible and facing away from the microphone.

90

FORUMS AND VIDEO CONFERENCING

To set up your PC for a video conference you need a sound card and microphone as well as a Web-cam attached to your PC (see *Additional hardware*, page 90). You then need to download and install some video conferencing software from a specialist service provider, such as the ones mentioned below.

Video conferences are generally held between people who already know each other and want to communicate on-line. But video chat forums let anyone join in and several of the services provide their own forums for general discussions.

Using the service

Once you have set everything up, you can begin your first video conversation. Apart from your Internet connection, there are no additional costs for placing a video call anywhere in the world.

PC-based video calls work best with smaller images on a low frame rate (the number of times the image is refreshed per second). Internet congestion often results in dropped frames and frozen images creating jerky or distorted pictures and sound. It is advisable to talk slowly and clearly to minimise the effect of any line distortion.

Eyeball (www.eyeball.com)

Eyeball offers free chat software that allows you to use your Web-cam to hold a video conversation over the Internet.

PalTalk (www.paltalk.com)

This works in a similar way to Messenger software in that it tells you when your address book contacts are on-line. It supports text, voice and video chats and conferencing between users. PalTalk also hosts video chat forums.

Microsoft NetMeeting
(www.microsoft.com/windows/ netmeeting)

Microsoft's application includes text chat, multi-point data conferencing and point-to-point audio and video conferencing. It is not the most straightforward application to use, but it comes as part of the Windows package.

PhoneFree (www.phonefree.com)

PhoneFree software supports free PC-to-PC voice and video calls over the Internet. It lets you receive video calls even if you don't have a Web-cam yourself.

Video forums

Video chat forums have yet to take off. One reason for this is the relatively poor level of technical quality when several people are participating. Many people also prefer the anonymity and security of standard chatrooms, where they can choose to be known by a nickname. Video chat reduces the degree of anonymity.

If you are ready to try out an on-line video chat forum, have a look at those provided by PalTalk, or just broadcast your image alongside normal forum contributions at Yahoo! Chat.

 Time Saver!

Time your video conferences for off-peak Internet traffic times to get the best performance and minimise the delays and disruption.

 Did You Know?

You can use your Web-cam to illustrate the subject under discussion. If you're talking about something you've made, you can put it in front of the camera.

Audio chatrooms

There are a number of services that now support audio chatrooms, such as Yahoo! Voice Chat (http://chat.yahoo.com). These are a little like a party telephone line in which anyone can dial into and join in the conversation. They are also ideal for partially sighted or blind computer users. The audio chats hosted at Audio-tips (www.audio-tips. com) are specially aimed at blind PC users.

SEE ALSO
- **What is e-mail?**
  – *page 26*
- **Take part in a newsgroup**
  – *page 92*
- **Use a bulletin board**
  – *page 96*
- **Use a chatroom**
  – *page 98*

Take part in a newsgroup

Read and post messages on **the Web**

A newsgroup is like an on-line notice board generated by people with common interests. Anyone can look at the notice board, add new messages and answer current ones. Newsgroups are a great way to swap thoughts, ideas and information about topics ranging from broad subjects such as education or gardening to specialised interests such as boat-building, archaeological digs, Star Trek and Polish literature.

Accessing newsgroups

Newsgroups are free to access. You can use your Outlook Express e-mail software to find a list of groups to choose from. Or you can search for newsgroups using a search engine such as Google (**www.google.com**), Deja News (**www.dejanews.com**) and Infoseek (**www.infoseek.com**).

What to expect

A newsgroup is a place for the free exchange of ideas, queries, gossip and news. The quality of a newsgroup depends on the people that use it. When a message is posted, you may get no answers or possibly hundreds; it could be the response you were looking for or something completely different. The lively, unpredictable nature of newsgroups is one of the main attractions for the millions of people who use this part of the Internet.

HOW TO: ACCESS A NEWSGROUP

To set up Outlook Express to access newsgroups, you will need your ISP username and password, which was chosen when you first registered for an account with your ISP.

The address of the ISP's news server will also be asked for. To get hold of this you'll need to call your ISP's support line (this is a commonly asked question) or check their homepage. For example, if you are registered with the BTinternet ISP, go to BTinternet (**www. btinternet.com**) and click on **My BT internet**. Under **Further Guidance** click on **My Account**, then **What are the BTinternet server addresses?**

If you used a CD-ROM to install your ISP, the newsgroup settings may already have been entered.

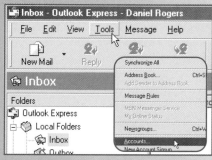

1 In Outlook Express, click on **Tools**, then select **Accounts** from the drop-down menu.

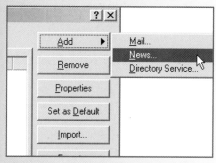

2 A new window will now open called 'Internet Accounts'. Click the **Add** button and select **News** from the menu that appears.

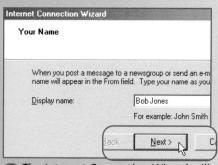

3 The Internet Connection Wizard will begin. Enter your name, e-mail address, news server, and account ID and password. Click **Next** to get to each new screen, then **Finish**.

4 You now have a news account (listed in the Internet Accounts window under the News tab). You will be asked if you want to download a list of newsgroups. Click **Yes** (see overleaf).

Spammers

Spam programs regularly extract all the e-mail addresses of newsgroup users to add to their bulk mail databases. It's a good idea to adjust your own e-mail address in an obvious way to fool the programs that the bulk mailers use but not individual newsgroup respondents. For example, **debbie.peters@kastracosmetics.com** could become **debbie.peters@remove-thiskastracosmetics.com** to avoid receiving junk e-mail.

 **Did You Know?**

If you want more features and facilities for accessing newsgroups, you can get specialist software at sites such as Jumbo (www.jumbo.com).

Conduct

Treat other people with respect when responding to newsgroup messages. Do not reply to any offensive or inappropriate comments because this could escalate into a row or 'flame war'.

HOW TO: FIND A NEWSGROUP TOPIC

Once you have downloaded the list of newsgroups, you are ready to take part in a discussion. The next step is to find a topic that interests you from the huge number available. As soon as the newsgroups have downloaded, you can begin searching through them by subject.

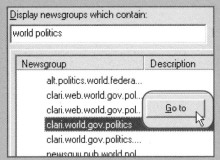

1 Enter a topic such as 'world politics'. A list of newsgroups with this text in the title will appear. Click on the one you want and click **Go to**.

2 A new list of message titles appears. Find one that interests you and double-click on it. Just as with an e-mail, the newsgroup message will then appear in a new window.

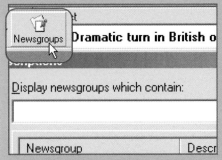

3 If at any time you want to look at different subject areas, click on **Newsgroups**, then repeat the process shown in step 1 above, choosing any other subjects that interest you.

NAMES OF NEWSGROUPS

Newsgroups are named using a convention. Each name begins with a series of letters or a word followed by a full stop. This describes the type of discussion the newsgroup contains, such as:

● **comp.** newsgroups that cover computers, technology and development.
● **humanities.** discusses fine arts, literature, music, philosophy and the classics.
● **news.** lists network news topics and Usenet itself.
● **rec.** shows a list of recreational pastimes and hobbies newsgroups.
● **sci.** is a forum where you can record and discuss scientific research and applied sciences.

● **soc.** deals with social issues such as history culture, religion, and lifestyle.
● **talk.** for on-line live group conversation with others.
● **misc.** carries topics that don't fit into any of the above groups.

This is followed by the name of the topic. For example 'politics'. Further sub-topics such as 'american' and 'federalism' may follow to narrow down the scope of the discussion, each separated by a full stop.

humanities.lit.authors....
humanities.lit.authors.y...
humanities.misc
humanities.music.com...

HOW TO: READ AND POST A REPLY

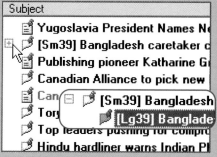

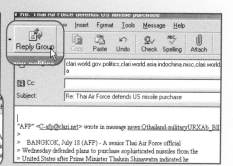

1 As well as reading newsgroup messages, you can reply to them or read others' replies. The plus sign to the left of a message indicates they have replies. Click on this sign to see them.

2 To add your own reply to a message, double-click on a message title to open the message window.

3 To reply to the author alone, click **Reply** and type a reply in the new window. Or, to send a group reply, click **Reply Group**. Either way, a new window will open for you to type your reply in.

SET UP A NEWSGROUP

It is easy to set up a newsgroup of your own. For example, if you are a keen classical music fan and can't find any suitable newsgroups, then post your idea to a USENET newsgroup called news.announce. newsgroups. Here your idea will be discussed and possibly voted on before it is accepted to go on-line.

It is a good idea to look at this newsgroup before you make any suggestions and also to check that there is definitely no newsgroup on the subject you are interested in. For more information on how to set up your own newsgroup, go to ZDNet (**www.zdnet.com**) and click on **Developer, Site Management** and then **Creating Your Own USENET Newsgroup**.

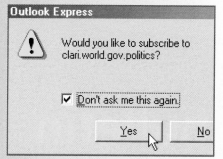

4 Once you have finished typing your message, click **Send**. It may take a short while for the message to appear in the newsgroup (if you have selected Reply Group).

5 If you close Outlook Express or try to access another newsgroup, you will be asked if you want to subscribe to the group you are leaving. Click next to 'Don't ask me this again' and make your choice.

Did You Know?

Raising a new topic within a newsgroup is known as 'starting a thread'. Any replies to the initial message are then added to that thread.

Jargon Buster!

Subscription
Subscribing to a newsgroup does not mean paying a fee or becoming a member. It means that the address of the newsgroup will be held in Outlook Express permanently.

SEE ALSO
- Spam and viruses – *page 56*
- Use a chatroom – *page 98*
- Do some research – *page 109*

Use a bulletin board

Swap **opinions** with other people **on-line**

A bulletin board (or BBS – Bulletin Board System) is an area on-line where you can exchange messages and opinions on a given subject. Bulletin boards work in a similar way to newsgroups, but unlike newsgroups they are Web sites, or part of Web sites. The term 'bulletin board' is now used loosely to mean any Web-based forum or message board, but when they were devised, they were completely separate from the Internet and used different technology.

PAST AND PRESENT

Across the board
Bulletin boards include messages on topics as diverse as international trading markets, dog shows and disability groups. There are also boards where consumers can post their good and bad experiences with businesses.

Dial-up
In the 1980s, before the Web was invented, you accessed a bulletin board by dialling up to its host computer directly rather than via the Internet. There are still about 40,000 dial-up bulletin boards, which you can access in this way.

These old-fashioned bulletin boards work very differently to Web sites. For example, you cannot use your mouse to move around a bulletin board and you have to type in special commands to perform simple tasks.

For more information and a list of bulletin boards of this type, go to The Directory (**www.thedirectory.org**). This site also provides links to download free bulletin board dial-up software.

Telnet
Later, bulletin boards were made accessible via the Internet using a system called Telnet, which you can still use today. To access one of these message areas, you need to have some Telnet software. Most Windows users should already have a program called HyperTerminal installed on their PCs.

Alternatively, you can find free Telnet programs at sites like Download.com (**www.download.com**). Packages to look for include CRT, mTelnet, NetTerm and ZOC.

World Wide Web
Today you can find bulletin boards all over the Web using nothing more than your standard Web browser. Many large sites, such as the CNN site (**www.cnn.com**) contain bulletin boards. Just look out for a link to a 'message board' or a 'forum'. Alternatively go to a search engine and enter 'bulletin board'.

Dial-Up Network
Home Networking
HyperTerminal
Internet Connection
NetMeeting
Phone Dialer

MESSAGE DETAILS

Most bulletin board messages are accompanied by a range of details to help you to decipher their content:
- the subject of the message
- the name of the person who posted it
- the date it was posted
- the number of people who have viewed it
- the number of people who have replied to it

- what sort of topic it is (new, active or 'hot' – a particularly popular talking point)
- an icon indicating the mood of the message, such as puzzled, amused or angry

Author	Replies	Viewed	Last Date Pos
smokey420	24	229	April 24, 2001 By: smokey
fetalcacti	3	26	April 24, 2001 By: RoxyPe

HOW TO: REGISTER WITH A BULLETIN BOARD

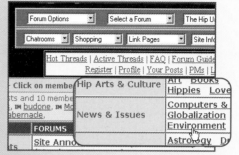

1 Go to Yahoo! (**www.yahoo.com**). Click on **Computers and Internet**, and select **Internet**, then **Chats and Forums**, and finally **Bulletin Boards**.

2 You will now be given a list of boards to choose from. Look for a subject or title that interests you (some also have a brief description to help you to decide). Once you've found one, click on it.

3 There may be a selection of bulletin board forums to choose from within the site. If so, find the one that suits you, and click on it.

4 You may have to register with a site. Look for **Register** and click on it. Fill out the required fields (usually your chosen username, password and e-mail address) and click **Submit**.

5 To read a message, click on your chosen topic. To reply, scroll to the symbols at the end of each message. You can choose to e-mail your reply directly, or post it on the bulletin board.

AVOID JUNK E-MAIL

To register with a bulletin board, you usually have to give your e-mail address. Unfortunately, many junk e-mailers send messages to addresses that they pick up from bulletin board sites. To avoid this problem, create a new e-mail address, perhaps a Hotmail one, and enter that when you register. Any junk e-mail will then be sent to that address, not to your 'everyday' mailbox.

Another way is to add a phrase to your e-mail address when you register with a bulletin board (i.e. turn michael@easynet.co.uk into michael@removethisbiteasynet.co.uk). This fools junk e-mailers who rely on a computer program to extract addresses and mail their messages. But it is easy for a genuine correspondent to work out your address and e-mail you.

Taking part

To post a new message click on **New Thread** (or similar) to open a new blank message form. Type in your message and click on **Submit** (or similar).

If you want to reply to a message, click on it to open a window containing the message and any replies that have already been posted. You will be presented with a list of options. Click on **Post Reply** (or similar) to open a ready-addressed blank response form.

Did You Know?

It is possible to find out what every icon on a page means. If the function of an icon isn't clear, place your pointer over it and after a few seconds a box should appear giving its title (for example, 'reply to this message').

SEE ALSO
● Take part in a newsgroup – *page 92*
● Use a chatroom – *page 98*
● Make new friends – *page 169*

Use a chatroom

Get **in touch** with other people who **share your interests**

Chatrooms are areas on the Web where people can exchange live messages about subjects that interest them, such as stamp collecting or a favourite sports team. They can be a stimulating way to get information and make conversation, or they can be a source of genuine help and support, as in the case of chatrooms for sufferers of a particular illness such as multiple sclerosis.

A chatroom is only as useful as the people in it, however. You'll find many filled with teenagers exchanging in-jokes. But if you are prepared to look for the right site, chatrooms can be a great way to discuss issues of interest.

Where to start
You can chat on the Internet in two ways. The first is to use a Web-based service like Yahoo! Chat, which needs no extra software. The second is Internet Relay Chat (IRC), a dedicated chatting network, for which you need to download some free software (see page 100). It is a good idea to sample chatting using the first method before trying the more involved IRC.

Chat subjects
Chat sites are divided into 'rooms' devoted to particular subjects. For example, people who like fly-fishing can talk to others with the same interest, while those who are new to chatting can choose to talk to other newcomers, rather than to people who've been chatting for years.

On-line personas
In a chatroom, people can be anyone they want to be. This can add to the fun, but you shouldn't always believe everything the person you're chatting to says. It might be that 21-year-old Janine from Canada is actually 50-year-old Hamish from Scotland. With this in mind, you should be very wary of meeting up with someone you've previously chatted to on-line.

Movies, TV

Featured Rooms
- Car Chat - From Buicks
- Music Lobby - Pearl Jar
- Surfing The Web - Got

HOW TO: FIND A CHATROOM

Sign Up For Yahoo! Chat!
s of people, hundreds of chat rooms, n download!

Sign up for your Yahoo! ID
Get a Yahoo ID and password for access to Yahoo! Chat and all oth

Yahoo! ID: aimz121877
(examples: "lildude56" or "goody2shoes")
Password:
Re-type Password:

1 Go to Yahoo! Chat (**http://chat.yahoo. com**) and click on **Sign Up For Yahoo! Chat!** Fill in the form and click **Submit This Form**. Yahoo will tell you when your details have been accepted.

Chat: hi

Voice: Hands Free | Talk

TOOLS
CHANGE ROOM ▶
CREATE ROOM ▶ | Send
SURF THE WEB ▶

4 To begin 'speaking', type into the box marked 'Chat:'. Click on the **Send** button to submit your message.

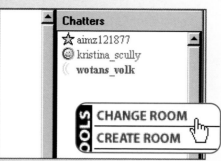

Continue to Yahoo! Chat
Complete Room List

· Teen
· Entertainment & Arts
· Movies
· Television
· Family & Home
· Games
· Government & Politics
· Health & Wellness
· Hobbies & Crafts
· Music
· Recreation & Sports
· National Basketball Association (NBA)
· National Football League (NFL)
· Women's National Basketball Association

· Bette - comedy
· Big Brother - I'
· e Vam
· the ne
· Dark Angel - sc
· Dawson's Creek
· Dharma and G
· Drew Carey - N
· ER - Be here T
· from the v
· Everybody Lov
· Felicity - Find
· Fraiser - talk ab
· Friends - Chan
· Gideon's Cross

2 Click on **Continue to Yahoo! Chat** and then **Complete Room List** to see a list of categories and rooms. Click on one that interests you. A chat screen will load within a few minutes.

Logging aimz121877 into the chat s
You are in **ER:1** (Be here Thursday r
🔊 **Welcome to Yahoo! Voice Chat.**
🔊 Use **Ignore** to mute another use
🔊 Click **HandsFree** to send your vo
🔊 Press the **?** button for more help
🔊 Voice is now active in **ER:1**
aimz121877: hi
aimz121877: is anyone out there?

5 Your text appears on screen beside your name. Anyone viewing that page can respond. If someone does reply, carry on the conversation by typing in another message.

Chatters
⭐ aimz121877
Ⓒ kristina_scully
« wotans_volk

TOOLS
CHANGE ROOM
CREATE ROOM

3 Once the screen has loaded, look at the right-hand side to see a list of other people in the room. If you are the only person in the list, click on **CHANGE ROOM** and choose another one.

Voice: Hands Free | Talk

TOOLS
CHANGE ROOM ▶
CREATE ROOM ▶
SURF THE WEB ▶
HELP ⌕ EXIT

6 When you feel like a change of topic, click on **CHANGE ROOM**, or on **CREATE ROOM** – to make your own room. You can use it to chat to friends if you arrange a time to meet beforehand.

Chatting to machines
The 'person' you are chatting to might not be human at all! Some programmers use chatrooms to test out programs designed to pass the 'Turing Test'. This determines the intelligence of a machine by its ability to appear human. You are unlikely to guess you are chatting to a program – unless its replies are so trite or contrived that they seem artificial.

Safe chatting
Choose your chatroom carefully. You'll find a diverse range of people when you join a chatroom. Some people are only there to be provocative or abusive. Try and avoiding these trouble-makers by choosing rooms devoted to a particular interest or hobby, rather than a general chatroom.

 Jargon Buster!

A/S/L? stands for *Age/Sex/Location, and is commonly used as an opening question in chatrooms when people are getting to know you.*

99

HOW TO: USE INTERNET RELAY CHAT

Internet Relay Chat (IRC) is a network of tens of thousands of chatrooms worldwide. The difference between IRC and Web-based chatrooms is that IRC requires additional software.

To use IRC, you'll need to download a free 'client' program which connects you to an IRC network. One of the most popular client programs is mIRC. Go to the mIRC Web site (**www.mirc.com**), click on **Download**, then on a server in your country (or a country close to you) to start the download.

1 When the file has finished downloading to your computer, double-click on the file's icon to start the mIRC set-up process.

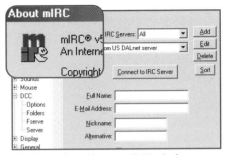

2 Close the 'About mIRC' window to open a 'mIRC options' window.

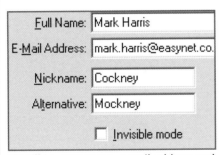

3 Fill in your name, e-mail address and nickname (the name you wish to be known by in the chatroom).

4 Click the arrow next to 'Random US DALnet server' and select a server geographically near to you – for a faster connection. Click **Connect to IRC Server**.

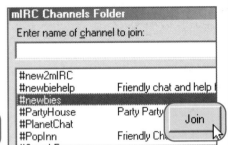

5 A list of chat channels (some with brief descriptions) appears. Choose one and click on **Join**. In this example, 'newbies', a newcomers room, was chosen.

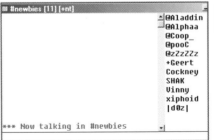

6 On the right of the next screen is a list of who is in the chatroom. The main section shows the current chat and the bottom line is for your message.

7 Type in your message and hit the return button. Your words will be displayed in the main window for everyone to see and reply to.

Watch Out!

Some sites say they have a 'chatroom', but in fact only have a message board. You can use these to exchange messages over a period of time – but it is not the same as live chat.

JOIN A CHATROOM

Netiquette

As with any social interaction, if you're communicating in a chatroom there is a certain etiquette (or Netiquette) you should follow closely.

For a good on-line Netiquette guide, go to The Netiquette Home Page (**www.fau.edu/netiquette/net**), but meanwhile, be sure to follow these general rules.

The Net: User Guidelines and Netiquette

● Always know where you are on the Web. Read the introductory passage when you enter a chatroom. This will explain what the subject of the room is, and whether there are any restrictions on language or other content.

● Try not to type in capital letters. It looks like SHOUTING and is considered rude.

● Address your comments to a specific person in the room – to save confusion about who is talking to whom.

● Chatrooms are not private. Other people, even children, may be present in the room. Moderate the content of your messages accordingly.

● Blasphemous words may be considered inappropriate – depending on the chatroom you are in. If you do swear, you may find a 'moderator' gives you a warning. This is the person who monitors language in the site – and if you continue to use bad language, you may find yourself evicted.

● If someone offends you in a chatroom, ignore them and hopefully they will leave. Some chatrooms allow you to evict someone. To do this, send a chat message of complaint to the room's moderator. Avoid arguing with whoever is offending you. Your attention may be exactly what the person is seeking.

Abbreviations

There are many abbreviations and acronyms commonly used in chatrooms and other Internet message areas. For a comprehensive list, see the Chatter's Jargon Dictionary (**www.stevegrossman. com/jargpge.htm#Jargon**).

It is not necessary to use these short cuts in a chatroom (many people prefer to use plain English), but they do save you time when typing messages.

AFAIK	As Far As I Know
IC	I See
BTW	By The Way
ADN	Any Day Now
GMTA	Great Minds Think Alike
B4N	Bye For Now
TNX	Thanks
L8R	Later
LSHTTARDML	Laughing So Hard The Tears Are Running Down My Leg

Chat for kids

Supervise your children when they use a chatroom to make sure they don't hand out personal details. You can also buy filtering software, which helps to prevent them from doing this.

EMOTICONS

'Emoticons' are combinations of letters and punctuation marks that are used to express emotion. They can add colour to a conversation – indeed many chat programs convert them to pictures automatically.

You do not have to use them, and may find them rather unnecessary. But for many people, they are part of the fun of on-line chatting, and are worth recognising. Try looking at the examples opposite with your head tilted to the left.

:)	a smile
;)	a wink
: (	sad
: – I	ambivalent
: P	sticking out your tongue
: – O	surprise
: *)	clowning
:–{}	blowing a kiss
(( )) : **	hugs and kisses
:O	in shock
: – &	tongue tied
: – \	undecided
> : – (	angry

SEE ALSO
● Filter out unsavoury sites – *page 52*
● Use a bulletin board – *page 96*
● Make new friends – *page 169*

2 Explore the Web

Explore the best sites on the Internet. Find information and inspiration on all kinds of subjects. And learn how the World Wide Web can make your life easier.

Advice and information

Learn something new

Use the Internet to further your education

The Web is a useful gateway to study. You can search for details of classes near you, or else enrol for an on-line course in another country. Perhaps you want to 'go back to school' and take a GCSE, get a professional qualification, or learn something just for fun. You can even do a complete university degree course. There are on-line courses offered in subjects ranging from accounting to wine tasting – ideal if you're tied to the home, or cannot travel far. Whatever you want to study, it doesn't take a high level of computer knowledge – if you can use e-mail, that's all the expertise you need.

What is on-line learning?

Studying on-line is much like taking a traditional correspondence course. The difference is that you have far more interaction with the tutor and the other students. Students access the 'classroom' through their own personalised homepage on a Web site. This is where students 'meet' to discuss the materials and review each others' work before it is reviewed by the teacher.

To find a course, you can use the listings sites mentioned overleaf, or conduct your own research using a search engine, such as AltaVista (**www.altavista.com**).

On-line colleges

You don't need to live in the same area – or even the same country – to take the class of your choice. Indeed, many on-line classes are offered by colleges in America. The University of California, Los Angeles (UCLA) is one of the biggest on-line providers (**www.onlinelearning.net**).

UK options are fewer – the Open University (**www.open.ac.uk**), for example, has course details, but no on-line study facility (see opposite).

QUESTION AND ANSWER

Before you start looking for a course, ask yourself a few questions. How much spare time do you have? Do you want a qualification at the end, or do you want to learn something without pressure? Can you afford to pay fees or are you looking for a free course? Do you want a course that offers a lot of feedback? If so, those offered by educational institutions will be better than those offered by enthusiasts.

Consider all these questions when choosing between courses. If you can't find the information you want on the college's Web site, look for a contact number or e-mail address. Admissions offices and tutors will be glad to help.

How do I organise classes?

Once you have signed up, the course centre creates a 'desk' for you – a homepage with icons that help you navigate through your classes.

Your course will usually be led by an instructor. There's a fixed start and end date, and you may use a textbook, which can be downloaded, purchased from a local shop, or ordered on-line from the course centre and mailed to your door.

At the University of Phoenix Online, for example (**www.uofphx.quinstreet.com**), classes are offered in sequence. Once you finish one course, you move on to the next, until all the degree requirements have been met.

You can begin a class at any time and work at any hour. Courses last five or six weeks.

Your weekly schedule

Typically, on the first day of the week, the instructor sends you the week's topics and sets assignments, such as writing an essay or reading from the textbook. He may also post a short lecture and provide discussion points. You can download the lecture and notes to read off-line, in your own time.

Times for conferences, when you can chat with your instructor and other students in the class, are organised through your

Course fees

Many on-line courses are free, and those with fees are often cheaper than a traditional course. With most courses, you register by filling out a form on a Web site, and pay fees by credit card.

It's still not too late to enroll in classes at University of Phoenix Online. Most of our degree programs are starting soon.

Business Professionals
56 classes including: Entertainment Studies, Business Basics, Award in General Business St. E-Commerce, and more...

Educators
85 classes including: Character Education, Tea English as a Foreign Language, Houghton Miffl Courses, Online Teaching Program, and more.

Computer & IT Professionals

desk. Each class shares a mailbox which serves as an 'electronic classroom'.

You and your instructor

When your work is due, you e-mail it to your instructor, who marks it and e-mails it back with comments. You take exams by downloading them and e-mailing them back in the specified time. Your grades are then sent to your desk.

YOUR DESK
Click here to log in to your desk.

Exams

If you are just doing a course for fun, you don't have to worry about exams. Just read, participate and learn.

 Watch Out!

Check the cost of your course before you enrol. Check, too, whether you are eligible for a grant.

CASE STUDY

Margaret enrolled for an on-line MBA (master of business administration) last year.

'I'd always wanted to go back to university and get my Masters degree, but I thought there was no way I could fit it in around my family.

'Then I was watching *University Challenge*. **The Open University were on it and I thought I might look up their Web site (www. open.ac.uk).**

'There were no

on-line courses available but it occurred to me that there might be other courses on-line. Searching with specific keywords through the Yahoo! search engine (www. yahoo.com), I ended up at World Wide Learn site (www. worldwidelearn.com) and it was there that the course at Oxford Brookes University (www.brookes.ac.uk) jumped out at me. Their MBA in Management Practice covered all I wanted to do and more.'

WHERE TO LEARN

Best place to start

**Education World
(www.educationworld.com)**
Start your search for education with an education-oriented search engine. Education World is a database of 110,000 educational Web sites. Another good alternative is the Distance Learning Resource Network (**www.dlrn.org**).

On-line education shop

**Hungry Minds
(www.hungryminds.com)**
With over 17,000 on-line courses at Hungry Minds, you can mix and match from different institutions. The site offers courses taught by American universities such as the University of Maryland. But it also gathers together courses from women's on-line network iVillage, employment supersite Monster.com and financial site Smart Money.com.

Courses around the world

**World Wide Learn
(www.worldwidelearn.com)**
The world of on-line learning is dominated by American institutions, but sites such as World Wide Learn make it easy to find courses devised elsewhere. Enter 'UK' into the search facility and you will find links to, among others, an on-line degree in Law from the University of London.

Virtual university

Virtual University (www.vu.org)
This is the world's largest on-line learning community, serving 500,000 students in 128 countries.

Once you register, an electronic desk is created for you. From your desk, you can sign up for classes, log into classrooms and access student chat rooms, with just a few clicks of the mouse.

One modest registration fee allows you to take up to three courses each term. Most courses are for continuing education credits. That means you'll have a certificate to prove you passed the course, but it will not count towards an academic degree.

You can also take classes just for fun (in which case, you get to sit out the final exam).

Best for children

**CyberSchool
(www.cyberschool.4j.lane.edu)**
CyberSchool offers on-line classes for secondary school students worldwide. Its team of tutors aims to complement and build on the traditional teaching that children receive in school. But it does not claim to offer an alternative.

Watch Out!

If you are taking a course leading to a final qualification – in accounting or law, for example – check that it is accredited by the relevant body for the UK.

SEARCH IT YOURSELF

Many colleges and universities offer their own on-line courses. If you have a specific university in mind, try typing its name into a search engine such as Google (**www.google.com**).

If you are looking for a course in a particular subject – for example, astronomy – then try entering the subject name, into a search engine. Entering 'online astronomy course' into the Google search engine, for example, retrieves a free course run by an enthusiast at **www.synapses.co.uk/astro**.

Another way is to click through the search categories at Yahoo! (**http://uk.yahoo. com**). Click On **Education**, then **Distance Learning** and **Courses Online** to see a list of subjects such as History and Psychology. Click on one to see a list of courses.

SEE ALSO
● **Do some research** *– page 109*
● **Help your child to learn on-line** *– page 132*
● **Study for exams** *– page 136*

Do some research

Surf the Web to **dig deeper** into a subject of interest

Unless you have unearthed a new manuscript by a famous author, or made a startling discovery in the laboratory, conducting original research is largely a matter of finding a new angle on the currently held facts, or making new connections between them. You can use the Internet to help you to find the facts, chase down leads, make contacts, exchange ideas and investigate related research in other disciplines. In the often lonely world of the researcher, it can provide you with the stimulation to make that all-important breakthrough.

Search If you are researching a particularly esoteric subject, the Web makes it easier to get in contact with the few people in the world who are working in the same field. A specific keyword search can unearth related Web pages, articles and news stories all of which can provide leads and contacts that you can follow up. Setting up your own Web site can also attract like-minded people to your work.

Archives Many newspapers, journals and magazines have on-line archives so you can search for the article you want and pay for a copy to be e-mailed or posted to you. Try The Newspaper Society (www.news papersoc.org.uk). This has links to more than a thousand papers around the UK, enabling you to find useful information such as the headlines on any specific day.

Official material Most government information is now on the Web. Go to www.ukonline.gov.uk for officially released material from all British government departments.

Multimedia You can also find text, speeches, photos, music, radio and video clips to use as source material.

 Watch Out!

Use a search engine, such as AltaVista (http:// uk.altavista.com) that lists the most relevant sites first. Some simply list all the relevant pages on their database, which is less use to serious researchers.

New angles

A good way to shed light on your subject is to use the findings of other academic disciplines – a mathematics student may find that a discovery in astronomy provides a perfect model for his theory. Someone interested in the diaries of an 18th-century duke may find an economic study of the period helps to explain the diarist's concerns.

GOOD PLACES TO LOOK

On-line library

Librarians' Index to the Internet (www.lii.org)
For a great variety of research sources, try the Librarians' Index to the Internet. A large team of indexers have chosen and annotated Web sources on a broad range of topics – so saving you valuable searching time. The Virtual Library (**www.vlib.org**) is also worth a visit. This consists of individual subject collections, from universities around the world.

Academic help

The Argus Clearinghouse (www.clearinghouse.net)
When you enter your search term at this site, the Argus Clearinghouse

responds with a list of sites, organised and rated by experts in that particular field. The sites are given marks for their level of information, description, evaluation, organisation and design.

Traditional resource

The British Library (www.bl.uk)
Copyright libraries, such as The British Library have long been invaluable to researchers. Among other services, you can search the library's public catalogue by author, title or subject.

Many documents are available to be photocopied and sent to you from the library's Document Supply Centre. Registration for the service is free but you pay for the copying and delivery charges of the items that you require.

Research advice

Expert Central (www.expertcentral.com)
If you can't find the information you are looking for, ask an expert for some help. Expert Central will link you up with a specialist who can answer questions on your subject of interest.

All Experts (**www.allexperts.com**) and Ask An Expert (**www.askanexpert.com**) also let you search their directories, which include hundreds of experts in a wide range of academic and general interest subjects.

MetaCrawler

If your research topic is obscure or you want to retrieve results from a variety of search engines with a single search, try MetaCrawler (**www.metacrawler.com**). This checks many search engines simultaneously and gives you a single list of sites.

CASE STUDY

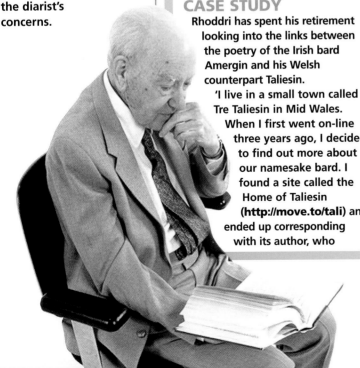

Rhoddri has spent his retirement looking into the links between the poetry of the Irish bard Amergin and his Welsh counterpart Taliesin.

'I live in a small town called Tre Taliesin in Mid Wales.

When I first went on-line three years ago, I decided to find out more about our namesake bard. I found a site called the Home of Taliesin (**http://move.to/tali**) and ended up corresponding with its author, who turned out to be a very nice young woman in Queensland, Australia! It was through her that I found out about Amergin, who was a druidic poet, reputed to have led an invasion of Ireland.

'When I read the Song of Amergin (**www.druidways.co.uk**), I was struck by the similarities with Taliesin's work. I'm no academic but I've since enjoyed comparing Amergin's work with other early Welsh poetry at The Index to Welsh Poetry in Manuscript (**http://maldwyn.llgc.org.uk**) and am now something of a bardic bore!'

RESEARCH METHODS

If you have hit a dead end with your research, try the following:

Keyword searching

This is the easiest type of search. Type in a word or words that relate to your subject in the 'search' box on your search engine or portal. Make keywords as relevant to your subject as possible: the closer the word to the subject, the quicker you'll find relevant material. To get the most out of your keyword searches, turn to page 60.

Academic resources

One way to kick-start your research is to look for details of a course in the subject which will provide you with a recommended reading list. This can be a great way to widen your list of sources. If you find that a particular academic is a specialist in your field, try entering his name into a search engine. You may find references to other books, journal articles or even a Web site.

Newsgroups and bulletin boards

Although there may not be a newsgroup or bulletin board dedicated to your exact area of interest, there is

likely to be one that is quite closely related. If you are looking for an answer to a particular question, it is worth posting it on a site just to generate some correspondence. This may provide you with the answer or a lead to follow up. Even just framing the question may help you to figure out a way round the problem. See *Take part in a newsgroup*, page 92 and *Use a bulletin board*, page 96.

There are also thousands of newsletters on the Internet. A search for 'genetics+ newsletter' for example, reveals several on the subject.

Links and Web rings

Most good sites have a page of links to related sites, or they may be part of a 'Web ring' – a loop of sites all carrying each other's addresses. This is one way to widen your research. Even obscurely connected links may open an avenue of thought that you haven't considered. Make sure you save every useful link as one of your favourite sites.

Site owners

If you find a useful site but it doesn't have exactly what you need, you should try e-mailing the site's author. Most would be thrilled to find someone who has visited their site and is interested to find out more. Sharing and exchanging ideas can be invaluable – especially with experts in an area that touches on the main body of your research.

bibliofind

Shopping Basket   Community   Reference   Help

me to   Search for Free!

Physical resources

The Web can also help you to find useful off-line resources. For rare books, try Bibliofind (**www.bibliofind.com**), which has a database of millions of secondhand and out-of-print books offered by booksellers around the world.

The Welsh town of Hay-on-Wye has the world's largest concentration of secondhand book shops (35 in all). Visit **www.haybooks.com** to search among the four million books stored there.

 Watch Out!

Small sites run by amateurs and enthusiasts can often disappear from the Web without warning. If you find some useful information on a small site, print it out.

Set up your own Web site

If you still can't find what you want on-line, why not set up your own site to attract people who might have the information you want? There may be others with exactly your interest waiting to discover such a site.

For more details on how to do this, turn to our *Making Web Sites* section (page 244).

SEE ALSO
- **Search the Internet** – *page 60*
- **Improve your browsing** – *page 72*
- **Trace your family's past** – *page 161*

Get the latest news on-line

Keep up-to-date with current events, expert analysis and commentary

The main advantages of the Internet over other media are that news is constantly updated and that you can read the latest news, when it suits you, rather than at times dictated by a TV or radio broadcast. Serious news addicts can even have newsflashes sent to them via e-mail or mobile phone. The other advantage of the Internet is personalisation – at many news sites you can choose to be shown only the subjects that interest you, without having to wade through screeds of irrelevant information.

Newspapers and TV
Most traditional news sources offer some sort of on-line coverage. The Internet allows newspapers and broadcasters to offer more in-depth coverage, with detailed explanations of news issues and links to related Web sites. Newspaper Web sites are also useful for researching old news articles.

News links
Excite and Yahoo! have categorised directories of news links, and constantly updated stories and headlines. When you register with a portal, you can enter your preferences so that the site displays just the topics you're interested in, such as sport, entertainment or foreign news.

BBC NEWS

News tickers
Many news sites offer a ticker – a small window that sits in a corner of your screen and displays scrolling headlines as the news unfolds, provided you're connected to the Internet. Look for a 'Ticker' link on a news site and follow the instructions to download the ticker program.

NEWS HEADLINERS

A daily newspaper

The Guardian (www.guardianunlimited.co.uk)
This site carries the news as printed in the daily newspaper, and much more. The Newslist section shows the day's top ten stories, complete with related links, so you can really explore the issues. You can have the *Guardian's* Newslist sent to your e-mail inbox or WAP phone daily. There are also specialised sections devoted to football, travel, money, films, education and other topics. And if you fancy yourself as a news expert, take the daily news quiz to test your knowledge of current affairs.

European news

CNN Europe (http://europe.cnn.com)
This is CNN's portal for European news. Click **Newscast on-demand** to see CNN headline news bulletins broadcast every 30 minutes. You can also access the bulletins at the Headline News site (www.headlinenews.cnn.com).

Customised news

Excite UK (www.excite.co.uk)
This portal is easy to customise, letting you decide what kind of news you want displayed. You can see local, national and international news, sport, entertainment or the latest share prices. Add your own reminder notes, receive local weather forecasts, or find out what's on at the cinema in your area.

Top ticker

MyYahoo! Ticker (http://my.yahoo.com/ticker.html)
The free MyYahoo! Ticker sits at the top of your screen and fits neatly into the title bar of an application, so you can see it while you are using Word or another program. You can choose the topics to be displayed – such as world

---

★ **STAR SITE**

For the most authoritative and current news on the Web, BBC News (**http://news.bbc.co.uk**) provides international coverage, with headlines updated live as they unfold. Follow the homepage links to sections on politics, health, education and sport. Click links marked **In Depth** for full coverage of stories, with strong audio and visual content. You can access Radio 4 and the World Service, plus TV news bulletins and BBC News 24. There's also a news ticker, offering more UK-based news than the Yahoo! service.

---

news, financial news or sport – and decide how often the ticker checks for more up-to-date versions of stories.

News around the world

Assignment Editor (www.assignmenteditor.com)
This site provides links to a large number of newspapers and magazines from the USA and around the world. Read today's news in Moscow or look at a local weather forecast from Tokyo.

The good news

If you want a break from bad news try Positive News (**www. positivenews. org.uk**), where you'll find only uplifting stories. For updates on more peculiar news events, try the Quirkies section at Ananova (**www. ananova.co.uk**).

📖 Did You Know?

*You can catch up with the latest parliamentary debates, including Prime Minister's Question Time, at the BBC's Parliament channel (**www.bbc.co.uk/ parliament**).*

HOW TO: DOWNLOAD A TICKER

1 Go to Yahoo! (**http://my.yahoo.com/ ticker.html**). Click on **Windows Users Click Here**. Follow the instructions to save the set-up program to your hard drive. Double click on it when the download is complete.

2 Read and accept the ticker's terms and conditions. Another window then appears offering to create a short cut to your ticker in your Start menu. Click **Yes**.

3 Enter your My Yahoo! log-in name – if you have one – or tick the box to sign up, if you don't. This will help you register later. Click **OK**.

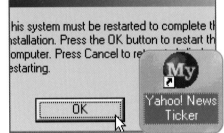

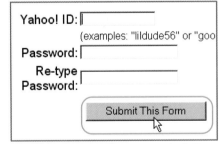

4 You are now asked to restart your computer. Click **OK**. Once you have restarted, double-click the **My Yahoo! News Ticker** icon on your desktop.

5 The ticker now starts running in the top right corner of your screen. At this point, you are asked to connect to the Internet and register with Yahoo!.

6 Fill in your details as requested, then click on **Submit This Form** at the bottom of the page. When your details are accepted, click on **Continue to Yahoo!**

7 To choose which topics the ticker displays, right-click on the **Y!** icon. Click on **Preferences**, then **News**. Select your topics, then click **Apply** and **OK**.

HOW TO: GET NEWS BULLETINS BY E-MAIL

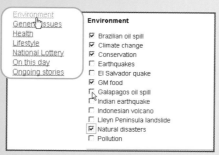

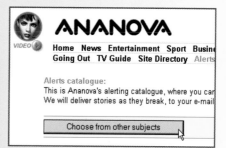

1 Go to Ananova (**www.ananova.com**) and click on **Alerts**, then **Alerts Catalogue** to see a list of news categories such as 'News', 'Business' and 'Entertainment'. Here we have clicked on **News**.

2 Now select from categories such as 'Consumer issues', 'Education' and 'Crime'. We have clicked on **Environment**, which brings up a list of related topics. Click on those you wish to receive news stories about.

3 After you have made your selection, click **Choose from other subjects** to return to the menu of news categories.

WATCH A NEWS BROADCAST

Several on-line news Web sites, such as ITN (**www.itn.co.uk**), BBC News (**http://news.bbc.co.uk**) and CNN (**http://europe.cnn.com**), make it possible to watch a news broadcast from your computer.

To watch a broadcast on the ITN site you need to download a media player. You can do this by going to Real.com (**www.real.com**) and downloading RealPlayer – see page 150 for more details. Once the download is complete, go to ITN and click **Watch ITN News Channel**. RealPlayer launches automatically, and after a moment the video broadcast will start up. Use the control

buttons to play, pause or rewind the bulletin. You can also access broadcast reports on the site.

At BBC News and CNN, you just click on the link next to a news story to launch the audio/video console – a separate window where the video is displayed.

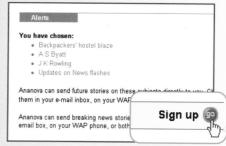

4 When you have finished, click **Sign up go** on the right-hand side of the page. You will then see a list of your alert selections.

5 If you are happy with your selection, choose a username and password, then click **Register**. You will then be sent news bulletins.

Time Saver!

*You can e-mail a letter to the editor to comment on a newspaper article the day it is published. To write to The Times, go to **www.the times.co.uk**, click **Contact Us** and then **The Newspaper Editor**.*

SEE ALSO
● **Take part in a newsgroup** – *page 92*
● **Tune into television** – *page 148*
● **Listen to the radio** – *page 152*

The Internet provides free advice on most areas of the law. But most legal Web sites deal with general enquiries, so finding advice on a complex case might be difficult. If you can't find what you need on-line, your area of enquiry may be too specific. In that case, go to a site such as Law Solutions (**www.law solutions.co.uk**) and e-mail your question to them. A barrister or solicitor will then get back to you with some preliminary advice.

Getting legal help

The Government offers free legal aid information. You can find advice in a wide range of areas, as well as legal aid to help you to pursue a case. The Citizens Advice Bureau (**www.adviceguide.org.uk**) is also very useful for free help, especially for consumer issues and minority rights. If you are in a difficult situation, this free information can be very helpful.

Find legal advice

Consult the Web for legal information and advice

The Web can't fight court cases for you. For that you will need a 'real' lawyer. But the Internet is a great source for researching information, locating solicitors in your area, and gaining free advice on many types of legal question. It may be that you want advice on a divorce or accident claim, or are looking for the right form for a rental agreement. You'll be surprised how much the Internet can offer, and how easy this information is to access.

Before taking any advice, ensure any Web sites you use are accredited by reputable organisations, and check your information with more than one source.

LEGAL SITES

Free advice

**Law on the Web
(www.lawontheweb.com)**
This site offers several different options for free legal advice. Each one involves filling in an on-line form. Then lawyers specialising in the relevant area read your questions and get back to you with an answer personally via e-mail.

Free advice is also available at UKLegal (**www.uklegal.com**), which provides a directory of legal resources, from solicitors to private investigators.

Legal forms

**DesktopLawyer
(www.desktoplawyer.co.uk)**
Many sites offer legal forms over the Internet. They range from tenancy agreements for when you want to let a property, to employment tribunal forms

for taking an employer to court.
DesktopLawyer offers free forms with a large range of interactive documents, including letters, court forms and agreements. You have to download some special software and the documents are automatically created as you work your way through simple questions.

On-line Services
• **Personal Injury**
• **Conveyancing**
• **Legal Support**

Best legal dictionary

Infoplease (www.infoplease.com)
If your solicitor seems to be talking a language you can't understand, you can make some headway through the maze of legalese with an on-line legal dictionary. Sites such as Infoplease will also help you to find answers to common legal questions, and provide detailed definitions of areas of the law.

SEARCH IT YOURSELF

A number of sites specialise in compiling links to legal sites. Start with Lawrunner UK (**www.lawrunner.com**) to help you to track down government agencies and legal organisations around the UK.

Infolaw (**www.infolaw.co.uk**) can help you to search for information, lawyer listings, law books and information regarding overseas laws. It is a good place to find barristers and solicitors near you, if you want to take your concerns further. Legal research

around the world can also be conducted using the Internet Legal Resource Guide (**www.ilrg.com**). This is an index organised by category, which includes more than 4000 Web sites.

Other sites

Even if you have to pay for a solicitor, there are other ways to use the resources of the Web that will save you time and therefore money.

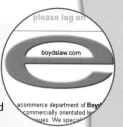

For a comprehensive guide to business on the Internet, with extensive legal advice on all aspects of e-commerce, you could try Boyds Law (**www.boydslaw.com/entiresolution**).

Briffa & Co (**www.briffa.com**) offer legal information relating to protection of copyright, designs, patents, trade marks, trade secrets and information technology. They will also design a business plan suited to your needs.

Another on-line firm, Sykes Anderson (**www.sykesanderson.com**) offers a 'pay-as-you-sue' scheme, which enables you to break down your fees and avoid expensive flat rates.

Problem Solver!
When you ask for legal advice, make your query as detailed as you can. Also, ask if there will be any fees involved or if you are required to come in for a consultation.

Watch Out!
Before you act on any free advice received over the Internet, get a second opinion from another advice service.

Look for a job

Using the Internet can make it easier to look for work

The Internet can play a useful part in your job search. You can search thousands of listings in the UK and abroad – and it only takes a few minutes.

Many sites offer useful tools to help you find the best job. You can read up on the latest industry news, get advice on how to apply for a job successfully and test out your suitability for different careers.

Some sites also allow you to design your CV on-line using their templates. You can even store your CV on the site for prospective employers to view and consider.

On-line listings
Companies advertise vacancies on their own sites, as well as at job listings pages. Register your job preferences with an employment site, and they'll e-mail you details of vacancies as they arise.

Jobs by email
We'll email you v you want - daily suitable vacan choice.

Applications Recruitment sites are full of advice on interview etiquette, and offer guidelines on how to write a good cover letter and CV. Some, such as Workthing (**www. workthing.com**), let you post your CV and a short profile on their site. Potential employers can read through the profiles and ask to see your CV. You can then choose whether or not you want them to see it.

Aptitude tests The Internet can help you to decide which career best suits your talents and personality. With on-line aptitude tests you can find out your personality type and preferred working environment. Tests such as these are especially useful if you are considering a change of career.

HARDWORKING SITES

Where to start

Monster.co.uk (www.monster.co.uk)
This is a comprehensive and user-friendly Web site for job-seekers, offering more than 16,000 UK job listings and 500,000 jobs worldwide. You can ask to be notified of vacancies according to your own preferences, then have the details of suitable positions e-mailed to you when they arise.

Other resources on the site include advice on improving your CV and interview skills, plus message boards and profiles of over 400 featured companies. There is also a handy 'Ask an expert' feature covering all aspects of job-seeking, which enables you to benefit from the experiences of others.

Job Search
Search more than **16,616** UK jobs
Search more than **39,000** European jobs
Search more than **500,000** Global jobs

Take a test

Reed.co.uk (www.reed.co.uk)
This site lets you take a test to determine your personality type and preferred working environment, helping you establish whether you are ready to move on and find another job.

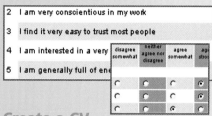

Create a CV

BradleyCVs (www.bradleycvs.demon.co.uk)
This site offers job-seekers a free guide to writing effective CVs, complete with samples that you can view on screen and print out. You can also learn how to

write better cover letters, how to search for jobs on the Internet, and how to negotiate a better salary within your current job.

Excellent advice

Workthing.com (www.workthing.com)
This site offers a wide range of easy-to-search job vacancies. It is also a good source of practical expert advice, such as tips on interview preparation from an experienced personnel director.

You can also use the site to get to the bottom of employment issues such as unfair dismissal and working conditions.

The site is broken down into different job sectors, in order to give you industry-specific information. You can register to have news of jobs e-mailed to you, and find out how to improve your skills in regard to all aspects of job-seeking.

APPLYING FOR JOBS

- Set yourself a weekly target, such as sending out five applications.
- Try to tailor your letter and CV for each application, making your skills seem as relevant as possible.
- Check your letter and CV for mistakes. Many applications are put straight into the bin for this reason.
- Write to companies even if they have not advertised a job. If it arrives at the right time, your speculative approach may succeed.
- Adopt a personal approach. Call the company and ask for the name of the head of the department that interests you, or the Human Resources manager.
- Keep a file of all your applications. Put the ad, your letter and CV in it. Refer to this when you receive replies to your applications.
- Don't give up. While you have applications out there, you are still in with a chance.

 Watch Out!

Don't just look for work on-line: not all companies rely on the Internet. Look in industry magazines, newspapers, job centres, and wherever jobs of interest to you might appear.

Did You Know?

Many people get a job through contacts rather than through an advertisement. Be sure to ask around about jobs and let people know you are available.

Personal profiles

A personal profile is a summary of your skills, personality, motivation and aims. Creating one can help you to focus on what you want to get from a job and so target your job applications more effectively.

HOW TO: CREATE A PERSONAL PROFILE

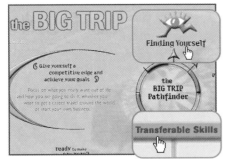

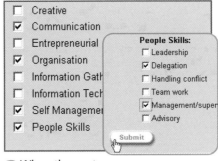

1 To create a profile of your skills, go to the Big Trip (**www.thebigtrip.co.uk**) and click **Finding Yourself**, then **Yes**. Then click **Transferable Skills** (skills that are useful in a number of different jobs).

2 When the next page comes up, select four areas in which you display strengths, and click **Continue**. Select two skills in each sub-section to narrow these areas further. Then click **Submit**.

3 Click **Personal Strengths** and choose the ten adjectives which best describe you. There are over 60 to choose from, so consider the subtleties carefully. Click **Submit**.

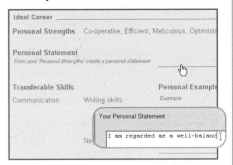

4 Click **Key Personal Values** and pick three values important to you. Click **Submit**.

5 Click **Your Personal Profile**. Fill in the form by clicking on the red areas to type your name and other details on screen. Or, you can print out the page to fill in by hand later.

6 You can add examples as well as comments about why particular values matter to you. You can now use your profile to rewrite your CV and to add focus to your cover letter.

Using employment sites

Some employment sites have thousands of jobs, and scrolling through an entire section can take far too long. You can speed up the search process by selecting only jobs in your region and your industry. Enter an area such as 'Midlands' and an industry such as 'Healthcare' to narrow down the responses.

HOW TO: CREATE YOUR CV ON-LINE

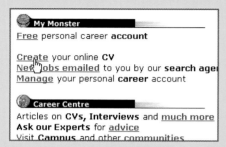

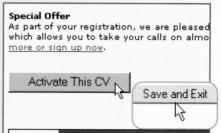

1 Go to Monster.co.uk (**www.monster. co.uk**) and click on **Create your online CV**. If you're new to the site, fill in the registration form. Otherwise, enter your username and password.

2 Click **Create a new CV**. At the bottom of the next page, click **Start** to activate the CV builder. Fill in the blank sections. Click **Save** to move to the next page. Fill in all the required pages.

3 If you want employers to be able to find your CV when they search the site, click **Activate This CV**. If you'd rather send out your CV as and when you want, click **Save and Exit**.

HOW TO: E-MAIL YOUR CV

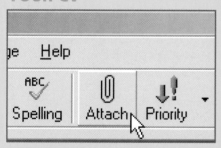

1 Compose your letter using your e-mail software, in this case Outlook Express. When you've finished, click on **Attach** on the toolbar.

2 The 'Insert Attachment' window will pop up. Browse your hard disk for your CV file, select it, and click **Attach**.

3 Your message window now shows the name of your CV file in the 'Attach' window. Click the **Send** button.

E-mailing your CV

If the person you're e-mailing your CV to has a different word-processing package, your formatting could be lost. Tell the recipient which format you used to save your CV, or save your work in a format suitable for their software. Go to the **File** menu and select **Save As**. Under 'Save as file type', choose a Format, name your CV, and click **Save**.

 Money Saver!

Before you pay for expensive training courses, take a free on-line tutorial at the Reed site (www.reed.co.uk).

 Time Saver!

Type out the main points of your CV before you go on the site, then cut and paste the information onto the form.

SEE ALSO
● **Set up Outlook Express**
– page 30
● **Find legal advice**
– page 116
● **File your tax return**
– page 196

Seek medical advice

Use the Internet to get help on a range of health issues

Should you fall ill, nothing can take the place of a consultation with a qualified professional. But the Internet is packed full of medical data and advice. It's especially helpful for those who are housebound by illness. The Web can offer self-care advice for mild conditions, information on over-the-counter and prescription medicines, and access to support groups. Most medical Web sites also offer e-mail newsletters covering recent developments in medical research.

Health on-line

On the Internet you'll find detailed explanations of diseases and conditions, signs and symptoms, and the range of treatments available. One of the best sites for general medical health issues is the MayoClinic (www.mayoclinic.com). The site has an A-Z of medical conditions, a first-aid and self-care guide and nutritional advice. Bear in mind that if a site is US-based, as this is, some products they recommend will be unavailable in the UK.

Help and support

The Internet offers support for people with similar health concerns. There are on-line groups and charities for almost all conditions, from asthma to arthritis.

Health questions

If you need more specific advice, some sites have interactive questionnaires to fill in on-line. Others let you ask a professional. At NetDoctor (www.netdoctor.co.uk), you can e-mail your question to receive a personal response.

BEST OF HEALTH

First place to go

HealthAnswers
(www.healthanswers.com)
An impressive all-round resource, offering health news, articles on key

health areas and an extensive reference section. Select a health topic, such as diabetes, cholesterol or women's health, for informative articles on the subject. For more detailed research, consult the **Library** section for information on diseases, medicines and nutrition and a guide to surgical procedures.

Advice and information

MDAdvice (www.mdadvice.com)
MDAdvice has an 'Ask An Expert' section where you can get advice from a doctor about common medical issues such as allergies and earache, and

less common ones such as Pickwickian syndrome (hypoventilation due to obesity). You can also search through the question-and-answer archive (many questions have been asked before). There is advice and information about health issues specific to groups such as children, women, men and the elderly, plus a news section with the latest information.

Medical and emergency information

NHS Direct (www.nhsdirect.nhs.uk)
This site has information on almost every health issue. See 'Health features' for in-depth studies of conditions such as depression or heart disease, including a rundown of symptoms and treatments and advice on finding support.

If you are unsure whether to consult a doctor about your symptoms, you can answer an on-line health test for some initial advice. Should you require a more personal touch, NHS Direct offers a 24 hour telephone helpline. Calls are charged at local rates.

Good hospital guide

Wellbeing.com
(www.wellbeing.com)
Click **drfoster** for the 'Good Hospital Guide', which you can use to compare your local hospitals – NHS and private. This and other information on the site is validated by the British Medical Association. There's also advice on coping with illnesses, plus the latest health news and reports.

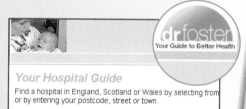

Your Hospital Guide
Find a hospital in England, Scotland or Wales by selecting from or by entering your postcode, street or town.

Cautionary notes

DON'T give out your medical history on-line unless you are sure of confidentiality.
DO remember that medicines and treatments may differ in other countries.
DON'T assume that another person's experiences of the same condition will be the same as your own.
DO get a second – or even third – opinion.

SEARCH IT YOURSELF

For information about health issues, go to a search engine such as AltaVista (**www. altavista.com**), then click the **Health & Fitness** option in the 'Web Directory' listing.

You will see a wide range of health-related topics, such as **Weight Management** or **Family Health**. Click any one of these to get to further sub-divisions, and keep clicking until you locate the precise subject. Sometimes there is a list of Web sites below the subject listings.

Click on one of these to go directly to a site. If you know precisely what you are looking for, type a word or phrase into the search window on the homepage. Then click **Search** to get a list of relevant Web sites. Click on a site name to go directly to it.

HOW TO: USE AN INTERACTIVE HEALTH TEST

There are lots of interactive health tests on the Internet, ranging from diagnostic tests to reviews of your overall health, diet and fitness. You fill in your details in the spaces provided and the Web site then assesses your entries and produces a likely diagnosis, or suggestions as to how you could improve your general lifestyle.

NHS Direct (www.nhsdirect.nhs.uk) has a thorough diagnostic questionnaire for you to fill in to establish the cause of your symptoms. In this case, the symptoms presented are raised, itchy areas on the skin.

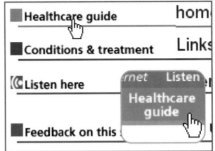

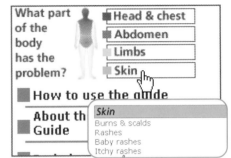

1 First go to the NHS Direct site (**www.nhsdirect.nhs.uk**), then click on **Healthcare guide** – either the underlined words, or the tab at the top of the homepage.

2 A new page comes up. Click **Skin** on the body map at the top left of the page, then select **Itchy rashes** at the bottom of the next page.

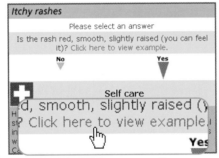

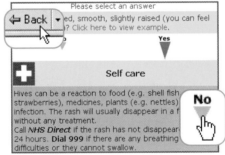

3 A question now appears. If you know your answer already, click **Yes** or **No**. If you are in any doubt, click on **Click here to view example** to see a photograph of the condition.

4 Click **Back** to return to the question. Clicking **Yes** will give you your diagnosis and a suggested self-care advice. Clicking **No** will call up a further question.

5 Continue to click **No** to get further questions which will narrow down an identification of your condition. When your answer is 'Yes', click **Yes** for your diagnosis.

Consult a doctor

If you remain in any doubt about an on-line diagnosis, telephone your GP or contact NHS Direct on 0845 4647. A health test such as this is no substitute for seeing a real doctor, and unusual conditions may require more specialised help.

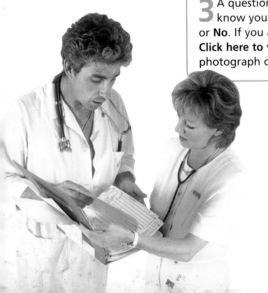

Time Saver!

The World Health Organization (www.who.int), like many other health agencies, makes leaflets available at its Web site. You can then download and print just the sections you want, saving yourself the bother of phoning or writing to the agency directly.

HOW TO: FIND THE BEST SUPPORT GROUP

On-line support groups provide a forum for meeting people with similar health concerns to your own. They can be a good place to exchange practical information on different medicines and treatments, care equipment and techniques, and benefit entitlements. Most importantly, they offer support for individuals and their families.

This example shows a search on the Lycos search engine (**www.lycos.co.uk**) for support groups for glaucoma sufferers requiring homeopathic treatments. If a search returns too many sites, you can narrow down your choices to get fewer, but more relevant, results.

1 Go to Lycos (**www.lycos.co.uk**). Enter the keywords 'glaucoma support group'. Click next to 'UK' if you want to limit your search to UK-based sites, then click **Go Get It!**.

2 Lycos displays over 700 glaucoma support group sites. To limit your results to sites about glaucoma and homeopathy, for example, scroll to the search box at the bottom of the page.

3 In the search box, delete 'glaucoma support group' and enter 'homeopathy'. Now click in the box on the right marked **Search these results**.

4 Click **Go Get It!**, and Lycos will now search the glaucoma support groups it found for ones that mention homeopathy. This will provide you with a smaller number of sites.

5 Click on any sites that interest you. If you still need further information, scroll back down to the bottom of the page and refine or alter your search terms to search again.

 Watch Out!

When looking up medicines on an American site, remember that generic and brand names in the US are often different to those in the UK – paracetamol, for example, is called acetaminophen in the USA.

Buying medicines from abroad

Some people buy medicines over the Internet from abroad that are not available in their home country. Always get medical advice before doing this – both for health and legal reasons. You should always check medical information against two or more independent sources, and if you still have any doubts at all, check again with a qualified doctor.

SEE ALSO
- **Improve your diet and fitness** – *page 126*
- **Enjoy the great outdoors** – *page 225*
- **Live the sporting life** – *page 238*

Improve your diet and fitness

Use the World Wide Web to organise a healthier lifestyle

The Internet cannot do the hard work of dieting and getting fit for you, but it can help you to get started and keep you on the right track.

You can use the Web to check out national fitness and health programs, find a personal trainer, get nutritional advice, or look up local health clubs and sports groups. Many Web sites will help you to devise a fitness plan to suit your lifestyle and physical constitution, while forums and newsgroups allow you to share your views, and your successes and failures with other, like-minded people.

Good health

For overall health, you should eat a sensible diet as well as exercise. There are Web sites that help you to do this. There are some where you can submit details of your eating habits and physical activity and receive suggestions for improving your lifestyle. Calorie counters can help you to monitor day-to-day eating, while body-mass calculators can help you to decide whether you are overweight.

Helpful programs

There are health and diet shareware programs available to download. Both Tucows (**www.tucows.com**), and Jumbo! (**www.jumbo.com**) provide software where you fill in a personal profile to track and report the items you eat and the nutrients they contain, and create a customised fitness regime. This is designed to help you to manage weight loss, diet sensibly and train effectively.

Precautions

Remember that information you find on the Internet is no substitute for a consultation with your doctor. If you are planning to lose more than 900g (2lb) a week, or if you have a pre-existing medical condition, you should consult your GP before embarking on any course of action.

BEST OF HEALTH

Fitness log

Just Move (www.justmove.org)
This site – maintained by the American Heart Association – has practical advice on maintaining a healthy heart as well as the latest health news.

The exercise diary is a useful starting point for anybody

Week	Time Goal
1	90 min
2	90 min
3	120 min
4	120 min
5	160 min

trying to get fit. The site provides specific feedback, which is based on your progress reports and statistical summaries of your fitness programme.

You can also sign up to a personal trainer service, which means you will receive messages of encouragement via e-mail.

Nutrition

Dietsure.com (www.dietsure.com)
This site offers a guide to nutritional analysis and a healthier lifestyle. You can store details of your food intake on-line and monitor the progress of your healthy eating program from anywhere. You can also analyse your diet by completing a questionnaire about your eating habits over the past week.

> Click here to analyse your diet

General health

Thriveonline (www.thriveonline.oxygen.com)
Thriveonline is a site for those who want an overall approach to their health. You can use its facilities to calculate calorie-intake and plan fitness schedules.

There are also more general resources to relieve the stress of everyday life, and advice on alternative therapies for more than 50 health disorders.

Dieting

Cyberdiet (www.cyberdiet.com)
This is a huge site packed with healthy eating information. There are handy facts on vitamins and minerals, and live discussion events hosted by health experts. You can also plan meals to suit your desired calorie intake.

Diet and fitness

Shape Up America! (www.shapeup.org)
A site which uses interactive technology to show you how to balance food with physical activity to maintain a healthy weight. Shape Up America! also has advice on what your daily intake of fat should be – based on details you supply – and healthy recipes to help you through the day.

> Welcome to
> *Shape Up America!*

SEARCH IT YOURSELF

Many Web-indexing services have categories that cover both health and fitness. These services organise Web sites by topic, making it easier for you to find what you need.

For example, go to AltaVista (**www.altavista.com**), and under Web Directory click on **Health & Fitness**. You'll see a range of sub-divisions, and below that a list of Web sites to visit. You can either

Search Tools
- 🔍 MySearch^AV
- ▤ Customise
- 🌐 Translate
- ⚡ Power Browser
- ▤ Text-only Search
- ❓ Help

Web Director
AltaVista Directory > Hea
Diet & Nutrition
Reference
Natural Therapies
Hospitals & Services
Conditions/Illnesses
Guides & News

choose a subject division to further narrow your search, or you can go directly to one of the listed sites by clicking on it.

Watch Out!

If a site is making grandiose claims – for example, 'drop a dress size in under a week' – then it's probably overselling itself. In the end it is you who have to put in the effort.

Did You Know?

*Sites such as Silver Hammer Publishing (**http://silver hammerpub.com**) and Health and Fitness Tips (**www. health-fitness-tips. com**) will e-mail you regular free diet and fitness newsletters.*

HOW TO: CREATE A FITNESS PLAN

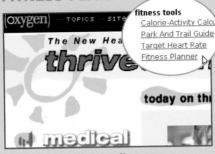
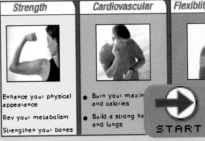

1 First go to Thriveonline (**www.thriveonline.oxygen.com**). Find the heading 'fitness tools' and choose the **Fitness Planner**.

2 You are now presented with a range of questionnaires – each targeted at different areas of fitness. Click on the **Start** button beneath one to continue.

3 Answer the on-screen questionnaire clicking on **Next** to move through the sections. Finally click on **Get prescriptions!** to see a suggested plan.

HOW TO: CONTROL YOUR DIET

1 Go to Cyberdiet (**www.cyberdiet.com**). Under 'Diet & Nutrition', click **Daily Food Planner**. On the next screen, type your daily calorie target, then click **Go**.

2 Use the chart to plan your meals. Click on the recipe titles to view extensive nutritional information, then click on the **I'm Finished!** button.

3 You'll be presented with a meal overview, recipes, a comprehensive shopping list and nutritional information to support your diet.

Time Saver!

*Print out your fitness and diet plans for easy reference. Go to the **File** menu and select **Print**. Or click the **Print** icon in your toolbar.*

Watch Out!

Before beginning a calorie-controlled diet, get advice on your individual calorie needs from your GP.

Join a gym

If you are advised by your doctor or by a Web site to get more exercise, it may be worth joining a gym. Search through on-line databases, such as Club Health (**www.club health.co.uk**) and Gym User (**www.gym user.co.uk**) to find a gym or health club that's right for you. You can search by area or postcode to find a gym nearby.

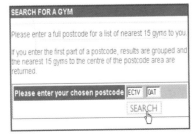

SEE ALSO
- **Seek medical advice** – *page 122*
- **Do your weekly shop** – *page 192*
- **Get cooking** – *page 236*

Solve computer problems

Enhance your PC using the Internet

One of the best places to look if you are having problems with your computer, or want to improve the way it works, is the Internet. Learning how to share problems and gain access to expertise on the Internet can help you to solve almost any computer problem – or at least tell you that the problem can't be solved.

Software bugs
Bugs are programming errors that cause your software to malfunction. It is not unusual for new versions of software to contain bugs. After the software is released, manufacturers soon learn about any bugs from their customers and some create mini-programs called 'patches' to solve them. You can download patches from the Net.

Hardware problems
Every device connected to your computer, such as a printer or scanner, needs software called a 'driver', which allows you to control the device. Often, when a piece of hardware isn't working properly, it is due to the driver malfunctioning.

Some drivers (for your keyboard, for example) are included in your operating system, but when you buy new hardware, such as an external 'zip' drive, you usually need to install a driver for it. If you don't have the right driver, or the driver is defective, your device won't work. Use the Internet to locate and download the right driver.

Identifying the problem
Often you won't even know what the problem is – you will just know that something is wrong. By sharing details of the symptoms with other Internet users, you can often diagnose the problem and take steps to solve it.

IMPROVING YOUR PC

Help with Windows

**Microsoft
(www.microsoft.com/windows)**
First click on your operating system to go to its homepage. In the case of Windows Me, click on **Support** and **Solution Center** to see FAQs, How-To and Trouble shooting sections, arranged by topics such as Hardware, Modems or Printing. From the Solution Center page you can also click **Product Guide** for an overview of WinMe, or click **Newsgroups** for a list of relevant forums. Whatever your Windows problem or version, you can also click on the **Microsoft Knowledge Base** to search for answers to technical questions.

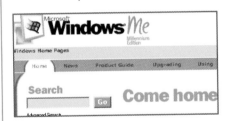

On-line tutorials

Cnet (www.cnet.com)
This site is useful for both new and experienced computer owners. One of the best features is its 'help and how-tos' tutorials, which give advice

and information on all sorts of hardware and software. If you want to perform a task, but can't work out how, this is a good place to start.

Ask an expert

Doctor Keyboard (www.drkeyboard.com)
Doctor Keyboard is a computer columnist at *The Times*. You can chat to the Doctor live or e-mail him questions and receive a response. Search the site for answers to previous questions and browse the Message Board – the sections include hardware, software, the Internet and Mac problems. There is a useful 'Jargon for Beginners' page and advice

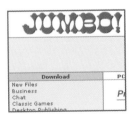

on 'Where to start when it all goes pear-shaped' – such as looking at the program's 'help' file or checking that all your cables are connected.

Computer newsgroups

**Cyberfiber Newsgroups Directory
(www.cyberfiber.com)**
This is a categorised directory of newsgroups. To find newsgroups on a computer topic, search by keyword or browse the subject listing. Click on **Computers (OS and Platforms)** if you

have problems with your Windows or Mac operating system (OS), and **Computers (Not OS Specific)** for other computer problems. Click on a newsgroup name to go to it. Browse the previous posts to find an answer to your problem, or post a question for the newsgroup members to answer. Alternatively, go to Google Groups (**http://groups.google.com**) and browse through the **comp.** newsgroups listed.

Shareware

Some programs, known as shareware (see *Software on the Web*, page 80) can really improve your PC's performance. At Jumbo (**www.jumbo.com**), programs are compared and reviewed so you can find what you want. See the useful Jumbo Guides for help on 'PC Essentials' or uses for an aging PC.

Did You Know?

The first computer bug was an actual bug. In 1945, Grace Hopper of Harvard University was working on an early computer, the Mark II Aiken Relay Calculator, when a moth became trapped in the machine and caused it to shut down.

Watch Out!

Make sure you have anti-virus software running to prevent any potential problems when you are installing new software.

FIND THE RIGHT DRIVER

Imagine a friend has given you an old printer that works fine on his computer, but not on yours – because you haven't got the right driver. How can you find one? Here are a number of routes to finding an answer.

Search engine
Go to a search engine site such as Google (**www.google.com**) and search under the make and model of your printer and the word 'driver', for example, 'Epson stylus color 400 driver'. The results page will list a lot of relevant sites, which you can sift through to find your driver.

Manufacturer's site
The best place to find drivers is at the manufacturer's Web site. At Epson (**www. epson.com**), you can click on **Download Library** to see a list of drivers arranged by type of hardware. Click on a category, such as **Inkjet Printers**, select the model and your operating system, then click **Search** to see any relevant drivers. Click **Download** to download the driver.

Microsoft site
There are links to most manufacturers' sites on the Microsoft Windows Me page (**www.microsoft.com/windowsme**). Click **Support** and scroll down under 'Archives' to **Finding Driver Information**. You can also search the whole Microsoft site at the Knowledge Base page (**support. microsoft.com**). Select your operating system and search under 'drivers'.

Bulletin boards
There are many bulletin boards where users can post and respond to computer problems such as missing printer drivers. To learn how to find one, see page 97.

Newsgroups
To search newsgroup postings for computer-related newsgroups at Google Groups (**http://groups.google.com**), click **comp.**, and look for an entry that matches what you need, such as **comp. periphs** (peripherals). To search for your driver in that newsgroup's 135,000 postings, enter your search term, select the 'in this newsgroup only' button and click **Search**. To post a message of your own, you need to subscribe using a news reader program such as Outlook Express.

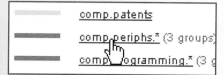

Alternatives
If you are still finding it hard to locate the right driver for your printer, you may be able to use another one that would work just as well. This will not apply in all cases, but it is worth looking up your printer model at UK Technical Support (**www.uktechsupport.f9.co.uk**) to see if there are any alternative drivers listed for it. You can read and post messages, or browse the site by manufacturer and model. There are also trouble-shooting tips and driver downloads available.

Frequently Asked Questions
If you want to find out something about your computer, one of the best ways to do this is by consulting Web sites with FAQs (Frequently Asked Questions). These will often have already covered all of the areas you want to know about, so – rather than e-mailing the site and then waiting for an answer – you can see if someone has asked a similar question before.

 Problem Solver!
If you find a site with instructions on how to solve a problem, print these out rather than saving them. It is easier to refer to a paper document when fixing your computer, especially if you need to turn your computer off during the process.

SEE ALSO
Are you Net ready? – page 14
Software on the Web – page 80
Download from the Web – page 82

131

Help your child to learn on-line

The Web offers a whole new medium for young children to do school work and satisfy their curiosity

There are many Internet learning facilities for children aged 6 to 11. These include on-line dictionaries, encyclopedias, thesauruses and sites on famous explorers, artists and politicians. Children can chat to each other or ask teachers for advice, and parents can ask questions of schools and the government. Some Web sites also offer educational software that you can download and use from home.

LEARNING IS FUN

The Internet can complement and support the education your child receives at school. You and your children can find out about schools around the country, visit the world's best museums and talk to teachers and students on-line.

Web resources

If your child needs a picture for a school project, there are millions of copyright-free images to choose from on the Web. If they're looking for ideas, they can read about any period in history and search through newspaper clippings from the past 30 years. They can even conduct science experiments from the safety of their Desktop.

Homework help

Difficult homework can be tackled with the help of the Internet. There are sites that provide answers to tough questions, from information on a specific author or historical figure to facts on cities or countries. Help with English grammar and spelling is available, as well as on-line foreign language dictionaries. There are also message boards and chatrooms where children can talk to people of their own age on any subject they want.

Just for kids

There are some great 'child-friendly' search sites that list a huge number of educational sites – and protect your child from finding offensive ones.

When your children are not on-line, they can benefit from educational software designed to improve their

subject skills. Find the best free and commercial software at the Superkids Educational Software Review site (**www.superkids.com**).

The Internet also offers help for parents worried about their child's education. Find out exactly what's required by the National Curriculum at the official site (**www.nc.uk.net**), which recommends sites related directly to your child's subject and stage of study.

THE BEST SITES

Where to begin

Ask Jeeves for Kids (www.ajkids.com)
A good place to start your search for educational information. Unlike most search engines, Ask Jeeves lets you type in a question in plain English, such as 'What are the rings of Saturn made of?' It then returns a set of questions, such as 'Where can I find an astronomy page about Saturn just for kids?' that you can click on for answers. It also filters out sites that are unsuitable for children.

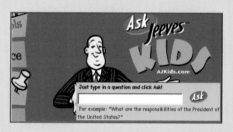

Learning support

Inclusion (http://inclusion.ngfl.gov.uk)
This site, from the National Grid for Learning, helps you to find the right type of education for your child. It provides a range of resources for carers, teachers, learners and parents. There's a list of discussion groups and documents covering special needs education.

Educational site

US National Museum of Natural History (www.mnh.si.edu)
This Web site's educational resources include 'electronic fieldtrips' on the Galapagos Islands, dinosaurs, gemstones and messages from outer space. Each section includes fun projects and activities for kids to take part in.

Fun way to learn

atkidz (www.atkidz.com)
Bright and colourful, atkidz is a great way to interest almost any child in learning – even in difficult subjects like maths. There are also games, an international chatroom, a parents' section about safe surfing and an on-line magazine with all sorts of competitions to enter. The educational pages include lots of useful links and fact files.

Read the latest review
Dinosaurs... ...volcanoes ...sharks ...famous landmarks we've got it covered!
Factfiles

Homework help

Homework High (www.homeworkhigh.co.uk)
This site is maintained by teachers for primary school children. As well as allowing children to ask questions (and get answers), the site lets them browse answers to previous questions and chat with each other.

SEARCH IT YOURSELF

One of the most accessible sites for finding educational resources is Looksmart (**www.looksmart.co.uk**). Although it's a general search engine, it also has a directory of selected Web sites with particular focus on children and education.

On the homepage, scroll down to **Library** and then click on **Education**. You will be presented with further options, such as 'Nursery – A Levels', 'For Parents' and 'For Teachers'. All of these options will link to UK-specific sites. But if you want to broaden your horizons further, simply click on the tab at the top of the homepage marked **The World**.

looksmart
UNITED KINGDOM
Monday, 26 March, 2001   Search the Web:
LookSmart Centres: Email | Insurance-NEW! | Jobs- NEW! | Shopping
wouldn't you like to make really cheap calls too?
Categories Quality sites, chosen by editors   The World   UK

Click on a category and further subcategories until you reach a list of sites, all with descriptions. Click on **Nursery – A Levels**, for example, then **For students**, to see links to sites such as the activity-filled Dodoland (**www.dodoland.com**).

Alternatively, use the search facility. Type the subject you're looking for in the 'Search the Web' box at the top of the homepage and click on **Search**.

SITE CHECKS

There are ways to determine if a site is child-friendly:
- Look for a link to see who runs the site
- Check for a link to the site's safety policy
- Read a few pages to check the language
- Check the links page for unsuitable sites
- Look for accreditation from official organisations

Watch Out!

For peace of mind, use a software package such as Net Nanny to filter out any unsavoury sites your children might encounter. See page 52 for more details.

HOW TO: E-MAIL A HOMEWORK QUESTION

Some Web sites allow you to send in a question and have it answered by a team of trained professionals. You should bear in mind that your question can usually only be answered when a 'class' is in progress. This is a live session concentrating on a specific subject, which means that teachers can often answer your question straight away.

There's a timetable of classes listed at the site, so you know when a teacher is available. Alternatively, you can look at previous questions to see whether your query has already been answered.

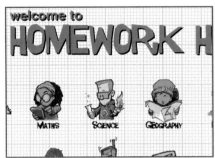

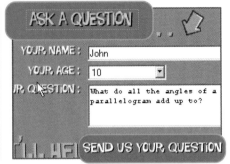

1 Go to the Homework High Web site (**www.homeworkhigh.co.uk**) and click on the subject that you wish to ask a question in; for example, Maths, English or Science.

2 On the next page, click on **ASK A QUESTION**. A screen will appear asking you for your name, your age, your question, and your e-mail address. Click on **SEND US YOUR QUESTION**.

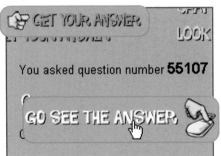

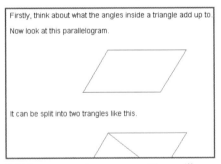

3 A list of other questions that have already been asked will appear. Check if yours is listed. If it is, click on the question for the answer. If it isn't, click **NOPE, MINE'S A NEW QUESTION**.

4 A message will now inform you of your question number. Write this down. Click on **GET YOUR ANSWER**, and enter your number in the box supplied. Then click on **GO SEE THE ANSWER**.

5 The answer to your question will appear and also be e-mailed to you. If there is a delay in replying, then **PLEASE CHECK AGAIN LATER** will show. Keep a note of your question number.

Book sites

For inspiration on books to buy for children, and to get them interested in reading, look up a Web site such as Puffin (**www.puffin.co.uk**) which has lots of information on subjects such as 'How a Book is Made' or the 'Education Zone'.

HOW TO: FIND USEFUL INFORMATION FOR A SCHOOL PROJECT

The Internet is excellent for finding useful information for your child's school work. A quick search using a child-friendly search engine can provide all sorts of relevant material, aimed at just the right level.

Good Web sites also provide links to sites that deal with other related questions and subjects. This can help your children to think around the subject, learn the value of creative research and get ideas and inspiration for their school work.

1 Go to Ask Jeeves Kids (**www.ajkids. com**). In the box in the centre of the page, type in a question, such as 'Where can I find information on the rain forest?', then click **Ask**.

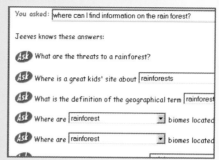

2 The site will bring up a list of questions similar to the one that you asked – 'Where is a great kids' site about rainforests?', 'What are the elements of a rainforest?', and so on.

3 If you are interested in the answers to any of the questions, click on the **Ask** button next to it, and a Web site will appear. You can then click on the subject that interests you.

4 If you want to return to the original range of options your question created, click on the the back arrow at the top of the page.

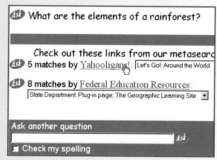

5 Scroll down to the bottom of this page for a list of other sites that will link to your question and give you more general information around the subject area.

Watch Out!

Web sites run by fellow students are prone to error. Where possible, double-check your information against another Web site or a reference book.

Cut download time

Many sites aimed at children contain a lot of pictures. But if you don't need the pictures you can set Internet Explorer not to show them. Click **Tools**, then **Internet Options**. Click the **Advanced** tab, scroll down to 'Multimedia', and untick the box next to 'Show pictures'. Pages will now load quicker. If you want to see a picture after all, right-click on the picture box and select **Show Picture**.

SEE ALSO
- **Study for exams** – page 136
- **Explore the natural world** – page 156
- **Keep the children entertained** – page 174

Study for exams

Learning and **revising** on the Internet

Students at GCSE and A-level standard can use the Internet to help with revision for exams. There is guidance on subjects ranging from history to business studies, and practice exam papers in all areas. Some Web sites even have an 'Ask a teacher' function for finding answers to tricky questions.
   And once the exams are out of the way, the Web can also help you to choose the right university, course or career, and advise you on how to apply for loans or sponsorship.

Revision There are Web sites that can help students set up a revision plan to take them through to the day of the exam. Some also suggest helpful concentration techniques, such as minimising distractions in your working area.

Exam tips Sites for students also provide downloadable practice exam papers and offer advice on grammar, spelling and how to write good essays.

Support Revising for exams can be a lonely business. It can help to know you're one of a crowd. Many revision sites have message boards and forums where students can have a good moan.

Next step Most colleges and universities have their own Web sites with information to help students to choose a degree course.

Careers There are a number of career advice sites, such as Monster (**www.monster.co.uk**) which can advise on the job market and how to apply for a position.

TOP OF THE CLASS

Where to start

S-Cool! (www.s-cool.co.uk)
A great gateway to resources for studying and revision (GCSE and A-level), S-Cool! is also good for career advice. The links pages are particularly comprehensive, with sites for everything from business studies to universities. The site also includes a guide to choosing A-level subjects, plus lively discussion boards covering revision tips, careers, problems at school and help on specific subjects.

Careering Out of Control?
An S-Cool guide to choosing your A-Levels

Choosing which A-levels to take?

How will it affect the degree you can take, or the care you choose?

This S-cool! guide should point you in the right directi

Exam and revision guide

Learn.co.uk (www.learn.co.uk)
This site covers maths, English literature, English language, French, business studies and science. Not only does it contain lessons on a wide range of core texts, concepts and facts, but it will also randomly generate a test on a chosen subject from its extensive on-line database.

Exam pressure

There are numerous sites to help students to cope with exam pressure. One of the best places to get help is Childline (**www.childline. org.uk**), which has a number of fact sheets giving plenty of common-sense advice. This includes everything from making flashcards to relaxing by taking deep, calming breaths.

Further education advice

HERO (www.hero.ac.uk)
Containing helpful articles on all aspects of the student experience, HERO also offers information on research, business, culture and sport. There are profiles of higher education institutions all over the UK, and advice and information to help you to choose a course and university to suit you. It also has articles on funding your study.

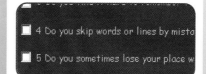

Grammar guide

The Blue Book of Grammar and Punctuation (www.grammarbook.com)
A useful guide to grammar and good writing, this site covers good, clear English usage and explains grammatical pitfalls such as the dangling participle ('Rushing to finish the essay, Bob's printer broke' implies the *printer* was finishing the essay, not Bob) and the dependent clause.

A useful collection of related links, includes Roget's Internet Thesaurus

(**www.thesaurus.com**) and GrammarNow (**www.grammarnow.com**) where you can e-mail in your specific grammar questions.

THE BLUE BOOK ACED AND DANGLIN
OF GRAMMAR AND PUNCTUATION

Rule 1. If you start a sentence with an action, place the acto

Incorrect While walking across the street, the bus hit her.

Correct While walking across the street, she was hit by a bus. She was hit by a bus while walking across the street.

Rule 2. Place modifiers near the words they modify.

★ STAR SITE

Study Skills (www.studyskills.soton.ac.uk)
This site helps you to gain the study skills you'll need at university. First take the Learning Styles test to see how you work best, then follow the site's advice on managing your time more effectively and studying more efficiently – leaving you more time for having fun!

4 Do you skip words or lines by mista

5 Do you sometimes lose your place w

 **Did You Know?**

You can buy past exam papers from your examining board. Find out which board your school is registered with and phone them up. They will send you a list and a form to fill in. Each paper will cost about £1.50. Allow two weeks for delivery.

 Watch Out!

Make sure you are studying the right material. Check the information at the National Curriculum site (www.nc.uk.net).

The BBC Schools Revision site offers help at GCSE level, AS level, and age 16+. It includes tests, revision material and an 'Ask A Teacher' feature so you can query anything that has not been covered. However, you may have to wait up to three days for a reply.

HOW TO: REVISE AND TAKE A TEST ON-LINE

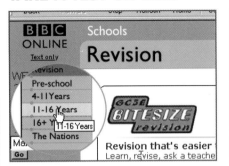

1 Go to the BBC Schools Revision Web site (**www.bbc.co.uk/education/ schools/revision**). Look at the left hand side of the page and click on the appropriate age range.

2 You will be given a list of subject areas. Click on the one that you need help revising.

11 to 14 yrs - Dear Nobody
Find out how Berlie Doherty's novel wa facts about teenage pregnancy.
KS3 - Bitesize Revision
Brush up your Shakespeare, fiction an
GCSE - Bitesize: English
Revise the GCSE English syllabus inclu cultures and non-fiction texts.

3 A list of revision topics and syllabuses will be shown. Click on the area you want to study.

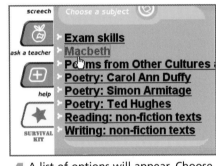

4 A list of options will appear. Choose a subject you want to revise and click on it.

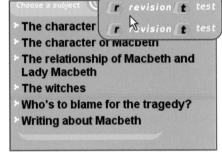

5 You can then decide to start with a Revision Bite which gives you detailed tips on how to tackle questions, or a Test Bite which tests you on the subject you have chosen.

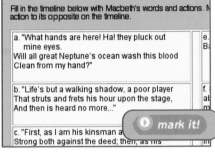

6 If you choose to take a test then at the bottom of the page click on **mark it!** and your work will be marked with the correct answers.

Better printing
Save ink and don't print unnecessary pictures. Copy and paste the relevant text into a Word document and then print it. To do this, highlight the text, go to the **Edit** menu and select **Copy**. Then open the Word document, go to the **Edit** menu and select **Paste**.

HOW TO: REGISTER FOR A REVISION NEWSLETTER

A revision newsletter is an excellent way to keep in touch with the most up-to-date news and advice for your exams and life at school and at home. Select the subjects that interest you most and the newsletter will keep you abreast of the most recent debates and developments within that field – such as the latest computer viruses or tips on buying your first car.

Depending on your stage of study, it can also help with advice for a future career or for further study in your chosen area.

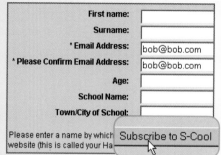

1 Go to S-Cool! (**www.s-cool.co.uk**). On the right-hand side of the page there is a section marked 'Join Mailing List!'. Click on the icon marked **Signup!**

2 Complete the form with your name, e-mail address, your 'handle' name (the name you will be known by), and your subjects of interest. Then click **Subscribe to S-Cool!**.

STUDYING ON THE WEB

There is plenty of useful information on the Internet which can be used in essays and other school work. But it is important to use it properly.

It is tempting to trust that everything that appears on the Web is correct. This is far from the case. Many sites have been designed and written by enthusiastic amateurs and the facts and views expressed are often questionable. It is always worth cross-checking all information with other sources.

Many students are also tempted to copy passages of text word-for-word in their essays. This is always easy for teachers to spot. It is far better to quote the Web site and comment on it. This indicates that you have conducted some research and formed an opinion of your own – both of which are good ways to gain marks.

Thank you for signing up with S-Cool!

Your password has been sent to you by e will be able to logon to the S-cool! site.

Click here to go back to the main menu and

3 After a couple of minutes you will receive an e-mail confirmation. This will contain your password to log in to the site as a member. You will now also receive the newsletters by e-mail.

Did You Know?

Using the grammar and spell check function in Word can help to eliminate mistakes in essays. But make sure the program is set to UK English and do not act blindly on its advice – if you mistype 'art' as 'act', for example, the program will not pick it up.

SEE ALSO
- **Learn something new** – *page 106*
- **Do some research** – *page 109*
- **Look for a job** – *page 118*

Hobbies and leisure

Go into outer space

Learn about the Universe on the World Wide Web

Thanks to the Internet, astronomy has come out of the observatory and into the sitting room. Anyone using a computer can become a space enthusiast or a witness to cosmic events such as eclipses and solar flares. Official and unofficial sites provide a mix of science, speculation, philosophy and fun. Amateurs can follow debates that previously raged in academic journals only. Does the discovery of ice on the Moon increase the chances of its colonisation? Do the marks on the surface of Mars signify an ancient civilisation?

Space travel You can catch the latest space mission news at the official sites of the National Aeronautics & Space Administration (**www.nasa.gov**), the European Space Agency (**www.esa.int**) and the British National Space Centre (**www.bnsc.gov.uk**).

Space images The Web is rich in exciting space images – both still and animated. NASA and ESA do not copyright their images, so they are freely available to download.

Astronomy The study of space is well served on-line at sites such as **www.astronomyforum.net** with star-gazers discussing their hobby.

Aliens Sites about aliens are very popular. One site (**www.hardcore linux.com/alien**) suggests that the Internet itself was devised by aliens to study the collective consciousness of the human race.

Simulations The Internet cannot take you into space, but you can try landing Apollo 11 on the Moon at the Apollo Project Archive site (**www.apolloarchive.com**).

SITES FOR THE STARS

Where to start
NASA (www.nasa.gov)
This huge, sprawling, US government department has an official site which is a massive network of individual sites. It has information on space travel and astronomy as well as material about such sciences as meteorology and navigation, which rely on space research and observation.

Eclipses, meteorites, life on Mars – it's all here. From the homepage, you can access the latest space news, or click on

links to historical archives, education, videos or children's pages.

Even the Russian Space Agency (http://liftoff.msfc.nasa.gov/rsa/rsa.html) can now be found on-line at the NASA site – reflecting the greater co-operation between the former Cold War rivals.

Space science
Zoom Astronomy (www.enchanted learning.com/subjects/astronomy)
This is a sensible, family oriented site with lots of information on the Sun, stars, Moon and planets.

Subjects such as solar eclipses are explained with the aid of clear

diagrams. There are also fun things to do, such as working out how much you would weigh on another planet.

Space news
Spaceflight Now (www.spaceflightnow.com)
Spaceflight Now carries news on all manned and unmanned space missions, as well as stories from the world of astronomy. Learn about the eruption on Jupiter's moon Io and see the latest deep space pictures from the Hubble Space Telescope. Click **Launch Schedule** for a comprehensive guide to upcoming launches throughout the world. You can view some of the launches on live Internet broadcasts. Click **Features** then **Video Vault**, for views from exciting rocket-based cameras.

Search for aliens
SETI Institute (www.seti-inst.edu)
The SETI Institute leads the field in the Search for Extra-Terrestrial Intelligence, analysing radio telescope data for unusual signals. The main purpose of the site is to convince you to lend the institute the power of your own computer to help to conduct this research (see overleaf).

But the site also feeds the public's voracious appetite for all things alien. You can read articles on what would happen if a signal was discovered and verified (the first person to be informed would be the secretary-general of the United Nations, in accordance with Article XI of the Treaty on Principles

Governing the Activities of States in the Exploration and Use of Outer Space, Including the Moon and Other Bodies).

If you think you have spotted an alien, you can report your sighting to Project: S.E.T.L.A.B. – The Study of Extra-Terrestrial Life and Answers from Beyond (**www.setlab.org**). This site is not intended to be funny, but you may need to suspend disbelief to enjoy it.

Best site for children
SpaceKids (www.spacekids.com)
With space news and features, plus pictures, videos, games and a Solar System Tour, this site is informative, lively and lots of fun.

The 'Ask Experts' feature allows your child to find out almost everything he or she has ever wanted to know about space.

SEARCH IT YOURSELF
Go to AltaVista (**www.altavista. com**) and click on the Web Directory tab. Then click on **Library & Resources**, then **Sciences**, then **Astronomy & Space** for a list of related sites.

Alternatively type a combination of keywords into a search engine:

Alien	Astronomy
Astrophysics	Extraterrestrial
Mars	Observatory
Planet	Space
Space exploration	Star

Watch Out!
Scan downloaded files for viruses before you open them, especially if they are not from a trusted source such as NASA. Most anti-virus software can be set to scan downloaded files automatically.

HOW TO: SEARCH FOR EXTRA-TERRESTRIAL LIFE

SETI@home (**http://setiathome.ssl.berkeley.edu**) uses millions of home PCs to search radio telescope data for unusual signals. To volunteer, you need to download a piece of software and a chunk of data onto your PC. The software runs when your PC is idle – generating a colourful graph that makes a great screensaver. The program then sends the results over the Internet to a research institution for evaluation, and downloads another piece of data.

Your PC needs at least 32Mb of RAM to run the software. To check this, right click on the 'My Computer' icon and select **Properties**.

WATCH SPACE FOOTAGE

The Apollo Project Archive (**www.apolloarchive.com**) has the best collection of images, sounds and video from the historic Apollo lunar landings. Video quality is better on the later missions, but all the clips are fun to watch.

1. Click **Multimedia** in the Table of Contents, and scroll through the archive.

2. Scroll down to the Apollo 11 section and click on the link for Neil Armstrong stepping onto the Moon's surface.

3. Windows Media Player will open up and the video will play – at first, only in small chunks at a time. This is because the Media Player is playing the video faster than your computer can download it. But after your computer has fully downloaded the video, you will be able to replay it in its entirety.

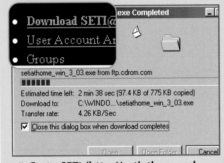

1 Go to SETI (**http://setiathome.ssl.berkeley.edu**). Click on **Download SETI@home**. From the next page, click on the Windows version of the program. Scroll down and click on **Download**.

2 Follow the on-screen instructions to download the installation program to your PC, then double-click the program icon on your desktop to install the software.

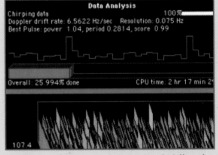

3 Now when your computer is idle, the SETI screensaver will start up, and begin analysing your chunk of data on-screen. Perhaps the first signs of alien life will be found by your computer.

Did You Know?

Apollo 13 astronaut Jack Swigert never said the famous words 'Houston, we have a problem'. In fact he said, 'Okay Houston, we've had a problem here'. Read NASA's full transcript of the mission at **www.hq.nasa.gov/office/pao/History/Timeline/apollo13chron.html**.

A dream come true

The European Space Agency is recruiting for missions taking place over the next few years. Visit **www.esa.int** and click **Frequently Asked Questions**. Scroll down to **How can I become an astronaut?** to see the selection requirements.

General Requirements

Applicants, male or female, must be nationals of an ESA Memb preferred age range is 27 to 37. Applicants must be within the heigh to 190 cm. They must speak and read English and have a univer equivalent) in Natural Sciences, Engineering, or Medicine, and pre three years' postgraduate related professional experience, or fly acquired as test, military or airline pilot.

Medical Requirements

SEE ALSO
- **Download from the Web** – page 82
- **Explore the natural world** – page 156
- **Keep the children entertained** – page 174

Take a virtual tour

Explore the world from the comfort of your own home

A virtual tour is a feature on a Web site that attempts to recreate the movement and interactivity of the real world on your computer screen. It uses sounds, pictures, maps, videos, animation and 3D images to give you 'virtual experiences' that would be far less accessible in real life – such as viewing the world's great art treasures, walking around Sydney Opera House or travelling back in time to visit a Roman fortress.

How it all works

Virtual tour sites often use video clips or panoramic images that you can 'walk' around. Some estate agents, for example, offer virtual tours of properties for sale. These can show you the inside of a house, allowing you to use on-screen buttons to rotate your view.

Many travel sites include these virtual panoramas. To find them, search under your destination and add the word 'panorama' – for example, 'rome and panorama'.

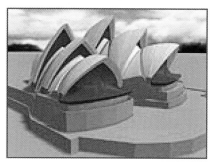

More complex virtual tour sites include impressively realistic three-dimensional imagery. You can walk around a 3D architectural model of the Sydney Opera House and other famous buildings at Great Buildings Online (**www.greatbuildings.com**).

Most virtual tours can be viewed using your usual Internet browser, but some sites require you to download additional software.

 Watch Out!

Different sites use different programs to create 3D images. This means that you cannot download one single program to view them all. Each site will provide a link to the software you require.

THE BEST SITES

Gallery tour

The Louvre (www.louvre.fr)
Take a closer look at great works of art such as the Mona Lisa. Select **English** as your language, then click **Virtual Tour** and select a gallery. You'll see a list of rooms. Click the **Q** icon next to each room to see a 360-degree panorama. You need QuickTime to view the rooms. Some rooms also have a high-resolution panorama (indicated by a large 'Q'), which offers a better quality picture.

New York's Museum of Modern Art (**www.moma.org**) lets you tour an image gallery with audio commentary. Click **Collection**, then choose a department, such as **Painting and Sculpture**, to open a thumbnail gallery. Click on one of these miniature images to see a larger version and hear the accompanying commentary.

Best collection of links

Ipix (www.ipix.com) is the company that makes the software used to view most 360-degree panoramic images on the Web. Click **Gallery** for links to various panorama sites. Look under 'Transportation' for links to tours

around a Boeing 777 plane or Julio Iglesias's private jet. Look under 'Events' for a link to the official site of the British Open golf championship (**www.opengolf.com**), with a video fly-by of every hole at St. Andrew's.

Best use of the Internet

EarthCam (www.earthcam.com) combines panoramic images with Web cams to bring you live-action video or still panoramic images which are updated every 60 seconds. Click **Times Square Video** to wander around New York's Times Square and take your choice of six cameras showing live still, panoramic and video images.

The EarthCam site also has an extensive directory of Web cam links. You can browse through categories such as 'Traffic Cams', 'Space & Science Cams' or 'MetroCams', featuring views of major cities around the world.

SEARCH IT YOURSELF

Click **Travel** at directory site About.com (**www.about.com**) for links to hundreds of travel sites. You can also use the site's internal search engine to find what you want. Searching under 'virtual south america' locates the Virtual Tour of South America, starting at Angel Falls, Venezuela.

Did You Know?

*You can follow a yellow cab around New York City by going to the Cab-Cam at **www. ny-taxi.com**.*

Troubleshooting virtual tours

Some virtual tours rely on a mini-program called Java, which works as part of your Web browser. To check that Java is functioning correctly, go to Microsoft's Java test page (**www.microsoft.com/windows/ie/most/howto/java. htm**). If you can see a pretty picture, Java is working. If you can't, Java may have become corrupted. Re-install Internet Explorer if you have it on a disc, or download another copy from the Microsoft Web site if you don't (**www.microsoft.com/downloads**).

CASE STUDY

Like many children, George and Grace were fascinated by the mysteries of ancient Egypt. Their father Mark was happy to encourage them and decided to spend some time looking for Web sites on the subject.

'I wanted to find something fun, interactive and educational, so I tried looking for a virtual tour. Once I found one, it took an hour or so to get all the right software, but I have since found a lot of other tours which use the same program, so I think it was worth it.'

Mark started his search at About.com (**www.about.com**). 'I like the way they check the sites out first'.

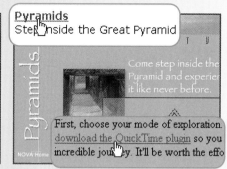

Find It Now: educational virtual tour Egypt

On the About Network:

African Field Trips
Information and resources pertaining to homework help and lesson plan resou
URL: http://kidscience.about.com/cs/africa/index

Online Field Trips for Homeschoolers
Take your children on educational and
URL: http://homeschooling.about.com/cs/fieldtrip

1 Mark entered 'educational virtual tour Egypt' into the search box. One of the results was another site which specialised in home schooling.

Pyramids
Step inside the Great Pyramid

Come step inside the Pyramid and experie it like never before.

First, choose your mode of exploration. download the QuickTime plugin so you incredible jou y. It'll be worth the effo

NOVA Home

2 One of the tours on offer was a trip around a pyramid. The introductory text stated that the tour required the free QuickTime plug-in, so Mark clicked the link to go to the QuickTime site.

Download the free player

QuickTime 5

Tell us who you are:

E-mail Address
mark.andrews@easynet

Downloading   VISE Data
7286K of 7364K

First Name
Mark

Last Name
Andrews

3 On the QuickTime site, Mark chose to download the PC version of the plug-in and spent an hour downloading the program, following the on-screen instructions to install it.

whole experience in
sage to room and back

4 Returning to the Pyramid site, Mark then downloaded the tour itself, which took about ten minutes. The tour was made up of a series of QuickTime virtual reality pictures.

5 Mark and his children used the mouse and keyboard to rotate the images and move through the passageways and chambers of the pyramid. George and Grace loved it.

Jargon Buster!

Plug-in A mini program, which is added to your Web browser, to open and run certain files such as 3D images.

Other QuickTime tours

The QuickTime Web site (**www.apple.com/quicktime/products/gallery**) contains a number of examples of virtual reality pictures, such as a night-time scene in Time Square, New York. It also offers links to other sites, which offer virtual reality tours using QuickTime. These include Neovisioni (**www.neovisioni.com**) which offers a great panoramic view from the top of the Jungfraujoch in Switzerland.

Tune into television

Find out everything about TV from your computer

Whatever TV programmes you like, you can use the Web to catch up on the latest plot-lines, find out the time and channel of a specific episode, or get behind-the-scenes information.

You can also download shows to watch on your computer – though the size and quality of video images on the Internet is poor. Many programmes, such as 'reality' TV shows, now have accompanying on-line content, including extra material not broadcast on TV, and round-the-clock coverage of events.

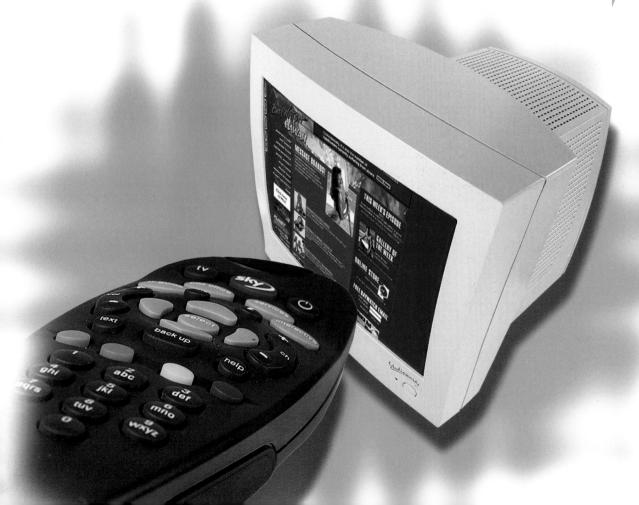

TV guides
The Internet makes it easy to look for TV guides. Listings can be personalised to suit your viewing preferences, and many sites offer a service that will e-mail you whenever your favourite programme is going to be on.

It's also worth visiting individual channels' Web sites for in-depth coverage. To find them, simply enter the station name into a search engine, or go to TV Show (**www. tvshow.com**) which has links to TV stations and networks worldwide.

Desktop TV
You can also watch a wide variety of live TV and Web broadcasts on your computer. You can download old series, watch live TV over the Internet or record cable programmes and play them back later.

Web cams
You can also watch live footage from cameras positioned in all sorts of places around the world, from ski slopes to the Elvis wedding chapel in Los Angeles. These cameras are known as Web-cams.

PRIME-TIME SITES

Where to start

TV Show (www.tvshow.com)
This site offers schedules from almost every country in the world, and links to sites about every aspect of TV programmes, news, stations and personalities, as well as sites about TV production (find out how to sell a TV script) and technology (discover how your TV works or how to fix the VCR).

TV listings

Radio Times (www.radiotimes.co.uk)
The BBC's main listing site contains listings, news, reviews and interviews. Listings cover all the channels, including satellite. There are features on presenters, and a search facility to tell you when programmes are on. The BBC also has a general site (**www.bbc.co.uk**) and sites for each channel (**www.bbc1. co.uk** and **bbc2.co.uk**) with links to everything Beeb-related.

Great Web-cams

**Discovery Channel
(dsc.discovery.com/cams/cams.html)**
The Discovery Channel presents a variety of Web-cams, showing live views of locations around the world and beyond.

You can look in on sharks and gorillas in their natural surroundings, an active volcano in central Mexico, or even view the surface of the Sun.

TV monitor service

TVEyes (www.tveyes.com)
If you don't want to sit glued to the TV, but do want to know when a particular subject is mentioned, use the TVEyes monitoring service. Their software monitors TV in real time and sends you a message via e-mail or pager whenever your keywords are spoken on television. You can then go on-line to view the programme's complete transcript.

Classic TV

LikeTelevision (www.liketelevision.com)
This site has hundreds of classic television shows, commercials, cartoons, movies and music videos for you to watch on your PC.

All you need to do is install RealPlayer to watch shows such as *Bonanza*, *Bugs Bunny* or *Superman*, or movies featuring stars like Charlie Chaplin.

 Time Saver!

If you use a TV monitor service, you can set it to send you several mentions of your keyword at once, rather than individually. Otherwise, you may receive an almost constant flow of e-mail.

SEARCH IT YOURSELF

For links to TV-related job opportunities, chatrooms, broadcasters' addresses, and fan pages of virtually every show ever made, from *I Love Lucy* to *Bob the Builder*, try TV Show (**www.tvshow. com**) or

UltimateTV (**www.ultimatetv.com**). TV Show has information on TV stations around the world.

Most TV stations, popular shows and networks maintain their own sites. You can quickly find most of these by entering their name into a search engine. This will work with many TV stars as well. Or, if you are really in a hurry, try simply entering the name of the show or person as a basic Web address, for example 'www.baywatch. com'. If you are looking for sites dedicated to the television shows of the past, try the links at TV Cream (**http:// TV.cream.org**) and Yesterdayland (**www.yesterdayland.com**).

RealPlayer

A program that plays video and sound files, RealPlayer also relays live video and audio Web-casts. You can download a free version from the maker's site.

HOW TO: DOWNLOAD REALPLAYER

1 Go to the RealPlayer Web site (**www.real.com**) and click **Download: RealPlayer**. Scroll down and click on **RealPlayer 8 Basic – is our free player**.

2 Enter your details into the RealPlayer download form and select the 'Bundle SPINNER with my free Realplayer' box.

3 If your computer meets the minimum requirements to run RealPlayer 8, click **Download FREE RealPlayer 8 Basic**. If not, go to 'Important Notes' to download an older version of RealPlayer.

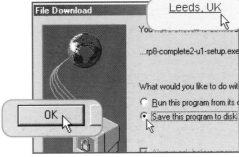

4 Click on the location nearest to you – the location of the computer you will be downloading from. The 'File Download' window will appear. Select **Save this program to disk** and click **OK**.

5 Choose where you want your file saved and then click **Save** to begin the file download. The download should take ten to fifteen minutes.

HOW TO: WATCH TELEVISION ON-LINE

1 Go to a site that offers TV and movies on-line, such as LikeTelevision (www. liketelevision.com). Click on **LikeTelevision** in the centre of the homepage.

2 You first need to sign up to the site. Click **VIP**, then **New Users Register Here!**. Fill out a short form and click **Register**. You will then receive an e-mail confirming your free registration.

3 Go to the list at the top of the page, and click on **Classic TV**. A page will come up, listing all the available shows. Click on the series you want to watch, for example, **The Beverly Hillbillies**.

---

1. Beverly Hillbillies - A Man for Elly
Description: LikeTelevision Fans · this episo... they've found the perfect man for Elly · Quirt "watching" machine). But big tough Quirt t... sponsor's son. Highly Recommended!

2. Beverly Hillbillies - Chickadee Return...
Description: LikeTelevision Fans · this episo... Laverne. Also starring Sharon Tate as Janet... Recommended!

4 A list of episodes will now come up, each with a description. Click on the episode you want to watch.

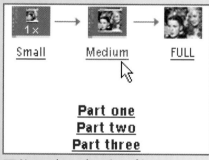

Small   Medium   FULL

Part one
Part two
Part three

5 Now select what size of image you want to watch – 'Small', 'Medium' or 'FULL' screen size. Choosing a larger screen size will reduce the quality of the image.

Beverly Hillbillies - A Man for Elly
Starring – Buddy Ebsen, Irene Ryan, Donna Douglas, Max Baer Jr., Raymond Bailey

LikeTelevision Fans · this episode · A Man For Elly · features Henry Gibson! The Clampetts think they've found the perfect man for Elly · Quirt Manley (Henry Gibson) · super stud cowboy from TV (Granny's new "watching" machine). But big tough Quirt turns out to be a product of Hollywood. The real Quirt Manly is the just sponsor's son. Highly Recommended!

Part one

6 To watch your programme, click on **Part one**. When that section has finished, click on **Part two** and so on.

---

 iMac

Most Macs come loaded with an alternative to RealPlayer, called QuickTime. But some sites may still require you to have RealPlayer. You can download a Mac version of the program from the RealPlayer site.

Web TV

Sony's WebTV (**www.sony.com**) is a kind of TV set designed to access e-mail and the Web without the need for a computer. WebTV uses your TV as a monitor and includes a remote control that is used to compose e-mail. You can watch TV in a small window while you are browsing on-line, or participate in Web-based activities built around a TV show. At the moment this is a US-only service.

SEE ALSO
• **Listen to the radio**
– *page 152*
• **Access showbiz news**
– *page 164*
• **Buy a book, CD or video**
– *page 201*

Listen to the radio

Use your PC to tune into Internet stations

You might think listening to the radio using a computer is unnecessary if you already own a radio. But Internet radio offers far more than the broadcasts available on a standard set. With the Internet, you can listen to diverse and stimulating broadcasts from all around the world. If you are living away from home, or have family or friends in other countries, it's easy to keep in touch with 'local' news. There are also special-interest Internet stations covering music or subjects that you cannot receive on a standard radio.

What do I need?

Most radio sites on the Web broadcast either for RealPlayer software or for the Windows Media Player. It's a good idea to make sure both are installed on your computer before you go looking for Web-casts. Most PCs already have Windows Media Player installed, but if not, you can install it from Microsoft's Web site (**www.microsoft.com/windows/ windowsmedia**) for free, and you can install RealPlayer from RealNetworks (**www.real.com**). There's also a free version of this software which is suitable for Internet radio, available from the same site.

How do I listen?

To listen to a radio station, you need to browse the Web and click on a suitable link. This opens up RealPlayer or Media Player, which start playing the station through your computer's speakers (see page 150).

What is available?

Many Internet radio stations only exist on-line. Type 'Internet radio' into your search engine to begin browsing through the many stations around the world now available.

RADIO SITES

Best place to start

Radio Now (www.radionow.co.uk)
This is an excellent place to look for a list of UK Internet radio stations. As well as providing general information about the content of each station, there are links to live Web-casts and to the stations' own Web pages. Information about digital radio services is also listed. Radio sites are listed by name and subject, making it easy for you to find what you want.

On-line-only station

LiveIreland.com (www.liveireland.com)
Live Ireland broadcasts only on the Internet. It provides several channels concentrating on traditional and contemporary music, and news and magazine programmes. The Live Ireland homepage also includes interviews, news and Web-cam feeds.

Station listings

Internet Radio List (www.internetradiolist.com)
This site provides links to hundreds of Internet radio sites around the world.

There is a 'featured station' every day, which gives you somewhere to start looking. Stations are organised by categories, such as music, news, sports and talk. There's also advice on building your own Internet radio station, covering the general, technical and legal aspects of broadcasting on-line.

Unusual radio site

Book Radio (www.bookradio.com)
Book Radio is not a radio station, in the conventional sense, but it shows what can be achieved using the idea of Web-casting sounds. The site is dedicated to all things book-related, and includes extracts from books, literary discussions, and interviews with authors. Book Radio is regularly updated with feature Web-casts on the latest works of fact and fiction.

★ STAR SITE

Live Radio (www.live-radio.net)
This site is the UK's most visited live radio site. It is the largest directory of links to radio stations broadcasting live on the Internet. All links on the site are monitored and updated daily, so you can be confident that you'll be able to hear all the stations listed.

The many thousands of national and international radio stations that broadcast over the Internet are grouped by world region, with each area having its own homepage, making it easy to find the country whose stations you are interested in.

You can also look for stations that broadcast only on the Internet. Browse the 'Net Only' section to locate stations such as Israel's Falafel Radio and Australia's Disco Channel, or Beethoven.com which broadcasts from Connecticut in the USA. When you have found a station of interest, click on the **Live Feed** button to start listening to a broadcast on your computer.

Did You Know?
You can listen to Internet radio by selecting stations from Web directories, but it's better to listen directly from their homepages, where you'll find additional news and information.

Time Saver!
For a list of Internet radio sites on the Web, and other radio-related information, visit the radio directory (www.radio directory.com).

HOW TO: TUNE IN TO INTERNET RADIO STATIONS

Once you have installed RealPlayer, you can use its own built-in listings to find a radio station. Another way to find stations is to use a search directory. Here are two routes to some good music.

1 First open RealPlayer. Then make sure you are on-line, go to the Radio menu and select **Open Radio Tuner**.

2 Wait for a few seconds until the tuner information appears. Then select a music type from the list. You will be shown a list of featured stations, and can click on one to hear it.

3 If the station you want is not listed, click **Find a Station**.

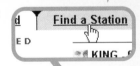

4 Enter information to help you to find a station you want, in this case a classical station in Minnesota, then click **Find**.

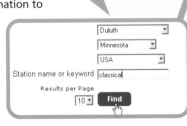

5 Look at the list of stations found, and play the one you want by clicking its name. The small player window will open, and you will hear the station broadcast.

1 Go to the Excite search engine (**www.excite.com**) and click on **Lifestyle**. Click on **Hobbies/Interests**, and then **Music**.

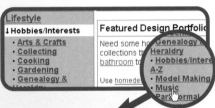

2 Type **Internet radio** into the search box and click **Go!**.

3 A list of radio sites will come up. Click on one that interests you, say, **Cajun Radio**.

4 Look at the links on the left of the page, and click on the option of your choice.

5 A list of further links comes up, informing you of broadcasting times. Choose a station, then click the **Listen Live** or **Listen Now** button. You will shortly hear the broadcast.

HOW TO: ORGANISE STATIONS IN REALPLAYER

There are so many radio stations available, that you will probably want to create a 'favourites' list. This is easy with RealPlayer. It is a bit like setting the pre-tuned stations on your car radio.

DIGITAL RADIO

Digital radio, or Digital Audio Broadcasting, is a form of transmitting radio of very high audio quality. Because of the way it is transmitted, digital radio stations can carry more information than the sound from the station itself.

Additional information could include weather and travel reports, or facts about the music being played at the current time.

Visual information can be broadcast too, and radios of the future could incorporate touch-sensitive screens which you tap to get more information whenever you want it.

1 To add any station to your list of favourites, simply click the plus sign near the name. You can do this without actually listening to the station.

2 When you want to return and listen to a selected radio station from your favourites list, click on **My Stations** and select a station from your list.

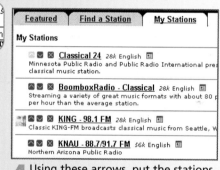

3 To change the order in which stations appear on the list, click the arrows to the left of each name. The 'down' arrow moves a station down in the listing, the 'up' arrow moves it up.

4 Using these arrows, put the stations you listen to most at the top of your favourites list.

Other on-line radio features

Any sounds that can be broadcast over the airwaves can be made available on-line. This means speeches, news reports and even events from space can be listened to as Internet radio broadcasts. Many radio sites have live Web-cam feeds showing the broadcast in action.

Did You Know?

While some Web-casts are live – that is, transmitted in real time – some are archived. Live and archived material are normally clearly marked and differentiated.

SEE ALSO
● **Take a virtual tour**
– *page 145*
● **Tune into television**
– *page 148*
● **Buy a book, CD or video**
– *page 201*

Explore the natural world

Access unique nature images and information

The Internet can take you to parts of the natural world, such as the inside of an anthill, that were previously almost inaccessible. It also provides information and research findings on plants and animals from around the world, and facts about ecological issues. And, if you're interested in wildlife, there are virtual zoos at which you can learn about animals and observe them through live Web-cam images.

Animals

The Internet can provide advice on keeping animals as pets and let you sponsor an endangered animal on-line. You can even visit a Web-cam of an anthill at the Natural History Museum site (**http://antcam.nhm.ac.uk**).

Plants

The Internet is also full of specialist factual information, such as the scientific (Latin) names of plants and flowers. You can get instant access to extensive databases and photos.

The environment

You can find debate on topics such as global warming, and explanations of natural phenomena in ecology and research centre sites. For example, there is a study of the Northern Lights (aurora borealis) including a beautiful film clip at Virtual Finland (**http://virtual.finland.fi/finfo/english/aurora_borealis.html**).

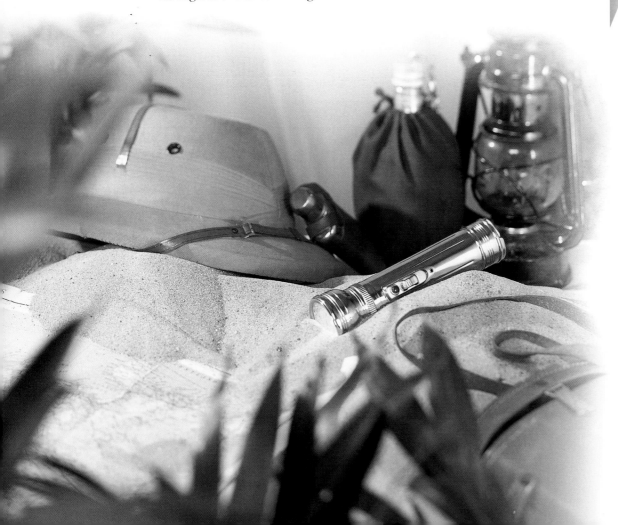

entre for this type of geophysical in Sodankylä, a small community in nish Lapland, at latitude 67.4 t is an excellent location for probing e earth's geomagnetic field. It was nnish Academy of Science and ied a geophysical observatory in e Sodankylä Geophysical GO) is run by the University of Oulu. esearch the observatory performs sical measurements at its different roduce ionospheric, geomagnetic and auroral data from Finland.

NATURE SITES

Research and exploration

National Geographic (www.nationalgeographic.com) Designed to accompany the National Geographic magazine and TV channel, this site is in some ways better than both. You can join a team of explorers on a virtual trek through the Congo Basin, reading their field notes and viewing their photographs as you go.

Or watch Web-casts of real-life explorers reporting back to the National

LOCATION:
Equatorial Africa

RESEARCHER:
Michael Fay, Conservationist

Geographic Society. The archive of Web-casts includes lectures on subjects such as *The Inca Mummies of the Andes*, but look out for new lectures which are broadcast live on the site.

Plant life

British Trees (www.british-trees.com) You don't need to go any further than the trees in your own road to find interesting natural phenomena. This site is dedicated to trees found in Britain. With many images of trees, and a species guide, you can find out which type of trees are in your garden or street, how old they are and what animals and plants live in and on them.

Natural phenomena

The Volcano Network (http://volcano.und. nodak.edu/vw.html) This site has all you could want about vulcanology, including video clips, links to current eruptions, and a 'volcano of the week' feature. You can also sign up to receive e-mail alerts whenever there is a new volcanic eruption.

Help the environment

Sponsor An Animal (www. howletts.net/helpus/sponsor.php3) Sponsoring an animal is an interactive way to care for endangered species. This site gives you a colour photograph and factsheet about your chosen animal, a certificate and a quarterly newsletter.

Click Here To Protect The Environment

Try Freedonation (**www.freedonation. com/envir**) if you are interested in helping the environment. You can make a donation with one click of a button. Your donation is paid for by sponsors so it is a free and easy way to give support to environmental campaigners.

Problem Solver!

Some Interactive museum sites or Web-cams require special software. The site should make it clear if you need particular software, such as QuickTime (see page 147) – and provide a direct link to a site where you can download it.

CASE STUDY

Paul found planning his weekend birdwatching trips was much easier through accessing up-to-date information on the Internet. Using a site such as Birdlinks (**www.bird links.co.uk**) or Birdwatching (**www. birdwatching.com**), he could get the latest bird news, and instantly book short breaks away. He could also share knowledge and sightings through posting and reading messages at the bird watching forum (**www.nature.net/forums/bird**).

Paul used Birdlinks to access the 'Regular rarities' section for current information about where rare species might be found. He liked the sound of the Galapagos Isles, so he

then went to WorldTwitch (**http://worldtwitch.virtualave.net**), a site which specialises in links relating to rare and exotic birds.

Through the site, Paul booked a two-week tour of Ecuador and the Galapagos Islands. He was delighted at the prospect of seeing some of Ecuador's 1500 species of birds.

SEE ALSO
- Take a virtual tour – *page 145*
- Support a charity – *page 206*
- Enjoy the great outdoors – *page 225*

Place a bet on-line

Try your **luck** and test your **skill** on the Web

As with any form of gambling, betting on-line comes with inbuilt risks. You may be tempted to risk more than you can afford and you may even become addicted. However, gambling Web sites help to prevent you from being pressurised into making mistakes. You can choose to compete against other people.

On the Web, you can open an account and play for real money, or have all the excitement of on-line gaming without the risk. Most sites allow you to sit in and play with pretend money, just to try it out. And the Web is also a great source of tips, systems, rules and odds.

Bookies William Hill and Ladbrokes have sites where you can bet on horse racing, football and just about any other sport. There are also specialist American sports sites such as Sportsbook (**www.sportsbook.com**).

Casinos Roulette and card games are on offer at casino sites such as VIP Casinos (**www.vipcasinos.com**). For the rules and odds of winning, consult The Gambler's Edge (**www.thegamblersedge.com**).

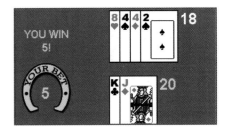

Registration To gamble or place a bet with real money, you need to register with a site and use your credit or debit card to place a deposit.

Support Always gamble within your means – if you ever need advice or support, contact Gamblers Anonymous (**www.gamblers anonymous.org.uk**).

YOUR BEST BETS

On-line casino

Casino On Net (www.casino-on-net.com)
Before you hand over your cash to an on-line casino, it pays to know that the site is legally sound. Casino On Net was one of the first on-line casinos, established in 1996.

You have to download their software to play casino games, but it is worth a few minutes' wait for their realistic 3D graphics and sound. There is a practice mode so you can try it out before you sign up. You can play privately or join a table with other players and chat to them while you're playing.

Traditional bookie

William Hill (www.willhill.com)
All on-line bookies allow you to place many different types of bets on numerous sports, but William Hill has the edge when it comes to variety. You can mix and match sports as you please, so that you could, for example, place a multiple bet on Premiership football, major league baseball and Formula 1 motor racing. You also have the option

to log in as a guest and place 'virtual' bets without any money changing hands. Once you have got the hang of it, you can go ahead and register to bet with real money.

Good for advice

The Gambler's Edge (www.thegamblersedge.com)
This site covers sports betting and just about every kind of casino game. The blackjack section, for example, covers the history and rules of the game, playing strategy, helpful tips and favourable and unfavourable rule variations. There are also blackjack links and game simulators.

On-line casino sites are also reviewed and rated so you can bet with confidence. There's a message board and a chatroom too.

The Gamblers EDGE
www.thegamblersedge.com

Live sports scores

Ananova Sport (www.ananova.com/sport)
Ananova Sport is a complete sport news and results site. Click the links to go to pages devoted to football, rugby, cricket, baseball, motor racing and numerous other sports.

News stories are constantly updated, as are the results and statistics. Click **Latest Headlines** for up-to-date breaking news, and follow the links for in-depth reports and analysis on, for example, all the top British and European football teams.

Most innovative site

Flutter (www.flutter.com)
The Internet now allows you to bet on anything, at any odds, against anyone. Sites such as Flutter invite punters to bet against each other. You can either suggest a bet of your own (10/1 that the Loch Ness Monster will be caught before 31 July?) and wait for someone to take you up on it, or you can take someone else up on their bet.

Paul says...	Juiz says...
Valencia will beat Arsenal 3-0 on Wed	Deportivo will thrash Leeds 4-0 on Wed
Take Paul on →	← Take Juiz on
Tony says...	James says...
Henry will score a hat-trick on Wed	The FTSE will finish up on Wed

SEARCH IT YOURSELF

Try the AltaVista search engine (**www.altavista.com**). Click on **Games** and then on **Gambling & Lotteries**. This opens a list of further sub-categories, including **Blackjack** and **Poker**. One of the categories is **Sports betting**. Click here for a listing of related sites.

Watch Out!

Only enter your credit or debit card details if you are sure that the site is secure. Turn to Shop safely on the Web (page 50) to know what to look for.

Money Saver!

Hedge your bets in roulette. Place one chip on the corner of numbers 7, 8, 10 and 11, another on red and another on the middle column. This gives you a 71 per cent chance that at least one of your bets will win.

HOW TO: PLACE A BET

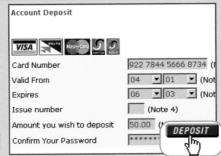

1 Go to **www.ladbrokes.com** and click on **Open Account**. A separate window opens up. Fill in the form provided and click **Open Account**.

2 Now enter your credit or debit card details and your deposit amount (minimum £10). Then click **Deposit** to return to the main part of the site and begin betting.

3 Click a link to a sporting event – here we have chosen horse racing at Ascot. A list of runners now appears with their previous and current odds. Pick a horse and click **Bet** next to it.

4 A window pops up showing your selection. Choose the type of bet – to win or each-way – and enter your stake. Then click **Bet Now** to place your bet. Good luck!

Don't forget!

Memorise your screen name and password. Some sites don't take your name and address when you register, so if you forget your screen name or password, the site will have no record of you. This would be disastrous if you won and couldn't claim your money!

 Watch Out!

Understand your bet before you place it. Go to www.ladbrokes. com and click on Help for brief definitions of every type of bet.

TRY AN ON-LINE CASINO

VIP Casinos (www.vipcasinos.com) Go to VIP Casinos, click **Free Demo** and fill in the short form to create a demo account. Then click on **Casino Games** and select the game you want to play. Your choices include roulette, blackjack and poker. You can start playing before you deposit funds into your account to get some practice without risking any money. When you select a game, a new window pops up and you will have to wait a few moments for the graphics to load.

The game graphics look like a real casino. For roulette, you will see the roulette wheel and board, and your chips. To place your bet, first float your cursor over a pile of chips. The farther down the pile, the greater

the amount that will be indicated. Click and drag your pile onto the board. It's not real money, so you can afford to be reckless! Put 500 dollars on red, and 10 dollars on number 14.

Click **Spin** to start the roulette wheel. The little white ball finally lands on 27, red. You lose the bet on the 14, but win on red. Now you can choose to let the bet stand by clicking **Same Bet**, add more chips and spin again, or clear the chips and make a new bet.

When you've had enough practice, you can deposit some money into your account by clicking **DEPOSIT NOW**. Fill in your payment details and then read and accept the terms of the site, before finally clicking **Submit**.

SEE ALSO
● **Filter out unsavoury sites** – *page 52*
● **Become a share trader** – *page 198*
● **Live the sporting life** – *page 238*

Trace your family's past

Use the Internet to find out about your family history

The Internet adds a whole new dimension to family history research. Information resources, such as census data and other public records are accessible over the Internet, minimising the time you spend tracking down resources. The Internet also makes it easier for you to share information with family members, link up with fellow researchers, track down individuals, and then publish your findings.

Genealogical societies

Organisations such as the Society of Genealogists (www.sog.org.uk) can help you in your search. The Society provides a collection of research material from their extensive library including family histories, civil registration and census material. They also offer lectures and courses designed to promote family history.

Software

Family history software enables users to scan in pictures, record information, create Web sites and construct family trees in several different ways. Some of the best software available is Family Origins (www.genealogy.com), Generations (http://shop.sierra.com) and Family Tree Maker (http://familytree maker.genealogy.com). For a review of family history programs, go to The Genealogical Software Report Card (www.mumford.ab. ca/reportcard).

Discussion groups

To exchange information, or ask others for help, try a newsgroup such as 'alt.genealogy' or an e-mail-based discussion list that covers family trees, surnames or genealogy. Hundreds of discussion groups are devoted to these subjects.

 Watch Out!

Don't assume your favourite family history Web resource has a record of everyone. Always use two or three different sites, and compare their results.

FAMILY FAVOURITES

Best place to start

GENUKI (www.genuki.org.uk)
Genealogical Information Service For
the UK and Ireland (GENUKI) is run by
volunteers as a virtual reference library
to provide basic general information
about family research in the British
Isles, including record offices and
surname lists. GENUKI provides
comprehensive links to other significant
Web sites which deal with British and
Irish family history.

Best newsgroup

alt.genealogy
The **alt.genealogy** newsgroup is
the best place for answers to
specific questions. Its members are
enthusiasts, who are happy to offer
answers to your queries. You can also
try the newsgroup **soc.genealogy.
britain** which is specifically devoted to
British genealogy.

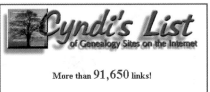

1. The 4 Contenders for the Best Genealogy
Listed here are the best (in my opinion) computer programs for genealogy.
powerful), (2) Family Origins (very easy to use and best liked) (3) Reunion

Good for software

**Louis Kessler's Genealogical Program
Links (www.lkessler.com/gplinks.shtml)**
Louis Kessler is a Canadian genealogy
enthusiast, who has gathered together
links to a wide range of software
resources. The list covers commercial,
shareware and free applications for
Windows, Mac, some handheld PDAs
(Personal Digital Assistants) and other
operating systems. There are links to the
Web sites of the software publishers, so
you can access more detailed
information. There are also links for back
issues of genealogical periodicals as well
as to newsgroups and mailing lists.

Genealogy resources

Cyndi's List (www.cyndislist.com)
Don't be put off by its informal name –
Cyndi's List is an enormous Web site
with more than 90,000 links to other
sites. It is an excellent site to bookmark
as a main research source. If you are
particularly interested in genealogy,
you might want to make Cyndi's List
your homepage. The resources listed at
the site span the globe and cover all
kinds of information, from census
details to royal lineages, ships'
passenger lists and military records.

Cyndi's List *of Genealogy Sites on the Internet*

More than 91,650 links!

- 82,650 categorized & cross-referenced links

SEARCH IT YOURSELF

**If you have an ancestor who died in
action in the First or Second World
Wars, you can search the records of
the Commonwealth War Graves
Commission to find out more.**

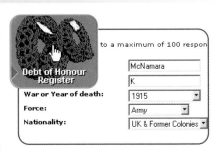

1 Go to the Commonwealth War
Graves Commission Web site
(**www.cwgc.org**) and click **Debt of
Honour Register** and then **Search**.

2 Enter your ancestor's name, and
initials if you know them. Enter his
year of death, or if you are not
sure, select either **First World War**
or **Second World War**.

3 Enter the force your ancestor
served in, and the nationality – of
the force, not the person. For
example, Australians who joined a
UK regiment are listed under UK
forces. Click **Search** to find records
under your ancestor's name.

HOW TO: FIND RECORDS OF YOUR ANCESTORS

Because of its belief that ancestors can be baptised posthumously, The Church of Jesus Christ of Latter-Day Saints, also known as the Mormon Church, maintains one of the world's largest family history archives. The International Genealogical Index (IGI) has around 600 million entries dated between 1550 and 1875. Records cover baptisms, marriages and census information, as well as letters and family Bibles. The data is also available on CD-Rom.

1 Go to the Family Search Web site at **www.familysearch.org** and click on **Search for Ancestors**.

2 Enter your ancestor's first and last name and any other information you know, such as spouse's name, parents' names or country. This will help to narrow down your search.

3 If you know the date of an event such as your ancestor's birth, marriage or death, enter this. You can search within 2, 5, 10 or 20 years if you're not sure of the exact date.

4 Click **Search** to display the results. You will see a list of Web sites that could lead you to information on your ancestor. These sites may be official records, personal Web sites or message boards.

5 The Church also maintains over 3400 Family Research Centers worldwide, where you can access their extensive library resources. Click the link on the home page to search for one near you.

Exchange information

You can buy genealogical software to help you share the findings of your family tree with other people. You should choose programs which can use the two most common family tree file formats – PAF (Personal Ancestral File), and GEDCOM (Genealogy Data Communications). Try **www.genealogy.com** for links to software sites.

Be thorough

When searching by a person's name, don't use a directory, such as Yahoo, which only looks through sites that it has previously listed. Use a search engine such as Google, which looks through the whole Web.

Did You Know?

You can take genealogy classes on the Internet. Genealogy.com (www.genealogy. com) and the Society of Genealogists (www.sog.org.uk) offer a wide range of classes.

SEE ALSO
● Search the Internet
   – page 60
● Take part in a newsgroup
   – page 92
● Do some research
   – page 109

Specific fan sites

There are many fan sites where you can find out information on a celebrity – even facts as obscure as their birth weight. Unofficial sites offer a great way to discover more unusual information and opinions. Unlike official fan sites, these are not endorsed by the featured celebrity.

General fan sites

There are also general fan sites, such as CyberSightings (**www.cyberpages.com**) which do not focus on specific personalities.

The Internet can help you to discover biographical details or find a fan club address. Or, find out what the stars say about themselves, or what fashions they are wearing. You can read on-line interviews, and, for a more interactive experience, join one of the specialist fan discussions in a chatroom.

Latest news

The Internet can help you to keep up with the latest music, theatre, film and video releases so you can follow celebrity careers. Or read fanzines on-line and keep up to date with who was spotted where, and with whom.

Access showbiz news

Learn about your favourite celebrity on-line

The Web is a great place to find celebrity news, on-line interviews and fan club chat. It allows you to read and swap trivia and opinions on celebrities more widely and quickly than ever before. Fans have also taken the opportunity to create their own, unofficial Web sites devoted to their idols, and virtually every film, TV show and other entertainment event has at least one Web site of its own.

CELEBRITY SITES

Guide to fans sites

Obsessive Fan Sites
(www.ggower.com/fans)
This site provides links to hundreds of fan sites that are funny, strange and often completely ridiculous. It filters

out unsuitable material and features the true fans' homages to their favourite personalities. Here you can find links to such obscure, fascinating sites as My Shrine to Kevin Costner and The Star Wars Trilogy Bloopers Guide. This is a fanatic's guide to mistakes in all the *Star Wars* films, such as an early scene in *Return of the Jedi* where the film runs backwards for a split second.

Gossip

People News
(www.peoplenews.com)
This site is filled with the very latest celebrity news and gossip. You can find out which celebrities were spotted where,

when and with whom, and pick up tips on the favourite haunts of the rich and famous. The site is made up of over 1000 pages and is updated 20 times a

day, making it a great place to keep yourself one step ahead of the gossip game.

Music site

Musicfans.com
(www.musicfans.com)
There is an enormous number of fan sites on the Internet for almost every band or artist you can think of. This is

the best place to start searching for information as it offers a comprehensive list of the best fans' sites. You can access this information either through the name of an artist or by a particular genre, such as rock or country.

Who starred in what?

Actors' Filmography
(www.geocities.com/Area51/Nova/
7320/ActorsFilmography.html)
Go to this useful site to find out every film a specific actor or actress, such as Humphrey Bogart or Jodie Foster, has appeared in. There are hundreds of entries, and more are added all the time.

CELEBRITY INFORMATION

- To find photos of your favourite celebrity go to AltaVista (**www. altavista.com**) and key their name into the search box.
- AltaVista also has a selection of movie and music video clips that you can view.
- For celebrity memorabilia such as autographs, clothing and other possessions try Auction Watch (**www.auctionwatch.com**) or the specialist Startifacts site (**www.startifacts.com**).
- Celebrity merchandise such as books, videos and clothing is also available for purchase on the

Internet at Celebrity Merchandise (**www.celebritymerch.com**).
- To join a fan club and get general celebrity news, gossip and reviews go to Eonline (**www.eonline.com**) or Popstazz.co.uk (**www.popstazz. co.uk/fanclubs.htm**).
- To locate the official celebrity sites try searching with celebsites (**www.celebrity-fun.com**) and Celebritybase.net (**www.celebrity base.net**).
- Search Excite's (**www.excite.com**) news article database for celebrity new stories.

Watch Out!

Some Web sites use the names of celebrities to attract visitors to sites which contain unsuitable material that has nothing to do with the star in question.

SEE ALSO
- Use a chatroom – *page 98*
- Tune into television – *page 148*
- Buy a book, CD or video – *page 201*

Enjoy the literary world

Use the Internet to access literature on-line

The Internet is helping to change the way we read and think about books, literature and the printed word. Using the Internet, you can purchase books at on-line stores, use an on-line library, or read books in electronic form. On the Web you will find articles about books and writing, literary quotations, information about setting up or joining book clubs, and details of how to publish your own work on-line.

Author, author!
If you are an unpublished writer, the Internet can help you to get your work seen. Sites such as Poetry.com (**www.poetry.com**) allow you to submit your manuscript to be read and evaluated by potential publishers and other writers. They also run regular competitions.

Prospective authors can also visit publishers' Web sites, which often give details about their policy regarding unsolicited manuscripts.

Literary groups
You can use the Internet to set up an on-line reading group. For ideas about books the group might like to discuss, visit booksellers and publishers' sites which often have reviews of new books.

Finding books
You can buy books at significant discount prices at book retail sites, and there are recommendations and features to read there too. You can also search the catalogues of secondhand and antiquarian booksellers to find specific old or out-of-print books.

LITERARY SITES

Read about books

BookEnds (www.bookends.co.uk)
BookEnds is an on-line magazine produced by Hammicks bookshops. It has feature articles, competitions, extracts from current books and interviews with writers. There are also separate areas for science fiction and for children's books. You can also buy books in the 'Bookplace' section.

Talk to other enthusiasts

WhatAmIGoingToRead.com?
(www.whatamigoingtoread.com)
A site devoted to literature, with reviews of new books, interviews with authors and an on-line reading group. Here, you can read and submit views on books under subject areas including 'Contemporary', 'Classics' and 'Poetry'. You can also receive e-mail newsletters containing details of new releases and suggestions of recommended reading.

Go to a library

Project Gutenberg (www.promo.net/pg)
A vast collection of electronic texts by authors who are out of copyright (because they died 50 years ago or more). Search for classic works of fiction, poetry, philosophy and reference. Download

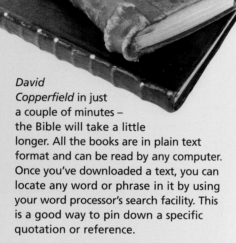

David Copperfield in just a couple of minutes – the Bible will take a little longer. All the books are in plain text format and can be read by any computer. Once you've downloaded a text, you can locate any word or phrase in it by using your word processor's search facility. This is a good way to pin down a specific quotation or reference.

Best publisher's site

Penguin (www.penguin.co.uk)
This site has articles on their recent publications, alongside in-depth author profiles and 'book of the day' features. You can take part in live discussions with

authors and there's some useful advice on how to start your own reader's group. You can search the entire Penguin catalogue by author, title or subject area, then order their books on-line. There is also advice on getting your work published.

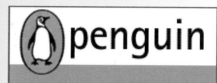

Improve your writing

Get Out There (www.getoutthere.com)
This site provides a chance for new writers to publish their work on-line and improve their writing skills. Click **Writing**, **Library**, then **Charts** to read popular current submissions and vote for your favourites. The site also has interviews with writers, monthly competitions and articles on how to write comedy, short stories or journalism. Click **Upload** to submit your work to the site.

SEARCH IT YOURSELF

Many authors have their own Web sites, and there are also a large number of 'unofficial' sites maintained by fans. You can use a Web directory such as Yahoo! to find them.

Go to Yahoo! UK & Ireland (**www. yahoo.co.uk**) and, under 'Arts and Humanities', click on **Literature**.

Now select **Authors**. If, for example, you are interested in

Margaret Atwood, click **A**. You can also choose to click on a subject, such as 'Canadian authors', instead of opting for a specific author.

Scroll down the list of authors until you come to the person you want to find out about. Click on the name. If the author has more than one site, you will get a listing of them all, otherwise you will be taken straight to the Web site.

 Did You Know?

*You can play poetry games on-line. Go to the Java fridge magnet poetry site (**http://prominence.com/java/poetry**) and create verses from the words given. You can also submit them to the poetry 'gallery'.*

 Problem Solver!

*If you are looking for a new book, but are not sure when it is due to be published, visit an on-line bookshop such as BOL (**www.bol.com**) for more information.*

difficulty, yet a motionless, unwearying struggle, congenial to his tastes.

Phileas Fogg was not known to have either wife or children, which may happen to the most honest people; either relatives or near friends, which is certainly more unusual. He lived alone in his house in Savile Row, whither none penetrated. A single domestic sufficed to serve him. He breakfasted and dined at the club, at hours mathematically fixed, in the same room, at the same table, never taking his meals with other members, much less bringing a guest with him; and

Did You Know?

New authors often make no money on their first book. But e-book publishers such as Online Originals give authors half of all sales. However, e-book royalties are lower than print books.

E-BOOKS–THE FUTURE OF PUBLISHING?

An electronic book (or e-book), is a text stored and read on a PC, handheld computer or dedicated reading device. But a traditional book is already small, light and convenient to carry around, so why try to improve on such a successful original?

E-books do offer certain advantages over print books. A single reading device can store the equivalent of ten books and a pile of newspapers and magazines – more than you could comfortably carry around with you. E-books can be bought and downloaded onto your reading device directly from the Internet at sites such as Ebooks.com (**www.ebooks. com**) – at prices lower than traditional printed books. There are also free books to download.

Reading devices

You can read e-books on handheld computers such as the Palm, Handspring, Symbian and Pocket PC, or specialised reading devices such as the Gemstar eBook. Online Originals (**www.online originals.com**) has a guide to some of the available devices.

However, you don't need a specialised device to read e-books. If you download the free e-book reader software from Adobe (**www.adobe.com**), you can read them on your home PC or laptop.

New versus old

Critics of e-books claim reading from a screen is difficult to do and e-books are less enjoyable to read than printed books. Manufacturers are aware of these issues and are investing a great deal of time and money to improve the technology and change our way of thinking.

E-books are bound to become more common. Students are already starting to embrace this technology. Not only can you carry around all your textbooks in one go, you can also search for particular chapters or passages more easily and make notes at the precise spot you need them.

Students can also save money by downloading (and paying for) just the chapters they want from a textbook or reference work, instead of having to buy the whole book.

OnlineOriginals
Discovering new literature

Get a Palm organiser (**http://www.palm.c** Online Originals in our special Palm format, bookmarks, touch-screen navigation and fin HotSync™ and you're ready to read -- on th anywhere. Try this realistic *demo* of our 'rea

Why Internet publishing?

Internet-only novel

An early attempt at Internet publishing was made by novelist Stephen King. Amid great excitement, the author placed installments of his Internet-only book *The Plant* on his Web site (**www.stephenking.com**). King relied on a trust system of payment, charging a small fee for each installment. But less than half the readers paid, so, to a chorus of disapproval from his fans, he stopped the experiment before the book was finished.

official STEPHEN KING web

SEE ALSO

● **Take part in a newsgroup** – *page 92*
● **Explore painting** – *page 172*
● **Buy a book, CD or video** – *page 201*

Make new friends

Use the **Internet** to find and make **new friends**

Although it can't replace face-to-face communication, the Internet can, if used with caution, open up new possibilities for finding friendship, rewarding long-term correspondence and even romance. You could easily come across someone interesting through a lucky encounter on a bulletin board, but you can increase your chances by making regular use of all the meeting points that the Web has to offer.

How to begin Rather than going to a site that specialises in getting people together, you could begin with a site or chatroom dedicated to your own interest, whether it's bridge, flower pressing or origami.

You can exchange friendly messages on the site's notice board or join a forum to discuss topics with like-minded individuals.

Penpal Web sites These specialise in setting up new friendships between people of similar interests from all over the world.

Dating agencies These operate in much the same way as their off-line counterparts, and have to be treated with a similar level of caution. There are also places, such as Yahoo, where you can post personal ads. As with their newspaper equivalents, these can be a hit and miss affair.

Clubs and groups Use the Internet to find out about clubs, teams or groups that you can join in your area.

Revive old friendships Search for old friends and long-lost school mates with one of the Internet's people-finder sites. A great place to start searching in Britain is the UK electoral roll at **www.192.com**.

 Did You Know?

*You can meet new friends around the world on Internet Relay Chat (IRC). Go to **www.irc help.org** to learn how to chat and to look up chat groups in your area or devoted to your favourite topics.*

THE BEST SITES

Penfriends

International Penfriends (www.internationalpenfriends.co.uk) International Penfriends is for adults and children who want to correspond with someone from another part of the world. It has over 300,000 members from 210 different countries, and you can write in English, French, German, Spanish or Portuguese.

Enter your personal details and preferences and pay a subscription fee to receive the names and addresses of people whose age group, hobbies and interests best match your own.

Personal ads

Excite Classifieds (personals.excite.com) This free service has over 200,000 personal ads. You can browse to find someone with similar interests or post an ad of your own. Look in the 'Just friends' section for 'Penpals', 'Sports' or 'Activities', where ads may include someone

looking for a bridge partner or a friend to go to concerts with. You can see a picture of the person placing the ad (if they have submitted one).

Dating agency

Dateline (www.dateline.co.uk) Dateline has been running since 1966 and is a computerised people matching service that covers the whole of the UK. To join, you'll need to complete and

submit a personal profile, and then Dateline will match you up with the most compatible people on their database. You can also ask them to

search just within your geographical area. It is then up to you to contact your matches by letter, telephone or e-mail.

People-finder

Friends Reunited (www.friendsreunited.co.uk) At this site you can search through a database of over 28,000 UK primary and secondary schools and colleges to find friends you have lost touch with. Register with the site and enter a name of a school or college to start your search. For people or businesses in the US, try Anywho (**www.anywho.com**).

SEARCH IT YOURSELF

To find a club, no matter what your interest, start searching through Yahoo! Clubs (clubs.yahoo.com). You could also try entering the name of your hobby into any search engine, followed by the word 'club', or 'online club', as in 'fly fishing'+online+club.

To find a mailing list, chat group or newsgroup on any topic, go to Topica (**www.topica.com**). For a list of the top one hundred Web chat channels, go to 100hot.com (**www.100hot.com/chat**), or to Forum One Communications (**www. forumone.com**), which can connect you with over 300,000 different chat groups.

To search for dating sites, look through the on-line database at Cupidnet (**www.cupidnet.com**). You can also try SingleSites (**www.single sites.com**), which contains links to thousands of on-line dating agencies around the world.

HOW TO: FIND OLD FRIENDS

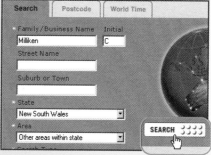

1 Go to WorldPages (**www.worldpages. com**). Click on **International**. On the next page, select a country (in this case Australia) from the drop-down list and click on **Search**.

2 A list of phone directories for that country will now appear. Here we have clicked on the link for **Telstra Australia White Pages**.

3 A new window opens to show the Telstra search page. Enter the name and area of the person or business you are trying to locate. Then click on **Search**.

MUSICAL MATCH

Like many of the other copywriters in his advertising firm, Nick also wrote in his spare time – in his case it was song lyrics.

"For a while, I was quite happy crooning away at the piano in my front room, but I reluctantly agreed to my wife's demands that I take things further.

"I didn't feel confident enough to advertise for musicians to make up a band. But I did want to get someone else to listen to the songs and find out if they were any good or not.

"A friend mentioned that there was a Web site where you could upload recordings of your songs (**www.allnoise. com**). He helped me upload a couple of songs and then I sat back to wait for the recording contracts to come flooding in.

"I didn't hear anything for weeks, but eventually a guy called Mark e-mailed me to say that he liked my lyrics but thought he could do a better job of singing them.

"We arranged to meet at a pub in London and hit it off immediately. We've since recruited a drummer and a guitarist from the personal ads at Q magazine's site (**www.q4music. com**) and recorded the songs again. The new versions have been on-line for a few months now and we're still not famous, but getting together to make music has been brilliant fun."

Results Listing 1 - 4 of 4	
You have searched for: milliken c M	
Name & Location	
Milliken C	
11 Stapylton St Holder 2611	
Milliken C & J	
67 Streeton Drv Metford 2323	

4 A page of results will appear, listing the names, addresses and phone numbers of the people who fit your search criteria.

Watch Out!

*Check out the dating safety precautions recommended by Dateline (**www. dateline.co.uk**), such as meeting in a public place or double-dating.*

SEE ALSO
● **Use a chatroom**
  – *page 98*
● **Do some research**
  – *page 109*
● **Trace your family's past**
  – *page 161*

171

Explore painting

Get creative through the Web

If you've always wanted to wield a paintbrush, palette and easel but have never known how to get started, why not take advantage of the Web to learn more about painting? You can look at works of art over the Internet, and access art supplies and tuition. You can also use computer programs to 'paint' on the screen instead of on canvas.

If you are an artist, you can post your paintings on a Web site so that other people can see your work. You can even put your paintings up for sale through an on-line gallery.

View art

Most museums have their own Web sites, displaying paintings and providing information on the artists and their work. There are also sites dedicated to the history of art, such as Art History Search (www.arthistorysearch.com), which offer specialist insights into art theory, history and techniques.

Art courses

There are free on-line art courses that offer tuition to people of all ability levels who may not have the time or money for conventional classes. But, if you prefer a mouse to a paintbrush, you can download a free painting program from sites such as Adobe (www.adobe.com).

Art lovers

The Internet can also help you to research painting holidays and workshops. Or, if you're an art lover and aspiring collector, The Art Connection Inc. (www.art connection.net) connects you to painters, and paintings for sale.

PAINTING SITES

On-line tutorials

WetCanvas! (www.wetcanvas.com)
This site sets out to bring 'art education to the masses'. Offering free on-line

courses, catering for children and adults of all abilities, WetCanvas! also includes a virtual museum, information on art supplies and services, and an on-line shop where you can purchase fine art.

Art supplies

ArtResource (www.artresource.com)
Head to ArtResource for painting classes and links to museums and galleries, plus

Fine Art Supplies
Artist's Brushes & Painting
Tools
Artist's Canvas &
Accessories
Artist's Finishes & Glazes
Artist's Paints
Artist's Painting Mediums
Block Printing
Easels & Sketchboards

a comprehensive art supply store that stocks paints, canvases, brushes and other materials.

Winsor & Newton (**www.winsornewton.com**) lets you order materials straight from the manufacturer.

Art history resources

The Mother of All Art History Links (www.umich.edu/~hartspc/histart/mother)
This award-winning site, put together by a university art history department, contains links to museums, on-line art, fine art schools, research resources and image collections.

Go to Artserve – The Australian National University (**http://rubens.anu.edu.au**) for surveys of great artists especially from the Mediterranean.

On-line gallery

Art Gallery Online (www.art-gallery-online.org)
This is a private, non-profit-making virtual art gallery devoted to showcasing the work of contemporary international artists. Browse artist portfolios and an on-line gallery.

SEARCH IT YOURSELF

To find out who painted what and when, look at the art database at ArtCyclopedia (**www.artcyclopedia.com**). World Wide Arts Resources (**www.world-arts-resources.com**) is also a good place to start.

For art museums links, try MuseumNetwork.com (**www.museumnetwork.com**) and Museums Around the World (**www.icom.org/vlmp/world.html**).

EXHIBITING ART ON-LINE

There are many options for painters, (amateur or professional), who want to show their work over the Internet. One way is to create your own Web site and place your images there.

To do this, you need to convert your painting into a digital image using a scanner. If your paintings are too big or delicate to fit on a scanner, you can get slides or photos made of them. Or, if you own a digital camera, you can take a picture of your work and then download it onto your PC.

Contemporary art Online (**www.contemporaryartonline.com**) arranges on-line exhibitions of international artists. World Wide Arts Resources (**www.wwar.com**) also invites submissions of work. If you e-mail your work to them, they will create an on-line portfolio of your art for free.

Exhibiting your work on-line ensures that your work gets seen by people around the world and saves you having to find a gallery. You can also correspond and receive feedback from the people who view your work, who would never have been able to view it in a conventional gallery. You never know who will come across your paintings on the Internet.

Problem Solver

*For answers to all your painting questions, try the on-line versions of comprehensive and world-renowned reference works such as The Grove Dictionary of Art (**www.groveart.com**).*

SEE ALSO
- Use a chatroom
  – *page 98*
- Enjoy the literary world
  – *page 166*
- Buy a book, CD or video
  – *page 201*

Keep the children entertained

Discover Web sites specifically for children

A t its best, the Internet is a useful educational tool as well as a playground. Most children will enjoy it both for learning and for fun. They can use it to play games on-line, download stories or read reviews of books. They can also get help with homework or set up an e-mail penfriend anywhere in the world. The Net will yield suggestions for activities to do in the holidays and chatrooms specifically for children. With good supervision and proper use of filtering software, children can spend time on the Internet safely and productively.

Before you start

● When you start an on-line session, use specialist children's portals – sites with extensive editorial content and a large collection of links, such as Zeeks (**www.zeeks.com**). These bring together a useful range of resources for younger users.

● Use child-friendly search engines such as Yahooligans! (**www.yahooligans.com**).

● There are sites, such as Kids Domain (**www.kidsdomain.co.uk**), that provide detailed advice for parents and carers on how to ensure that their children surf the Web safely.

● If you are really concerned about your children finding unsuitable sites on the Internet, make use of filtering software (see page 52) and set up security measures for your browser (see page 48).

FUN SITES FOR CHILDREN

Where to start

Kids Domain (www.kidsdomain.co.uk)
For primary school-aged children, Kids Domain is a great Web site. It has a wide range of information on subjects such as how to get into the *Guinness Book of Records*, and ideas for cooking and craft activities. There is the chance to download icons of creatures such as unicorns, dragons or cartoon characters.

There are on-line games and colouring activities, and reviews of books, computer games, and films. Other activities have both on-line and off-line components, such as the many stories at the site – to which your children can add their own.

There are separate areas for adults, teachers and children, with the adults section offering, among other things, useful guidelines to help younger users get the most from the Internet.

Children's shareware

Tucows (www.tukids.tucows.com)
Children can use the Web to download shareware and play on-line games. Downloading will save on time spent on-line. The download site, Tucows, has a

section specially for children. It offers a range of on-line games (reviewed and rated by children), activities, such as on-line colouring, and jokes and riddles to make the whole family groan.

A large shareware library offers software – both educational and games – for downloading. Shareware is grouped according to target age, so it is easy for all age groups to find suitable material. There is also a section offering shareware for teachers.

Before you can access the site, you have to indicate where you are in the world and pick a site from which to download.

Internet communications

Kidlink (www.kidlink.org)
This site offers an immediate way to interact with children from all over the world. There are e-mail discussion

groups in the Kidcafé area. If you prefer live on-line chat then head for the Kidcafé conferences section. There is also a gallery of computer art where children can submit their own work.

Penfriends

Kids' Space Connection (www.ks-connection.org)
This site encourages children to explore and communicate using new technology. It is particularly good at connecting penfriends from around the world.

Choose the **Penpal Box** link from the main page, and you'll see a list of prospective penfriends grouped by age.

You can also access the **Class Box**, which encourages whole classes of children to correspond and learn about other cultures in an informal and interesting way.

Swap messages

Bulletin boards are an alternative to live on-line chat. You leave messages here to be commented on by other bulletin board members later. For a selection of bulletin boards for children, which they can contribute to, visit Zeeks (**www.zeeks.com**).

Did You Know?

*You can copy text from a Web page into a Word document. To do this, highlight the text, go to the **Edit** menu and select **Copy**. Then open a blank Word document, go to the **Edit** menu and select **Paste**.*

Money Saver!

*It is worth making sure that children print out Web pages and read them off-line to save on phone call charges. To do this, go to the **File** menu and select **Print**, or click on the **Print** button on the toolbar.*

MORE KIDS' SITES

On-line activities

Crayola (www.crayola.com)
Crayola make colouring pens, crayons and other art materials. They run an excellent art-activity Web site full of

creative ideas and fun things to do, such as the 'idea generator', which creates silly sentences to set the imagination in motion. There are many pictures and craft projects which you can print out and complete off-line, and an inspiring ideas

section. This has a changing range of activities which you can view by topic, target age, and length of time the activity will take. There is also a section for creating printed and e-cards.

TV tie-in

**Bob the Builder
(www.bobthebuilder.org)**
Many children's TV shows have tie-in Web sites that offer activities and

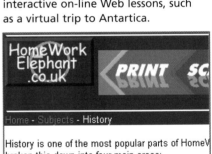

information related to the show. The Bob the Builder site is particularly well thought out. It offers exciting on-line activities for younger users, featuring characters from the show. There are jigsaws, on-line drawing and colouring exercises, and various other activities which encourage skills such as

co-ordination. For example you can help fix the jug that Pilchard has broken by dragging the mouse over each piece, or assist with spelling in Mrs Percival's lesson. This is a good site for children to use with an adult. It will help younger users to get familiar with computers and the Internet.

Homework help site

**The Homework Elephant
(www.homeworkelephant.co.uk)**
This is an index of Web sites that can provide high quality information to give assistance with schoolwork.

As well as covering all the main school study topics, the Homework Elephant has links to on-line encyclopedias, newspapers, and language translation sites. You can also access exciting interactive on-line Web lessons, such as a virtual trip to Antartica.

Time Saver!

Bookmark your favourite children's Web sites and organise the bookmarks in a folder in your Web browser. This makes it easy to return to them at a later date.

HOW TO: COLOUR A PICTURE THEN E-MAIL IT TO A FRIEND

There are many Web sites, such as Up To Ten (**www.uptoten.org**) which provide pictures for children to colour in on-line, or to print out and colour in. Some also allow you to send images that have been coloured in on-line to friends and family, or to point those people to the Web site where the images are stored.

1 First go to the UpToTen homepage (**www.uptoten.org**). Then click on the icon **Coloring 4 kids UpToTen**.

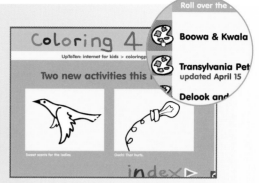

2 A new window will open, offering a range of colouring choices. You can either choose one of the projects on the page or view the 'Index' and then choose a project.

3 A selection of images will appear. Colour them in using the palette on the left. Drag the paint brush at the top right onto a colour. Click on the part of the picture you wish to colour in.

4 When you have finished, click the aeroplane icon on the menu and fill in the form with your name, e-mail address and your friend's e-mail address. Then click **Send**.

5 A short animation will let you know that the e-mail has been sent to your friend. Now wait for the response from the recipient.

Sounds like fun

Make your PC more enjoyable for children to use by setting it up to play sounds when it performs various tasks, such as opening a folder or receiving an e-mail.

Go to the **Start** menu, select **Settings** then **Control Panel**. Double-click on the **Sounds and Multimedia** icon, scroll through and click on an event from the 'Sound Events' list. Click on the arrow to the right of the 'Name' box, scroll through and click on your preferred sound.

Money Saver!

If you pay for phone calls when connected to the Web, try to keep on-line activity within the cheap-rate times. If your children need to be on-line in peak times, ISPs offering a flat monthly fee with no phone charges can be less expensive.

Ask around

Don't just use the Internet to find an e-pal for your child. Ask your family, friends and colleagues if they know anyone with a child of a similar age. Having some common ground may help the children when they begin to correspond.

HOW TO: FIND E-PALS

Penfriends have always been popular among children. With the Internet it is also possible to have e-friends, or e-pals – contacts around the globe who can be e-mailed rather than written to. Corresponding with an e-pal is a less formal relationship than with a traditional pen-friend. There is not the same requirement to enter into a long-term commitment.

Selecting an e-pal Web site

It's easy to make new e-pals, as there are many Web sites offering contacts. Some adults are concerned about the kinds of contacts children might make on the Internet. However, you can minimise the risk by selecting the site for them.

What to look for

● Try to find sites that are aimed specifically at children, rather than those for all age groups.
● Look for a site that is regulated by an official body, such as the Children's Online Privacy Protection Rule (COPPR).
● Find a Web site with a wide and varied selection of prospective e-pals on offer – preferably from different countries around the world. Help your child choose one.

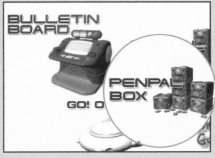

1 Go to Kids Connection (**www.ks-connection.org**) and click on the **Penpal Box** on the right hand side of the homepage.

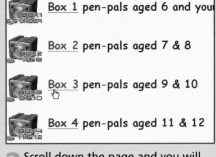

Box 1 pen-pals aged 6 and you[r]
Box 2 pen-pals aged 7 & 8
Box 3 pen-pals aged 9 & 10
Box 4 pen-pals aged 11 & 12

2 Scroll down the page and you will be given a choice of boxes which specify penpals' ages. Click on the box of the age group you want.

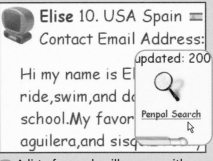

Elise 10. USA Spain
Contact Email Address:
updated: 200
Hi my name is El
ride,swim,and do
school.My favor
aguilera,and sisq

Penpal Search

3 A list of penpals will appear with their e-mail addresses. To narrow your search, click on **Penpal Search** at the top right and specify the country, age range and gender of your penpal.

Submission Form

Submit Form

4 You can also submit your own details. At the top of the page, click on **Submission Form**, complete the form and then click **Submit Form**.

Learn a language

If your child is just picking up a new language such as French or Spanish, encourage them to get an e-pal in the appropriate country and start some writing. This will make learning the language much more enjoyable.

ORGANISE A CHILDREN'S PARTY ON-LINE

The Internet can be extremely useful when it comes to organising children's parties. In fact, it can provide everything you require without the bother of trailing around the shops. If you need inspiration or to buy presents, decorations, games or food for a kids party, here's how the Web can help.

Presents

Many Web sites provide gifts for children's parties. Large stores such as Toys "R" Us (**www.toysrus.co.uk**) have their own sites from which you can order birthday presents. These will then be delivered directly to your house.

Decorations

You can order balloons and unusual gifts on-line – such as an inflatable cat – at Not Just Balloons (**www. notjustballoons.co.uk**).

Themes

Get inspiration for party themes, ranging from a Dinosaur Dig to a Pirate Party at Amazingmoms.com (**www.amazingmoms.com**).

You can also book an entertainer, such as a clown or a magician. Many entertainers have their own sites which you can book through directly. If you don't know of any entertainers in your area, try the listing at the Party Store (**www.thepartystore.co.uk**).

Entertainment

For games and other entertainment ideas to keep the partygoers happy, visit Totally Party (**www. totallyparty.co.uk**). Here you will find a good list of party games, a pre-filled party bag service, the chance to order party food boxes as well as helpful tips on organising celebrations for children.

Design your cards

If your child would like to design an original invitation, why not use an on-line drawing or colouring site, such as Cory's PaintBox (**www.corypaints.com**), print out the drawn or coloured picture, and use that as the basis of a printed invitation.

Party venues

To find a venue outside of your home, go to Party venues (**www.partyvenues.co.uk**). Click on **Advanced Search** and tick the box 'Suitable for Children's Parties' for ideas.

PARTY CAKES

You can get a special cake designed by Jane Asher at her Web site (www.jane-asher.co.uk). Order on-line from a great selection, or e-mail a design, photograph or text and it can be printed onto your cake in edible ink. The cake will also be delivered directly to you.

SEE ALSO
● Download from the Web – page 82
● Help your child to learn on-line – page 132
● Play games on-line – page 186

Go motoring

Get on the road with the information superhighway

On the Internet, you can find any number of official and unofficial sites devoted to every aspect of motoring. If you like to get your hands dirty, there are tips and guides for maintenance checks to help to get your car through its MOT, and bigger jobs such as repairing your brake calipers. Or you can find local mechanics to handle the servicing for you.

Anyone who wants to buy a car will find reviews and dealers for all the latest models and classified adverts for secondhand motor cars. You can also advertise your own car for sale.

Buying and selling Checking on-line classifieds is far more convenient than poring over magazine adverts. You can search for the exact model and year you want, and view only offers in your local area and your preferred price range. When selling a car, on-line adverts also allow you to reach a huge potential audience, free of charge or at low cost.

You can also get an evaluation of any new or used car to help you with your purchase or sale.

Mechanical advice Use the Web to find test reports, repair guides and checklists to deal with all types of DIY work. If you own an older model, you can also search for that elusive chrome wing mirror or a set of original hubcaps.

Other enthusiasts You can join a car club and meet new people at motoring events, or you can take part in on-line discussion boards to swap tips and gossip with fellow experts and amateurs.

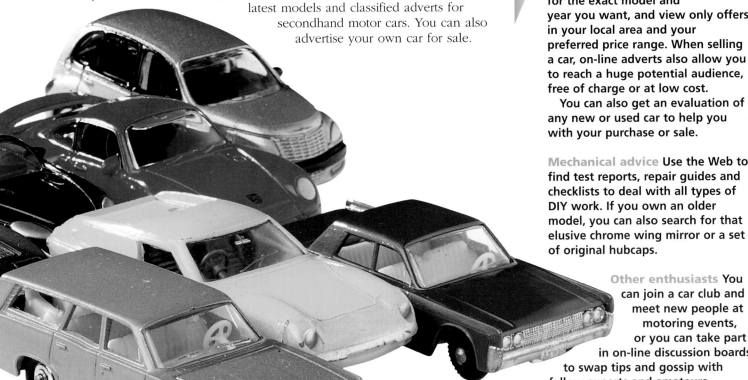

TOP OF THE RANGE

Where to start

About (www.about.com)
The About site is a categorised guide to the Internet compiled by experts in fields as diverse as Hinduism, cats and photography.

The Autos section is a good base for exploring cars on the Web. Follow the links for all the major owners clubs, car manufacturers and motoring organisations.

Best for buying and selling

Parker's Online (www.parkers.co.uk)
The publishers of the Parker's car price guides have produced an excellent Web site for anyone who is interested in buying or selling a car in the UK or from abroad. One particularly useful feature is the valuation section. Enter the make,

model, year and mileage of the car you want to buy or sell and the site will give you a range of the prices you can expect – depending on the condition of the car.

There are also comprehensive reviews of old and new models and plenty of special features such as a checklist you can print out and take with you when inspecting a secondhand car (look for irregular wear of the tyres, which may point to misalignment of the steering system).

Car DIY advice

Car Care Clinic (www.carcareclinic.com)
This is the place to go for advice on any repairs you are undertaking. You can pick the problem you are trying to solve from an alphabetical list or e-mail your question to the site. There is also a free helpline for advice on all motoring issues and a discussion forum to swap tips with other enthusiasts.

Advice with a smile

Car Talk (www.cartalk.cars.com)
This is the site of a hugely popular radio show, which is broadcast on hundreds of stations in the United States.

It offers an addictive mix of wacky motoring humour and sound mechanical advice. Check out the bulging mailbag of car questions, and e-mail for specific advice on your own particular automotive problem.

When you've done that, have a look at the Ten Worst Cars of the Millennium. Apparently the best attribute of the winner was the heated rear window.

Selling a car on-line

- First get your car valued. Go to a site such as Parker's Online (www.parkers.co.uk) and enter in your car's details.
- Check the listings at a site such as Autotrader (www.autotrader.co.uk) for similar cars to see if the price is realistic for the current market.
- Now choose a price, giving yourself room for negotiation by adding 'or nearest offer' (ono).
- Take a digital photo of the car or get a normal photograph scanned in to use when advertising your car.

- Advertise your car on-line for free (see overleaf) as well as in local newspapers and trade magazines.
- E-mail the details of your car to your friends and colleagues. Ask them to circulate them.
- Read the advice in the 'Sell your car' section at Autobytel (www.autobytel.co.uk), for warnings about scams such as thieves who take the car for a test drive and never return.

Time Saver!

You can get free maintenance tips e-mailed to you. Sign up to Car Adviser (http://car adviser.cars.com).

Watch Out!

When searching US sites, use American English. Try 'auto parts' rather than 'car parts', 'hood' rather than 'bonnet', and 'trunk' not 'boot'.

HOW TO: ADVERTISE YOUR CAR FOR SALE

1 Go to Excite Classifieds **(http://classifieds.excite.com)**, and click on **Place Ads** and then **Place Vehicles Ad.**

2 On the next screen, click **Cars**. Select your make of vehicle from the list and then click **Continue**.

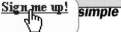

Personalization Information-
Information to provide customized features horoscope, and other helpful features. (At Excite we value your privacy and guarantee to

First Name: Simon
Last Name: Garner

3 You must now give your Excite membership details. If you are not a member, click **Sign me up!**. Then fill in the form and click **Done**.

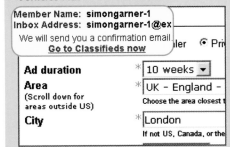

Member Name: **simongarner-1**
Inbox Address: **simongarner-1@ex**
We will send you a confirmation email.
Go to Classifieds now

Ad duration * 10 weeks ▾
Area * UK - England - ▾
(Scroll down for areas outside US) Choose the area closest to
City * London
If not US, Canada, or the

4 A welcome page now appears. Click **Go to Classifieds now**. Use the form to enter the details of your car.

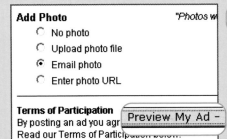

Add Photo "Photos w
○ No photo
○ Upload photo file
● Email photo
○ Enter photo URL

Terms of Participation
By posting an ad you agr
Read our Terms of Participation below.
[Preview My Ad –]

5 If you have an electronic image of the car, click to indicate how you will send it in (see Problem Solver!, left). Click on **Preview My Ad** to see your ad.

[Continue]
Exterior Color - Blue - Dark
Interior Color - Gray
6-cyl.
Two Door
Automatic Transmission

Seller Info
Member Name: simongarner-1
View seller's other ads
For sale by Private Party
London, UK - England - Southeas
[Send message]

6 You will be told again about sending in your photo. Take note and click **Continue**. You can now see your free ad. If you're happy, click **Place My Ad**.

Problem Solver!

*If you are unsure how to send in your picture to the Excite site, click on the **Help** tab and select **Photo Questions**.*

Did You Know?

*You can pick the brains of other car owners through a newsgroup. In Outlook Express, click on **Tools** and **Newsgroups**. Enter the make and model of your car to bring up a list of relevant groups.*

CASE STUDY

John recently retired and finally had the time to devote to his beloved MGB GT, which had languished unused in his garage for many years.

He also used his new-found free time to improve his PC skills, and soon found that his two hobbies coincided when he came across the MG Owners' Club Web site (**www.mgcars.org.uk/mgoc**). 'I saw the site and joined the club on-line right

The MG Owners' Club

away,' said John. 'I was able to get advice on repairing the transmission that really helped me get my MGB back on the road. I drove it to the MG Owners' Club day at Silverstone race circuit. It was such a good day out that I've already signed up for next year!'

SEE ALSO
● **Send e-mail attachments** – *page 42*
● **Take part in a newsgroup** – *page 92*
● **Buy and sell at auction** – *page 208*

Improve your home

Plan a new look for your house and garden

The Internet is a great place to find ideas and inspiration for maintaining your home, inside and out. You'll find instructions for DIY plumbing, home decorating hints and horticultural tips. Find just the right plants for your location and type of garden, buy home accessories, tools and garden furniture locally or from abroad, or locate a recommended builder in your area.

Do-it-yourself You can get advice on every type of job around the house. There are step-by-step guides for you to print out and guides on what products to use.

DIY supplies Browse the Web for all your DIY and home furnishing supplies – tools, paintbrushes, kitchen units, lighting and more. See what's available before you head for the shops, or order speciality or professional goods on-line directly from the supplier.

Gardening tips Consult The Royal Horticultural Society (www.rhs. org.uk) for seasonal tips, such as how to protect young plants from late spring frosts. You can also look up on-line plant encyclopedias for details on different plants and the best ways to care for them.

Garden supplies Many sites offer specialised plant finders to locate exactly the right plant for the climate, light availability and size of your garden. You can then order delivery of the appropriate plants.

THE ROYAL HORTICULTURAL SOCIETY
GATEWAY TO GARDENING

PLANTS   EVENTS   GARDENS

 Did You Know?

Is the glue on stamps kosher? Is it vegetarian? Find out the answer, and learn how to glue anything to anything else, at This to That (www. thistothat.com).

 Money Saver!

Quote Checkers (www.quote checkers.co.uk) will check a builder's quote for you so you don't pay over the odds.

SITES TO HOME IN ON

Home improvements

HomeCentral (www.homecentral.com)
A good place to start your home improvement research is HomeCentral. The site has articles on design,

decorating, completing a total look, techniques and safety tips. It also has special calculators to help you work out exactly how much wallpaper and paint you need to buy.

DIY solutions

Homebase (www. homebase.co.uk)
This site will help you choose the best home and DIY products, paints and tools for your needs. You can buy all the products directly from the Web site. Check the site's 'Ideas' section for inspiration, and see 'How-To' for step-by-step instructions for common household projects, such as repairing a dripping tap.

Great garden advice

Garden UK (www.garden-uk.org.uk/reference.htm)
A compilation of gardening reference sites, including the Encyclopedia of Plants, searchable by common or botanical name, and Gardener's Guru, with advice on growing organic produce.

Pick of the plants

The Postcode Plants Database (www.nhm.ac.uk/science/projects/fff)
If you want to create a garden using native species, go to The Postcode Plants Database, a site affiliated to the Natural History Museum. Enter your postcode to find a list of native species specific to your region.

Garden shopping

Greenfingers.com (www.greenfingers.com)
This is a gardening superstore that also provides 'workshop' advice on subjects such as taking a softwood cutting and renovating an old lawn. You can buy rare plants and seeds, fountain kits or gardening equipment and accessories, and there are regular sales throughout the year.

Alternatively, you can buy direct from The Royal Horticultural Society's shopping site (**www. grogro.com**). You'll find the plants exhibited at the RHS's shows, plus greenhouses, garden furniture, lighting, books and tickets to the Chelsea Flower Show.

Did You Know?

Horticultural therapists have developed tools and techniques to help you to avoid getting back pain in the garden. Go to Fred's shed (www.fredshed. co.uk) for details.

SEARCH IT YOURSELF

For specific advice, look for a specialist site. The Kitchen Specialists Association (**www.ksa.co.uk**) is a great place to plan your new kitchen, find your nearest retailer and get advice on costs and appliances.

To create a 3D plan of your new bathroom before going shopping, visit BathWeb (**www.bathweb.com**).

If you are after that elusive finishing touch, the Internet is a great way to track items down. A quick search at **www.google.com** for a 'crocodile doorstop' reveals a small company that imports unusual items for the trade. You can phone them for the name of the manufacturer.

If you draw a blank on your search, post a message on a forum at one of the big home sites, such as Home Arts (**www.homearts.com**). Someone else may know where you should try.

Double Galley

HOW TO: USE AN ON-LINE PLANT SELECTOR

Plant selectors are simple to use, and enable you to find the perfect plant for your garden. But, before you buy any plants, find out what type of soil yours is – soil-testing kits are sold at garden centres, and the test is easy to perform.

Crocus (**www.crocus.co.uk**) has a plant selector and allows you to order their goods on-line, with advice from the experts. And if you do buy a plant from the site, Crocus also offers an optional e-mail service that gives you seasonal plant care advice, to keep your garden healthy all year round.

1 To find plants suitable for a shady garden with slightly acidic soil, for example, go to Crocus (**www.crocus.co.uk**) and click on **plant search**.

3. plants to suit you
In 'plants to suit you', Helen has devi best suit your gardening style.

based on your experience or ambitio

based on the type of garden you hav

4. planting ideas

2 There are five ways to search, by plant name, type or suitability, plant ideas and bargains. Under 'plants to suit you', click **go** next to 'type of garden you have'.

3 Now click on **A shady garden**. Other options here include water garden, a garden with boggy patches, a sunny garden and a rock garden.

4 A list of suitable plants appears with symbols denoting their best soil type, season and so on. Hover your mouse over each symbol for an explanation.

Japanese Skimmia
'Skimmia japonica Veita

A quick growing garden

size 3lt Pot
price £10.75
available 7-10 Working Days

5 For a shady garden with acidic soil, popular favourites such as camellias are suitable, as well as more unusual choices such as Japanese Skimmia and Big Blue Lily-Turf. To buy a plant, click on the shopping cart icon next to it.

AS SEEN ON TELEVISION

Most of the home and garden improvement programmes have an on-line presence. Go to the BBC site (**www.bbc.co.uk/homes**) to see the Changing Rooms and Home Front Web sites. Click DIY SOS for step-by-step instructions and videos on plastering a wall, hanging a door and other DIY projects.

STEP BY STEP

PLASTERING A WALL

Watch the video for how to plaster a wall.

For a non-embedded player click here.
You can download Realplayer for free here. Follow
RealPlayer 8 Basic.

Don't forget
There is always a risk in buying plants by post because you can't check whether they are healthy.

 Watch Out!

*Avoid botched jobs. The BBC's Good Homes site (**www.goodhomes. beeb.com**) has a long list of approved dealers and tradesmen.*

SEE ALSO
● **Shop safely on the Web** – *page 50*
● **Get a mortgage quotation** – *page 204*
● **Buy and sell at auction** – *page 208*

Play games on-line

Use the Web to play almost any game imaginable

Whatever games you like to play, the chances are you can play them on the Web. You can play virtually every video game, sport or board game, either alone or against other players – and even chat to them while you're doing so. There are also trivia quizzes and puzzles for you to ponder. There is plenty for children too, including sites with child-safe games for them to enjoy.

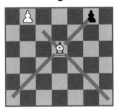

Play on-line
Most games work with your normal Web browser, but some may require you to download a small program. Many games can be played for free, but some charge subscription fees.

Types of games
On-line games include solitaire, crossword puzzles and arcade games such as pinball – with sound effects and flashing lights – as well as classic video games such as Space Invaders and driving games. There is also a range of simulation games, where you manage a city or build civilisation from scratch.

Playing off-line
If you're worried about the expense of your Internet connection, you don't have to play games on-line. There are free downloadable games, such as blackjack, to play off-line, many with high quality 3D graphics.

GAMES SITES

Best place to start

About.com's Internet Games section (internetgames.about.com)
This site provides an introduction to games sites. Categories include cards, action and role playing games. Most are free, and there are also other free games to download and play off-line.

Games to play off-line

FreewareGaming (www.freewaregaming.com)
Choose from hundreds of free downloadable games in categories such as **Puzzle/Logic**, **Sport**, **Card/Casino** and **Action/Arcade**. Games are rated and reviewed, and each listing shows the file size and system requirements.

Video games

Smiley's Game Emporium (www.clickets. com/targets/games/games.htm)
This site has over 20 free games for you to play on-line. It's strong on classics such as Asteroids and Breakout and many games, such as Carpet Golf 3-D, feature exciting and realistic graphics.

Playing against other people

MSN Gaming Zone (zone.msn.com)
Hundreds of games you can play with others on-line are offered by MSN. To play bridge, for example, click **Card**, then **Bridge** and enter one of the listed game rooms, divided into Social or Competitive. Pick a social room to start with: you'll find that the locals are friendly. In all the games, you can chat to each other as you play. Each game's homepage has a 'Getting Started' guide, plus tips, strategies, and technical help.

Games for children

Rainy Day Playhouse (www.pen-web.com/rainyday)
This site offers fun, easy-to-play games. Click **Alex Warp** to bend the faces of famous celebrities, such as Leonardo Di Caprio, into bizarre new shapes. Or choose from arcade and puzzle games and send an electronic postcard.

SEARCH IT YOURSELF

SimCity is a computer simulation game that allows you to become the ruler of existing cities or create a dream city from scratch. To play, go to a search engine such as Google (www.google.com) and search for 'SimCity'. Some hits will be articles containing the word SimCity, but most will relate to the game.

The rules of SimCity are based on city planning, resource management, human factors, strategic planning, unemployment, crime and pollution.

Your city is populated by Sims – Simulated Citizens – and to keep your city running profitably you must keep the Sims happy.

For a guide to the latest computer simulation games, go to About.com (**www.about.com**) and click on **Games** and then **Computer Simulation Games**.

Problem Solver!

*If a game won't load, your browser may be unable to read the script language used by the makers of the game. Go to **Tools** and **Internet Options**, select the **Security** tab and click **Custom Level**. Under both 'Active scripting' and 'Scripting of Java applets', click **Enable**, then **OK**.*

HOW TO: PLAY A SINGLE-PLAYER GAME ON-LINE

Many games can be played on-line by single players. At various sites on the Web you can play against computer opponents – card games such as hearts or euchre, or board games such as chess, Othello and backgammon. You can also try your hand at trivia quizzes and puzzles such as crosswords and word-searches.

FUTURE ON-LINE GAMES

On-line games are as old as the Internet. Researchers began playing simple on-line strategy games in the 1970s, and millions of gamers now play on-line. There is even a professional league – the Cyberathlete Professional League.

Most on-line gamers are American, because Internet connections are cheap or free in the USA. As Internet access becomes faster and cheaper elsewhere, on-line games will be increasingly available to players in the rest of the world.

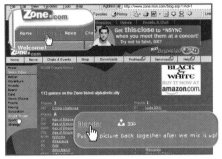

1 To play single-player games at MSN Gaming Zone (**zone.msn.com**), click **Games**, then **Single Player**. Click a game on the list to play it, such as **Blender**.

2 When the page loads up, click on **click to start**. The picture squares will then scramble. You have a set length of time to put it back into order, depending on the puzzle's difficulty.

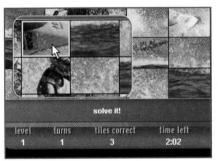

3 To solve the puzzle, click on the square you wish to move, then on the square where you want to position it. Monitor your progress by checking the details at the bottom of the window.

4 Repeat the process until the puzzle is completed. If you don't succeed before the time limit runs out, you will get a message saying 'game over' and the option of starting a new puzzle.

HOW TO: PLAY A MULTI-PLAYER GAME ON-LINE

At The Station (www.station.sony.com) you can play a number of on-line games against other players, including the hugely popular Trivial Pursuit.

When you join up to play Trivial Pursuit, you will be automatically assigned to a table. There are three players to each table, so you may need to wait a short while for a group of three to assemble. Because tables are assigned automatically, it is difficult to organise a game with someone else you know. But, if you wish, you can leave a game at any time in order to join another.

Most players are English-speaking, although they could be from anywhere in the world. You can see only the character name of your opponent, not their real name. However, there is a chat window on the page which lets you speak to the other players, and you can make your character smile or frown, as appropriate, while you chat.

To begin playing Trivial Pursuit, you must first download a small program (see right).

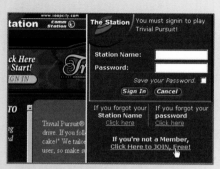

1 Go to The Station (**www.station. sony.com**). Click **Trivial Pursuit**, then **Sign In** and **Click Here to JOIN, Free!** to register as a new user.

2 Choose a user name and password, complete the registration process, then click **DOWNLOAD**. During the installation a Security Warning will pop up. Click **Yes** to accept the software.

3 When the download is complete, you'll see 'PLAY' at at the top left of the page. Now choose an avatar – a character to represent you. Click **Avatars**, select one from the list and click **Accept**.

4 Click **PLAY**. The Trivial Pursuit board appears and the game starts. Click **Throw** to throw the dice and click on a square to move to it. Answer your questions in the pop-up window.

Did You Know?

At ChessKids (www.chesskids. com), young chess players can take free lessons, chat with other users of the site or play against a computer opponent.

SEE ALSO
● **Download from the Web** – *page 82*
● **Place a bet on-line** – *page 158*
● **Keep the children entertained** – *page 174*

Money and shopping

Do your weekly shop

Order your groceries **from home** and get them **delivered** to your doorstep

More and more people are saving valuable time by using the Internet to have their weekly shopping delivered to their door – especially heavy goods that can be bought in bulk, such as canned and dried food.

Once you have an account with an on-line store, you just log in to the site, select the goods you require, enter your payment details and select a delivery time. When you get to know the system, each weekly shop can take just 10 minutes.

SITES TO TRY

Tesco (www.tesco.com)

Tesco's is probably the best UK on-line supermarket for usability, layout and features. Registration is straightforward and shopping is easy – click on a department and choose from the virtual aisles, such as 'Bakery and Cakes', 'Convenience Foods' or 'Beers

and Spirits'. You choose your groceries, then you select a delivery time (you can look at the slots anytime). Items are arranged on a clear and colourful grid.

Asda (www.asda.co.uk)

There are no distracting 'extras' on the Asda site. Enter a PIN number,

choose a delivery time and then go shopping.

As soon as you proceed to the checkout, a screen appears with most of your details already entered. All you have to do is enter your payment details and confirm your order.

All deliveries are £3.50 except on orders over £99 which are free.

Sainsbury's (www.sainsburys.co.uk)

The Sainsbury's site is easy to find your way around. Once you've logged in, you can choose to start a new order, use a Sainsbury's list, or finish off a previous, incomplete order.

You select your grocery items in the standard way. It is easy to book a delivery time, and there's a straightforward one-page confirmation and payment section.

SPECIALITY GROCERIES

Sometimes a 'spoon of opalescent roe from the belly of a 100-year-old sturgeon' is the only thing that will do. For beluga caviar and many other gourmet foods, head to **www.gourmet2000.net**.

For some old-fashioned home baking, try the Bakewell Pudding Shop (**www.bakewellpudding shop.co.uk**). You can pay to 'post a pudding' anywhere in the world.

If you're feeling brave, go to Mad Bob's Hot Sauce Shop

(**www.mad bobs.co.uk**) and order the hottest chilli sauces on Earth.

Mad Bob 'doesn't do mild', so take his advice and keep some cool yoghurt close to hand. Water, it's said, only makes things worse.

YOUR SHOPPING GUIDE

Several high street supermarkets offer on-line shopping, including Tesco, Sainsbury's and Asda (see left). But their services are not available in every part of the country, so this is the first thing you should check. You can do this by entering your postcode in the appropriate section of the site.

In choosing a shop, you should also look at the service offered. Iceland, for instance, only processes orders of over £40 but delivers for free, while Tesco and Sainsbury's charge a flat fee of £5 for delivery.

register **today**

* required info

* postcode
* title   Please select...
* name
* surname
email

Registration

All the major supermarkets' registration systems are similar. They request your name, address and a contact telephone number, and then you get to choose a password or PIN number to help to protect your account details.

Range of goods

On-line supermarkets offer almost everything that you would find on their shelves – fresh fruit, canned food, even a newspaper. If you find products you want are routinely missing from your site, try a larger supermarket chain.

What to buy

Many people choose not to buy goods that are easily damaged, such as eggs, or biscuits. Some also prefer to choose their own fresh fruit and vegetables, rather than rely on the choice of a supermarket employee. However, most on-line supermarkets do allow you to indicate the size and ripeness of the fruit that you want.

Buying bulk items such as canned food, pasta, pet food or nappies is a great way to save money, both in special deals and by cutting down on the number of times you need goods to be delivered.

Substitute items

Most on-line supermarkets give you the chance to say what should happen if one of your items is not available. You can choose to accept the nearest substitute or simply not to receive the item or any replacement.

Pick the most appropriat
No substitute please
Pick the most appropriat

r Order' button. The infor
e debited from your acc

The choice of a suitable substitute item is in the hands of the supermarket, which can create problems. You have to be prepared to find that the nearest alternative for your order of Ardennes pâté might be a jar of beef paste.

Bargain-hunting

Most sites alert you to cut-price goods that you might miss in the bustle of the supermarket. So while you might miss out on the fun of spying them in the aisles, you won't miss out on the bargains.

Shopping lists

You can save your shopping lists and use them to place repeat orders. It is also possible to save your order halfway through and come back to it later. So, while your first shopping trip may take some time, the next one will be quicker.

Booking delivery

As you can't always be in to receive your groceries, supermarkets let you pick the time of the delivery (usually, a 2 hour time slot). Afternoons are very popular, and can be heavily booked. But evening slots are often free.

Dealing with problems

If you do not receive the expected quantity and quality of goods, you should contact the shop by e-mail or on a helpline to get a refund or replacement goods. The charge to your card is normally made on the day the goods are sent out rather than when you ordered them. This allows for changes in availability and price. You will be charged only for the available items at their price on the day of delivery. Again, contact the shop if this causes you problems.

Broaden your options

For an extensive list of UK-based shopping sites offering all sorts of goods and services, take a look at British Shopping (www.british-shopping.com).

 Time Saver!

When you go back to a shopping site after you have registered, it will recognise who you are. This means that you don't have to re-enter all your details – you just have to enter a password or PIN number.

193

Shopping account

The process of setting up an account is similar for all on-line supermarkets. Here we have set up an account with Tesco.

HOW TO: SET UP AN ACCOUNT

1 Go to **www.tesco.com**. Click on **groceries** and then **register**.

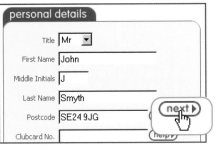

2 Use the next screen to enter your name, postcode and (if you have one) your Tesco Clubcard number. Click **next** to continue. Your postcode is now used to locate your street details.

3 Now choose your house number. The site will provide you with a list to choose from. Click on your address to select it. Enter your phone number and e-mail address. Then click on **next**.

4 Choose a password and click **next**. Indicate if you want to receive promotional material and if you want your details passed on to other companies. Then click **next**.

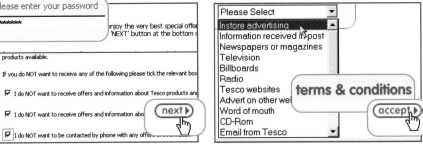

5 Now select from a list to say where you heard of Tesco's on-line shopping service and click **next**. Then read the site's terms and conditions and click on **accept** to continue.

6 You have now completed your registration. Make a note of your customer ID number password and other information. Then click **shop online now** to start shopping.

Organic groceries

Most of the major on-line supermarkets offer some organic produce. For a more specialised service, try Organics Direct (**www.organics direct.co.uk**) or the Fresh Food Company (**www.freshfood.co.uk**).

Organics Direct stocks more than 450 organic products including handmade breads, fresh pizzas and even a range of baby foods.

food as nature intended - from the farm to your doo

HOW TO: CHOOSE AND PLACE AN ORDER

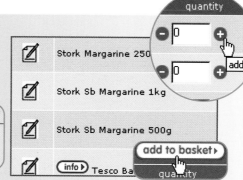

1 Go to Tesco (**www.tesco.com**) and click on **Groceries**. Enter your password and click on **sign in**. The on-line store will now load. This may take a few minutes.

2 Now click on **Departments** in the left column. Click on one to open it, then click on a food type – this is like pushing your trolley along the various aisles of your local supermarket.

3 You will be shown a list of products and prices in the main part of the screen. To select a product, click on the '+' button (click twice to select two lots of the item). Then click **add to basket**.

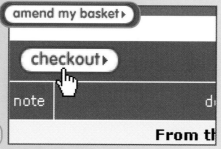

4 Continue clicking through the aisles, selecting products and adding them to your basket. To check what you have chosen, click on **view my basket**. Use the '+' and '-' buttons to alter the amounts you have chosen.

5 When you are happy with your choices, click on **amend my basket** to confirm them, and then click on **checkout** to make your purchase.

6 Now select a delivery time. Click on the appropriate square of the grid provided. The checkout screen now appears. Fill in your credit card details and click **confirm my order**.

Problem Solver!

If you have difficulty using a shopping site, consult its help section, where you will find answers to all the most common questions.

Weighty problem

At first you may find it disconcerting to shop without being able to view the products properly. Most sites offer pictures of some of their goods, but it can still be hard to visualise quite how much 500g (1lb 2oz) of margarine is.

One solution is to save the supermarket receipt (which shows all the weights) for your last shopping trip and use it to compose your first on-line shopping list. You can then save this and refer to it every time you go shopping.

SEE ALSO
● **Shop safely on the Web** – *page 50*
● **Improve your diet and fitness** – *page 126*
● **Get cooking** – *page 236*

File your tax return

Get **on-line advice** and **forms** for completing your own **tax return**

Everyone in the UK who is sent a tax return in the post is now obliged to fill out an annual self-assessment tax form. The government is dedicated to making this task as easy as possible. To this end, they have set up the Inland Revenue Web site (**www.inlandrevenue.gov.uk**), which deals with every aspect of the taxing procedure. The Inland Revenue site also offers three different options for filing your tax return.

Getting the forms in the post
You can file your tax return in the traditional way by waiting for the self assessment forms to arrive through the post. You then complete the forms and send them back to Inland Revenue. If you have any queries regarding your tax return, you can consult the Inland Revenue Web site (**www.inlandrevenue.gov.uk**).

Downloading your tax forms
The second way to file your tax return is to download your forms directly from the Inland Revenue site. All you have to do is print out the forms and fill them in. The forms are available in  a special format called PDF (Portable Document Format). To use PDF, you need to have the Adobe Acrobat Reader software, which you can download free from the Adobe site (**www.adobe.com**).

To download the forms from the Inland Revenue site, click on **Self Assessment** and then **Self Assessment Web Site** to open up the relevant section. Scroll down to the section marked 'The Tax Return' and click on **Download the forms**.

There are hundreds of forms for every kind of tax status, but to download the standard self-assessment form, select **Tax return (SA100)**.

Filling in your form on-line
A third way to file your tax return is to fill in a form on-screen and submit it over the Net. To do this, you will have to register with the Inland Revenue site (see opposite). They will then send you a User ID through the post, which you need, along with your chosen password, to log on to the service.

To fill in the form and send it back to Inland Revenue, you'll need to buy some software such as TaxSaver 2001 Deluxe, which costs £30 (see opposite). The Inland Revenue Website has a list of suitable programs with links to  their sites. You can order a program and have it sent to you in the post on a CD-ROM. You then use the program to help you fill in a form on-screen and either send it to the Inland Revenue over the Internet or print it out and post it.

HOW TO: REGISTER WITH THE INLAND REVENUE SITE

Inland Revenue

Self Assessment Tax Return

Welcome to the Inland Revenue to use compatible software and

Register here

To register please enter the following details:

Please do not use spaces or dashes between characters.

Your Tax Reference   2751751966   The ten d[...] front of yo[...]

Your Postcode   EC1V 0AT

Continue

- The password must be between 8 and 12 characters long and contai[...] letter
- You can use capital letters
- **Do Not Use** Postcodes, Tax Reference numbers and special charac[...] '?)

Enter your password   ••••••••

Repeat your password   ••••••••

OK   Clea[...]   OK

1 Go to the Inland Revenue on-line assessment site (**www.ir-efile.gov.uk**) and click on **Register here**. (If you are in doubt at any stage, click on the **Help** button at the bottom of each page).

2 Now fill in your tax reference (the 10-digit number found on the front of your tax return), your postcode, your National Insurance number and your e-mail address. Then click **Continue**.

3 Next enter a password for the service. Read the instructions carefully, enter a password and click **OK**. You will now receive confirmation of your registration by e-mail.

HOW TO: PURCHASE THE INLAND REVENUE SOFTWARE

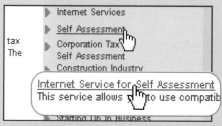

tax
The

Internet Services
Self Assessment
Corporation Tax
Self Assessment
Construction Industry

Internet Service for Self Assessment
This service allows [...]to use compatib[...]

Starting Up in Business

- An introduction to the Internet service for S[...]
- Register for the Internet service
- Software and Online Forms available.
- Frequently A[...]d Questions from taxpaye[...]
- How to pay your Self Assessment tax by[...]
- Alternative payment methods for Self As[...]
- How to ch[...]   **www.taxcentral.co.uk**

Welcome to TaxCentral

If you receive a Tax Return, you can complete-it-yourself with our TaxSaver Deluxe CDROM software, or if you prefer the personal touch we'll even find you a tax adviser.

Try our selection of tax tools, read our regular interview Being Frank with Francesca and see the latest tax news. Check your payslip and even compare your tax bill with the rich and famous with our celebrity tax meter!

1 Go to the Inland Revenue site (**www.inlandrevenue.gov.uk**). In the right-hand column of contents click on **Self Assessment**. Then click on **Internet Service for Self Assessment**.

2 Click on **Software and Online Forms available**. A new page opens listing suitable software. Click on **www.tax central.co.uk** to purchase TaxSaver Deluxe 2001. Keep in mind it costs £30.

3 You'll be taken to the TaxCentral site. Simply click on **Products** and then on **TaxSaver Deluxe**. Scroll down to the bottom of the page and click on **Buy TaxSaver 2001 Deluxe today!**

Other useful sites

There are other Web sites available besides Inland Revenue's. The Yahoo! tax centre (**uk.biz.yahoo.com/tax/home.html**) is a good all-round resource and Moneyweb (**www. moneyweb.co.uk**) is a well-organised financial site. Click on **Tax** to access the relevant section. If you want tax advice, on-line calculators help with tax terminology or any other information.

Taxing!
Sir Elton John pays £28,451 in tax a day! Check out the celebrity tax meter at the Digita tax centre (**www.digita. com**) for some light relief from those tax forms.

Time Saver!
Keep all your financial papers together and have them close to hand. This will save you time when filling in the form on-line.

SEE ALSO
- **Become a share trader** – *page 198*
- **Get a mortgage quotation** – *page 204*
- **How e-commerce works** – *page 296*

Become a share trader

Own and **manage shares** using the **Internet**

Stocks and shares information was once the exclusive property of brokers and stock market traders. But the Internet has opened up the possibility of share trading for everyone. Many Web sites give you straightforward answers to basic questions such as which shares can be traded and how the actual purchasing process works. These sites also provide key information for first-time traders, such as how to reduce risks, trading tips, plus guides to the current performance of shares to help you to make investment decisions.

Where to begin

You can either register with an on-line broker who will deal with shares for you or – to cut out the middle man – register with a share trading site to start researching share performances yourself.

Choosing investments

Most Web sites will warn you about risky investments. The usual advice for beginners is to invest in shares from reliable companies on which you have current information.

Reduce risks

You can put your money into a variety of shares or join an on-line collective fund – which is a group of people who invest together – usually for about £25 a month.

Trial run

There are Web sites that let you practise trading on-line. These offer 'fantasy' share buying and selling facilities where you can find out how good you are at spotting potential stock market winners without spending any money.

SHARE TRADER SITES

Practice site

Fantasy Stock Market (www.fantasystockmarket.com)
If you are not sure whether trading shares on-line is for you, play the fantasy stock market and buy and sell stocks using virtual money. You start trading with a set amount of 'cash', with the aim of increasing this amount. Buying and selling is very similar to those at real share dealing sites, so it is a good way to get a feel for the process.

Pre-trading site

The Motley Fool (www.motleyfool.co.uk)
Before you begin share trading, it is wise to do some research. Motley Fool provides information and advice on all

aspects of financial management, including on-line share trading. The articles at the site are written in a clear, easy-to-understand language. Motley Fool also provides a breakdown of the fees and charges of a range of on-line share trading services.

Share news

Advanced Financial Network (http://freeserve.advfn.com)
One of the keys to successful share trading is keeping up to date with financial news. This Web site includes a streaming service which displays a continuous stream of share values on your computer screen. You can configure this to show your up to 110 shares, and their prices. You can also launch the service as a separate browser

window, so you can carry on surfing other Web sites while your share information continues to be displayed.

Share history

UK Share Net (www.uksharenet.co.uk)
This is a comprehensive on-line shares service for people interested in stocks and shares. It has financial and business news, as well as more general news stories. There is also detailed share information on the history of particular shares. The site offers a useful 'powersearch' facility where you can enter a search term, such as 'Vodafone' into the search box and a search will be conducted within a number of UK financial Web sites simultaneously.

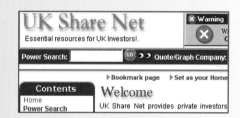

SEARCH IT YOURSELF

To find out more information about the variety of share dealing services available, try using a search engine. Search engines that let you specify whether you want to search sites from the UK, Europe or the whole world are useful for share broker and share trading information.

1 Go to Excite (**www.excite.co.uk**).
2 Type in **share trading sites** if you want to begin researching share

information yourself. This will give a list of trading sites with advice and information for the private investor.
3 Alternatively, if you would prefer a share broker to deal for you, then type in **share broker**, which will give you a list of on-line brokers.

 Did You Know?

Short term investment is risky and if you want to get out in a hurry you may not get a good price. It is better to invest over a period of at least five years to minimise the effect of fluctuating share prices.

 Money Saver!

Make sure you know the costs of share trading. The Motley Fool Web site (www.motley fool.co.uk) compares charges of some of the top UK on-line share traders.

HOW TO: LEARN TO TRADE

Before having a go at proper share dealing, first try it with a practice portfolio. This operates in exactly the same way as a real portfolio but you can see how your shares perform without investing a penny. It is best to spend at least a week, or preferably more, using the practice portfolio. You can then consider the pros and cons of share-trading – whether you have the time to devote to it and whether it is easy to use the particular system offered by your broker. If you are happy with the way things are going, it will then be time to open a real portfolio.

To open a practice portfolio, you need to register with the share-dealing site.

1 Go to the Web site of a broker, such as Virgin Money (**www.virgin money.com**). Click **REGISTER HERE** then **REGISTER HERE GO**. Complete the form. Click **PLEASE REGISTER ME GO**, then **GO**.

2 Once you are registered, click on **STOCKS AND SHARES** and then **START A PRACTICE PORTFOLIO**. Then click on one of the practice portfolios assigned to you under **Portfolio Number**.

3 Click **Add New Holdings**. Type in the name of a company and click **Search**. To buy shares in the company, click the company name, enter how many you want to buy and click **Add to Portfolio**.

4 To see how your shares perform, you need to return to the site at regular intervals and view your portfolio. If you decide you want to open a 'real' portfolio click **APPLY TO TRADE**.

REAL PORTFOLIO

When you click **APPLY TO TRADE**, you need to fill in a form on-line and provide access to some funds (in other words provide access to a bank account).

Once you've set up an account, shares can be bought and sold using the same proceedure applied in your practice portfolio. Your on-line broker will issue information about your shares, but there are other services which keep an eye on share prices. Refer to news on-line from your share trading site and use the help buttons to guide you through any other questions about share dealing.

Watch Out!

When buying shares on-line, always make sure to double check any information you enter into forms. An extra zero accidentally added to a figure, for example, could end up being very expensive.

SEE ALSO
● **Do some research** – *page 109*
● **Find legal advice** – *page 116*
● **Place a bet on-line** – *page 158*

Buy a book, CD or video

Access searches, information and previews before buying on-line

The Internet gives you fast and convenient access to the largest selection of books, music and videos available to buy anywhere in the world. There is no longer any need to spend time and money telephoning or travelling to shops. You can do it all from home. You can find shops which specialise in out-of-print books, textbooks, foreign books, CDs, old vinyl records, and virtually every film ever made both on video and DVD. There are also on-line shops which have reviews, links, samples, ratings and news to help you decide what to buy – this service is also a great way to get inspiration for gifts for people of all ages.

Most wanted
New and recent titles are easy to find on the Net, but where the Web really comes into its own is with obscure or out-of print books and records. You can scour the world in an instant to find that first edition of Brighton Rock, or some German pressing of early Beatles hits. You can also access Web sites with information and prices on converting old film to video.

Previews
Some on-line video and DVD shops offer small preview clips of films, so you can see what to expect before you buy. Many on-line bookshops offer sample chapters on-line.

FEATURED STYLE: Novelty

THE BEST SITES

Overall shopping

Amazon (www.amazon.co.uk)
For the world's largest on-line collection of books, music and films, go to Amazon. The site has many innovative options, for example, it will generate a list of titles it thinks you will like (based on previous purchases). It can be quite an eye-opener to

discover the kind of reader Amazon's computer thinks you are.

Amazon often provide discounts which means that despite delivery costs, their products are usually cheaper than most shops.

Rare items

Alibris (www.alibris.com)
This was the first on-line site dedicated solely to selling hard-to-find books. Rather than storing the books, the site links thousands of sellers from around the world. With a database of millions of books, you can search by title, author or subject area.

Price guide

On-line Price Guide (www.onlinepriceguide.co.uk)
This site searches UK on-line shops for the best prices on books, CDs, videos and DVDs, saving you time, money and effort. Search the site for the item you want, and the Guide will come up with its price, and a link to that item at various on-line shops.

Vinyl site

Global Electronic Music Market (http://gemm.com)
Although vinyl records are becoming more rare in the shops, they are easily available on the Internet. At this site

you can search through the world's largest catalogue of music with listings of over 11 million new and used records for sale. Supply your own 'wants list' or browse the selection on offer by artist, category or era.

Review site

The Internet Movie Database (www.imdb.com)
Virtually everything you want to know about any film or actor can be found on this site. Film buffs can also create a personalised database to help them keep track of when favourite films are on TV or are released on video.

SEARCH IT YOURSELF

If you can't find what you are looking for at one of the large on-line shops, try searching through speciality database sites. For a worldwide resource of booksellers, try Bookweb (www.bookweb.org/bookstores), or Books (www.books.co.uk) for a selection of shops in the UK. Bookfayre (www.bookfayre.com) contains a UK-based searchable database of rare and hard-to-find books.

For an exhaustive music database, try the All Music Guide (www.allmusicguide.com). For answers to movie questions, go to the Movie Review Query Engine (www.mrqe.com) and Cinemachine (www.cinemachine.com) for search engines devoted to movie sites.

Money Saver!

Shopping on-line can save you money, but the postal costs can easily add up. If you are buying several items, make sure any items already on order are sent in the same package as the items that are immediately available.

HOW TO: BUY SECOND-HAND BOOKS ON-LINE

There are many second-hand book sites accessible via the Internet. Bibliofind (**www.bibliofind.com**) is one of the best. The site is linked with Amazon.com and can provide immediate access to millions of rare, used and out-of-print books from around the world.

You can search by title and author or, if you don't know or can't remember those, by keywords. Because the titles are found internationally, always check where the book is being shipped from and how much that will cost.

1 Go to the Bibliofind Web site (**www. bibliofind.com**). Type the title and/or author of the book, or any keywords in the search box, such as **Moby Dick 1st edition**. Then click **GO!**.

2 You will be presented with all the matches for the title, author or keyword you've typed in. Click on **Sort listings by:** and choose a start date or price category. Click **GO!**.

3 A list of titles will appear with the price or date and the retailer. Click on the title you want to buy. You will then be given details of the book, including its state of repair.

4 Click on **convert this currency** to see the price in the currency of your choice. Scroll down for **Item Purchase Information** which gives details of accepted payment methods.

5 At the top of the page, click **Buy now from Seller**. Fill the form out with your e-mail address and create an Amazon password. You will then need credit card details and a postal address.

Time Saver!

Some Web shops boast huge catalogues, but in fact they only order an item from their supplier once you have purchased it. This can slow down your order. The better on-line shops, such as Amazon, check their stock levels before confirming your order.

SEE ALSO
● **Shop safely on the Web** – *page 50*
● **Do some research** – *page 109*
● **Enjoy the literary world** – *page 166*

Get a mortgage quotation

Use **the Internet** to get the finance for your move

Most building societies and banks advertise their mortgage products on-line, so if you are looking for the best deal, it makes sense to try the Web. It will be quicker and simpler than traipsing up and down the high street or sending off for brochures. You can use the information you find as a basis for discussion with brokers or financial advisers. Some lenders even allow you to make your application on-line.

Find out about a mortgage

At most lenders' Web sites you can view details of the policies on offer and, if you find one that suits you, make an initial application on-line. By answering the questions on the on-line form, you'll get an instant reply informing you of your eligibility. On-line applications can save you time and trouble. An application form is sent to you by post with your details filled in. All you need to do is read, check and sign it.

Choose a mortgage

When choosing a mortgage, you don't have to search through all the lenders' sites. Use an independent site such as Your Mortgage (**www. yourmortgage.co.uk**) to compare rates and products. Most mortgage sites let you specify your exact requirements and then search their database for suitable mortgages.

Calculate your mortgage

Many sites let you enter details of your mortgage and then calculate what your monthly payment will be. Or, you can enter the monthly amount you want to pay, and find what you can afford to borrow.

If you're looking for a place to buy, you can use the Web to find properties and calculate what your own home is worth.

TOP MORTGAGE SITES

Mortgage comparisons

**Charcol online
(www.charcolonline.co.uk)**
This Web site has a searchable database of more than 500 mortgages from 45 lenders. Charcol online provides buyers with information on how to find the best mortgage for you. The site also lets you select several different mortgages and compares their pros and cons.

Narrowing your choice

**Your Mortgage
(www.yourmortgage.co.uk)**
This site offers the latest mortgage deals. Because there are many mortgages to choose from, Your Mortgage has a

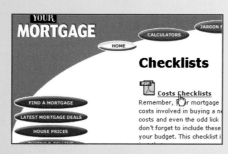

'Wizard' function that allows you to narrow your choices. Complete four simple stages, by clicking on statements that best describe your situation (such as whether or not you're a first time buyer) or entering figures (such as how big a deposit you can afford), to begin your search. If you already know which type of mortgage you want, you can conduct a search of their database.

Mortgage news

**FTyourmoney
(www.ftyourmoney.com)**
Part of the Financial Times, this site also has a Mortgage Wizard to help you to

find a mortgage to suit your individual needs. The site also has the latest financial news and features to keep you up-to-date with mortgages, taxation, property and more.

Financial advice

moneynet (www.moneynet.co.uk)
As well as mortgages, this site covers savings, pensions, insurance and loans. The search facility provides details from major mortgage operators helping you locate the information you need. The site presents an extremely thorough overview of virtually every aspect of the financial market.

 Watch Out!
Even if you are eligible for a mortgage deal, don't commit to more than you can afford.

Problem Solver!
If you are still looking for a home, go to Up My Street (www.upmystreet.com). View local maps, typical property prices, council tax rates, lists of local amenities and the area's best schools.

SEARCH IT YOURSELF

Yahoo! (www.yahoo.co.uk) has links to most banks and building societies in the UK.

Go to the 'Regional' heading and click **UK**. Select **Business and Economy**, then **Shopping and Services**. Click on **Financial Services**, then **Banking**. To complete the search, click on **Banks**.

To locate mortgage brokers, click on **Back** until you return to

Financial Services, then click **Personal Finance**. Next, you need to click **Mortgage Loans**, and finally **Brokerages**.

SEE ALSO
• **Find legal advice** – *page 116*
• **Improve your home** – *page 183*
• **Open an on-line bank account** – *page 212*

Support a charity

Help and find out about charities using the Web

The Internet has opened up new ways of donating to charity. The Web has made it easier than ever before to find out about a charity, and volunteer to help. On-line fund-raising also means that charities can spend less time and money campaigning and more time applying their funds where they are most needed.

Shop and click to donate

One of the best ways to donate money over the Internet is through shopping. Each time you purchase from a retailer listed with a charity on the Internet, that retailer will donate a percentage of the sale to the charity. At other sites, such as the rainforest site (**www.therain forestsite.com**) you can click on a button to have a donation made for you by the site's sponsors – making it easy for you to help a cause.

Other ways to help

You can also give your time. The UK Charity Directory (**www.charec.co. uk**) has a large list of vacancies at all levels within a selection of charities.

Legitimate charities

There are sites where you can check which charities are registered with the Charity Commission. They also explain how much of your donation will go towards administrative costs.

CHARITY SITES

Research

United Devices (www.ud.com)
To participate in scientific research that may eventually help to cure cancer, you can download a screensaver from United Devices for the National Foundation for Cancer Research. The screensaver will process scientific research data while your computer is idle. The technology, pioneered by the Seti@home project (see *Go into outer space* – page 142), uses the program to link up millions of home computers, creating a virtual super-computer. This then screens millions of

chemicals for their usefulness in fighting cancer by using the vast amounts of unused computing power in your PC.

Shopping

iGive.com (www.igive.com)
This is a shopping portal with a directory of links to on-line retailers. Shoppers can select the non-profit organisation or

charity that will receive up to 26 per cent of the value of their on-line purchase. The directory includes major charities, as well as smaller ones, and many high street retailers.

E-greetings

Say it with ease
(www.say-it-with-ease.com)
This site donates money to a charity every time you send an e-card. There is no cost for this service. The money comes from corporate sponsors who see this as a new way to give. Most charity

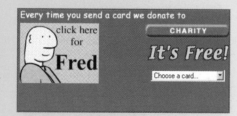

e-card sites give to a specific charity or list of charities, so you should shop around to find one you want to support.

Auctions

All Star Charity
(www.allstarcharity.com)
On this site you can bid for exciting once-in-a-lifetime experiences – such as a spot on a sitcom or a studio session with a famous musician. Or, bid for memorabilia such as signed scripts and original works of art. All proceeds go to non-profit-making charities chosen by the star who donated the item.

MAKE A CHARITY SITE YOUR HOMEPAGE

You can use a charity site – such as World Vision (**www.worldvision. org.uk**) or The Hunger Site (**www. thehungersite.com**) – as your homepage. Open Internet Explorer and click on the **Tools** menu. Select **Internet Options**. Type the charity site's address in the address box, then click **OK**.

Watch Out!

*If you are unsure whether a charity is legitimate, look up UK charities through the Charity Commission (**www.charity commission.gov. uk**) and US charities through the Federal Trade Commission (**www.ftc.gov**).*

Charity shopping centres

On-line charity shopping centres – such as iPledge (**www. ipledge.net**) or free2give (**www.free2give.co.uk**) – are Web sites which provide links to other retail sites. You first select a charity and then click on one of the links.

If you visit an on-line shop by this route (rather than by entering the shop's Web address directly) and then buy an item, the retailer will automatically donate some money to the charity you selected.

SEE ALSO
• **Use a chatroom** – *page 98*
• **Get the latest news on-line** – *page 112*
• **Seek medical advice** – *page 122*

Buy and sell at auction

Find out how you can **bid for almost anything** over the Internet

One person's trash is another person's treasure. No matter what it is, you can be sure there's someone out there who collects it. The Internet has made auctions open to anyone. If there is something you want, you can probably find it, and often at a bargain price. Equally, you can sell virtually anything at an Internet auction site – perhaps an antique figurine or a pile of old comics. Transactions need not involve money, since the Internet can also be a useful 'swap shop'.

HOW IT ALL WORKS

On an auction site such as eBay, a seller places an ad for an item, listing a minimum bid and a closing date for the auction. Buyers enter their bids by filling in a form on screen and the highest bidder at the close of the auction wins. At this point the auction site notifies the winner and the seller by e-mail and the two parties make arrangements to complete the transaction.

Other ways to bid Some sites such as eWanted (**www.ewanted.com**) let you state how much you want to pay for an item, and then notify you if anyone accepts your offer. Other sites, such as Ybag (**www.ybag.com**), let the buyer specify an item and a price they are willing to pay and then search through hundreds of merchants for one offering the item at the buyer's price.

You can also use a 'sniping' service, such as eSnipe (**www.esnipe.com**). These sites place your bid in the last few seconds before an auction closes – a process known as 'sniping'. This keeps prices down by masking your interest in an item and so avoiding bidding wars. Users have sniped manually for years, but eSnipe automates the process and increases your chances of success.

At sites such as Swap Shop (**www.swapshop.com**) you can exchange items with other users of the site. And at NetShop-UK (**www.netshop-uk.com**) you can barter for items rather than bid.

HOW TO PAY SAFELY

Depending on the seller, you can pay by cash, cheque or credit card. Paying by credit card gives you more rights as a consumer, but most private sellers can only accept cheques or cash.

Most sellers are above board but there are always a few dishonest traders. Regardless of how you pay, the best way to ensure that you are not defrauded is to use a payment company that acts as a middle man between you and the seller. These are known as Escrow companies (after a legal term for a fund held in trust).

TRADENABLE
FEARLESS COMMERCE

Instead of paying the seller directly, you pay an Escrow company such as Tradenable (**www.tradenable.com**), who inform the seller that they have received the money. The seller then ships the goods to you and, if you're satisfied, the Escrow company pays the seller. They charge around 4 per cent of the transaction price for this service.

TOP AUCTION SITES

Lot number one

eBay (www.ebay.co.uk)
Of the hundreds of on-line auction sites, eBay is the biggest – think of it as the world's largest flea market. Coins, toys, books or gems, even cars, boats and houses – it's all here. Buyers and sellers can register for free. Items can be put up

Featured Items
89.00 LEATHER GYM BAG CLOSEOUT O
30 HIGH GRADE SILVER DENARII - FRE
LADIES 3/4 LEATHER COAT BLOWOUT!!
MENS SIZE XXL LONG LEATHER TRENC

for sale for a small fee plus a percentage of the final sales price.

One of the best things about eBay is its feedback system, which rates sellers according to the number of positive comments posted by buyers. Most sellers are in the USA, but eBay has 11 country-specific sites and users in 150 countries. To reduce shipping costs, choose the eBay nearest to you.

Another big name

**Yahoo! Auctions
(http://auctions.yahoo.com)**
If you are looking for a particular item, the bigger the auction house the better.

Yahoo! Auctions is close in size to eBay. The UK section of the site alone has over 250,000 items for sale (**http://uk.auctions. yahoo.com/uk**).

Yahoo! also hosts auctions on behalf of various charities, such as Oxfam. Make a successful bid for a first edition of Charles Kingsley's *The Water Babies* and your money goes directly to a good cause. There are also many other items on the site which are being auctioned for smaller charities. Enter 'charity' into the search box on the site to see a list.

Finding an item

AuctionWatch (www.auctionwatch.com)
If you're looking for a very specific item – say, old football club programmes – try this site. They will search through all the auction sites for you and let you know

as soon as the item you are interested in has been located. Similar services are offered by Web sites such as Bidfind (**www.bidfind.com**).

Auction guide

AuctionGuide (www.auctionguide.com)
Full of handy explanations of auction procedures and terminology, this is a great site for learning auction basics. If you have any doubts about auction pitfalls such as hidden costs, consult the 'Tips 'n Hints' section.

Use your browser

The iMac version of Internet Explorer 5 has a feature called Auction Manager, which monitors the status of auctions that you are interested in, and notifies you when someone places a higher bid than you and when the auction closes.

To find out more, go to the **Tools** menu, select **Auction Manager** and then click on the **Help** button for an on-screen tutorial.

 Did You Know?

eBay set up the first on-line auction in 1995. Electronic auctions now generate annual profits of around £38 billion.

SOLD TO THE HIGHEST BIDDER!

Auction sites can be a good way to get the best possible price for any items you want to sell.

Be it the watch worn by grandad in the trenches, or an ancient map of your county – someone, somewhere, will want it. For an object you know to be genuinely precious, consider contacting Sotheby's (**www. sothebys.com**) for a valuation and also to browse their on-line auctions to check the prices of other similar objects.

If you are selling an item that seems to defy the categories of most auction sites, you can search for a speciality auction by typing 'auction' and your subject (such as 'thimbles', 'stamps' or 'railways') into a search engine.

Bidfind (**www.bidfind. com**), and Bidville (**www.bidville.com**) also offer a range of speciality auctions to try.

HOW TO: TAKE PART IN AN ON-LINE AUCTION

Most auction sites let you browse through the listings without registering. You can also check the bidding on an item you're interested in. Bookmark the page and return to it periodically to see what the highest bid is and how much time is left in the auction. You need only register with the site when you want to place a bid or to put an item up for sale.

All the auction Web sites operate on largely the same principles. Here we have shown how to register with eBay, locate an item and bid for it.

Auction aficionados

It is possible to make a living by selling at auction. But finding items to sell, organising lot descriptions and photos, posting auctions, handling queries, notifying winners, taking payment and shipping the goods will make it a full-time job. Successful sellers work 10 to 16 hour days.

Watch Out!

If a seller does not deliver an item as arranged, contact the auction site. Some will try to resolve the dispute for you. Many sites also offer some form of guarantee.

 Step 1 - eBay UK ...nformation below and click the ...are shown in green.

...ail address
username@aol.com

jon.asbury@planet
Note: AOL and WebTV
the domain suffix (@aol
username is joecool, you

1 Go to **www.ebay.co.uk** and click **Join**. Select a country of residence and click **Begin the registration process now**. Fill in the form and click **Continue**.

By clicking "I Accept" below, you agree:

1. that you have read, understand and agree to abide reference;
2. you intend to form a legally binding contract by cli
3. a print out of the Agreement and the documents it applicable law or regulation.

[I Accept]   [I Decline]

Click "I Accept" to accept this User Agreement. When yo

3 When the e-mail arrives, note down your ID number and click on the link provided to go back to eBay. Read the site's terms and click on **I Accept**.

Please note that you must create a **new** password now, from the confirmation code sent to you in the confirma

Your E-mail Address: | silversurfer@Rea...

The confirmation code sent to you in the confirmation instructions. | 2245687

Click **here** if you need eBay to resend your confirmation instructions.

Create a **new**, permanent password:
Type your **new pa**...

Complete your registration

4 Enter your e-mail address and ID into the form provided and choose a password. Note them down and click **Complete your registration**.

SPEARS SKITTLE GAME DATING FROM THE 1930S. CONDITION IS OUTSTANDING AND CO AND ARE 15CMS HIGH. THEY ARE ALL BEAUTIFULLY HAND PAINTED AND IN SUPERB OR REALLY PRETTY SET. BUYER PAYS POST/PACKING. WILL SHIP WORLD WIDE. PAYMENT BY BANK CHARGES APPLY TO NON UK TRANSACTIONS.

Click on

6 You are now shown details of the item, including a picture, its price and the name of the seller. If you want to make an offer, click **Bid**.

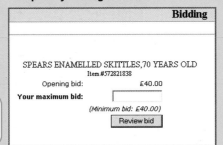

Bidding

SPEARS ENAMELLED SKITTLES, 70 YEARS OLD
Item #572821838

Opening bid: £40.00
Your maximum bid:

(Minimum bid: £40.00)
[Review bid]

7 Now enter the maximum amount you are willing to bid (here, it is in pounds sterling), and click **Review bid**. Check your details and click **Place bid**.

 ...ration - Step 1 Complete!

You have successfully completed step 1 of the eBay

Important! You cannot begin buying or selling on eB

Step 2 - Receive Confirmation Instructions
eBay will send you an e-mail message (within 24 hour received within 24 hours.

Step 3 - Confirm Your Registration

2 Check your information and click **submit**. eBay then processes your registration and e-mails you an identity code. This is normally done in minutes.

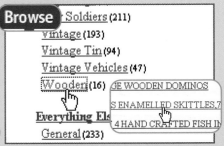

Browse ... Soldiers (211)
Vintage (193)
Vintage Tin (94)
Vintage Vehicles (47)
Wooden (16)   GE WOODEN DOMINOS
                S ENAMELLED SKITTLES,7
Everything Els   4 HAND CRAFTED FISH IN
General (233)

5 To bid for an item, click on **Browse** and look through the categories to find an item of interest. Here we have chosen a set of antique skittles.

8 You will immediately receive a message telling you whether you are the highest bidder – if you are not, you can reconsider your offer.

You will then receive an e-mail every day until the auction closes, telling you whether you are still the highest bidder – and finally whether you have been successful with your bid.

If you have, you are bound by contract to contact the seller (using the details given on the site) and arrange payment and delivery of the item.

AUCTION TIPS

Every auction site offers a guide to its own bidding system – both for sellers and buyers. You should always refer to this for specific help and advice. But there are several useful tips worth bearing in mind:

DO watch an auction before joining one yourself. This way, you can get a feel for how they work without having to bid.

DO make sure you know the shipping costs before you make a bid, by checking the auction house's FAQ page. Shipping fees vary widely, even though all auction houses use standard courier services. Shipping costs and insurance, if taken, can vastly increase the price.

DON'T bid for a product before investigating its retail price. Sites such as ConsumerReview (**www.consumer review.com**), and the Product Review Site (**http://productreviews.esmartbuyer.com**) help you check.

DO pay taxes on your auction earnings. If you are regularly going to sell at auction for profit, UK law stipulates that you will have to pay tax. If you buy an item from abroad, you may also have to declare it and pay duty.

DON'T sell an item at auction without first setting a reserve price at the minimum amount you want to get. Bids that don't reach the reserve price are rejected. That protects you against being forced to sell an item if the highest bid is very low. An agreement between a buyer and seller is a legally binding contract.

DO learn how to spot and protect yourself against scams such as artificially increasing the bid price. See the Tips guide in AuctionGuide (**www.auctionguide.com**).

DON'T buy any item you feel has been poorly described. You want to be sure you know exactly what you are getting. A photo is helpful.

DO check the site for feedback left by previous buyers to see if the seller is honest.

DO ask for help if you are a victim of auction fraud. **Amazon.co.uk** will reimburse you if you are defrauded on their auction site. Other sites are also willing to fight fraud.

GOING, GOING...

It is no exaggeration to say that just about anything you can think of can be bought at an Internet auction.

One of the most bizarre items ever sold through eBay was a Second World War submarine, put up for sale by a small town in New England that decided it no longer needed it.

Someone once tried to sell a missile through eBay. Although the auction company thought the sale was only a prank, the federal authorities in Washington, DC advised them to keep the sale open, then made the winning bid themselves and arrested the would-be arms merchant.

Perhaps the strangest item ever put up for auction was a soul. eBay eventually cancelled the sale when they could not decide how the winning bidder would take delivery.

Money Saver!

Compare prices for similar items at different auction sites before you bid, or you might waste money paying more than you need to.

SEE ALSO
- Shop safely on the Web – *page 50*
- Improve your home – *page 183*
- File your tax return – *page 196*

Open an on-line bank account

Do your **banking** business **whenever** it suits you on the Web

Most major banks and building societies now offer instant on-line access to your finances at any hour of the day. On-line banking services range from checking your balance to making transfers, payments and managing your investments. You can apply for loans, new accounts, credit cards and even a mortgage on-line. You can move money electronically from your on-line high street bank account to a high-rate savings account, and transfer it back again later – without having to give notice.

Service your accounts >>
View all your latest acc transactions and balan

What is on-line banking?

There are two kinds of Internet bank – high street banks, such as Barclays, that allow you to access your existing accounts on-line, and Internet-only banks, such as Egg.

An Internet-only bank has no high street branches, so you can't pop in to pay in a cheque or get face-to-face advice. You have to make all your financial arrangements on-line.

Is it free?

Both kinds of Internet bank may charge you for using their service, which can be a monthly, annual or full initial payment. It can be a few pounds a month – and is one of the first things you should check when comparing banks.

What banking can you do?

You can check your balance, see which payments have been made and which are about to go out, view and change your standing order and direct debit details, and apply for overdrafts and loans.

There are some things you can do that were not previously possible, such as moving funds between banks and paying bills – telephone, utilities, council tax and so on – on-line.

THE KEY QUESTIONS

How do you bank on-line?

If you have an account with a high street bank, you can get on-line access by going to the bank's Web site and filling in an on-screen form. The bank will send you more details about the service through the post together with your user ID for the site. You may also receive a telephone call from the bank to confirm that you are who you say you are. The process for an Internet-only bank is similar except that you are also applying to open an account.

Register here for banking

How do you take cash out?

With a high street account, you can continue to withdraw money from a cash machine or over the counter as usual. But, with an Internet-only account, you do not have this option. For this reason, many people keep a separate current account with a high street bank and use an Internet-only bank for their savings.

Some Internet-only banks, such as Egg, do provide you with a debit or credit card, which you can use to make payments.

How do you pay money in?

If you have on-line access to your high street bank account, you can still pay in

Welcome to **smile** the internet bank

- **smile** has been designed and built for the Internet and is part of the Co-operative Bank p.l.c
- it's not just an add-on Internet banking service
- it's not just one account

only cheques and cash by going into your branch or sending it in the post.

With an Internet-only account, you either have to post your cheques using the bank's pre-paid envelopes, or take them to another bank (approved by your on-line bank), which will transfer the amount to your account – often for a small charge. Smile customers, for instance, can pay cheques in for free at any UK Post Office.

The only way to use the Internet to pay money directly into an account is to transfer it from another on-line account. If you normally have your salary paid directly into your bank account, you can still do this with an Internet-only bank.

What are the interest rates?

Because Internet-only banks have less overheads, they can offer better rates on

savings accounts, loans and overdrafts. Together with ease of access, this is the biggest advantage of such accounts.

What if I have a problem?

Most Internet-only banks offer a 24 hour helpline, which you can call in the event of any problem. You can also check the Help section of the bank's site, and e-mail less urgent queries.

Will my account be secure?

All banks offer a secure service. There is a rigorous system of passwords and access criteria to establish your identity. And all the personal data sent to and from your computer is encrypted, making it virtually impossible for a hacker to break.

Security

We'll reimburse you in full if any funds are removed from your account subject to our no risk policy

Our no risk policy
How we do it

	BANK OF SCOTLAND
Technical	HOBS (this has
Cost	£4 per mo
Features	•View your three mont Investment accounts • a pay-in bo
Available	Launched
Futher details	Bank of S

BARCLAYS

PROS
- Instant access to your account
- Instant loan and overdraft applications
- Good savings rates
- Instant change of direct debit and standing order details

CONS
- No face-to-face assistance
- No cash withdrawal
- Cheques have to be sent in by post

CASE STUDY

Grant, a self-employed property developer, has just come back from his first holiday in five years.

'I'm a control freak. I need to know if all the rents have come in, and the contractors have been paid. A holiday was out of the question.

'In the end my wife made me get on-line access to my Barclays accounts and then took me to an Internet café in town. She whipped a sombrero out of her bag, stuck it on my head and said "Pretend you're on holiday".

'I gave it a try and found that I could be a control freak anywhere in the world! In fact we spent the next hour or two browsing for a holiday and booked one there and then!'

EASY-TO-USE SITES

Barclays Bank

www.ibanking.barclays.co.uk
This site includes a clear demonstration of both business and personal services, and links to other related services.

If you are an existing customer, applying for an on-line account is a matter of answering a series of simple questions. The pages load quickly and there's a freephone helpline.

You can apply for an overdraft or a savings account, e-mail Barclays with queries or service feedback from any screen, and there's help for iMac and Netscape users.

Egg

www.egg.com
Egg offer services from savings accounts to shopping and insurance. Everything is done on-line – you can apply for an Egg card and receive a decision in seconds, or you can view your account details and latest transactions.

Egg's help pages are comprehensive and they even give you tips on setting up your PC and getting started.

Lloyds TSB

www.lloydstsb.com
The Lloyds TSB homepage is clearly laid out and easy to navigate, with a wealth of features, including a branch locator and a list of rates and charges. The banking page offers a choice of seven different bank accounts and travellers' services.

The Lloyds site will check whether your browser is compatible with their on-line banking and you can register for all their on-line services from one page (see opposite).

First Direct

www.firstdirect.com
First Direct was the UK's first 24-hour, branch-free bank – all business being conducted over the telephone. Their years of experience in telecoms-based banking shows on their Web site.

It has quick-loading pages that include information about services offered, demos and help. Accounts and features are easy to use and there is a great deal of on-line support available.

SEARCH IT YOURSELF

A basic keyword search such as 'Internet banking' will bring up thousands of sites. It's better to start with a well-known banking name such as:
Halifax: **www.halifax.co.uk**
HSBC: **www.banking.hsbc.co.uk**
NatWest: **www.natwest.com**
Royal Bank of Scotland: **www.rbs.co.uk**
Smile: **www.smile.co.uk**

Time Saver!

Make your on-line banking or Internet account site one of your Internet Explorer Favorites and add it to your toolbar for fast access.

Watch Out!

Keep all your passwords in a safe place or, better still, memorise them and destroy any hard copies.

HOW TO: GET ACCESS TO YOUR ACCOUNT ONLINE

1 To access your Lloyds bank account on-line, go to the Lloyds TSB site (**www.lloydstsb.com**), and click on **Register here for Internet banking**.

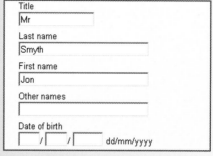

register for Lloyds TSB online
Complete the online application form to join the service

logon to business banking
Helping your business succeed

registration process
The ins and outs of the registration process

2 In the next window that appears, scroll down and click on **register for Lloyds TSB online** to open a form for you to fill in.

Title
Mr

Last name
Smyth

First name
Jon

Other names

Date of birth
/ / dd/mm/yyyy

3 Now enter your personal contact and bank account details. Try to complete all the boxes if possible – many are mandatory.

Please enter the password you would like to use for Ll

Please enter password
(between 6 and 15 characters - letters and numbers on

Please retype password

PhoneBank telephone banking

If you are registered to use our Phonebank service, ple password in the box below to allow us to register you

4 Scroll down and choose a password that is not too obvious to anyone that knows you – this word will allow access to your account, so it should be absolutely secure.

Please read the Legal Conditions for Lloy

☑ **Please tick the box to confirm you**

By clicking 'Send', I confirm:
a) that the details I have provided in t
b) that I have read and agree to the L service.

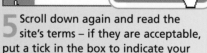

5 Scroll down again and read the site's terms – if they are acceptable, put a tick in the box to indicate your acceptance and click the **Send** button.

6 A screen will now appear, giving you a **reference number** and a telephone number. Call the phone number so that the bank can check that you are who you say you are and set up a secure account for you.

The bank will then arrange to send you a Welcome Pack in the post with your **user ID** and more information about using the service. You will need to enter your user ID on the site before you can start using the service.

Get it in print

Opt for e-mail notification whenever you use your Internet account for important transactions, and then print out the e-mails. This ensures that you have hard-copy evidence of your account activity should any problems arise later. These documents also act as a handy back-up should your computer ever suffer a fatal crash.

Money Saver!

To help you choose between accounts, create a table in Word or Excel to compare the features and interest rates of all the accounts you are interested in.

Watch Out!

If you log on in a public place, such as a Web café, make sure no one can see you type in your password.

SEE ALSO
● **Security on the Internet** – page 48
● **File your tax return** – page 196
● **Get a mortgage quotation** – page 204

Great days

Mark a special occasion

Find the **perfect way to celebrate** every type of event

Sending a card over the Internet is a great idea. It's virtually free, you can choose from thousands of musical and animated designs, and you can do it at the very last minute and still not miss the big day. If you tend to forget birthdays and anniversaries, there are Internet services to remind you. You can also buy gifts on-line and find other ways to mark a special day. You can have balloons, flowers, chocolate, food and all sorts of novelty items delivered to almost anywhere in the world.

E-cards

Many sites offer free Internet greetings cards, known as 'e-cards'. You can choose a card, add your message, enter the e-mail address of the recipient, and the e-card will show up in their inbox a few minutes later. Sending an e-card is an easy and immediate way to keep in touch with friends and relatives in other countries.

Real cards

If you would prefer to send a real card, there are Web sites that will do this for you as well. Select a card and a message and they will put it in the post for you.

Gifts

The Internet is also the place to track down gifts. You have to pay for the item and for delivery, but this can still be worthwhile for convenience alone. What's more, Web sites often offer real bargains because the overheads involved in running a Web site are much lower than those of a real shop.

CELEBRATE IN STYLE

Best e-card site

Cards4You
(www.cards4you.co.uk/ecards.html)
This site offers an astounding range of greetings cards and enables you to send colourful and entertaining e-cards extremely easily. You can even propose with a 'will you marry me?' card. Many cards are animated and you can personalise your choice with a

message or photo. You can also add music and change the background and colour of your card according to taste.

Real card Web site

Clinton Cards (www.clintoncards.co.uk)
If an e-card does not feel personal enough, you can still order 'real' cards over the Internet. One of the best Web sites for sending cards anywhere in the world is Clinton Cards. This site lets you create customised cards and then posts them for you. Alternatively, they will print personal messages on the cards, stamp them and address them, then forward them to you to sign and post yourself. All this is closely comparable in cost with what you would pay for a card in one of Clinton Cards' high street shops.

Reminder service

Greetsomeone.com
(www.greetsomeone.com)
If you have a hard time remembering birthdays, anniversaries and other events, try this site for a complete reminder service. Once you've entered all the dates you want to keep track of, the service will remind you before every important event on your calendar.

You can choose whether they send your reminder by e-mail, to your pager or to your palm-top computer. You can be notified on a particular day before the occasion or every day for a week beforehand.

Unusual gift ideas

Star Registry
(www.starregistry.com)
For a really unusual gift, go to Star Registry to have a star officially named after a person of your choice. The star name will then be copyrighted and listed in the international star registry, and you will be provided with precise co-ordinates for locating your star in the sky.

London Zoo
(www.zsl.org/londonzoo/adopt.html)
For an unforgettable present, adopt an animal at London Zoo. From as little as £25 for a hamster, or as much as £6000 for an elephant, you can adopt an animal for a year. You also have the option of sharing an animal for just £35.

Romantic gift service

Sayitwith (www.sayitwith.co.uk)
Using this site, you can arrange for flowers, chocolates and champagne to be sent anywhere in the UK. The delivery price is included. A reminder service is provided to help you to monitor any important dates you need to remember.

Delivery times

When ordering a delivery of gifts or flowers on-line, check with the company to find out how long delivery will take. Services such as Lastminute.com (**www.lastminute.com**) that offer quick delivery, can still take up to eight to ten hours. If you are trying to surprise someone with flowers or a gift at work, it is best to order the day before to ensure delivery on time.

 Money Saver!

You can send an e-card to as many people as you like. This makes it a cheap way to make a special announcement, such as 'We've had a baby girl'.

Watch Out!

Before sending an e-card, double check you have typed the recipient's e-mail address correctly. Otherwise the card might be sent to the wrong person, or returned to you undelivered.

219

Watch Out!

Remember that an e-card will arrive instantaneously. There is no need to send the card ahead of time.

HOW TO: SEND AN E-CARD

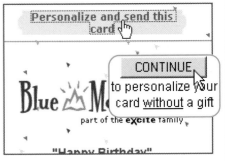

1 Go to Blue Mountain (**www.bluemountain.com**) and click on a category, such as **Birthday**, on the homepage.

2 A new page opens, showing a selection of cards available within the 'birthday' category. Click on any card you like the look of, for instance, **Happy Birthday!**.

3 Scroll down the page and click on **Personalize and send this card**. A new page will appear click **CONTINUE** to personalize your card <u>without</u> a gift.

4 Fill in the recipient's (and your own) name and e-mail address, a personal message and click **Continue**. Select a delivery date, or whether you wish to have notification of the delivery.

5 Edit any changes to your card and then click **CONTINUE**. A new page now opens, telling you whether or not delivery has been successful.

Receiving an e-card

When your card arrives at its destination, the recipient will receive an e-mail message from the card company. This will inform them that you have sent the card, and will supply a Web address link which they can then click on in order to view it.

If the recipient wants someone else to see an e-card, they can send the address to them. After viewing the card, they can also click on a link to reply with an e-card of their own.

HOW TO: USE A REMINDER SERVICE

1 Go to GreetSomeone.com (**www. greetsomeone.com**). Scroll down the page and click on **Reminder service**.

2 A new page appears. Scroll down to the bottom to fill in the form provided. Select how many days in advance of the occasion you would like to be reminded of it.

3 Select the month, the date and the year on which the occasion occurs. Fill in the 'Remind me for' box to help you to remember the occasion for which you need a reminder.

4 Finally fill in your name and e-mail address and click **Register**. A new page will now appear confirming that your reminder has been activated.

SEARCH IT YOURSELF

On-line florists

For flower delivery in the UK, go to Internet Flowers (**www.internet flowers.co.uk**), which provides links to many sites offering on-line ordering. Organising a delivery in this way costs no more than ordering by phone or in person.

For deliveries worldwide, go to Interflora (**www.interflora.com**). The company has outlets in more than 150 countries, which means that it can offer same-day delivery even in remote locations such as the Cook Islands or Guam.

E-greetings cards

Posty City (**http://postycity.net**) saves you time by searching greetings cards sites until it finds a card that matches

Product: 3135, Stargazer Lily Wreath

the specifications that you enter. For a personalised photo card, visit CardStore (**www.cardstore.com**).

Other on-line gifts

The Chocolate Lover's Page (**http:// chocolate.scream.org**) have a database of links to 800 sites around the world dedicated to chocolate.

 Watch Out!

When searching for gifts on-line, enter the most specific search terms you can. If you were searching for toiletries, for example, type in 'scented soap' rather than just 'soap', so that you do not get a list of sites about TV soap operas.

 Did You Know?

*There are card and gift shops on the Web, which give their profits to charity. For charity e-greetings, go to say-it-with-ease. com (**www.say-it-with-ease.com**).*

SEE ALSO
● **Shop safely on the Web** – *page 50*
● **Buy and sell at auction** – *page 208*
● **Find a fun night out** – *page 222*

Find a fun night out

Use the World Wide Web to find out what's on where

When you are stuck for ideas for a place to meet friends, where to go on a special occasion, or a last-minute evening out, you can find all the information – and usually book the tickets – on-line. Forget about buying listings magazines and restaurant guides. All the tools you need are on the Internet.

On-line guides

If you are not sure what you want to do, a good place to start is an on-line listings guide such as Event Selector (**www.eventselector.co.uk**), where you can search by event, venue and place. Time Out (**www.timeout.com**) has entries on theatres, restaurants, cinemas, clubs, pubs and bars in London and other major cities all around the world.

Capital site

To plan a night out in the capital, visit This is London (**www.thisislondon. co.uk**) for details of where to eat and what to see. To find out about tickets, schedules and maps for the tube, train and buses, go to the London Transport site (**www.londontransport.co.uk**).

Foreign breaks

To make the most of your stay in Paris, pay a visit to the French capital's tourist office before you go (**www. paris-touristoffice.com**). France Tourism (**www.francetourism.com**) has details of what's on around the country. If you're off to Germany, visit the national tourist board's English-language site (**www. deutschland-tourismus.de/e**).

NIGHT LIFE

All-round entertainment information

What's on Guide (www.whats-on-guide.co.uk)
This detailed site has extensive listings for events, theatre, sports, nightlife, exhibitions, eating out and shopping. Unlike many UK listings, which focus on London, this guide has a comprehensive listing of events all over the UK. You can search by city, region and date.

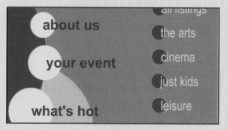

Eating out

Taste (www.taste.co.uk)
At Taste you can find thousands of ideas for where to go for great food in the UK and Europe. Click on **restaurants** on the homepage. You can search restaurants by name, location, cuisine or price range. The site also has reviews, celebrity chef features and recipes to try out. You cannot make bookings through the site, but it provides you with all the information you need to book by telephone.

Night out planner

ConciergeDesk (www.conciergedesk.co.uk)
This site offers an all-round planning service for your night out and there is no charge for any of the services on the site. Let someone else find you a great restaurant, get you tickets to a sold-out concert, obtain an invitation to a private opening, and pick up your laundry.

ConciergeDesk do all this as well as arranging private guided tours (which range from £200 to over £1000), and offering mobile phone hire, the answers to questions about opening times, or chauffeur services where you can be collected from the airport in style.

Theatre guide

Whatsonstage.com (www.whatsonstage.com)
You can use this site to decide which play to see and find out where and when it is showing in the UK. The site allows you to search by play title, venue, region or date. It also offers reviews, competitions and features as well as an on-line ticket buying service for selected shows.

DETAILED SEARCH

Our listings database is searchable by all of the following possible, you can narrow or broaden your results to the pr

Performance Name: Blood Brothers

☑ Play ☐ Musical ☐
☐ Opera ☐ Dance/Ballet ☐
By Genre:
☐ Cabaret ☐ Festival

Last-minute ideas

lastminute.com (www.lastminute.com)
This site can help you to get late reservations at restaurants, tickets to theatre, dance and sporting events. The 'Favourite Deals' section has ideas on what to do. Prices are given with each listing, so you choose what you can afford. For cheap eats, the 'Dine for Under a Tenner' category is also useful.

SEARCH IT YOURSELF

If you already have an idea of where you would like to go – for example, a visit to the Royal Opera House – try searching for that venue in a search engine. Most theatres, clubs and restaurants have their own Web sites. Check theatre, dance and concert availability from the many on-line brokers such as Ticketmaster (**www.ticketmaster.co.uk**), Aloud (**www.aloud.com**) and tickets-online (**www.tickets-online.co.uk**).

Or, search through a dedicated site like Whatson stage.com (**www. whatsonstage. com**). If you're a keen clubber, try Night Out (**www. night-out.co.uk**). If you have no idea what you want to do, go to unmissable.com (**www.unmissable. com**) for unusual or far-flung events, like the Verona Opera Festival in Italy.

Watch Out!

As with paying for anything on-line, make sure you are buying tickets on a secure site. Look for the padlock in the Status Bar at the bottom of your browser window and make sure the site has a refund policy.

HOW TO: BOOK A NIGHT OUT ON-LINE

▼ search by
- **REGION**
- **NEW EVENTS**
- **BEST SELLERS**
- **ROCK**
- **DANCE**
- **CLASSICAL**
- **THEATRE**
- **POP**
- **CLUB**
- **COMEDY**

Simply fill in one or more of the f[...] list of events currentl[...]

Artist: Van Morriss[...]

the W·A·Y·A·H·E·A·D box office

Simply fill in one or more of the following fields to get a [...] of events currently on sale.

Artist: Van Morrison
Town/City:
Start Date: dd / mm / yyyy
End Date:

search

‖ TRACK YOUR TICKET ‖ FREE EMAIL NEWS SERVICE ◄

ticket availability

Van Morrison, Warwick Castle, Warwick, 21/07/2001

Start Time: 19:30   **Doors Open: 18:00**

ticket price   face value   p&p   ticket type   no. o[...]

£33.25   £30.00

no. of tickets   order

2   order now

Event Information

Children under 5 are not adm[...]

Enter the number of tickets y[...] the **Order Now** button to proce[...]

---

1 Go to a ticket purchase site. The best ones such as Way Ahead Box Office (**www.tickets-on-line.co.uk**) also have ideas on what to do, and list hundreds of events and shows.

2 On the homepage, you can search by entering an event name, a venue, a location or an artist (such as Van Morrison shown above) and then clicking **search**.

3 A new page lists the events that meet your criteria, with times and locations. Click **order** by an event to see more details. Then type in how many tickets you need, and click **order now**.

FINDING A FILM

One great feature of the Internet is being able to find out what films are on in your area just by entering your postcode.

For listings of films showing in cinemas near you and their times, go to the film section of The Guardian newspaper"s Web site (**http://film.guardian.co.uk**).

You can search for a film by entering its title or your postcode in the boxes provided. Enter the area of the cinema you wish to visit in the 'What's on near me' box, then click **Go**.

A list of cinemas in your area will now appear, giving the address, box office number and showing times for all the films playing at each cinema. You can click on any cinema you are interested in, and a new page will come up giving you more details of film times and the ratings for each film playing. You can click on a film title for more information about it, read reviews or even submit one of your own.

Ritzy Cinema

Coldharbour Lane, London SW2 1[...]

Information: 020 7733 2[...]
Bookings: 020 7733 2[...]

The Adventures Of Pino[...]
Babe: Pig In The City (U[...]
Blow (18) Sun mat 1.00p[...]
Dinosaur (PG) Sat mat 1[...]
Dr Dolittle 2 (PG) 11.45a[...]
Le Gout des Autres (The[...]
Intimacy (18) late 9.20pm[...]

Tickets £33.25 each

find seats

have available in the

choose again | buy these

4 You are now asked to select your seats. Click **find seats**. If you're happy with them, enter your payment details and click **buy these**. A confirmation page tells you how to collect your tickets.

⏱ **Time Saver!**

Many sites have graphics that are time-consuming to download in your browser if you don't need to see all the images. Find a 'low graphics' or 'text only' version of a page or turn the graphics off.

SEE ALSO
- **Access showbiz news** – *page 164*
- **Mark a special occasion** – *page 218*
- **Book a perfect holiday** – *page 228*

Enjoy the great outdoors

Look on the Internet for inspiring holidays and days out

The Internet makes planning an outdoor activity less difficult and time-consuming. It can also help you decide where to go if you are running low on ideas. There are enough dedicated travel sites on it to inspire a year of trips. And you can find information on virtually any place you want to visit around the world.

Tourist sites

Begin your research at a site such as Travel England (**www.travel england.org.uk**). Here, you'll find details and links on places to visit, accommodation, and events happening around the country. You can also sign up for e-mail updates. Local tourist board sites have more detailed information on walking,

outdoor sports and places of historical interest. National and local walking clubs' sites are also a great source of information.

Finding accommodation

To find what you need, search by town and type of accommodation – stately homes, bed and breakfasts and self-catering cottages are all available, and you are not limited to the UK. Numerous tour operators offer walking and activity holidays worldwide. Book a guided trek in the Himalayas on-line, or an outdoor holiday in Spain, where the climate is suitable for year-round walking. Consult official and unofficial sites in each country for more information.

OUTDOOR SITES

Best official site

The Ramblers' Association (www.ramblers.org.uk)
Full of practical information, this site covers safety issues, route planning, map-reading, and equipment. There's detailed regional information and a 'Walk of the Month' feature. The many links include national parks, government agencies, clubs, voluntary groups and accommodation. The site also offers guided walking and sightseeing holidays for people with disabilities.

SEARCH IT YOURSELF

If you are looking for places to go hang gliding, first go to MSN UK (http://search.msn.co.uk). Under 'Lifestyle', click **Sport, Other Sports A-Z, Sports C-K** and then **Hang-glide**. Click on **Resources** to see links to a list of sites on the subject. Go to The National Sites Guide (**http://nsg.intracus.com/ nsg/index.html**) to find out where in the UK you can fly, and to find a list of hang gliding clubs you can join. Or, if you feel like having a go at hang gliding somewhere more exotic, over the Alps for example, click the **International sites** link, then choose **Switzerland** from the list of countries.

Equipment shop

Field and Trek (www.fieldandtrek.co.uk)
Purchase the best outdoor equipment on-line at this site. You can find everything you need for an outdoor activity, and buy specialist items such as a Global Positioning System. It is also well worth consulting the site's 'Technical Guide' for information about choosing suitable outdoor clothing and equipment for your trip, such as an extremely light gas stove or a climbing rope which will not break.

Walking guide

African walking safaris (www.zambezi.co.uk/walking)
This site focuses on walking safaris in Zimbabwe, Zambia and Botswana. You can choose from wilderness trails, bush camps or lodge-based walks. There are maps showing the prime walking safari areas in Southern Africa and background information on the different destinations and what they

have to offer.

There is also a guide to the walking seasons, a list of essential items to take with you and useful answers to frequently asked questions.

Camping site

Campsites in Europe (www.interhike.com)
Try this site for a handy guide to camping and hiking in Europe with details of campsites in countries such as Greece or Switzerland. Visit the new Travel Forum where fellow campers give advice and information.

You can also access this campsite database by WAP phone.

Outdoor sports guide

Adventure Activities A-Z (www. reviewing.co.uk/outdoors/links.htm)
This site provides links to UK outdoor sports and activities sites, plus the Countryside Commission, The National Trust and Ordnance Survey. Links are listed alphabetically, enabling you to quickly access sites on the subject of your choice, from archery to yachting.

Find news and information, as well as weather forecasts, safety tips and details on how to buy the essential equipment for your trip.

HOW TO: PLAN A WALK

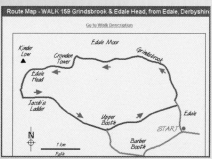

Walking Britain

WALK 159 Grindsbrook & Edale Head, from Edale, Derbyshire

SITE SEARCH
HOME PAGE
Go Back a Page
THE WALKS ENGLAND
THE WALKS SCOTLAND
THE WALKS WALES
ORDER BOOKS & MAPS ONLINE
EMAIL

Length : 7.5 miles - 12 km Ascent :
Click here for deta

The Kinder Plateau provides a wonderful excuse for pu
the main car park in Edale (grid ref 124853) and for on
Edale station served by trains on the Manchester and S
two contrasting sections of scenery with the wild moorl
Edale. All of the route is over clear footpaths although a
Kinder plateau. In addition, you sample part of the Pen
original start to this long distance footpath while you re

Parking in Edale can be a problem especially at weeke
probably a good idea. From the car park (or station) he
Tourist Information Centre on the right hand side of the

1 Go to Walking Britain (**www.walking britain.co.uk**). Look for a walk that interests you. Walk lengths and difficulty are given, with route descriptions and a link to a sketch of the route map.

2 To find a more detailed map for any walk you are considering, go to the Ordnance Survey (**www.ordnance survey.co.uk**) site.

3 Click **Get-a-map**, then either search for areas by name, or click the UK map and zoom in repeatedly for more and more detail.

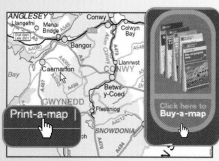

4 Click **Print-a-map**, for a printer-friendly version of your chosen map section. Click **Buy-a-map** to purchase the map on-line.

CASE STUDY

Keen walker Darren, could never get his wife, Rachel, interested in a trekking holiday. They'd been on a few day walks, but disliked carrying heavy rucksacks making longer treks almost impossible.

Darren went to the Walking Tours in Britain and Ireland site (**http:// walking.about.com/cs/ toursbritain.**) and posted his problem on the site's forum. Within a day he had a reply from an American journalist, Dennis, who had walked the West Highland Way the year before. He had used a baggage-transport service called the Sherpa Van Project

(**www.sherpavan.com**), which operates along the UK's long distance paths, picking up and carrying bags to any destination.

When Darren e-mailed back to thank him, Dennis offered to send him a newspaper article he had written about the walk. Reading the article clinched the deal for Rachel, so Darren booked a trek and the baggage service for later in the year.

Then it was just a matter of searching the Web to solve the much harder problem of how to ward off those Highland midges.

Did You Know?

Mount Everest is beyond the reach of most amateur climbers, but you can enjoy an interactive journey from base camp to the summit at The Tech Museum of Innovation (www.thetech.org/ exhibits_events/ online/everest).

SEE ALSO
● **Explore the natural world** – *page 156*
● **Book a perfect holiday** – *page 228*
● **Finding a great day out** – *page 232*

Book a perfect holiday

Plan your break away on the Internet

You can use the Internet to research and book a holiday – it is great for both last-minute deals and pre-arranged breaks at home and abroad. The Internet can help you to book a flight, find out about the best places to see, hire a car, check up on the local cuisine and language, and investigate exchange rates. Using the Internet can be much faster than ploughing through brochures, and when you have found what you want, you can book and pay for your holiday on-line.

On-line travel

It's easy to book a holiday with on-line travel agents and airlines. Travel agents such as Thomas Cook (**www. thomascook.com**) offer flights, accommodation, insurance, car hire and travel guides. Or you can find and book a flight directly from an airline's Web site.

Guides

The Internet offers travel guides from official tourist agencies such as the French Tourist Office (**www. franceguide.com**), independent organisations, and even individuals who publish their holiday experiences on the Web.

Passports and visas

If you are a UK national, you can fill out your passport application on-line by visiting the UK Passport Agency (**www.ukpa.gov.uk**). The site aims to help new applicants and existing passport holders by providing information on all aspects of application and renewal. A pre-printed form is sent to you to sign and return with photos and you can then check its progress on-line.

The site also provides information on what types of visas UK passport holders need when travelling abroad.

HOLIDAY SITES

Directory information

**Country Connect
(www.countryconnect.co.uk)**
Country Connect provides UK addresses for the tourist boards of many different countries. If you want to travel to Brazil, for example, this site will give you details of the Brazilian Tourist Office in London and tell you where to make visa enquiries. The site will also give you links to ABTA travel companies, travel guides and useful advice.

Accommodation

The AA (www.theaa.co.uk)
This site is helpful for booking a short break in the UK – it provides lists of hotels and bed and breakfast accommodation, searchable by location and price range. Each place to stay is shown on a map, with detailed information about facilities, and you can

Car hire

Most on-line travel agents offer a car hire service, but it may be cheaper and easier to go about it yourself. Leading car rental companies such as Avis (**www.avis.co.uk**), Hertz (**www.hertz.co.uk**) and Budget Rent-A-Car (**www.budget-rent-a-car.co.uk**) allow you to book and pay for car rental on-line.

make a booking on-line. The site also has a database of things to do around Britain and a route-planner to help you to find the best way to get there.

Cheap air fares

cheapflights.com (www.cheapflights.com)
This site scans a range of airlines to find the best deals. Flights may be from no-frills budget airlines, or may be discounted fares from the major carriers. When you enter your destination and departure dates, cheapflights.com lists a selection of available flights. Telephone numbers are listed for those companies that don't offer on-line booking. The site also includes accommodation, car hire, insurance, package holidays and cruises.

Last minute holidays

lastminute.com (www.lastminute.com)
As the name implies, this is a great site if you've left your holiday plans to the last minute, but you can also book holidays up to a month in advance. It offers a wide range of package holidays, flights and accommodation. If you suddenly find yourself with a free weekend, click **this weekend** for a selection of exciting ideas and offers.

Tourist information

lonely planet (www.lonelyplanet.com)
Here you can find detailed information on a wide range of destinations around the world. Browse the site by city or country, or use the search tool. Enter a destination or keyword to see relevant entries from the site's guides, as well as from the extensive Travellers' Reports – comments submitted by users.

SEARCH IT YOURSELF

At Excite (**www.excite.co.uk**) you have two search methods. Click **Travel** under 'Excite Channels' for a categorised directory of sites. Or search the Web yourself by entering a keyword (such as 'travel' and your destination) into the Search window and clicking the **Search** button. If you want to find only UK-based Web sites, make sure you select the 'UK sites' option.

 Watch Out!

To ensure you're protected against the failure of your airline or travel agent, make sure the Web sites you are using are approved by Air Travel Organiser's Licensing (ATOL) (www.atol.org.uk) or the Association of British Travel Agents (ABTA) (www.abta.com).

HOW TO: FIND AND BOOK A FLIGHT ON-LINE

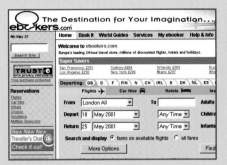

1 First go to a site where you can compare prices and book flights, such as Ebookers (**www.ebookers.com**). Let's say you want a week in Amsterdam.

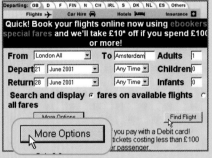

2 Enter your flight details. Remember to enter in a city name, not just the country. When you're finished, click **Find Flight**. You can use more advanced search tools by clicking **More Options**.

3 Scroll down and examine the list of flights shown and decide if any interest you. If one does, click on the price of the flight to get more details.

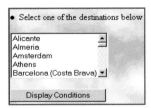

4 A list of flights and flight times will appear. Scroll down the page to see a breakdown of costs. When you have made a choice, select a delivery method for your tickets, then click **Continue**.

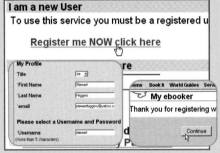

5 If you are not registered with Ebookers, click on **Register me NOW click here**. Fill in the 'My Profile' registration form, click **Register** and then click **Continue**.

6 Enter in the passenger details and click **Continue**. Enter your payment and contact details and an address your tickets can be posted to. Finally, click **Continue** to purchase your tickets.

Watch Out!

Discount flights may not go to city centre airports and may arrive at unsociable hours. If you arrive at London Stansted at 2am, you won't be able to get a train into central London for hours.

Time Saver!

*Many travel retailers have their own Web sites with timetables and direct booking. Book trains to Paris at Eurostar (**www. eurostar.co.uk**) and coach journeys in North America at Greyhound (**www. greyhound.com**).*

Weather check

Check the weather at your selected destination before you depart. Try Weather Information Pages (**www.ukweather.freeserve. co.uk**), or the Met Office (**www. meto.gov.uk**).

CASE STUDY

When seventeen-year-old Jim Harrison spent a weekend near his home helping to excavate a Roman fort, he couldn't wait to get back to the dig during his Easter holiday. But his mum and dad were intent on going abroad, and didn't want to leave Jim at home on his own.

Not wanting to discourage Jim's interest, his dad David suggested they try to find a compromise. So they went on-line to look for an archaeological dig abroad, where they could all enjoy a family holiday.

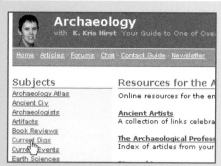

1 The Harrisons began their search at About.com's Archaeology page (**http://archaeology.about.com**), which has a hand-picked list of relevant Web sites. They clicked on a link for **Current Digs**.

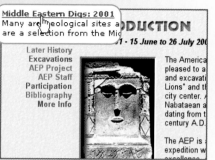

2 A link for **Middle Eastern Digs** caught Jim's eye. He found a site asking for volunteers on a dig in Petra in Jordan (**http://todacosa.com/petra/aep.htm**). But Jordan was too expensive for a holiday.

3 They decided to look for volunteering options in Europe but could not find anything suitable on About.com. David decided to search at Yahoo!, keying in 'international archaeology volunteering'.

4 Clicking through the results, they found a site for the Earthwatch Institute (**www.earthwatch.org**), a group that arranges digs and conservation projects all over the world.

5 Jim volunteered for an excavation of neolithic remains in Andalusia. The whole family went to Spain, and Jim spent a week on the dig before joining his parents on the coast.

Counting the cost of knowledge

Hard work and scraped knees aren't the only costs of volunteering – it can also be expensive. Apart from air fares to faraway locations, volunteers must also pay a fee to cover food, accommodation and training. To get more for your money, look for digs that offer courses and lectures, which in some cases can be counted towards a university degree.

Did You Know?

*The Foreign and Commonwealth office Web site (**www.fco.gov.uk**) has information on vaccinations, visas and other issues for British citizens planning a holiday abroad.*

Finding a great day out

Surf the Web for inspiration as well as information

It is not easy to find an activity that the whole family can enjoy, especially when parents and children all have their own idea about what makes for a good time. But even if you have only a vague idea about what you want to do, the Internet can help. If you ask the right questions and look in the right sites, you will find that the Net is good for more than just addresses and opening times – it is a great source of fun ideas for a family outing.

Where to start

All the traditional sources of travel information – tourist offices, guide books and travel agents – can be found on the Web. But the best place to start is a general travel site (see opposite).

Travel sites

The advantage of such sites is that they are moderated: that is, someone has taken the trouble to trawl the vastness of the Web, and assess and organise the many thousands of travel-related sites – so you don't have to.

A good travel site is like an all-knowing librarian: it will lead you quickly to the information you want.

KEW PALACE
The smallest royal palace
A hidden treasure in the
Royal Botanic Gardens, Kew

SITES FOR A DAY OUT

Official site

**British Tourist Authority
(www.visitbritain.com)**
An official site is one that is set up and run by an authoritative organisation. For example, there is an official British Museum site, but you will find a lot of other sites about the museum – good and bad – by people who have no actual connection with it.

Official sites can usually be relied on to provide correct factual information, but since they are in the business of promoting their organisation, they are not necessarily the place to look for a warts-and-all assessment.

Visitbritain.com is the official site of the British Tourist Authority. It is comprehensive, reliable and easy to navigate. It has many useful links to other sites, and a good search engine which makes it a fine starting point if you have only a rough idea of what you are looking for.

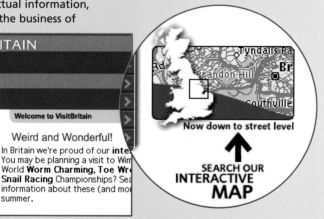

SEARCH OUR
**INTERACTIVE
MAP**

Practical help

**Sightseeing.co.uk
(www.sightseeing.co.uk)**
This site allows you to search for destinations in a natural, user-friendly way.

You specify the part of the country and the type of attraction you are interested in (for example castles, or gardens), and it creates a list of possible trips within easy travelling distance.

With each suggestion come contact and location details, admission prices, maps and travel tips. There are also links to other sites devoted to each attraction.

A second opinion

The UK Guide (www.ukguide.org)
When you are planning to visit a place you have never been to before, it is a good idea to get a view from an independent source. This is a no-nonsense site with very few graphic or pictorial elements – but is is full of good

content including maps and links. The site has basic information designed to be helpful to visitors from abroad.

Best of the rest

Association of Leading Visitor Attractions (www.alva.org.uk)
This site provides links to a selection of Britain's most popular tourist sites, with separate sections on 'museums and galleries', 'heritage', 'cathedrals', 'leisure attractions' and 'gardens and conservation'.

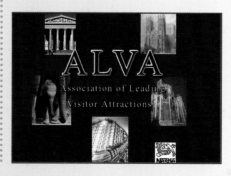

 Problem Solver!

*Forgotten the address of a site you visited earlier? Click on the **History** button at the top of the Explorer window. This shows you a complete list of all the pages you have visited. Click on the page you want, and you will go straight to it.*

Watch Out!

Many good Web sites state the last time they were updated. It is a good idea to check this before using any information you find on the site.

WHERE TO GO: START WITH YAHOO!

All the sites on the British Yahoo! (http://uk.yahoo.com) are organised into a vast directory or family tree. You narrow your search by clicking down through the levels. There is no right way to find your way to the specific site you need, but here are two possible approaches to finding a good day out.

1 One of the main headings on the Yahoo! homepage is 'Recreation & Sport'. That might lead to a fun way to spend the day.

& Media
…n Coverage, Newspap…

Recreation & Sport
Sport, Outdoors, Travel, Mo…

Reference
Libraries, Dictionaries, Phon…

Regional
…d, Countri…

Regional
UK, Ireland, Countries, Regions…

Science
CS, Biology, Astronomy, Engineer…

Social Science

1 If you know that what you want is a day by the sea, you can start your search by specifying the part of the country you are in. Click on **Regional** and then **UK Cities and Towns**.

- **Amusement and Theme Parks@**
- **Automotive** (6194) NEW!
- **Aviation** (882)
- **Booksellers@**
- **Chats and Forums** (7)
- **Cooking@**

2 The most likely headings under 'Recreation' are 'Amusement and Theme Parks' and 'Travel'. Try **Travel**: if it is no use you can always come back to **Theme Parks**.

Bourne@
- **Bourne End@**
- **Bournemouth@**
- **Bourton-on-th…**
- **Bovey Tracey…**
Bowdon@

2 There are over 2000 cities and towns listed, so first click on a letter in the A–Z list and then make a choice: Bournemouth is in driving distance.

- **Destination Guides** (28693) NEW!
- **Directories** (52)
- **Disabilities@**
- **Ecotourism** (26)
- **Family Travel** (30)
- **Health and Medicine@**
- Hitchhiking (14)

- **Family Camping@**
- **Tour Operators@**
- **Travelogues@**

3 Under **Travel**, the 'Destination Guides' and 'Family Travel' options seem the most useful for an outing with kids. Try **Family Travel** first. Then search by either category or site listings.

welcome children.
- About: Travel With Kids…
- Adoption Travel - resourc…
- BabyCenter: Travel With…
- Family Travel Files - offer…
- Family Travel Forum - inc…
- Family.com: Travel - cont…
- Fodors Family Travel Ce…

4 Under site listings is About.com: Travel with Kids which has a page called Children's London. It's an American site, but full of good ideas.

- Bournemouth - details o…
- Bournemouth and Poole…
- Bournemouth Holidays…
- Bournemouth Web - fe…
- Bournemouth-Info.com…
- Everything Bournemout…
- In And Around Bourne…

4 In the 'Local Guides' section there is a site that lets you navigate round virtual Bournemouth – a fun way to plan a seaside outing.

- **Business and Shopping** (92)
- **Community** (16)
- **Education** (23)
- **Entertainment and Arts** (12)
- **Health** (9)

- **News and Media**
- **Property** (1)
- **Recreation and S…**
- **Travel and Tran…**

3 There are several dozen sites divided into categories such as 'News and Media' and 'Recreation and Sport'. Click on **Travel and Transportation**.

CASE STUDY

The Johnson family wanted a day in the fresh air – somewhere they could explore and have a picnic. They were unsure where to go and thought it might be good to search for inspiration on-line.

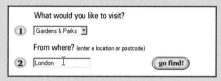

1 They began by browsing at **www.sightseeing.co.uk**, looking for interesting gardens and parks in London: the children wanted more than nice scenery.

2 Third on the list of results was Kew Gardens, which looked the kind of thing they wanted. They thought that Kew Palace in the grounds would be worth seeing.

3 There was no Web site listed for Kew Palace. The Johnsons wanted to be sure it was open, so they did a search for 'Kew Palace' at Lycos.co.uk (**www.lycos.co.uk**).

1. http://www.hrp.org.uk/kew/indexkew.htm
Official information for London's **Kew Palace** and information for visitors, travel trade and re
http://www.hrp.org.uk/kew/indexkew.htm (100% - 4k)
org.uk

2. Kew Palace
Kew Palace
http://sol.brunel.
brunel.ac.uk

3. ROYAL PALA
HM Tower of
Queen Charlo
http://www.hrp.org
org.uk

4 There was a page on Kew at the official site for Historic Royal Palaces. It said that there was renovation going on – so they decided to look at another of the palaces featured on the site.

5 When they saw the Hampton Court site, they knew it was the right place to go. The maze would keep the kids happy, and the gardens looked fantastic.

Homes and gardens
Britain has many historic and well-known homes and gardens which are open to the public. Plan a day out to one with Historic Homes of Britain (**www.specialtytraveluk.com/about.htm**). They organise tours for groups and individuals with special private visits to houses that are not open for public viewing.

Time Saver!
If you want to find information about a particular town, it is worth starting at the relevant local authority's site. The address will usually take the form:
www.town.gov.uk
(replace the word 'town' in the address with the name of the place in question).

Recipe sites
Many Web sites offer a unique way to compare and choose from a selection of recipes without having to open a single book. You can look up a recipe site that will suggest a meal you can make from left-over ingredients in your cupboard, or browse hundreds of popular cookbooks at The Ultimate Cookbook (**www.ucook.com**).

Food from abroad
The Internet also gives you instant access to food you can't buy in the local shops, such as Custard Apples from Australia. You can arrange for exotic or gourmet foods from all over the world to be delivered right to your doorstep.

Cooking courses
Whether you are an experienced cook or not, you can benefit from on-line cooking courses and instructional videos – for both everyday and entertaining ideas.

There are dedicated sites for vegetarians and vegans, wine buffs, curry fans and Italophiles.

Get cooking

Find good food information on the Internet

The Internet offers facts and advice about food and drink which would be difficult to find anywhere else. Discover how to order left-handed cooking implements, perhaps, or join a recipe and food-related newsgroup. Or, get last-minute advice on wine for a particular dish you are cooking. However much you know about culinary matters, you will always be able to learn a lot more on the Web.

DISHES OF THE DAY

Food and drink
Epicurious (www.epicurious.com)
This American site is full of culinary articles, from advice on alfresco entertaining to tips on how to keep

steaks from curling, as well as step-by-step on-line cooking demonstrations.

There are tens of thousands of recipes, each one with a feedback and ratings section so that people who have cooked the dishes can comment on them. The site also has links to cookware sites and articles on subjects as diverse as choosing the right wine glass for a dinner party and locating the best places to eat in Tuscany, Italy.

Original idea
Takeaways.com (www.takeaways.net)
Browse menus from thousands of restaurants that will deliver to your door. Search by area, cuisine, restaurant name or your preferred price range. The site will then display the phone number you need to place your order.

Restaurant searches
**Restaurants.co.uk
(www.restaurants.co.uk)**
This site lets you search for places to eat by either region or cuisine. There is an extremely thorough

listing of restaurants with reviews and featured places to eat from all over the country. There is also a chatroom where you can comment and read customers' opinions of particular restaurants.

Food demonstrations
**The Food Network
(www.foodnetwork.com)**
Learn all the techniques and tips you need for fabulous cooking at The Food Network – a site devoted to teaching you how to cook. Once you have RealPlayer or Quicktime (which you can download from the site), you can watch their film clips and learn cooking techniques from the experts. You can also save the clips to your computer and keep them for reference.

Recipe tips
**The Cook's Thesaurus
(www.foodsubs.com)**
This site is a cooking encyclopedia which offers information on thousands of everyday and unusual ingredients, as well as advice on the kitchen tools you need to cook them with. You can also find substitutes for fatty, expensive or hard-to-find ingredients.

SEARCH IT YOURSELF

For a comprehensive database with more than 10,000 food and drink related sites, try Kitchen Link (**www.kitchenlink.com**). To help you to choose a site, you can get reviews at Seasoned Cooking (**www.seasoned.com**).

To find the Web sites of celebrity chefs and their recommended recipes and tips, head for the homepages of the TV channel on which they are broadcast. Or, for information on your favourite food writer, try searching the homepage of the newspaper or magazine they write for.

If it is unusual kitchen utensils and equipment you require, search at The Cook's Kitchen (**www.kitchenware. co.uk**) or Lakeland Limited (**www. lakeland.co.uk**). At these sites you can order items such as 'Aquatronic' weighing scales (which measure liquids and solids), a hachoir set, or a blowtorch for finishing off those crèmes brûlées.

 Did You Know?

If you love spicy food, you can find out everything you've ever wanted to know about chilli peppers, such as why they are hot and which is the hottest, at The Chile-Head's Home Page (http://chileheads. netimages.com).

SEE ALSO
● Seek medical advice – page 122
● Improve your diet and fitness – page 126
● Do your weekly shop – page 192

Live the sporting life

Use the World Wide Web to find out almost anything about sports

With up-to-the-minute results, plus facts and figures from the archives, the Internet will help to satisfy your sporting cravings, whether you're a keen player or a committed armchair enthusiast. Every sport on earth – even tug-of-war and camel racing – have dedicated Web sites, created by participants and fans as well as official governing bodies. Or if you want to take up a sport as a player or official, the Web is useful for learning rules of games or finding local coaching sessions.

Footy fever

Football is the world's most popular sport and there are thousands of sites devoted to it. At the official sites of the top English and European clubs you will find news, match reports and fixture lists, along with multimedia elements such as panoramic tours and live Web-casts.

Sport for all

Browse through any Web directory and you'll find sites on every conceivable sport and quite a few you've probably never heard of, such as tchoukball (a little like basketball but with two small square net goals on the floor) or yukigassen (an organised snowball fighting game popular in Finland, Norway and Japan).

Events

For sports trivia buffs, there are challenging quiz sites, such as League Lineup (**www.leagueline up.com**) as well as lists of fascinating statistics.

And if you want to attend sporting events in the UK or worldwide, you can use the Web to buy tickets on-line.

SPORTING GREATS

Best all-round resource

BBC Sport (www.bbc.co.uk/sport)
BBC Sport brings you the most complete sports coverage available. The homepage shows the day's biggest sporting stories, and there's more detail available in each sport's own section, while the 'Other

BBC SPORT	
Front Page	Wednesday, 28 March, 2001, 15:31 GMT
Results/Fixtures	LATEST: Australia's Adam Gilchrist and Glenn
Football	McGrath fined after first one-dayer in India.
Cricket	
Rugby Union	**Hoddle is new Spurs**
Rugby League	**boss**
Tennis	Southampton chairman Rupert
Golf	Lowe confirms Glenn Hoddle's
Motorsport	decision to become
Boxing	Tottenham's new manager.
Athletics	
Other Sports	
Sports Talk	

Sports' section takes in cycling, swimming, netball, curling and more.

The site is strong on multimedia, with audio and video reports, live Web-casts and a global sports round-up from the World Service. Click **Sports Talk** to see debates on the day's hot sporting issues, and add your own comments to the message board by clicking **Click here**.

Latest sports news

Ananova Sport (www.ananova.com/sport)
Ananova Sport is a comprehensive sports news service. Click on **Latest headlines** to see breaking sports stories. Or click on an individual sport, such as **Athletics**, **Tennis**, **Horse racing**, or **Golf** to see the latest news.

For some sports, you can also see live score updates as the action unfolds. On the sport's home page, look for a 'Live scores' link. Continuously updated scores are displayed in a small window that you can keep open in a corner of your desktop while you work on your computer.

Best site for spectators

FanZone (www.fanzone.co.uk)
This is the perfect Web site for the travelling sports fan, with information on every English, Scottish and Welsh football league ground, plus non-league

football, rugby, speedway, horse racing and more. Each entry includes directions, a local pub and food guide and links to team sites. Click **Printer** for a shorter version of the information to print and take with you.

Meet the players

Icons.com (www.icons.com)
Icons.com hosts the official sites of many top UK and European footballers. Click under 'Player sites' to browse by player, country and club, or select a player's name from the A-Z list. Each player's page has his life story, told in his own words, plus a regularly updated personal diary. You can contact the player by e-mail, and – if you're lucky – be nominated 'Fan of the Month'.

For information on other sports stars, go to Yahoo! (www.yahoo.co.uk), click on **Sport** in the directory section and then **Athletes**. This brings up a list of sports. Click on one to see a list of sites devoted to stars of that sport.

SEARCH IT YOURSELF

If you want to participate in a sport, a good place to start is your national Sports Council site. For example, to find out about canoeing in Scotland, go to the Scottish Sports Council site (**www.sportscotland.org.uk**). Scroll down the homepage, and under 'Do you want to take up a sport?', click on: **Governing body contact details are available here**, then the letter **C**. When the page comes up, scroll down to see the information

for the Scottish Canoe Association. Click the link to go to their official Web site (**www.scot-canoe.org**). Click **Coaching** on the homepage to see details of canoeing courses on offer and find out how to get in touch with the course organisers.

Did You Know?

*To search for local sports information go to a search engine such as Google (**www. google.com**) and enter the sport you are interested in and your home town. For example, 'hockey+Bristol'.*

Did You Know?

Sports news can be tailored to your interests and e-mailed directly to your computer, or sent to your WAP phone, as it happens. Visit a general sport site and look for an 'e-mail alerts' link.

HOW TO: FOLLOW A LIVE SPORTS EVENT

Many sport sites let you follow the action with a live audio or video Web-cast. Look for a link that says something like 'Internet Radio' or 'Live Matches'. The procedure is broadly similar for all sites that offer this facility. You may be asked to download QuickTime or RealPlayer before you can access these services (see page 150). If your audio broadcasts skip from time to time, try closing your browser window and listening just using RealPlayer, which takes up less memory.

This example shows the site for the Wimbledon tennis tournament, which, during the competition fortnight, offers live audio and video features, virtual tours, archived video clips and a Web-cam ('Slamcam') with a choice of robotic camera angles that you can control.

1 To see the latest scores in a match, go to **www.wimbledon.org** and click on **INTERACTIVE** then **Live and Interactive**. Click on **Live Scoreboard** then **Launch the Enhanced IBM Real-Time Scoreboard**.

2 When this has loaded, you can see the latest scores. Scores are updated point by point – though not instantaneously. You can also read news, interviews and schedules from this page.

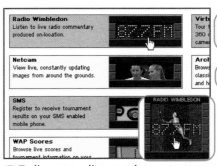

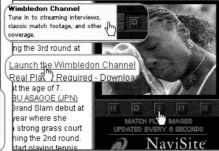

3 To listen to a live match commentary, return to the Live and Interactive page and click **Radio Wimbledon**, then on the radio icon. Within seconds you will hear the broadcast begin.

4 To watch a broadcast, click back to the Live and Interactive page again and click **Wimbledon Channel**, then **Launch the Wimbledon Channel**. Click the play button to see the action unfold.

Web-cast limitations

Although you can watch and listen to 'live' video and audio broadcasts from sport Web sites, the technical limitations of the Internet mean that the broadcasts may be jumpy and 'live' scoreboards may take a while to update. The quality and immediacy of standard radio or television broadcasts remains higher. However, sports coverage on the Internet is more interactive – for example, you can control camera angles. The quality is also likely to improve as connections to the Net become more efficient.

SEE ALSO
● Improve your diet and fitness – page 126
● Take a virtual tour – page 145
● Play games on-line – page 186

Plan a wedding

Make **the big day** go with a bang

Arranging a wedding is stressful and time-consuming, but the Internet can help to ease the burden. On the Web you can seek inspiration for music, flowers, cakes and speeches, research venues and organise gifts. Specialist wedding Web sites provide many of these services, and are a great place to go for information and advice.

World Wide Wed

The Internet provides a single convenient point for finding caterers, photographers, printers, dressmakers and musicians – even poets who will write a few special verses for your big day. You can also get help on choosing venues, managing money and meeting important deadlines.

Some sites even allow you to store all your notes and plans on-line for easy reference.

Helpful advice

There are sites to help you to produce and circulate your wedding list and others that offer advice on speechmaking or writing your own vows. A good place to start your research is the Wedding Links Galore directory (**www.wedding linksgalore.com**).

 Time Saver!

If you circulate your wedding list on-line you can manage it so that friends and relatives see what they each have given and don't duplicate gifts.

 Did You Know?

*If you are unsure about the role of the best man or how to seat divorced parents of the bride or groom, consult the guide at the Wedding Etiquette & Helpful Hints site (**www. i-do.com.au/ editorial/Tips/ etiquette.htm**).*

PLAN THE PERFECT DAY

Best on-line planner

Confetti (www.confetti.co.uk)
This site offers almost everything you need when planning a wedding. Confetti gathers together a wide range of suppliers, so you can hire your suit, book musicians, organise a venue and so

on. The site has advice and information on etiquette, speechmaking and writing your own vows, as well as legal matters such as managing joint finances after you are married.

Confetti offers helpful message boards so you can swap information and ask other people for advice – for example, on pre-nuptial agreements or the worst things that can go wrong. The site also includes an area where you can safely store all your planning information, such as managing the budget or organising the seating plan and gift list.

Finding wedding services

Wedding Service
(www.wedding-service.co.uk)
This is the ideal place to find services in your area of the UK. It is a vast directory, covering

Fireworks . . Florists	Party Party Party
For Sale & Wanted	Photography UK
Gift List	Planted Personal Logos
Harpists	Questions pre wedding
Hats & Tiaras	Question to ask bands
Hen & Stag	Shoes
Honeymoons	SHOPPING CENTRE
Horse & Carriage	Stationery . . . . Spam
IceSculpture	Speeches/Toastmaster

everything including calligraphers, balloon shops, cake-makers and jewellers. You can even hire a country house to hold your wedding in. Providers don't have to be on the Internet to get listed – many just have a phone number. Where they do have a Web site, you can link to it direct.

FOUR MONTHS BEFORE
Confirm church arrangements and calling of banns.
Apply for passports/check yours are still valid.
If changing name, allow at least six weeks for a new
Arrange visas and vaccinations.
Make wedding day appointments with hairdresser/be
Arrange clothes for mothers.
Choose music and hymns - get these approved by th
Send invitations.
Choose wedding rings and gifts for attendants.

Best advice guide

The Wedding Planner
(www.weddingplanner.co.uk)
If you are concerned about all the things to be managed in the build-up to a wedding, then visit Wedding Planner. The site has almost everything you need to know to plan a wedding and provides all kinds of information and advice.

There is, for example, a useful countdown checklist that starts a year before the wedding and ends with the tidying-up jobs after the wedding itself. This sits alongside advice on the roles of various key people such as the best man, bridesmaids and ushers. There is also help with music, flowers, stationery, photography and much more.

Budget wedding

TrumpMoon Weddings
(www.trumpmoon.ltd.uk)
You don't need to spend a lot of money to have a stylish wedding. Trumpmoon is a site for those with limited funds, and offers lots of excellent ideas about keeping the costs of your wedding down.

For example, you can learn how to bake your own cake or make your own dress and veil. There are suggestions on how to decorate your chosen venue within a small budget, as well as tips on amateur photography and how to look your best in photographs. The site is small, but it is inspiring and will give you lots of ideas.

A-Line
Disguises a thick waist and is also good if you are on the short side as it projects the illusion of height.

SEARCH IT YOURSELF

When looking for wedding-related Web sites, there are so many to choose from that it pays to be specific when using a search engine. For example, if you are looking for some ideas for wedding cakes, use 'wedding cakes' as your search term, rather than just 'wedding', to narrow down the subject area.

Wine

If you supply your own wine for the reception, you can save a lot of money. You can save even more by taking a day trip to France and buying in bulk. If you can't manage that, try ordering it at Buy wine on-line (www.buywine online.co.uk). But remember, if your reception is in a hotel, you may be charged corkage.

CREATING AN ON-LINE WEDDING LIST

There are many on-line wedding list services. Confetti.co.uk (www.confetti.co.uk) is comprehensive and easy to use – and does not require that everyone buying a gift has access to the Internet.

The bride and groom will need to register with Confetti, where they can create their wedding list from an on-line catalogue. Gifts start at under £10 and go up to thousands.

To make a purchase, family and friends can use the Internet or make a phone call to Confetti. The site will organise the purchase, and make sure that the gifts are wrapped and delivered to you.

1 Go to Confetti (**www.confetti.co.uk**) and click on **planning tools**. On the next page, click on **my confetti gift list**.

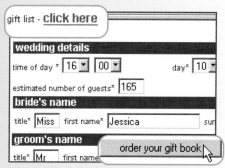

2 On the next page click on **click here** to register your gift list. Fill in your details on the registration form and then click on **order your gift book**.

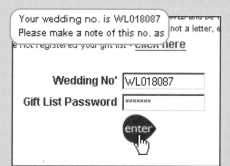

3 You'll be given a wedding number. Write it down, as you'll need it to access your gift book. Click **sign me in now**. Enter your wedding number and password, then click **enter**.

4 To select gifts, click on **browse gift book**. Click on the images of the gifts you like. This will open a pop-up window; enter the quantity you want and then click **add to gift list** to add it to your list.

5 To view your list, click **view gift list**. Here you can adjust the quantities and preview the gifts. When you've finished, click on **save changes**. Your list is now available for guests to view.

Did You Know?

After the big day you can make an on-line wedding album using personal Web space provided by your Internet Service Provider. Scan in your photographs so anyone who was unable to attend can see the event (see Add a picture to your page, *page 264).*

How guests can access your list

Once you've set up a list, send the site address and your wedding number to all your guests who have Internet access. They can see your list by clicking **Gift lists**, then **View couples' gift lists**. When they enter your number, the list will come up. On-screen instructions will explain how to buy an item. You should also send your guests the site's phone number, so that if they aren't on the Net they can speak directly to someone at the site.

SEE ALSO
● **Get a mortgage quotation** – *page 204*
● **Mark a special occasion** – *page 218*
● **Book a perfect holiday** – *page 228*

Making Web sites

Design and set up your own Web site and make sure people see it. Add sound, pictures and home movie clips, to make it stand out. And learn how to create an on-line business.

What is a Web site?

Find out how **Web sites** and **Web pages** work

Look at any newspaper or magazine advertisement, or watch almost any television commercial, and you will see references to Web sites. A presence on the Web has become an essential part of most companies' marketing and sales strategies, and they're keen to make sure you know where to find them. But the Web isn't just for big companies. Most sites are actually run by individuals to promote an interest or hobby, or to keep in touch with their families. If you've got something to say or share, why not start your own site?

How the Web works

The World Wide Web is a huge conglomeration of Web sites, each made up of Web pages. A Web page is a document stored on a computer (known as a 'server' or 'host') that is permanently connected to the Internet, so that it can be viewed by anyone at any time.

Web pages are written in a computer language called HTML (HyperText Markup Language) that allows separate documents to be linked together. A collection of linked pages forms a Web site, which in turn can be linked to other sites around the world – forming the World Wide Web itself.

Making your own site

You don't need to know about HTML in order to make your own Web site. You can design your site using a basic word-processing program such as Word and it will do all the HTML programming for you (see *Build a Web page in Word*, page 256).

Once your site is designed and written, you can then store it on a computer connected to the Internet. This means that you don't always have to be on-line for your site to be seen. For more information on making your own site, see *Designing your own site* opposite.

Time Saver!
Learn from other sites as you surf the Web. If you see a design feature or idea that you like, think how you could do something similar.

HOW TO ANALYSE A WEB SITE

Think of a Web site as being like a magazine. A good magazine has interesting stories or articles displayed over a number of pages using text and graphics. A good Web site delivers a similar product, but its pages are stored on a computer connected to the Internet.

Like magazines, Web sites are generally dedicated to exploring a specific theme or a related group of themes. Both can be 'browsed' rather than read from beginning to end and both hope to capture the interest of the reader so that they return again in the future.

The documents that make up a Web site are 'published' by being loaded onto an Internet server computer (see *Upload your page*, page 262). The

pages are then available to anyone who enters the appropriate file address into their Web browser (see *Start browsing*, page 22).

Web pages have greater flexibility than printed pages because you can include moving images, links to related Web sites and interactive features such as bulletin boards. You can also print the page out, copy and paste useful text into a word-processing document or e-mail the page to a friend.

Designing your own site

If you are considering making your own Web site, the most important thing to think about is its content. Who is the site for? What will a visitor to your site want to get from it? What is the most important information you want to provide? Even interesting content is not necessarily enough. It also needs to be accurate and up to date. Visitors to your site will soon notice if your material is stale and may not visit again. You should expect to have to update

your site regularly – or use material that will not go out of date.

Once you have settled on your content, you then need to create a design that suits your needs. For information on how to create a well-designed Web site, see *Web design basics*, page 254).

HOME OF THE McKAY FAMILY

Sign My GuestBook | View My GuestBook

Hello, and welcome to the McKay family homepage, we decided to build this homepage for something to leave our childeren, grandchildren, and greatgrandchildren. We will be including many family photographs taken over the years with some stories attached to them, we hope that this homepage will be added to in future years by those mentioned above, in a way it will be a family tree, my wife and I would like to include some of our personal stories about where we were born, what we accomplished in our lifetime, and what we are doing now. We sincerely hope you enjoy this homepage, and I hope it will be added to in the many years to come.

Why have a Web page?

If you have an extended family you could use your site to keep in touch by publishing photographs and family news. If you're a collector or have a lot of knowledge about a particular subject, you could use a Web site to share your experience with the world, making new contacts and friends along the way. If you run a small business or have a freelance or part-time career you could use a Web site to promote yourself.

SEE ALSO
● **What is the Internet?** – *page 10*
● **Web design basics** – *page 254*
● **How e-commerce works** – *page 296*

How are Web sites made?

The **nuts and bolts** of Web design

To create your own Web site, all you need is a software package which will help you to design your site, and Web space that will ensure the Web pages are available to the rest of the Internet. You then need to think about the plan and layout of the site, how people will navigate their way around it, and the look of your site – which involves deciding on what kinds of text, graphics and colour to use.

Web design software
You can use a basic word processing program such as Word to design your site, so if you can use Word you're halfway there already (see *Build a Web page in Word*, page 256). If you feel inspired to create a more intricate Web site, you can buy a more complex program such as FrontPage (see *Other design programs*, page 294).

Web space
The final step is to place your site on an Internet server, called a 'host'. This is a computer that is constantly connected to the Internet – so making your pages accessible to all Internet users. Sending your files to this computer is called 'uploading'.

In order to upload files, you need to have a section of the host computer allocated to you. This area is called Web space (see opposite).

Design your page on-line
You can also use software on specialist Web sites to design your pages. Some Internet sites boast that it can take as little as ten minutes to create your own Web site on-line (see *Design a Web page on-line*, page 288). These sites also provide Web space for your site as part of their free service.

Watch Out!
You should check how much Web space comes with your ISP account. Some ISPs offer an unlimited amount.

HOW TO: FIND WEB SPACE

Your ISP
You may already have some Web space allocated to you by your current Internet Service Provider (ISP) as part of your Internet access agreement. This could be a few Megabytes (more than enough for an average homepage) or several hundred Megabytes. If you want to create a commercial site, check whether your ISP will let you use the space for business.

Other sources of space
If your ISP does not provide Web space, there are many other host companies to choose from. Go to

Looking for a web host? Let us help!

HostSearch has the tools that can help you find a w search on the most comprehensive and accurate di

🔍 **Host Search**

Host Search (**www.hostsearch.com**) for a list – and reviews – of these. Many companies provide free Web space while others charge significant amounts. Choosing the right host for your Web site will depend on the level of service you require. If you

need guaranteed availability, fast response times and security, for example, in order to support a business, one of the subscription companies with clear service levels will be appropriate. If your pages are not commercial and access times and availability are less important to you, one of the free services might be

Addr.com Web Hosting

Services | Why we are the best | Have you

acceptable. But some of these free hosting companies will automatically add advertising to your site in return for the service.

The amount of Web space you can obtain with a specialist host varies from a few to several hundred Megabytes (Mb). You only need a lot of Web space if you want to enhance your site with high-quality graphics, video or other large files, which use up a lot of computer memory. For most personal homepages, 5Mb is more than enough.

USING PHOTOGRAPHS ON YOUR SITE

If you want to use your own images, you need to have them as graphic computer files. A scanner or a digital camera will be useful for this – especially if you are making a site with a lot of family or local content.

Scanners
A scanner transfers your paper images and photo prints into graphic files that you can edit and use on your PC. Some new PCs come with scanners included. You can also buy them from sites such as ZDNet (**www.zdnet.co.uk**), which also include product reviews, or from a high street electrical shop, such as Currys (**www. currys.co.uk**) or Dixons (**www.dixons.co.uk**). Scanners vary in price from about £50 upwards.

Digital cameras
These cameras take photographs without using any film. The picture is stored as a graphic file that you can transfer directly to your computer. They cost from about £90 upwards and can be bought from sites such as PC World (**www.pc world.co.uk**), or again, from high street shops.

Other options
You can get your standard camera film transferred to CD-ROM when it is developed, or have pictures scanned at a shop specialising in copying and reproduction.

SEE ALSO
• Upload your site
  – page 262
• Link to more pages
  – page 270
• Set up a business site
  – page 298

Web site ingredients

Discover ways to make your **Web site** exciting and unique

There are many useful resources on the Internet, such as images, sounds, animations and Web page builders, which you can use when designing your site. Some are protected by copyright, which means that you have to pay for them or get permission to use them. Others are available free of charge and almost all can easily be added to your site. Remember: the more interesting your site, the more likely it is that people will return to it and recommend it to others. But don't go overboard, a well-designed Web page won't need more than one or two special features to impress.

Sound
Adding a spoken commentary, background music or just an interesting sound effect to your site is easy and adds impact (see *Add sound to your page*, page 276).

Animated images and text
The easiest way of adding some movement to your page is to include an animated GIF image. This is a series of pictures saved into a single file that are shown in quick succession to create the impression of a moving image. There are thousands of such animations available free of charge on-line (see *Add a picture to your page*, page 264).

Streaming video
With the faster Internet connections now available, you can add video clips to your site without slowing up or crashing your visitors' computers. By connecting your video camera to your computer, you can save your own video clips, edit them and put them on-line (*Add a video to your page*, page 282).

HOW TO: FIND IMAGES ON-LINE

General multimedia

Photographs, sounds, animated icons, streaming video, desktop wallpaper, screensavers, music files and ClipArt are all available on the Web. The quality is often excellent and the best sites are those that have broken their content down by theme so that you can quickly find the subject matter you need.

WorldAtlas.Com (www.worldatlas.com/clipart.htm)
An excellent site for free ClipArt graphics of world maps and flags.

**Cheryl's Image Gallery
(www.artbycheryl.com)**
Thousands of themed hand-drawn images are available at this site. They are free to use on personal or commercial Web pages.

Extra features

The CD-ROM that accompanies this book includes a selection of pictures, buttons, backgrounds and borders for you to use on your Web site, organised within themes such as Sport or Music. You can browse through the various themes to find the images you want to use. Then right-click on the image and select **Save As** to save the file onto your computer.

**American Memory
(http://memory.loc.gov/ammem/amhome.html)**
This site has seven million historical and cultural items from the USA – including photographs, manuscripts, maps, recordings, and moving images – most of which have no copyright restrictions.

Free Graphics (www.freegraphics.com)
An index of dozens of sites which have a variety of free image resources.

NASA (www.nasa.gov/gallery/photo)
NASA's Web site provides a vast collection of space exploration images which are free to use for educational and non-commercial purposes.

Web design elements

Many sites offer buttons, borders and backgrounds designed specifically for use on Web pages. Some sites offer packages of these features all designed to complement each other.

ABC Giant (www.abcgiant.com)
An excellent site for free graphics, ClipArt, animation, buttons, bullets, borders, fonts and other Web graphics.

Backgrounds Archive (www.backgroundsarchive.com)
This site provides small images that can be used repeatedly across the screen to create attractive textured backgrounds.

Free Buttons.com (www.freebuttons.com)
Find themed buttons for all Web page purposes at this site. The buttons are free to use, but you have to provide a link to the site on your Web page.

Technical resources

For more advanced Web page design, you can find programming generators for HTML and JavaScript. You'll also find Flash and Shockwave animations, but remember that your visitors will need to have the Flash viewer plug-in installed.

Flash Kit (www.flashkit.com/movies)
Try this site for hundreds of Flash animations, movies and tutorials.

CNET Builder (http://builder.cnet.com)
The CNET site has extensive scripting resources for programming languages such as DHTML (Dynamic HTML) and JavaScript.

HOW TO: FIND INTERACTIVE FEATURES

There are many lists of Web resources on the Internet, but a good place to start looking for additional features for your Web pages is the CNET download service (**www.webware.com**), where you will find files and links to sites providing tools for all the ideas listed here, plus many other possibilities.

Before you choose any particular on-line service to add to your site, see what it looks like on a couple of existing sites and be sure that you can make it work with your overall design. Many of these free services are funded by advertising, so check that the sponsors are appropriate for the visitors you'll be inviting.

Bulletin boards

world crossing (www.worldcrossing.com)
You can make your site interactive by adding a feature like a bulletin board – a place for visitors to place notices, ask questions and generally discuss the site subject matter. World crossing is a provider of free message boards which are easy to customise to your own design.

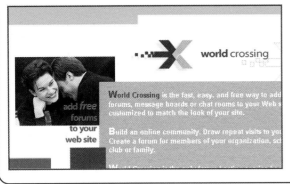

Guest books

Getstring.com (www.getstring.com)
Invite people to comment on how interesting or useful they found your site by adding a guest book. The Getstring Web site contains no advertising and has a control panel where you can change the configuration details.

Opinion polls

MyComputer.com (http://ezpolls.mycomputer.com)
Engage your visitors by asking them a question relevant to the subject of your site and presenting them with a multiple-choice checklist to provide an answer. The software for this activity is freely available and is simple to configure. Using this site you can ask a question and set up to 15 choices.

Hit counters

thecounter.com (www.thecounter.com)
A hit counter tracks visitors and identifies where they came from. It provides you with many useful facts and figures about who comes to visit your site and when, and which pages they are viewing, so that you can work out which pages may need changing. To add a counter, you only need to add a few lines of HTML to your existing Web page. There are several styles of counters to choose from.

Sound advice
Placing unexpected sounds or music on your site can be unwelcome, particularly if your visitor is browsing from a shared location, such as an office or café. Make your sounds optional by providing a button to turn them on and off.

HOW TO: GET ADVICE ABOUT YOUR SITE

Ask an expert

If you need advice on designing your Web page, the Internet provides forums and expert sites on most subjects. However, you should proceed with caution when following this advice. Many of the contributors to these sites are fellow Web-users who, however well-intentioned, may not always possess the expertise you need.

Pose a problem

BigNoseBird.Com (**www.bignosebird.com/bbs.shtml**) is a message board which aims to help you learn about Web page design. The site features a range of forums on related topics, so that visitors can pose questions and learn from others' questions and answers. Try the Open Forum for general issues, and the specific forums dedicated to HTML, graphics and JavaScript for more specialist enquiries.

About.com (**http://webdesign.about.com/compute/webdesign**), meanwhile, has a wealth of tips and information about how to create your site, plus Web design forums, chatrooms and an expert whom you can e-mail with specific technical problems and queries. The information here is clearly explained and laid out in well-organised subject categories, such as 'content' and 'legal issues', so you can find what you need to know quickly. There are also examples of Web site designs to give you inspiration.

Ask for feedback

Another useful place to visit is SiteCritique.net (**www.sitecritique.net**). This site requires you to register, but there is no charge for this. It then allows you to submit your own site for criticism by other members, according to categories including 'navigation', 'usability', 'graphics', and 'content'. Awards are given out each month for the sites which receive the best reviews.

HOW *NOT* TO DESIGN YOUR SITE

Web Pages That Suck.com (**www.webpages thatsuck.com**) details exactly what its name suggests – badly-designed sites. You can learn a lot about Web page design from other designers' mistakes, and the site's compiler – US Web designer Vincent Flanders – has scoured the Net for them.

The examples are all commercial sites, since Flanders considers personal Web pages too subjective to criticise. There is a 'daily sucker' feature highlighting a different site every day, as well as countless examples of sites which are hard to read or use because of jarring combinations of colourful graphics, over-elaborate fonts or unnecessary features.

The site isn't merely negative, though. Flanders uses examples to show how you can fix similar problems with your own site. You can also submit suggestions for sites to be considered, although you can't get feedback on the design of your site.

Celebrating 5 Years of Sucking!
Web Pages That Suck.com
Where you learn good Web design by looking at bad Web design.
Fast Company magazine calls WPTS the "Best for Improving Your Si

SEE ALSO
● Avoid computer viruses – *page 54*
● Download from the Web – *page 82*
● Solve computer problems – *page 129*

Web design basics

Find the **most appropriate way** to present your site's content

In Web design, as in any kind of graphic design, it is important that the visual elements enhance the message rather than hinder it. If your site is about flower arranging, for example, you should avoid spinning graphics, sound effects and flashing text. The design of the site should always highlight its main features and make it easy for the visitor to use.

Before you begin designing your site, take time to consider its main aims, the material that is going to be on it and how it will be organised.

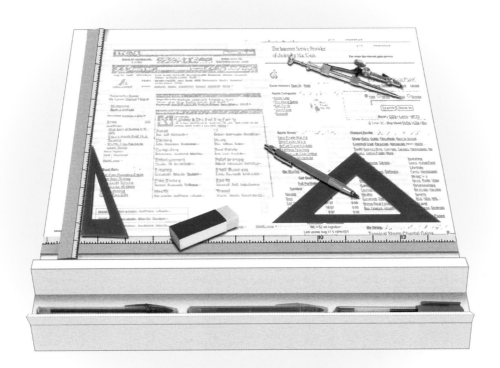

The golden rule
Don't overcomplicate. This applies to every aspect of your design – fonts (typefaces), colours, effects. Too many competing visual items can put the user off.

Colour
Make your site easier on the eye by limiting the number of colours you use to three or four. Also use colour consistently – one colour for links, one for headings, one for text. This gives the user a visual sense of how your site works.

Backgrounds
Keep the background simple. For example, a patterned background often makes it difficult to read the text. Research suggests that the human eye is most comfortable reading green text on a black background, whereas white on a colour is hardest to read.

Fonts
Use only two or three fonts on your page. Any more will make it look messy. You should also only use fonts that other computer users are likely to have on their computers, such as Verdana and Helvetica. If you use an unusual font, it may not display correctly on all computers.

Did You Know?
*If you're feeling confident, you can put up your site for a Web design award, which can help attract more visitors. For details on how to apply, go to Website Awards (**http://websiteawards.xe.net**).*

FIRST STEPS IN WEB DESIGN

Before you start designing your pages on a computer, you should first draw sketches of what you are aiming to achieve. This forces you to work out how each page will be structured, what will appear where, and the numbers of words and images you will need.

Draw a table

When you create a Web page in Word, it is best to create a 'table', which acts as a framework for everything you want to include on the page (see *Build a Web page in Word*, page 256). Without a table, the positions of your text and pictures on your Word document may differ from the way they will appear once your page is on-line.

Once you have drawn a sketch of your Web page, divide each element into different segments (marked in red on the sketch shown). This will form the basis of your table. Now count the number of columns and rows the table will need and keep this information to hand before beginning to design your page in Word.

Make it easy for the visitor

When sketching out your site, ensure that you create distinct 'signposts'. Include a clear title and unambiguous explanation of what your page is about. Give some space to a list of contents to direct visitors around the site – this will be especially useful when you start to create additional pages (see *Link to more pages*, page 270).

Keep it interesting

Provide one or two attractive images to add visual interest to the page. But don't overdo it: too many pictures will make the page load slowly. If you can find an image that is informative as well as appealing (for example, a picture of the stamp collection that your site is about), use that.

Always try to provide links to other sites of interest. It can be annoying for visitors to find that your site is a cul-de-sac.

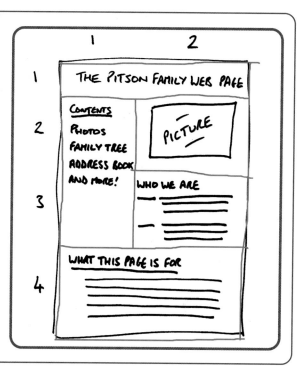

HINTS AND TIPS

DON'T have long lists of links, as they are not user friendly. If you want to offer many links, split them into smaller groups by theme.

DO consider adding a site map. This is a visual representation of how the pages on your site link together. It can be a great help to the visitor.

DON'T use yellow for text. It doesn't display well on many monitors and is almost always difficult to read.

DO design your pages so that as much as possible can be seen on screen at once. Your site users will quickly tire of scrolling down or across to see the rest of your page.

DON'T align large blocks of text to the centre. It makes it harder for the visitor to read.

DON'T try to fit too much on a page, especially in a small type size. Dense pages are off-putting. If you want to include a lot of material, split it into separate pages, then link them.

SEE ALSO
● **Build a Web page in Word** – *page 256*
● **Add a picture to your page** – *page 264*
● **Add sound to your page** – *page 276*

Build a Web page in Word

Creating your own pages is easier than you might think

Microsoft Word is ideal for creating your own simple Web pages. If you already use Word for creating your paper documents you will be familiar with its menus and options. Word also includes some powerful tools to simplify putting together Web pages. You can do it all just by keying in text and pointing and clicking with your mouse. There is no need to learn any complicated programming techniques.

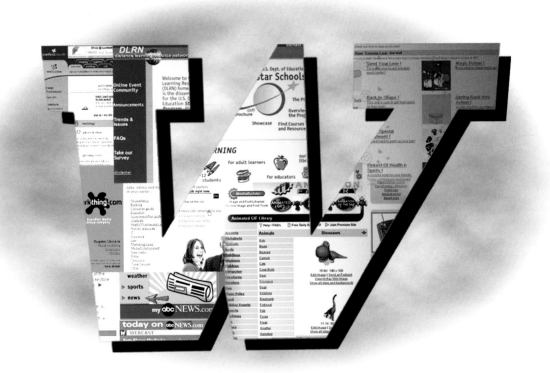

Using Word

Creating a Web page in Microsoft Word is very similar to creating a normal paper document. You position all your text and images manually using the standard document editing menus. Word then translates your page into HTML automatically.

Before you start

It is worth taking a few minutes to sketch out on paper a brief design of what you want your page to look like before you start up your software. This will be a useful reference point when you start creating the electronic version. See *Web design basics*, page 254 for more details on how to do this.

Using the CD-ROM

The CD-ROM supplied with this book includes a variety of background images, borders, buttons and artworks that you can use to make your site. Before you begin the step-by-step process shown here, it is worth inserting the disk into your computer's CD-ROM drive and looking for any images that you want to use. Then follow the instructions on the CD-ROM to save the images ready for you to use.

Watch Out!
Don't use more than three or four colours, and use colours consistently – one colour for text, another for links, and so on. That will make your page easier to read.

HOW TO: STRUCTURE YOUR WEB PAGE

One of the main differences when you are preparing a document for the Internet, rather than for print, is that you need to take extra care to ensure that all the elements of the page are correctly positioned. Otherwise they will not be properly displayed on other people's Web browsers.

   The easiest way to do this is to place all the text and images in a table, using the table's rows and columns to act as boundaries, and set the position of each item. You can use your sketch to work out the number of rows and columns you need.

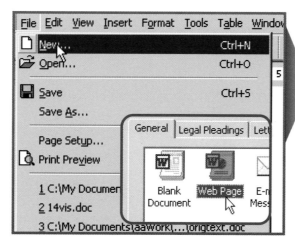

1 Open Microsoft Word. Go to the **File** menu and select **New**. Under the 'General' tab, click on **Web Page** and then click **OK**.

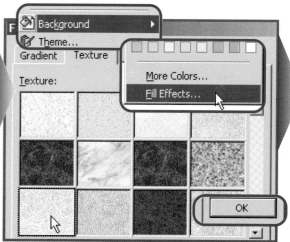

2 Begin by adding a background to your page. Go to the **Format** menu and select **Background** then **Fill Effects**. Click on the Texture tab, then select a texture that you like and click **OK**.

Use Word's own guide

Word 2000 also has a Web page-generation Wizard, which leads you through all the options required to make a Web page.

   If you want to try this method rather than the step-by-step guide above, go to **File** and select **New**. Click on the 'Web pages' tab, then on **Web Page Wizard** and follow the instructions.

Problem Solver!
*If you want to add a row to your table, click in the row above where you want to insert it, go to the **Table** menu and select **Insert** and then **Rows Below**. You can insert a column using the same principle.*

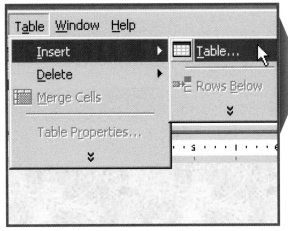

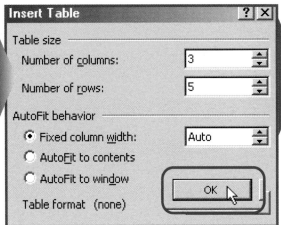

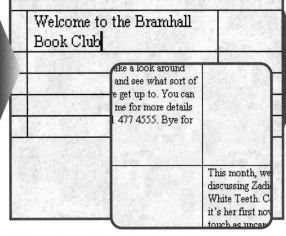

3 Now insert your table to help to position the various items that will appear on your page. Go to the **Table** menu and select **Insert** and then **Table**.

4 Then select the number of columns and rows you require, and click **OK**.

5 Now click in the first section of the table in which you want to write some text, and type it in. The height of the row increases to accommodate the text. Type in the text for each section of the table.

Did You Know?
*You can find free site building resources, including ClipArt, sounds and other add-ons, at Reallybig.com (**www.reallybig.com/reallybig.shtml**).*

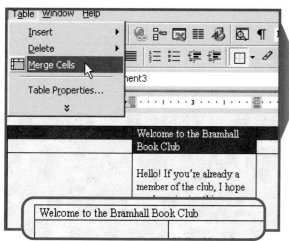

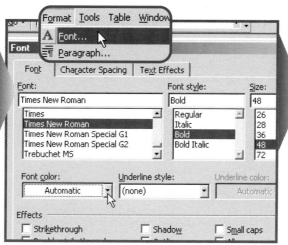

6 You can remove the divisions between parts of the table to allow text to run right across. To do this, highlight the top three cells by clicking and dragging across them. Go to the **Table** menu and select **Merge Cells**. Then do the same for the second row.

7 You are now ready to style your text. Highlight the text in the first section of the table. Go to the **Format** menu and select **Font**. In the next window, select a font, style, size and effect. Then click on the arrow beneath 'Font color'.

8 Click on a colour from the pop-up menu that appears. Then click **OK** to apply your changes to the highlighted text.

Themes

Instead of using a background colour, there are a number of pre-set themes you can apply to your page. Go to the Format menu and select Theme. Then click on a few of the options from the list to see the available effects. You cannot use a theme and a background colour together.

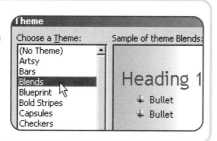

Problem Solver!
If you can't find an appropriate piece of ClipArt in the Word gallery, have a look on the CD-ROM accompanying this book and try some of the sites mentioned in Web site ingredients, *page 250.*

9 Now align your text either to the left, right or centre. Highlight the text and then click on the appropriate button on the toolbar. Repeat steps 8 and 9 to style and then align the rest of the text on your page.

10 Once all the text is prepared, you can add some images to liven up the page. Word has a gallery that you can pick from. Click in the appropriate section of the table, go to the Insert menu and select **Picture** and then **Clip Art**.

11 Click on a category, then on an image that you want to use. A small toolbar appears. Click on the first button to insert the picture. Click the close button to return to your document.

You can also change the width and height of each row and column of the table to suit your text. To do this, hover the cursor over the border-line between sections. When you see a double-headed arrow, click and drag the cursor to move the border.

Watch Out!
*If you double-click on your saved Web page, it will open in your Web browser. To open it in Word, you need to go to Word's **File** menu and select **Open**.*

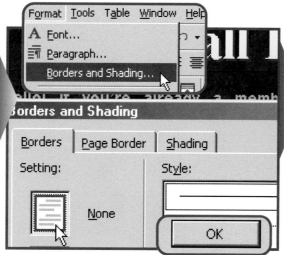

12 The picture will now appear in the table. To re-size it, click on it and then click and drag one of the corner handles which appear.

13 You can now make your table invisible so that it won't appear on your Web page. Highlight the table by dragging across it and then go to the **Format** menu and select **Borders and Shading**. Click the icon next to 'None' and then click **OK**.

14 Go to the **File** menu and select **Web Page Preview** to check your page in your browser. If you are not happy, close the browser window and make changes to the Word file. When you are ready, go to the **File** menu and save your page (see below).

SAVING YOUR HOMEPAGE

When you save your page, call it 'index'. The main page of your site should always be named in this way, because browsers automatically look for (and open) the 'index' page when they go to a site address. If you call the page something else, you would have to add that name to your basic Web address in order for people to access it. For example, if you called your first page 'welcome', an address such as **www.geocities. com/stephenmannion/welcome.htm** might be used.

SEE ALSO
● **Upload your site**
– *page 262*
● **Design a Web page on-line** – *page 288*
● **Ensure your site is seen** – *page 306*

Upload your site

Get your **Web site on-line** for all to see

Once you have created your Web pages you can upload your site onto the Internet. This process uses specialist software to transfer copies of your Web page files from your computer to the Internet server you have chosen to host your pages. You may already have this software installed on your computer – Microsoft provides a free simple file transfer program called the Web Publishing Wizard.

Getting your Web site on-line is straightforward, but it is critical to prepare your pages carefully. You also need to have accurate notes of the names and locations of all the files required to make your site complete.

Preparation
You will find it is much easier to upload your site, and to maintain it, if you ensure that all the files comprising your site are stored in the same folder. Keep this folder exclusively for your Web site files so that you can upload the entire contents of the folder to publish your site.

If your site contains images, store these in a sub-folder within your main Web site folder so that they can be easily located by the Web Publishing Wizard.

File names
It is good practice not to use spaces or upper-case (capital) letters for your file names – some browsers and servers are case-sensitive and will not find a file if the wrong case is used.

Web host information
When you sign up with a Web host company you will be provided with a Host Address/FTP Server. This is a computer that is always connected to the Internet and is where your Web pages will be stored. You will need the URL for this server to access your Web site. You will also need the username and password you chose when you logged in.

Time Saver!
Different Web hosts have different procedures for uploading pages. Always read the 'help' pages provided by your Web host.

Jargon Buster!
FTP (File Transfer Protocol) is a method for copying files between computers. It is most commonly used for transferring Web site files from your PC to an Internet server.

HOW TO: PUBLISH YOUR SITE ON THE WEB

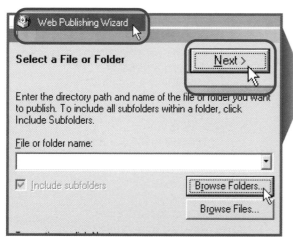

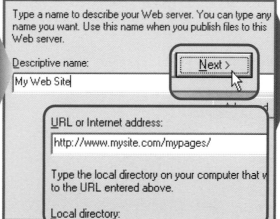

1 To start the Web Publishing Wizard, click on **Start**, **Programs**, **Accessories**, **Internet Tools** and then **Web Publishing Wizard**. On the next screen, click **Next**, then select your Web site folder by clicking **Browse Folders**.

2 Type a name to describe the server that will host your page, then click **Next**. Enter the full address of your server. The folder containing your Web page files is already entered below. A copy of this folder will be sent to your host server. Click **Next**.

3 The Web Publishing Wizard will now connect to the site. Type in your username and password, then click **OK**. The Wizard will log-in to your server. Click on **Finish** to put your files on-line. To update the site at any time, see below.

CHECK YOUR WEB SITE

Once you have finished uploading your page, you should check that it looks correct and that all the elements have been properly published. Open your Web browser and enter the URL of your Web page. Then click on the **Refresh** button in case the browser is loading an earlier copy of the page from your computer's memory.

Updating your site

To update your site, make the changes to the original Word file and save it. Open the Web Publishing Wizard, and click **Browse Files**. Locate your new Word document and click **Next**, then follow the procedure from step 2 above (some of the details you entered earlier will appear automatically). Click on **Finish** to upload your files and close the Wizard. Any existing file with the same name will be replaced automatically by the updated file you have selected.

SEE ALSO
● Link to more pages – page 270
● Design a Web page on-line – page 288
● Set up a business site – page 298

Add a picture to your page

Enhance your Web site with the **images of your choice**

Once you have created your own Web site, you can add pictures to it. These can be images of your own – family photographs, for example – or pictures found from other sources, such as Internet downloads. Using a scanner, you can add any kind of image – from pictures found in books to images printed in newspapers and magazines.

Preparing an image
Once you have an image that you want to use on your page, you need to make sure that it is suitable for your Web site. This involves checking that the picture is saved in an appropriate file format, and that it has been properly sized to fit the page. It should also be 'optimised' (see page 267).

Image size
The optimising process is also necessary to ensure that your pictures load as quickly as possible. Graphics that are not optimised often have very large file sizes and will therefore take a long time to download. This may result in visitors to your Web site losing patience, and going elsewhere before they have even seen your site.

Copyright
Most printed material is covered by copyright laws, and is not freely available for you to scan in and use without the permission of the copyright owner.

Did You Know?
A number of Web sites let you download images for free. You can then use these on your own site. For more details, see page 251.

HOW TO: GET YOUR IMAGE ONTO YOUR COMPUTER

Scanners

Scanners are ideal for turning your favourite pictures into images you can use on your Web page. A scanner takes a digital copy of an image and then displays it on your computer screen This means you can transfer photographs, or pictures from newspapers or books, to your own computer. Using image editing software (see below), some of which may come with your scanner, you can then manipulate this picture in various ways – changing its size, colours and other properties to create a new and different image.

You can also decide at which image resolution you wish to make your scan. Resolution describes picture quality and is measured by the number of dots per inch (dpi) that make up an image. The greater the dpi, the better quality the picture, and the more memory it uses.

Most scanners designed for home use plug into the back of your computer – in either the parallel or USB (Universal Serial Bus) port. Some computers now come with scanners supplied, but for details on how to buy a scanner, see *How are Web sites made?*, page 248.

Digital cameras

A digital camera takes photographs without using film. Instead it stores images as graphic files, such as JPG (see *Image file formats*, page 266) which you can transfer directly to your computer. A cable, which connects the camera directly to your PC, is supplied with most new cameras. You can then edit your image in any graphics package.

The other main advantage of digital cameras is their immediacy. There is no need to wait around to finish a film and then develop it. You can see your 'photographs' immediately and use them as soon as you connect your camera up to your computer. You can also review your photographs on the camera before you transfer them to your PC.

IMAGE EDITING SOFTWARE

There are a variety of specialist and general Web graphics tools you can use to prepare your pictures for your Web site. The appropriate application will depend on just how much you want to achieve on your Web site and your available budget. It is worth going to the manufacturers' Web sites to download trial versions of these tools before you invest in any graphics package.

Xat Image Optimizer

Image Optimizer is a low cost shareware program that takes you step-by-step through the image preparation process. You can download a 30-day evaluation copy from xat.com (**www.xat.com**).

Paint Shop Pro

This is a popular shareware graphics program that also includes all the tools that you will need to optimise images for the Web. It is good value and suitable for people who don't have previous photo-editing experience. Go to **www.pspro.aphid.net/guide/intro.html** to download the 30-day trial version.

Adobe Image Ready

If you need a top-of-the-range application, then try Image Ready, which is included with Adobe Photoshop (**www.adobe.com/support/downloads**). However, this is more suited to advanced Web designers, rather than beginners.

Problem Solver!
If you are not sure how much to compress your image, put several different versions onto your Web page and look at them in your browser. The one that has been compressed the least will look the best, but you should choose the one that has been compressed and yet still looks acceptable.

HOW TO: PREPARE AN IMAGE FOR A WEB SITE

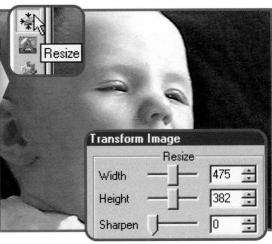

1 Download the Xat Image Optimizer from **www.xat.com**. Start the program and open the original image file. This example uses a scanned bitmap (.bmp) file, which, with a 3.2Mb file size and measuring 1200x900 pixels, is too large for Web use.

2 First you need to crop the image to discard any unwanted sections of the picture. Click on the **Crop** tool and drag the mouse to define the area of the image you want to use, then click on the **Crop Image** button.

3 Now resize the image. Click on the **Resize** button and set the image width you want by using the slider. As most browsers are set for a maximum width of 800 pixels, with some as low as 640, a setting of 475 is usually adequate for a large image.

CHOOSING IMAGE FILE FORMATS

When you save your image, you are offered a number of different file formats. The one you choose depends on the kind of image you have and what you will be using it for.

.gif – Limited to 256 colours or less and therefore suitable for buttons or simple graphics on a Web site. Other features include transparency (the ability to add a see-through background) and animation.

.jpg – Ideal for photographs, this produces a compact file, up to 100 times smaller than the original, by merging similar colours into a single tone to save space. It is unsuitable for images with few colours.

.png – A relatively new format not yet widely used on Web pages. It aims to eventually replace the .gif format. Some older browsers will not display .png images correctly.

Jargon Buster!
Optimising. Balancing the size and quality of a file to make it suitable for use on a Web site.

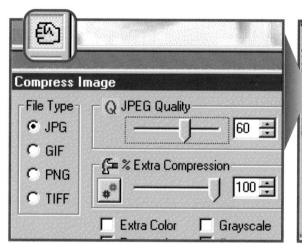

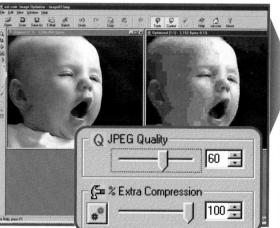

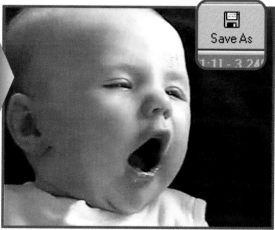

4 Now click the **Compress Image** tool and select a file format from the left of the window. This is a photograph, so a .jpg format will be appropriate (see *Image file formats*, page 266).

5 Now move the sliders to reduce the image quality to the lowest acceptable point (called optimising). In this case, 60% JPEG and 100% extra compression settings produce a result which is 6K in size. Further reduction would reduce the quality too much.

6 To save the image, click on the **Save As** button and save your new optimised JPEG image to the Web page folder you created earlier (see below).

STORING YOUR IMAGES

Keep a copy of your original image in a separate folder to the one where your optimised version is stored. If your Web page has a lot of images, store all the optimised versions together in an 'images' folder created within your main Web page folder. This will make things much easier later when you come to upload your site.

Did You Know?
Only minor sizing adjustments should be made to your image at this stage, as major changes can lead to a poorer quality image. It is best to get the size right in your image editing program (see page 266).

HOW TO: INSERT YOUR IMAGE

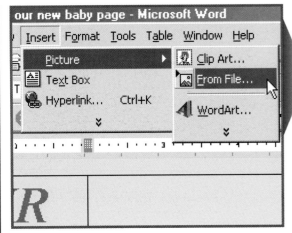

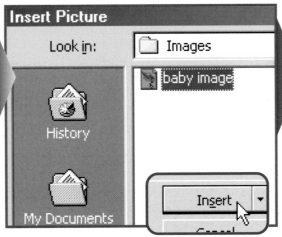

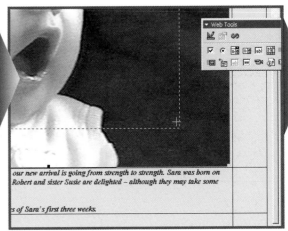

1 First open your Web page in Word. Click in the part of the table where you want to place the image, then go to the **Insert** menu and then choose **Picture** and **From File**.

2 Locate the image and click **Insert** to add it to your Web page. A copy of the picture will also be made in your Web page files directory (which Word creates when you first save your page), and it is this copy that is displayed on your page.

3 You can now make minor adjustments to the size of the image so that it fits into the design of your page exactly. To do this, click on the corner of the image and then drag it to the size you want.

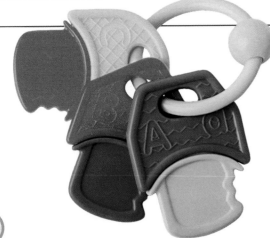

Did You Know?
*An optimised image is also
perfect for sending by e-mail.
Just enclose it as an attachment with
an e-mail message (see* Send e-mail
attachments, *page 42).*

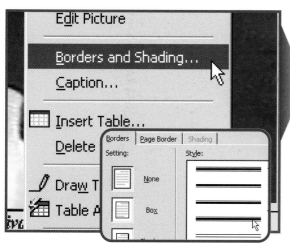

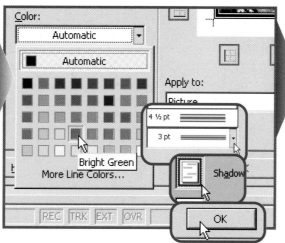

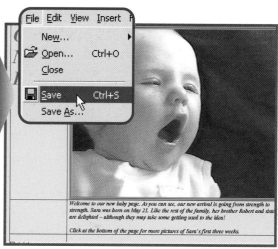

4 You can now add a frame to your picture. To do this, right-click on your picture, then click **Borders and Shading**. Select your border style by clicking on one of the options available.

5 Then choose a colour for your border, and specify its width. You can then choose a setting, for example, **Shadow**, which gives the illusion that the picture is sitting slightly above the level of the page. Click **OK** to apply your selections.

6 To save your document, go to the **File** menu and select **Save**. If you want to, you can go back later to edit any of the new features you have added.

SETTING YOUR DESKTOP

You can scan in your favourite picture and use it as Desktop wallpaper. This is a great way to personalise your computer. Go to the Start menu and select Programs, Accessories and then click Paint. Go to the File menu and click on Open. Find your picture then click Open. Finally go to the File menu and select Set as Wallpaper, then click OK to apply your change.

SEE ALSO
● Web site ingredients
  – page 250
● Link to more pages
  – page 270
● Ensure your site is seen
  – page 306

Link to more pages

Connecting your **Web page** to other sites on the Internet makes your page more **useful** and **fun to visit**. It also means that you are **adding** to the **accessibility** of the Web

A link, or 'hyperlink', is an item on a Web page which, when you click on it, takes you directly to another page anywhere else on the Internet. The World Wide Web is a collection of inter-connected sites, and links are the basis of how it works. Following links on Web sites is a great way to access related information on a subject. Using Word, you can link your site to your favourite sites on the Web, and create links between all the separate Web pages that make up your site.

HOW TO: ADD A LIST OF LINKS TO OTHER WEB SITES

One of the most common features on all Web sites is a list of links to other related sites. These could be your favourite sites or sites that cover similar material to your own.

Once you have decided which sites you want to put on your list and have their Web addresses to hand, the first step is to add a list of their names to your Web page.

If you have enjoyed this site, you can find more information on champion dog breeding grooming techniques and shows at:

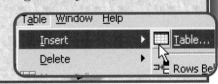

1 Open your Web page in Word. Click on the page at the point where you want to insert your list of links. Then go to the **Table** menu and click **Insert** and then **Table**.

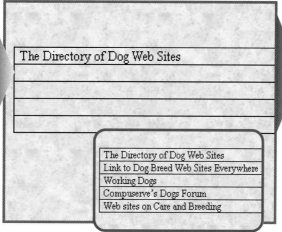

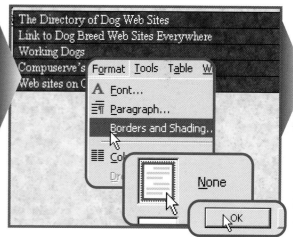

2 In the 'Insert Table' dialogue box, specify one column for the site name, and as many rows as you have sites to include. Then click **OK**.

3 A table now appears on your page. Click in the first section and type in the name (not the address) of the first site you want to include. Then add the other site names to the other sections.

4 Now make the table grid invisible. Highlight the table by dragging across it, then go to the **Format** menu and select **Borders and Shading**. Click on the icon next to 'None' and then click **OK**.

ADDING EXTRA ROWS

If you decide to add more rows to your table (to add more sites, or to provide a description for each one you mention), click in the row above where you want to insert a new one. Then go to the **Table** menu and select **Insert** and then **Rows Below**.

271

Did You Know?
You don't have to place your links in a separate table. You can refer to another site within a paragraph of text, highlight the reference and turn that into a link.

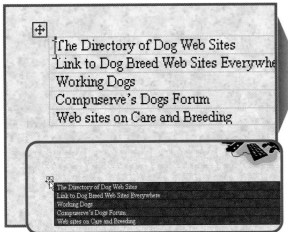

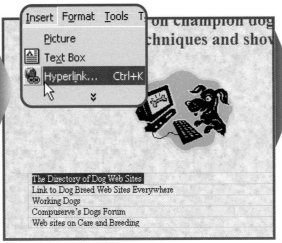

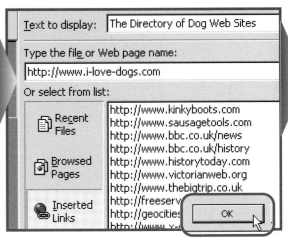

5 You can move the table anywhere on the page by hovering your cursor over the table until a four-way arrow appears at its top left-hand corner. Click on the arrow and drag the table to where you want it to be.

6 Now highlight the name of your first Web site, go to the **Insert** menu and select **Hyperlink**. This opens up a hyperlink dialogue box.

7 Click in the text box beneath 'Type the file or Web page name', and enter the full Web address of the site. Then click **OK**.

Create links automatically

Word can be set up to automatically recognise a Web address and turn it into a link – colouring and underlining it accordingly. This is a quick way to create a list of links. To activate this function go to the **Tools** menu and select **AutoCorrect**, then click **AutoFormat As You Type**. In the 'Replace as you type' section, tick next to 'Internet and network paths with hyperlinks' and then click **OK**. Then type the addresses of your links in the table rather than the site names.

Time Saver!
*A quicker way to insert a
hyperlink is to highlight the text
and then press the 'Ctrl' and 'K'
keys at the same time.*

Watch Out!
*Once you have uploaded your Web
pages, it is always worth checking them on-line
by putting the Web address in your browser.
It is possible that you will spot a problem that
was not obvious before.*

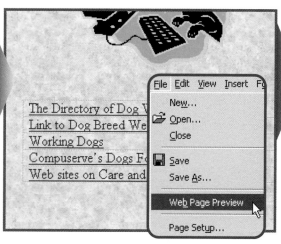

8 The name of your site now appears in blue
underlined type. When you move your cursor
over it, the cursor will change into a pointing finger
indicating that it has found a link.

9 Repeat the process for each Web site in your list
and then save your page. To test that your new
links are working, go to the **File** menu and select
Web Page Preview.

10 Now click on a link – in a moment your browser
should open and display the relevant page. If
it does not, check the address that you entered in
the hypertext dialogue box. You can now upload
your new page (see *Upload your site*, page 262).

Change the colour of a link
Word automatically displays links in blue underlined
type. If you don't want them to appear this way,
highlight the text, go to the **Format** menu and
select **Font**. Then choose the colour and underline
style you want. Be careful though – people expect
to see links as blue underlined text and may not
notice the link if you change it.

Did You Know?
*You don't always have to make it
clear that a word or graphic is a link.
Sometimes it's fun to create a secret link
for the sharp-eyed visitor to find when
they move their mouse over it.*

HOW TO: LINK PAGES TOGETHER

You can also create links between Web pages
that you have created yourself. Say you have a
homepage on dog breeding, you could then
create another page about grooming, and a
third about dog showing – then link them
together to make a more useful and
interactive Web site.

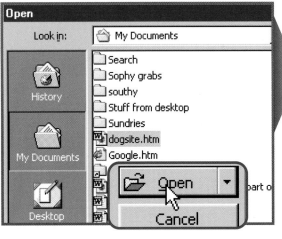

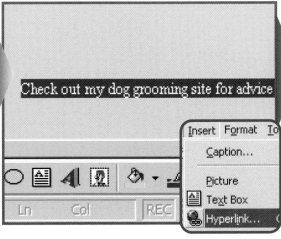

1 In Word, go to the **File** menu and select **Open**.
Use the window that appears to locate your
original Web page file and click **Open**.

2 At the bottom of the Web page, type some text
inviting the reader to visit your second page.
Next highlight the text, go to the **Insert** menu and
click on **Hyperlink**.

TURNING OBJECTS INTO LINKS

You can also turn images and graphics into links. Right-click on the
image on your page and select **Hyperlink**. The hyperlink dialogue
box will appear. Now enter the location of the Web page you want
to link to – just as you did to link your two Web pages above.
Images that look like buttons can look particularly effective.
There are some in the CD-ROM accompanying this book and others
in the ClipArt gallery offered by Word.

Did You Know?
You can edit a hyperlink
(to change the Web address)
by right-clicking on it and then
clicking **Edit Hyperlink**.

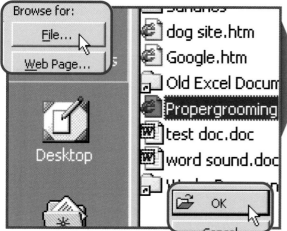

3 You now need to locate your second page on your hard drive. To do this, click on **Browse for File**, locate your links page and click on it. Finally, click **OK**.

4 The name of your file will appear under 'Type the file or Web page name'. Click **OK**. Save your Web page and then close it.

5 Now, follow the same procedure to add a link from your second page back to your original Web page. Finally, save your second page and close it.

Taking it further
If you have enjoyed and mastered the process of creating links, you can now make more Web pages and expand your site. You could create pages for every member of the family, a page of photographs or links to sites run by other relatives. You will find your ISP has provided plenty of space.

SEE ALSO
- Design a Web page on-line – *page 288*
- Build a Web page in Word – *page 256*
- Add sound to your page – *page 276*

Add sound to your page

Enhance your Web site by **creating audio** features

A few well-chosen sound effects can enhance the appeal of your Web site. If you have pictures of a new family member on your site, you could have happy baby noises to accompany them. Or, if your site is more serious, you could add some music appropriate to its tone. You can find all sorts of audio effects and music clips on the Internet, many of which are free to download and use on your Web site. You can also create sounds of your own using your PC's Sound Recorder facility.

How it works

There are two simple ways to add a sound file to your Web site. The first is to add a sound that plays automatically as soon as someone visits your site. The second is to add the sound file as a link. This means that a visitor can hear the sound by clicking on a picture or piece of text.

The second method is considered better among Internet users, because it allows the visitor to choose whether or not they want to hear the sound. A sound that plays automatically can be quite annoying for the unsuspecting visitor – especially if they are listening to music of their own or trying not to disturb other people in their home or office.

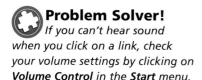

Problem Solver!
If you can't hear sound when you click on a link, check your volume settings by clicking on **Volume Control** *in the* **Start** *menu.*

> The text on many Web sites is never proof-read. As a result, you will find that, as here, words are often spelt wrongly or inconsistently – sometimes within the same Web page.

HOW TO: FIND A SOUND FILE ON-LINE

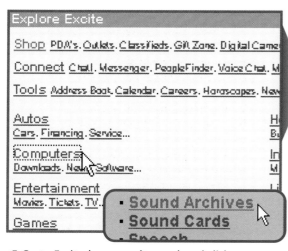

- MIDI Sound   to applications. Purchase those of in
- Military.com - Military Sounds - Do and air raid sirens. Most are in .wa
- MSU Vincent Voice Library - Libra download some of them here. Also
- Multimedia Sounds - Directory for ommercials to Star Trek. Hours o
- Sonarchy - Archives of sound, mu section of sounds from around the

Download comple

The file 'C:\My Download Files\Porche.au' wa downloaded successfully.

More Info will show software that works with th The file type will be transmitted back to RealN for the purpose of providing you with the corre execute the file.

real download   Run

1 Go to Excite (www.excite.com) and click on **Computers** then **Multimedia, Music & Sound** and **Sound Archives** to find a list of sound file sites.

2 Click on **Multimedia Sounds** to open up a list of sound categories. Click on a folder to open it – for example, **sound_effects/**.

3 Click on a sound to download it with RealPlayer. In this example, **Porsche** was chosen. The 'Download Complete' window will appear. Click on **Run** to hear the sound.

SITES FOR SOUND

There are many sites on the World Wide Web that you can access to download sound files of all kinds for your site.

Partners in Rhyme   (www.partnersinrhyme.com)
Sounddogs.com   (www.sounddogs.com)
Sound Effects   (www.stonewashed.net/sfx.html)
Ultimate Sound &
Music Archive   (www.ultimatesoundarchive.com)

Save your sound

When you find a sound you like, save it by right-clicking on the link for it. Select **Save Target As**, pick a folder on your hard drive and click **Save**.

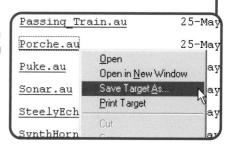

HOW TO: ADD A LINK TO A SOUND FILE

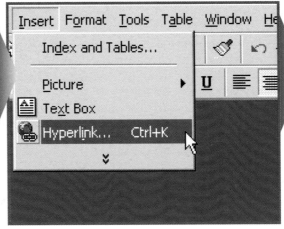

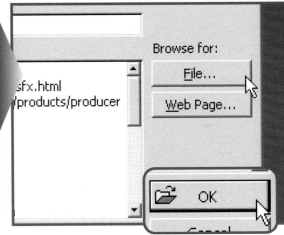

1 Open your Web page in Word. Click on the item that will act as the link. Here, a picture of a car has been added.

2 Go to the 'Insert' menu and select **Hyperlink**. If you want to use some text as a link, rather than a picture, highlight the text and do the same.

3 In the dialogue box, click on **Browse for File** and locate the sound file (select 'All Files' in the 'Files of type' box to see all of the files listed). Then click **OK,** and **OK** again. Finally, save your Web page and close Word.

No sound?
If visitors to your site don't have the correct plug-in, they may not be able to hear your sound. When they click on the link, their Web browser will offer them the option to visit a site, where they can download the necessary plug-in.

Did You Know?
*If you are using the Real Player plug-in you'll need the free program (**www.realnetworks.com/ products/producer**) to convert other sound file formats to the RealAudio format.*

HOW TO: ADD A SOUND THAT PLAYS AUTOMATICALLY

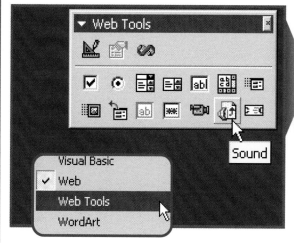

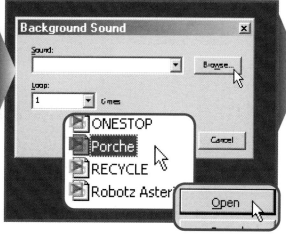

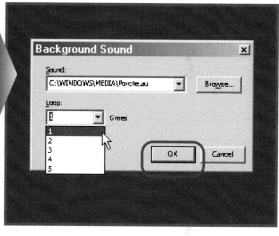

1 Open your Web page in Word, go to the **View** menu, select **Toolbars** and click on **Web Tools**. When the toolbar appears, click on the **Sound** button.

2 The 'Background Sound' dialogue box will appear, click on **Browse**. Look through your hard drive to locate the sound file you wish to use and then click **Open**.

3 Click in the 'Loop' box and select the number of times you want the sound to play. Finally, click **OK**. Save your Web page and then close it.

TESTING YOUR SOUND

Double-click on your Web page to open it in your Web browser. If you added an automatic sound, it should play as soon as the page appears. If you added a link, click on it and the sound should start playing.

   You are now ready to upload your updated Web page onto the Internet. See *Build a Web page in Word*, page 256 for more information.

279

HOW TO: CREATE SOUNDS

You can also record your own words, noises and tunes using your computer. This can be good for adding a personal welcome to the Web site, or for adding a tune played by one of the children.

Before you start

Make sure you have plugged your microphone into the sound card at the rear of your computer system unit. The microphone socket will be marked 'mic' or perhaps it will have a picture of a microphone next to it. Remember to switch the microphone on, and check that it has a battery – if it needs one.

SOUND FORMATS

There are many digital sound formats available for use on your computer. You can tell the format of a sound file by looking at the 'file extension' – the last section of the file name:

.au Audio is one of the least common formats used by PCs, but is widely used on the Web.

.wav Wave is a format used for everyday sounds played by your computer as you use it. It is perfect for short sounds on Web pages and is compatible with most browsers.

.mid MIDI (Musical Instrument Digital Interface) format is a set of instructions that tells your computer to re-create a tune using instrument sounds stored in its own hardware

.ra (Real Audio format) is the best sound format for longer excerpts of recorded music.

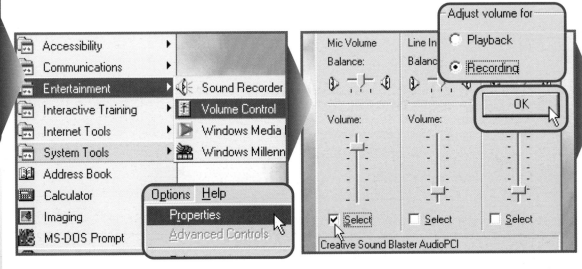

1 Go to the **Start** menu and select **Programs**, **Accessories**, **Entertainment** and then **Volume Control**. Go to the **Options** menu and select **Properties**.

2 Click the **Recording** option and then **OK**. Make sure the 'Select' box beneath 'Mic (Microphone) balance' in the 'Record Control' window is ticked. Now Windows knows you will be using a microphone.

What you need

To record your own sounds on your computer, you need a sound card inside your system unit (if you have speakers, then you already have a sound card), a microphone and the Sound Recorder software, which comes as a standard feature of Windows.

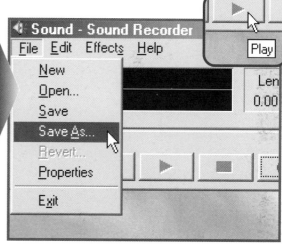

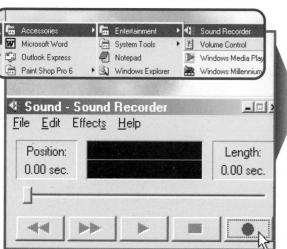

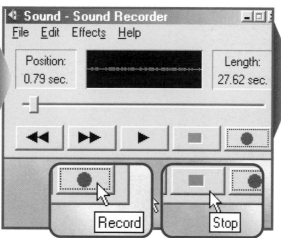

3 Now go to the **Start** menu and select **Programs**, **Accessories**, **Entertainment** and finally **Sound Recorder**. Your computer is now ready to record any sound you enter.

4 Click the **Record** button and speak into the microphone, or start a CD or tape. The green line in the sound recorder distorts, giving a visual image of the sound. Click **Stop** when you have finished.

5 To hear your sound, click the **Play** button. If you are happy with it, go to the **File** menu, click **Save As** and save it. You can now use the sound file in your Web page. To re-record, go to the **File** menu, select **New** and click **No** to delete and start again.

GET THE EQUIPMENT

You can buy microphones on-line or from high street computer retailers. Expect to pay up to £30 for a suitable model. Try going to ZDnet (**http://computershopper.zdnet.com**) or CNET (**http://computers.cnet.com**).

SEE ALSO
- Listen to the radio – page 152
- Web site ingredients – page 250
- Link to more pages – page 270

Add a video to your page

A movie clip can add **a whole new dimension** to you site

Adding a video clip to your Web site can be a great way to personalise your page. It is not possible to upload a long full-screen video, but many sites now include short clips that play in a small window on your computer's Desktop – everything from home movies of the family to a product demonstration. To add a video clip, you need some additional hardware to get video footage from your camcorder or VHS player onto your computer and some additional software to prepare the film for showing on your Web page.

Transferring video

To transfer video pictures from a standard camcorder or VHS video recorder to your computer you need to add a video capture card to your system. This is a similar size to an internal modem and it slots inside your PC's system unit. It is easy to fit, and will come with installation instructions.

A good card for beginners is the Studio DC10 Plus from Pinnacle (**www.pinnaclesys.de/uk**), or the Pinnacle Studio DV if you have a digital video camera. You can expect to pay up to £150 for a card. You then plug your camcorder into the video capture card to begin loading your video onto your computer.

Loading video files

Video capture cards come with video capture software which you need to open before you try loading the video onto your computer. The software allows you to copy a section of the video and save it as a computer file.

You can also use the same software to edit the video clip. Alternatively, you can use the more limited Windows Movie Maker program that is included with Windows Millennium Edition.

HOW TO: LOAD AND SAVE YOUR VIDEO

The following procedure will help you to transfer a short film (of no longer than two minutes) from your video camera onto your computer, then prepare it so you can add it to your Web page. Depending on the type of camera, computer hardware and software you are using, the process will vary slightly. Always check the appropriate manuals for clarification before you start.

Watch Out!

Be careful when loading video onto your PC. Two minutes of video footage can consume up to 500Mb of your disk space – so make sure you have that amount free. If you are likely to work with video regularly, it may be worth investing in a second hard drive.

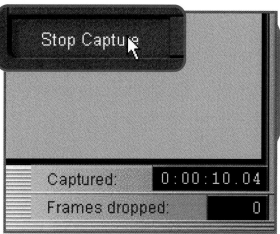

1 First open the video capture software that came with your capture card and start playing your video. Enter a file name for the clip and click on **Start Capture** just before the segment you want to transfer commences.

2 Click **Stop Capture** just after the sequence you need ends and then check the display beneath the video window that no frames have been dropped. Dropped frames are frames from the film that have been missed by mistake.

3 Now cut unwanted seconds from the start and end of your film clip. Use the movie view slider to line up the entry point where you want your film to start, then select **Split clip** from the menu.

PREPARING YOUR VIDEO

You need to do two things to prepare your video for the Web, resize it and compress it. You resize and compress your video so that it takes up less disk space. This means it can be downloaded by visitors to your site in less time. Resizing means altering the dimensions of the size of the window the video will play in. Compressing reduces the file size of the video still further by saving it in a different way.

Jargon Buster!
Pixel An individual dot on a computer screen. All images on the screen are made up of these dots.

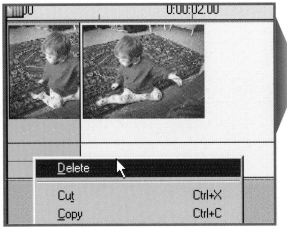

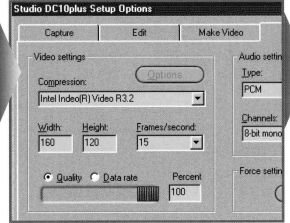

4 Select the unwanted segment and delete it to leave the exact length of film required.

5 You now need to change the settings for your film so that it is suitable for putting on your Web site. Click on the **Make Movie** tab and click on **Settings**.

6 The film needs to be as small as possible but remain viewable. Click in the boxes beneath 'Width' and 'Height' to select the size of window your film will play in. A good, small Web-friendly size is 160x120 pixels.

Video formats

The standard video format for PCs is AVI (.avi), but there are a number of other file formats that can also be used for Web video, including RealVideo (.rv), MPEG (.mpg), and QuickTime (.qt).

Many sites include two versions of a movie on the site. The first will be a small version, probably in RealVideo format and the other a much larger downloadable version in AVI or QuickTime format.

Watch Out!
Try to keep your video file below 2Mb in size. If most of your visitors have a standard 56K modem, a video clip of this size should take less than ten minutes to download.

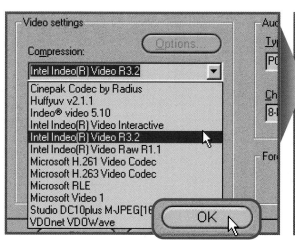

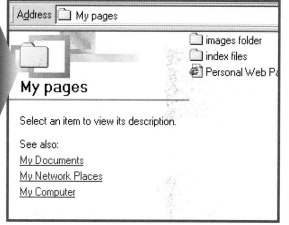

7 Now tell the program which compression software you are using (see below). Make your choice from the drop-down menu in the Settings window, then click **OK**. This software is then automatically used to compress your finished movie file.

8 Now give your movie a name and click on the **Make File** button. The software will now compile your film (compressing and saving it as it does so). Even a short film may take a few minutes to compile.

9 Once your clip has been compiled, close down the video capture software. Then move your movie file to your Web site folder ready to place on your page.

COMPRESSION SOFTWARE

Once you have resized your video image, you should then lower its file size still further by using a compression program. Radius Cinepak and Intel Indeo are fairly common and will provide a good rate of compression. If you are using Windows 95 or any later version, these will already be installed in your PC.

Problem Solver!
*To ensure that you are getting the most out of your hard disk space, go to the **Start** menu and select **Programs**, then **Accessories**, **System Tools** and finally **Disk Defragmenter**. Click **OK** to get your computer to reorganise the way it stores all your files.*

HOW TO: ADD YOUR MOVIE TO YOUR PAGE

Now that you have prepared your movie, you can add it to your page. This works in the same way as inserting a normal image but Word also provides a toolbar for working with movie files.

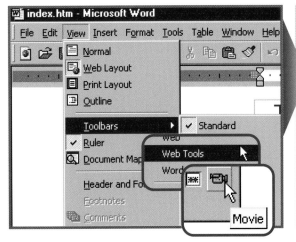

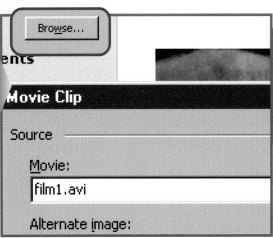

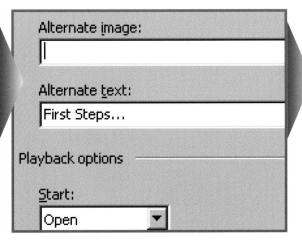

1 Open your Web page in Word. Go to the **View** menu and select **Toolbars** and then **Web Tools**. position your cursor where you want your movie to appear and then click on the **Movie** icon.

2 A dialogue box will appear. Click on **Browse** and locate the movie file you wish to play.

3 In the 'Alternate image' and 'Alternate text' boxes, you can enter the name of another graphic image and a message to display if the visitor's browser can't play movies (see below for more details).

Entering a graphic image

Not everyone may be able to view your movie, so you can use the alternate image and text boxes to display a picture or text instead. Simply write your message into the Alternate text box or use the file browser to select an image file from your Web folder (don't forget to upload this picture too).

Watch Out!

It is polite Web etiquette not to set your film to play as soon as a visitor opens your site. It is better to inform visitors of the size of your video file, its length and its content, so that they can decide if they want to play it.

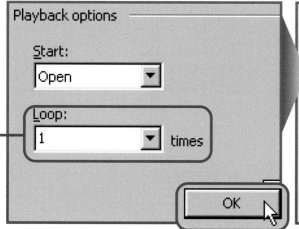

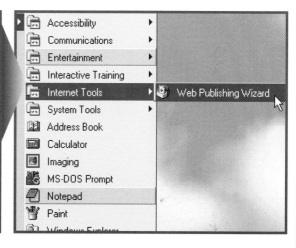

4 In the 'Start' section, select how the movie will be played – either 'Open' so that the movie plays as soon as you open the page, or 'mouse-over' which allows the user to decide to play the movie (see *Watch Out!* above). Then click **OK**.

5 You can preview your video by right-clicking on the movie panel and selecting **Play**, then save your page and close Word.

6 You can now open the Web Publishing Wizard and upload your Web page, together with the movie file, to your Web space (see *Upload your site*, page 262).

Loop:

| 1 | ▼ | times |

The 'Loop' section allows you to specify how many times you want the movie clip to play. Once is normally enough.

SEE ALSO
- **Link to more pages**
  – *page 270*
- **Add sound to your page**
  – *page 276*
- **Add a video to your page**
  – *page 282*

Design a Web page on-line

Use the Internet to **design your own** site in a **matter of minutes**

There are many on-line services that help you to create your own Web site without the need for Web-authoring software. The GeoCities sites (**www.geocities.com**) provide all the tools and Web space you need to create your own site. There is also plenty of help and support available, and a huge community of existing users, many of whom have developed sophisticated Web sites from which you can learn many helpful tips and tricks.

Get started

GeoCities is part of Yahoo!. It provides an on-line community where you can design and post your Web pages. It is a free service, but in return you have to carry advertising on your site. These adverts generally appear in a separate small window on your Web page.

Design your site

Once you've signed up, you will be provided with 15 Megabytes of disk space (plenty for the average user), which you can develop in a number of ways. GeoCities provides a simple Web page generator called PageWizard, and a version for making more complex sites called PageBuilder. It also offers template designs you can alter to suit your needs. You can also use this service to publish pages developed off-line, so if you have already created your page with Microsoft Word, for instance, you can still use GeoCities as your host.

Develop your site

Once you have got your basic page together, GeoCities provides several easily added tools, including search boxes, forms, clocks, visitor counters, menus, news headlines and weather forecasts.

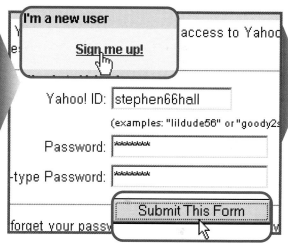

Time Saver!
When deciding what to put on your Web page, go to the GeoCities Members Directory to see other members' sites and how they have used their pages.

HOW TO: SIGN UP TO GEOCITIES

Registering with GeoCities only takes a few minutes and you can begin designing your site immediately afterwards. So before you go on-line, save yourself time and money by making a few preparations.

First, decide what you want to appear on your Web site. Then create a Word document containing any text that you want to include. You can save time by copying and pasting the text in during the on-line design stage.

Finally, save any pictures you want to use in their appropriate formats. For more information on this, see page 264.

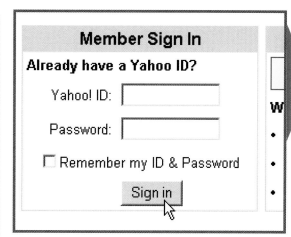

1 Go to the GeoCities homepage (**http://geocities. yahoo.com**). You now need to register as a Yahoo! member. To do this, click on **Sign in**.

2 Now, under 'I'm a new user', click on **Sign me up!** This opens up a form for you to fill in. Choose an ID – a name of your choice, ideally composed of letters and numbers to make it unique – and a password. Fill in your other details and click **Submit This Form**.

Other on-line Web site providers

There are several places on the Internet that offer free Web space, site building tools and links to other free providers.

FreeWebspace.net (**www.freewebspace.net**)
Tripod (**www.tripod.com**)
FortuneCity (**www.fortunecity.com**)

Watch Out!
Be careful to choose suitable advertising for your site. Go for something that complements your pages and that will not offend your visitors.

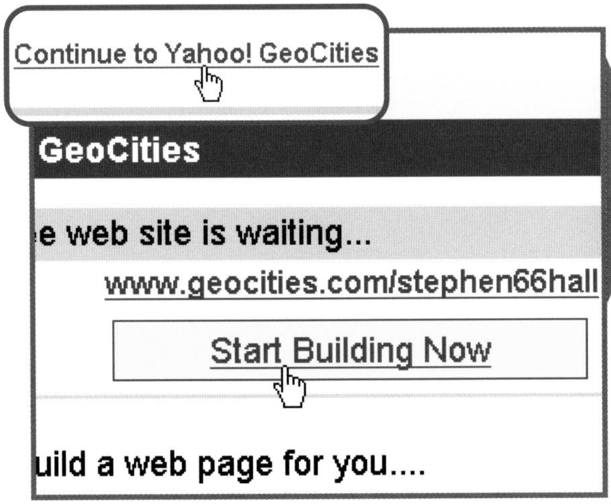
Continue to Yahoo! GeoCities
GeoCities
e web site is waiting...
www.geocities.com/stephen66hall
Start Building Now
uild a web page for you....

3 Make a note of your Yahoo ID and click **Continue to Yahoo! GeoCities**. Once the site appears, click on **Start Building Now**.

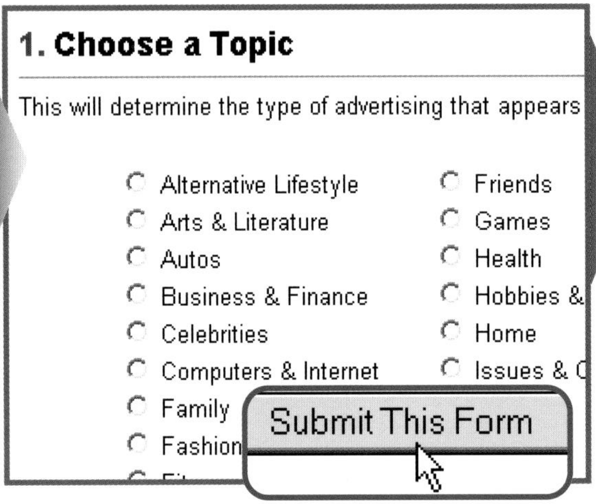
1. Choose a Topic
This will determine the type of advertising that appears
Alternative Lifestyle
Arts & Literature
Autos
Business & Finance
Celebrities
Computers & Internet
Family
Fashion
Friends
Games
Health
Hobbies &
Home
Issues &
Submit This Form

4 This opens up a form asking you to specify what type of advertising you want to appear on your site. Follow the on-screen instructions and then click **Submit This Form**.

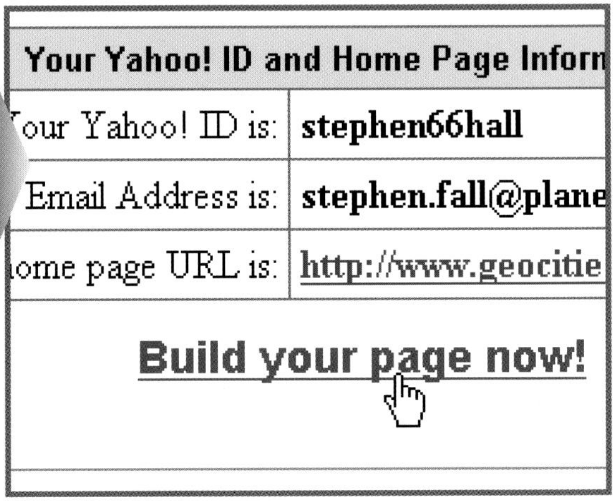
Your Yahoo! ID and Home Page Inforn
our Yahoo! ID is: stephen66hall
Email Address is: stephen.fall@plane
ome page URL is: http://www.geocitie
Build your page now!

5 Now make a note of the Web address (URL) of your Web page. Then click **Build your page now!** to get started.

YAHOO! DIRECTORY

To include your site in the Yahoo! directory, so it can be found by anyone in the world, go to www.yahoo.co.uk for the appropriate directory category. At the bottom of the page, click on Suggest a Site and follow the instructions. You will then have to wait for your site to be reviewed and selected by Yahoo! before your listing appears.

Did You Know?
If you design your site at GeoCities or another on-line site provider, you can have it ready and on-line in about 20 minutes.

Time Saver!
Add the GeoCities site and your own Web page to your 'Favorites' list for easy access. Go to each site, then go to the Favorites menu and click on Add to Favorites.

HOW TO: CREATE A SITE ON-LINE

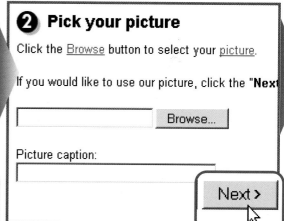

6 Click on **Yahoo! PageWizards** to see a selection of template designs. Click on the design of your choice, then click **Begin** and **Next**. A Web page design Wizard now opens.

7 Enter the title of your Web page as you want it to appear on screen, and then under Enter text, paste in your prepared text for the page. When you've finished, click **Next**.

8 Select a picture to illustrate your page. Click **Next** to use the one already on the template (as here), or click **Browse** to find out how to use a picture stored on your PC. The image will be copied to your GeoCities Web space when you click **Upload**. Click **Next**.

Editing your site

To make changes to your site once you have created it, re-run the GeoCities Wizard and select **Edit existing page**, rather than 'Create new page'. Select the page you want to edit from the drop-down list and go through the original creation steps, making any alterations you require.

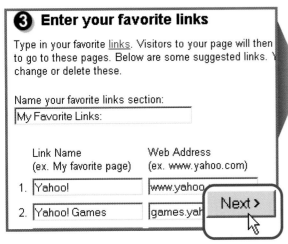

Watch Out!
Think before you place your contact details on your Web site. You may prefer to withhold these details in order to protect your privacy.

List your site
To list your site for other GeoCities members to see, first sign in at GeoCities, then click on **or list your own** under 'Member Pages'. Enter a keyword that describes your site, then select a category in which it will be listed, write a short description of your page and finally, click **List Page**.

❸ Enter your favorite links

Type in your favorite links. Visitors to your page will then to go to these pages. Below are some suggested links. change or delete these.

Name your favorite links section:

My Favorite Links:

Link Name (ex. My favorite page)	Web Address (ex. www.yahoo.com)
1. Yahoo!	www.yahoo
2. Yahoo! Games	games.yah

Next >

Page name: mygardeningclub

My Gardening C

Welcome to my gardening club. This site is for anyone interested in creating the perfect garden. Tips, advice and helpful information are all here. From small gardens, to huge ones, I will informed on everything you know. Look at links to other

Preview

Congratulations!

You have finished creating your own Quick Start Web Page and your friends can now view your page at the web addres below!

Please write down your web address for future reference.

http://www.geocities.com/stephen66hall/
mygardeningclub.html

If you'd like to make changes to your page, press the "Bac button. At any time in the future, you can run this Wizard t changes to this page.

9 Now enter the links that you wish to appear on your site. Click **Next** and then enter your own contact details so that visitors can send you e-mail messages. Then click **Next** to continue.

10 Finally, give your page a name. This will be used in its Web address. Click on **Preview** to check the design of your page and then click on **Done** to exit the Web page design Wizard.

11 The Web address of your new page will now be confirmed. Make a note of it and e-mail it to your friends so that they can look at it.

12 Your finished Web page is now available for all to see. Click on the link provided to view it yourself. If you spot anything you want to change, you can edit your page using the Web page design Wizard as described previously.

My Gardening Club

Welcome to my gardening club. This site is for anyone interested in creating the perfect garden. Tips, advice and helpful information are all here. From small gardens, to huge ones, I will keep you informed on everything you need to know.

Look at links to other useful Web sites I have selected, or scroll through my own advice, on subjects as diverse as installing fountain, keeping your lawn in shape, and cutting down trees.

Project planners help you to choose and complete a task at the right time of year

Tall, bright yellow sunflo everyone and c

My Favourite Garde

Crocus

HOW TO: ADD EXTRA FEATURES

One advantage of using an on-line Web page creation service is that there are usually many extra interactive features you can easily add to your page. In GeoCities, you can use the Yahoo! PageBuilder to edit your page and add any extra features. This makes editing your site very easy.

To download PageBuilder, go to the GeoCities homepage and click on the link provided. The program can take several minutes to load onto your hard drive.

Watch Out!

Don't add extra features to your Web site just because it is easy. They should be relevant to your page and not distract from its main themes.

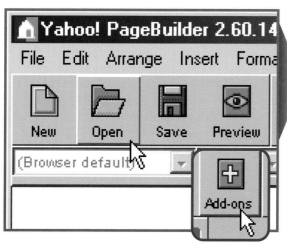

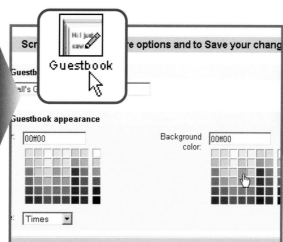

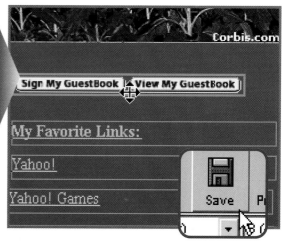

1 Open PageBuilder and then click on the **Open** icon. Select the Web page that you created using the PageWizard. Click on the **Add-ons** icon to access the additional features.

2 Click on a category in the left-hand menu, such as **Interactive**. Then click on one of the add-ons displayed, such as **Guestbook**. Select the text style and colour of the guest book and click **OK**.

3 Now drag the Guestbook icon onto your page. To do this, left-click on the **Guestbook**, hold down the mouse button and move the cursor across to your page. Release the mouse button to add the item. Then click the **Save** icon to save and publish your changes.

Extra features

You can use the process shown above to use all sorts of add-on features, including a counter to show how many visitors you have had to your site, a weather forecast or an opinion poll. Some you can drag straight onto your page without going through the second step above. For others, follow the on-screen instructions.

SEE ALSO

- What is a Web site? – page 246
- Build a Web page in Word – page 256
- Ensure your site is seen – page 306

Other design programs

Use **Web-authoring** software to **create** a site with more features

You can make a great Web site using Word, but most of the exciting and stylish Web sites you see on-line are made with specialist Web-authoring programs. These offer features not found in Word, such as buttons that change shape when you click on them. They are more complicated to use, as most require some understanding of HTML, the programming language of the Internet. Some Web-authoring programs are designed for professionals, but there are also inexpensive or free programs written with amateurs in mind. So if you are serious about Web design you may consider them worth a try.

Learning HTML
You don't need to know any HTML to work with most features offered in Web-authoring programs. But the more complex you want your site to be, the more likely it is that you will need to learn something about the underlying language. Perhaps you will have some faulty HTML code that needs to be edited out, or you need to ensure that a page element can be viewed by all browsers. In these cases, you may need to edit the HTML code manually.

HTML help
Web-authoring programs can help you to learn HTML by giving you an instant preview of what the page will look like, as you make your changes in the code. For an on-line tutorial in basic HTML, consult the Beginner's Guide to HTML (**http//archive.ncsa. uiuc.edu/General/Internet/WWW**).

WEB DESIGN PROGRAMS

Microsoft FrontPage
(www.microsoft.com/frontpage)
FrontPage is aimed at beginners and advanced users alike. Because it is a Microsoft program, the layout and buttons should be largely familiar to you. It is also easy to drop in tables and other elements from related programs such as Word and Excel. It costs about £130 and can be purchased at local computer retailers or on-line.

Microsoft FrontPage
Create It,
Control It, Cultivate
Build exactly the site you want with FrontPage and management solution. Find out more.

Netscape Composer
(www.netscape.com)
Users of Netscape Communicator or Netscape 6.1 (both of which include the Navigator browser) will already have this program. It is a simple HTML editor that is suitable for beginners and offers more features than Word – such as automatic conversion of images into Web format.

It is also available free. You can download the latest Netscape package from the Netscape Web site.

First Page III
bring your code to new heights.

Evrsoft 1stPage 2000
(www.evrsoft.com)
This is a professional Web-authoring program that is free to download. You can edit HTML text and preview the results in a built-in Internet Explorer browser window, or in three other browsers. Features include an image viewer and layout and design tools.

Sausage HotDog PageWiz
(www.sausagetools.com)
HotDog PageWiz is an HTML editing program that is aimed at beginners and intermediate Web authors. Whether you need to correct mistakes in your site's code, or you just want to experiment

Turn yourself into a Web Wizard!
hotdog Pagewiz

with HTML, this program makes it easy. You can preview the results of your HTML changes as you make them. Features include the ability to download an entire Web site, make changes and upload it again. Download a free 30-day trial from the Sausage Web site or buy it for about £50.

Try
Free Trial Version of Macromedia Dreamweaver
Download a free 30-day trial of Dream today. You can download version 4 of in English or Japanese or version 3 o

Macromedia Dreamweaver
(www.macromedia.com)
Dreamweaver is an HTML editing program aimed at serious designers, but it is not difficult to use – especially if you follow the built-in tutorials. The program is especially good for such tricky elements as tables, forms, rollovers and animation, and includes the basic tools required for editing images. It costs about £270 from retailers or the Macromedia Web site, where you'll also find a free 30-day trial. Click **Downloads** then **Dreamweaver**.

Jargon Buster!
HTML Editor This is another name for a Web design program. When you make a change to your design, the program makes the relevant changes to the underlying HTML text.

Money Saver!
Using free trials of programs is a good way to evaluate them. Once you know what you will be getting, you can then decide whether it is worth paying for the full version of the program or not.

Deciding on a program
For further advice on Web software, go to CNET's 'Spotlight on production tools' page (**http://builder.cnet.com/webbuilding/pages/Authoring/ProdTools**). You can read a selection of useful reviews and product comparisons.

A CNET Builder.com Topic Center
SPOTLIGHT ON
production tools
advertisement
Outpost.com
Picture this!
Weekly Camera Deals
Sony's new CDRW Cameras!

You can build a Web site with a simple text editor. In fact, a lot of today's production tools and the complexity of Web sites, you c... To help you choose, we've gathered resources on all the major W list of tools–just the ones we think are the most useful for professio

Code-based HTML editors

SEE ALSO
● **Build a Web page in Word** – *page 256*
● **Add a picture to your page** – *page 264*
● **Add sound to your page** – *page 276*

How e-commerce works

Turn the **Internet** into a source of **profit**

The collapse of the 'Dot Com' boom has demonstrated that making money out of the Internet is not as easy as some people thought. When the Internet has been successful, it has usually been because it has been used as an additional channel to reach the customer, along with traditional routes such as high street outlets and mail order. If you want to make money out of the Web, there are ways of doing so – but they almost certainly won't make you a millionaire overnight.

What is e-commerce?
E-commerce is no different from everyday commerce: it just means using the Internet as part of your business strategy.

How do I start?
Your first step should be to create a business plan setting out the nature of the enterprise, how much money you need to invest, and the target revenues you hope to attract. Identify your customer base and the unique selling point of your business.

Many commercial sites fail because their expectations of visitor traffic and sales are unrealistic. They end up paying more to attract visitors and run the business than the visitors are spending.

On-line business advice
Before you start, go to ZD-Net (**www.zdnet.com/enterprise/e-business**) and The E-commerce Times (**www.ecommercetimes.com**) for news and advice concerning the latest trends and developments in on-line business.

Jargon Buster!
Click-through Advertisers pay by assessing the percentage of visitors to a site who click on their ad. Click-through rates are falling (as little as 0.2% meaning that 1 in 500 visitors clicks on an ad) so advertisers are paying less.

E-COMMERCE MODELS

You will need to think about the nature of your business before you decide how to present it on the Net. Is it a 'hobby' enterprise intended to generate a small amount of extra money. Or, will it be your main source of income, which would need to cover your living expenses and possibly pay staff salaries?

A successful e-commerce site will probably develop revenue from a combination of the models below.

Specialist product sales

Develop a niche market for selling unique products on-line – for example, rare collectible items. Use the Web to promote and handle orders and deliveries. Unique products give your business the best chance of success in a crowded marketplace.

General product sales

If you want to sell goods cheaper or with faster delivery than other services, you will need to compete with the likes of Bigstar (**www.bigstar.com**). Selling reliable plumbing or furniture removals can be as lucrative as selling goods.

On-line products

If you have the technology, you could choose to sell electronic services, such as downloadable software, images, music and other material. Load Music (**http://loadmusic.com**) is a good example of this.

Advertising

Design a site which will appeal to people on a worldwide scale and then sell advertising space to other firms.

Affiliate model

Provide links on your site to other on-line retailers and receive a commission for any sales they make to customers who have come from your site. If you have a specialist site on astronomy, for example, you could provide affiliated links to Amazon (**www.amazon.com**) for visitors to buy books recommended by your site and for which you would receive a small commission.

On-line subscription service

A subscription entitles the customer to regular access to the site content. This is a particularly effective model for sites offering specialist information, such as distance learning sites and financial data.

Customer data model

A specialist site can collect detailed information about its visitors that can be sold on to other businesses targeting the same market. Any site that presents you with a registration questionnaire is probably intending to generate some income in this way.

BUSINESS TIPS

● The Internet is not a magic money maker. Products that won't sell in shops are unlikely to sell any better on-line.

● Would your business still work if it relied on printed catalogues and telephone orders? If not, why would it do better on-line?

● Set targets that will keep you in profit and monitor your success against them. Be prepared to make changes and look at other ways of promoting your site.

● Many consumers don't like buying certain products on-line. Sales that rely on trying things on, such as footwear, don't work well.

● Some consumers are reluctant to buy expensive goods, such as jewellery, because of the fear of fraud or counterfeiting.

● Conversely, low-cost goods may not be economically viable on the Web, once delivery and credit card commissions have been met.

● Always seek professional financial advice at every stage.

SEE ALSO
● Shop safely on the Web
– *page 50*
● Find legal advice
– *page 116*
● File your tax return
– *page 196*

Set up a business site

Use **the Web** to improve your company

Having considered the pros and cons of e-commerce, you may decide to take your business onto the Web. To do this, you need to decide how best to reach your market through the design and publicity of your site. The worldwide accessibility of the Web means that an on-line business has the potential to reach a much larger market, whether it is selling a service, a product or information.

Design your own site

The Internet can be used both to sell a service such as plumbing or joinery, and to sell goods such as fresh flower arrangements. If your product or service can be effectively promoted and illustrated with basic text and pictures, then the simplest option is to design a site yourself (see *Design a Web page on-line*, page 288). Otherwise you may need to hire a Web designer or consultant to help you to create a more complex design.

Business software

There are a number of Web sites offering basic Web design templates with easy-to-follow instructions on how you can insert your own product pictures and text to produce customised Web pages. These sites can also help you to establish a secure way for customers to complete transactions on-line. However, you have to pay for this part of the service, so if sales volumes are likely to be low, you may prefer to take orders over the telephone instead.

Watch Out!

Only promise what you know you can deliver. Reputation is important on the Web, and if you let your customers down, word will quickly get around through newsgroups and forums.

BUSINESS ADVICE

Get your product right

In recent years, a number of companies who were confident of making a profit from the Internet have gone out of business. There are several lessons you can learn from these failures.

In the rush to get on-line, many businesses failed to realise that their ideas were not viable for a Web-based business. It has been found, for example, that people are often reluctant to buy tactile items over the Internet, such as clothes and furniture, preferring to see and try them for size in the shops before making a purchase.

It has also been difficult for some businesses to persuade people to order expensive items such as handmade jewellery over the Internet. This is partly because of the 'must see' shopping preference, but also due to the fear of fraud or counterfeiting. While well-known shopping brands already have an important recognition and trust factor, new Web-based shops have to earn and build this up from nothing (see *Shop safely on the Web*, page 50).

Don't expect miracles

Some businesses have considered going on-line as an attempt to address marketing and profits problems of an off-line venture.

It is important to ask why your business might be more successful on the Internet if it is not working well in its

current format. Who are the customers that will come to you over the Web that don't come to you already? Can you actually deliver the goods or service you are offering, and how quickly?

Don't overdo the design

Web site design has been a clear factor in the success or failure of some ventures. An ambitious interactive multimedia presentation might look great on a test machine,

but your potential customers aren't going to hang around wasting time and money while huge graphics and animations download.

Boo.com (**www.boo.com**), for example, have made an attempt to provide a virtual equivalent of the 'touch' experience by offering interactive 3D animations of their products.

However, because these images and animations required powerful hardware in order to be viewed properly, the site could not be used efficiently by all customers, and Boo.com have struggled to make a success of their business.

Hire a designer

If you don't have the time or expertise to design your own business Web site, you can employ a company or designer to build a unique site for you. However, this is usually a fairly expensive solution and even a small site can cost from upwards of £500.

PLANNING YOUR SITE

A business site needs to be organised so that visitors can find their way around it easily, locate services or goods that interest them, and place orders or make appointments simply and with confidence. You will need to attract people into your site and be able to gather information about them and their interests while they're visiting. Many of the issues you need to address are the same as if you were opening a high street shop.

Did You Know?
*You can find impartial advice about on-line and off-line business at NewBusiness Magazine (**www.newbusiness.co.uk**).*

Designing the site

Your site, and in particular your opening homepage, needs to be welcoming, clear and helpful.

Keep it simple. Don't use huge graphics or animations that slow things down. Get your message across quickly and have a clear navigation system that can be easily understood. Try to have a short statement that clearly sets out your site's objective, and choose a memorable Web address.

For instance, a name such as 'Flowersthatlast', tells you pretty much all you need to know. More esoteric names are likely to need a bigger budget to get brand recognition – would you associate Amazon.com with books if you had not seen their adverts?

Attracting customers

It is important that you determine how customers will be able to place orders for your products so that both you and they can conduct the transfer of goods and money with confidence. Your prospective customer might appreciate being given a choice of ways to order.

You can subscribe to a secure credit card acceptance service for on-line payments, but you might also want to offer telephone, fax and mail orders as well – particularly if your on-line business has an off-line counterpart.

Orders and deliveries

Once you've made a sale, you need to ensure you can deliver the goods. Consider whether or not you can cope with worldwide orders, how the delivery charges will be calculated and included in the overall costs, and what delivery times you can promise.

Fulfilling orders is a fundamental customer satisfaction criteria for making an on-line purchase. People want to know how quickly their items will be

delivered and be confident they can check on their order status during the interim.

You also need to arrange insurance so that customers can be compensated for non-delivery or damaged goods.

Promoting the site

Publicity is very important. You should include all the 'tags' that will help to get your site listed by search engines (see *Ensure your site is seen*, page 306), and spend time registering with as many as you can.

Build a great web site online in 10 minutes!

Payment

To accept credit card and cheque orders through your Web site you need a secure Internet Payment Gateway and an Internet Merchant Account. On-line shopping malls (see opposite) offer links and sometimes free access to this service.

| Commerce Settings | Instant Credit Cards | eBay Listing Tool | Resource Centers |
| Community | Catalog Maintenance | Business Profile | Webstore Promotion |

HOW TO: USE WEB DESIGN SITES

One way to simplify the Web site design process is to join an on-line shopping mall such as FreeMerchant, Bizhosting or Bigstep. These sites will get your shop or service on-line for the minimum amount of money and trouble.

While these services offer free start-up packages to get your Web site on-line, if you want your business site to be able to receive secure payments on-line you will need to start paying a monthly fee.

Jargon Buster!
Shopping cart The program that tracks customers' orders as they move around a shopping site, then allows them to 'check out' through a payment and delivery module, ensuring the transaction is secure.

Web-building module

Bigstep.com (www.bigstep.com)
This site offers an excellent step-by-step Web-building module that allows you to create an attractive-looking Web site to your specifications. Or, you can ask a Bigstep consultant to do it for you (for a fee). You can have your own URL attached to the site and register your shop or service with the major search engines. You can also have an e-mail database to keep in touch with your customers.

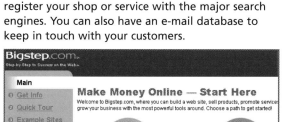

If you need a sales section on your site, you can use the shopping cart function whereby you can have payments made though a secure server with on-line order tracking. You can also receive detailed breakdowns of user activity on your site, so you can see which parts are most successful.

Promotion

FreeMerchant.com (www.freemerchant.com)
Working in a similar way to Bigstep, FreeMerchant's Web page design tools are also easy to use. However, unlike Bigstep, you will need to make your own arrangements for credit cards to be accepted on your site.

Two advantages of using this service is that your FreeMerchant shop can be listed at Internet Mall.com (**www.internetmall.com**) – a site which promotes FreeMerchant stores, and you can also use a link to the eBay auction site to list your goods or services for auction there. This will help to promote your site and increase sales.

Control

Bizhosting.com (www.bizhosting.com)
Providing a full range of point-and-click design tools, Bizhosting helps you to build a free site for selling goods and services by phone and mail. You can upload an existing site into your Bizhosting Web space, rather than design a new one on-line.

Upgrade your site to accept credit cards from either your own Merchant Account or through the Bizhosting service. Although the site's monthly charges are low – upwards of about £10 – it has higher transaction charges.

LEGAL ISSUES

Before trading on-line, you will need to check the Terms of Service associated with your Web host, since you are obliged to comply with local laws regarding employee and stock conditions. For example, copyright laws need to be considered if your trade is in music or books.

There are consumer groups concerned about how e-commerce companies use information about visitors and shoppers, and legislation to protect the rights of customers may follow. If you are in any doubt, seek legal advice on the Web. The E-commerce Law Source (**www.e-commercelawsource.com**) is a good starting point.

Watch Out!
Consult your bank manager or financial adviser before creating a business site. Find out how much you can afford to invest and whether there are other conditions involved.

HOW TO: REGISTER FOR A FREEMERCHANT STORE

Use the process shown here to register with FreeMerchant. You can then start building a simple on-line shop. However, it is worth remembering that you may not be able to accept orders on-line with some trial services. And if you upgrade to a membership package you may need to make arrangements for accepting credit card transactions.

All the services mentioned on this page have similar procedures and you could experiment with the free trial services of all of them before making a final choice about whether one of them is suitable to host your business.

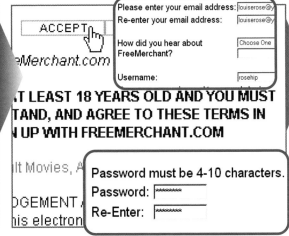

1 Go to the FreeMerchant Web site (**www.freemerchant.com**). Click on **30 Day Free Trial**, then on the next screen, click next to **30-Day Free Trial** and click **next**.

2 At the next screen read the terms of service, click **ACCEPT**, then fill in your e-mail address and username. Click **Continue**. Enter and re-enter a password, then click **Next**.

Be prepared
In the e-commerce world computer problems are also business problems, and need to be solved fast. Make sure that you know where you are going to get help before you need it – whether it is concerning Web design, hosting or performance. Have a fall-back position ready for each of your service providers in case things break down irretrievably.

Money Saver!
Don't forget that many of the extras offered by hosting firms will come at a price. Check the potential total cost for all your requirements in advance and allow for different volumes of transactions to see which host offers the best deal for your business.

Company Name:	silver daisy
Address:	229 Old Marylebone Road
(line 2):	
City:	London
State:	Please Select a State
Province/Region (only required for non-US):	London
Zip/Postal Code:	NW1 4AE
Country:	United Kingdom
Phone:	0207 251 6634
Fax:	0207 251 6635
Number of Employees:	11-50
Annual Revenue:	$10,000,001 - $1
Industry:	Publishing

Next

☑ **Total Merchant Services**
Free Merchant Account Set Up!
To accept credit card and check orders through your website
This can be a lengthy, expensive task. TMS makes it easy a
your website today!

☐ **TeamOn**
E-mail and Online Office - It's free to get started!
Enhance your existing e-mail to create an online office for yo
mail, documents, contacts and calendars anytime, anywher

☑ **Office.com**
Whether you're about to launch a business or take it to the r
for a free newsletter from Office.com!

☑ **WishList**
WishList gift registry service for your sto

Next

FreeMerchant.

Please verify the

PowerTools
We have found some of the
advantage of these extra too
detailed information of how d
☐ Yes, I want mo

Hosting Packag
30-day FREE tr
● **$99.95/year**

Bron
All th

Enroll!

3 Now enter your personal details, and the name of your business. Then click **Next** at the bottom of the page.

4 A variety of additional options will appear – which includes the choice of setting up the use of credit cards through your Web site. Tick your preference and click **Next**.

5 Finally, confirm that you are registering for the 30-day free trial – you will be charged $99.95 a year after the trial period, remove the tick from the PowerTools check-box, and click on **Enroll!**. You are now registered with FreeMerchant.

Using different currencies
If you are paying over the Internet by credit or debit card, it does not matter what currency the product has been priced in. Your bank will simply debit the equivalent amount of sterling from your account. Equally, if you are selling an item, you can advertise it in any currency – the appropriate amount of sterling will be credited to your account once the transaction is complete.

Time Saver!
Create all your graphics and text before you build a shopping site and store them in a desktop folder. If you have a range of items, divide them into categories and submit one group at a time.

HOW TO: DESIGN YOUR BUSINESS PAGES

You can design your page using the main menu of FreeMerchant or a similar company. Creating your shop is a straightforward process. You will need to specify the category of the items you wish to sell, and then describe them in slightly more depth. In this example, 'still life art work' is the category of items to be sold on the site.

You can also add text, colours and graphics, such as digital photos, to ready-made templates.

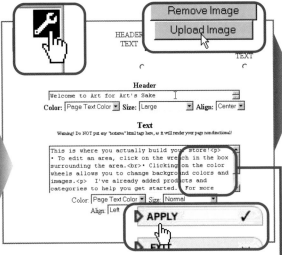

1 Click on the **Store Builder** icon. A layout appears with a toolbar and panels. Each panel has a spanner icon, which you click on to edit that section. The template has an upper panel to introduce the site and lower panels for products or services.

2 Click the spanner in the top panel to edit the introduction. Type your headings and text into the boxes or paste it in from a document you created off-line. To add your own graphic, click on **Upload Image,** fill in the path and file name, Click **APPLY**.

3 You can change the look of the page by clicking on the **Change Template** icon on the main toolbar and then selecting a new template from the options.

POINTS TO REMEMBER

- Make sure you clearly describe the items or services you intend to sell
- Keep the page design as simple as possible
- Give contact details that will make it convenient for customers to reach you
- Add images only if they help to make your site easier for people to use

HTML tags
As you enter your text, FreeMerchant will automatically add in these text markers for its own benefit. Don't worry – they won't appear on your site.

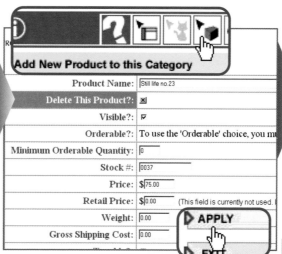

Category Name:	Still Life Art Work
Delete This Category?	☒
Has Subcategories?	○
Has Products?	◉
	Note: Categories may have subcategories OR products, but not both
Products Orderable?:	To use the 'Orderable' choice, you must enable the shopping cart feature
Visible?	☑
Description:	Unique and limited edition photgraphic and digital artwork. Prices from $75
Image:	Upload Image / Remove Image
	Current Image:

APPLY

EXIT

Add New Product to this Category

Product Name:	Still life no.23
Delete This Product?:	☒
Visible?:	☑
Orderable?:	To use the 'Orderable' choice, you m
Minimum Orderable Quantity:	0
Stock #:	0037
Price:	$ 75.00
Retail Price:	$ 0.00 (This field is currently not used.
Weight:	0.00
Gross Shipping Cost:	0.00

APPLY

EXIT

Example Product 2

a product.   To edit this product, click
wrench and you can set price,
 options, weight, and other options.
    $ 2.00

Still lif
$ 7.

Limited art

a phone or mail order by calling 0207 549 6678 or write to 129
London NW1 5AE

Publish Store

4 To add a category (i.e. a product type) in the lower panels, click on the spanner. Fill 'Category Name' and 'Description', upload an image to illustrate and click **APPLY**.

5 Now click on the new category. You can add products within your category by clicking on the **Add New Product** option on the toolbar. Now fill in a form describing your specific product. Click **APPLY**.

6 Add as many products as you need. Then click in the space provided at the bottom of your page and add your contact details. When your shop is ready, click the **Publish Store** icon at the top of the screen to save the pages.

Viewing your shop

Now that you have finished creating your business pages, you can view them on-line by typing in the URL you entered when registering with FreeMerchant (see page 302).

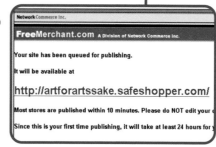

Network Commerce Inc.

FreeMerchant.com A Division of Network Commerce Inc.

Your site has been queued for publishing.

It will be available at

http://artforartssake.safeshopper.com/

Most stores are published within 10 minutes. Please do NOT edit your

Since this is your first time publishing, it will take at least 24 hours for

SEE ALSO
● **Find legal advice** – page 116
● **Become a share trader** – page 198
● **Link to more pages** – page 270

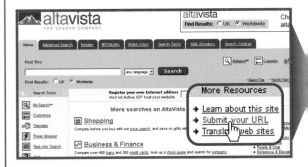

1 Go to AltaVista (**www.altavista.com**). Scroll down towards the bottom of the page and click on **Submit your URL** within the 'More Resources' section, then **Add Your Web Site to AltaVista**.

Ensure your site is seen

Get your **site noticed** by **registering** with a **search engine**

When you register your site with a search engine, you are effectively alerting the search engine to the existence of your Web page and its contents. Then, if someone uses the search engine to look for the type of content you offer, your site will be one of the ones listed among the search results. Most search engines do not charge you to register with them. Registration is straightforward – but, due to the volume of sites on the Web, it can take a month before the search engine catalogues your site so that it will appear in searches.

Jargon Buster!
URL stands for Uniform
Resource Locator – it is the
technical name for a Web address.

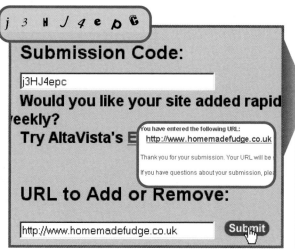

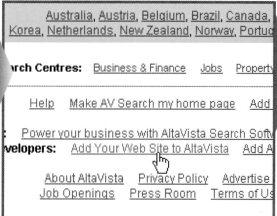

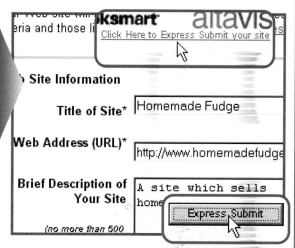

2 You will be given a unique submission code. Type this into the box, enter your Web site address, then click **Submit**. Your address will be confirmed and your site will be registered with AltaVista.

3 AltaVista also provides a directory service, though this requires a one-time payment of about £150. To get your site listed, return to the AltaVista homepage and click on **Add Your Web Site to AltaVista**.

4 Click on **Click Here to Express Submit your site**. After reading and accepting the charges and conditions, click **Express Submit**. Finally, complete the on-line registration and your payment details – you can pay by either cheque or credit card.

MULTI-REGISTRATION WEB SITES

Many Web-based and software application services specialise in automating the submission of sites to search engines.

Ineedhits.com (**www.ineedhits.com**) will submit your site to over 25 search engines, including Google and Lycos, free of charge.

Microsoft's Submit-it service (**www.submit-it.com**) provides a subscription-based service which registers your site with hundreds of search engines from a single form and includes tools to check that your keywords are the best ones to use.

HOW TO: MAKE SURE YOUR SITE GETS LISTED

Once you have registered with a search engine, you can take steps to ensure your site appears higher than other sites on the list of results when someone enters a relevant search term.

To do this, you need to add a brief description and a list of keywords to your site. These words will be invisible to someone viewing your site, but can be read by the search engine. However, you can only do this by manipulating the HTML code underlying your page. This may turn out to be the only HTML work you ever do, or it may whet your appetite to try some more. But it is worth doing so that your Web site gets seen by people who are interested in your subject area.

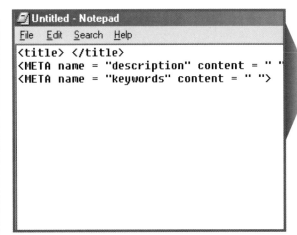

```
Untitled - Notepad
File  Edit  Search  Help
<title> </title>
<META name = "description" content = " "
<META name = "keywords" content = " ">
```

```
Untitled - Notepad
File  Edit  Search  Help
<title>Homemade Fudge</title>
<META name = "description" content = " "
<META name = "keywords" content = " ">
```

1 First open your Notepad program. Go to the **Start** menu and select **Programs**, then **Accessories** and **Notepad**. Type in the text shown above. The items enclosed in < > are known as tags. They are the building blocks of HTML (see below).

2 Now type the name of your Web site between the two **<title>** tags. For example, type: **<title>**Homemade Fudge**</title>**. Make sure that the title clearly describes what your site offers.

HOW HTML WORKS

All HTML instructions are enclosed within markers called 'tags'. There are many types of tag, each referring to different areas of the page. Most tags come in pairs and are positioned before and after the text or item that they are referring to. For example, the first title tag would look like this: <title> and the second like this: </title>. The forward slash indicates that it is the second of the tags.

Problem Solver!
In order to come up with every keyword someone might use to locate your site, go to **www. thesaurus.com** *and get a list of every variant on each word you use.*

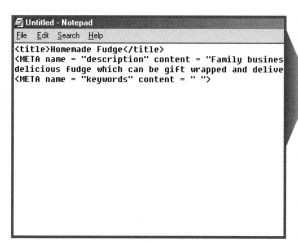

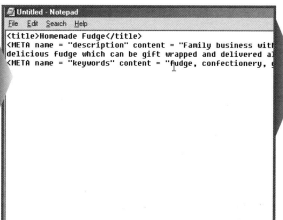

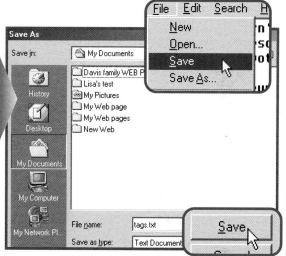

3 Then, between the inverted commas of the first <META> tag, enter a description of your site. This text summarises the content of your site and appears beneath your site name in the search result list, so use this text to attract visitors to your site.

4 Between the inverted commas of the second <META> tag, enter a list of keywords associated with your Web site. Separate each by a comma. Try to anticipate what keywords someone might put into a search engine and type them in.

5 Now go to the **File** menu, and click on **Save**. Save the Notepad file as 'tags.txt'. You are now ready to insert these tags within the rest of the HTML that makes up your Web page.

Choosing keywords

The main keywords should directly reflect your site content. If you sell home-made chocolates, your list would start with 'chocolates' and perhaps be followed by 'fudge', 'truffles', 'milk', 'dark', 'white', 'confectionery', 'sweets' and so on.

Do not repeat words. Include different tenses and plurals such as 'chocolate, chocolates' to cover all the combinations people might search for.

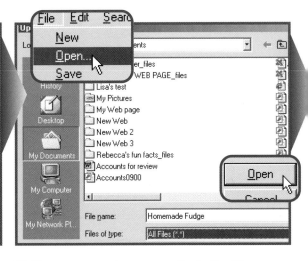

iMac
*The equivalent of Notepad on an iMac is SimpleText. To open this, double-click on your **Hard Drive** icon, then **Applications** and finally **SimpleText**.*

HOW TO: ADD THE TAGS TO YOUR HTML PAGE

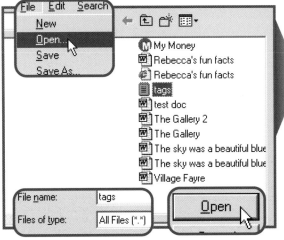

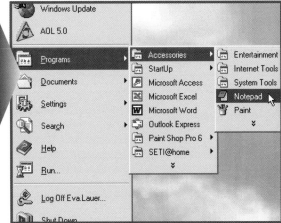

1 Open your tags.txt file in Notepad by going to the **File** menu and selecting **Open**. Choose **All Files** from the 'Files of type' drop-down menu, locate your file and then open it.

2 Next, open a second Notepad Window. To do this, go to the **Start** menu, select **Programs**, then **Accessories** and finally **Notepad**.

3 Now open your homepage. Go to the **File** menu and then **Open**. Choose **All Files** and select your homepage. Click **Open**.

Publicise your site

Search engines are only one way to publicise your site. Getting a link to your site from a popular site – for example, a birthday present site such as Hard2Buy4 (**www.hard2buy4.co.uk**) – is one good method, or a well-placed off-line promotion can attract visitors too. E-mail your preferred site and ask them if they will create a link to your site, and whether there will be a fee.

Did You Know?
*If you want to find out more about HTML and how it works, there is an excellent site on the subject called WEBalley (**www.weballey.net**).*

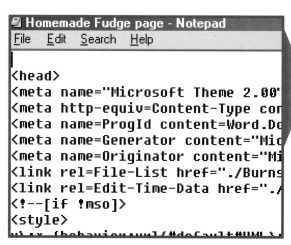

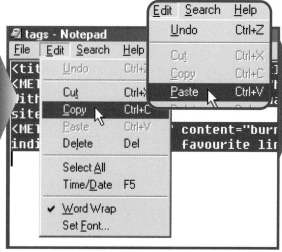

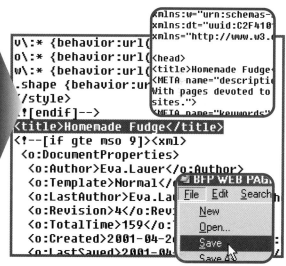

4 Scroll down to the tag that marks the beginning of the 'head' section (it will look like: **<head>**). Click after the tag and press the **Return** key to add a blank line beneath it.

5 Then, switch back to your tags.txt document and copy all the text. Return to your homepage document and paste the text into the blank space under the **<head>** tag.

6 Word will already have inserted a 'title' tag, which you now need to delete. Scroll down the document until you see **<title>...</title>**. Delete the tags and anything between them. Then save your Web page, ready to upload it to the Web.

SEE ALSO
• **Build a Web page in Word** – *page 256*
• **Upload your site** – *page 262*
• **Add a video to your page** – *page 282*

Web Directory

All the Web sites mentioned in the book are listed with an accompanying page number so that you can refer to them for additional detail. Remember that Web site addresses change frequently and without warning.

A
Advertising
Classifieds
Autotrader
(www.autotrader.co.uk) 181

Classifieds
(http://classifieds.yahoo.com)
Find jobs, flats, cars, even true love – all over the world.

Loot
(www.loot.com)
Thousands of privately placed small ads for flights, antiques etc.

Recycler.com
(www.recycler.com)
100,000 new ads every week, in useful categories such as home improvement.

Personal
100hot.com
(www.100hot.com/chat) 170

Anywho
(www.anywho.com) 170

Cupidnet
(www.cupidnet.com) 170

Dateline
(www.dateline.co.uk) 170

Excite Personals
(http://personals.excite.com) 170

Forum One Communications
(www.forumone.com) 170

Scoot
(www1.scoot2.co.uk) 170

SingleSites
(www.singlesites.com) 170

WorldPages.com
(www.worldpages.com) 171

Yahoo!Clubs
(http://clubs.yahoo.com) 170

Yahoo! Personals
(http://personals.yahoo.com)
Find a soulmate by location, interest or relationship type.

Art
Architecture
Great Buildings Online
(www.greatbuildings.com) 145

Westminster Abbey
(www.westminsterabbey.org)
Conduct your own virtual tour of this magnificent building.

Artists
Art Advocate
(www.artadvocate.com)
Gallery of new art for sale.

Artist Show
(www.artist-show.com)
Add your own site to this huge list of art links.

Artshow.com
(www.artshow.com)
Artists' portfolios, and resources for artists in many media including tuition and workshops.

Arts and crafts
Adobe
(www.adobe.com) 172

The Art Connection Inc.
(www.artconnection.net) 172

Contemporary Art Online
(www.contemporaryartonline.com) 173

About.com Arts and Crafts Business
(http://artsandcrafts.about.com/hobbies/artsandcrafts)
How to start up a craft business.

ADAM
(http://adam.ac.uk)
A catalogue of Web sites and mailing lists for students of fine art, design and architecture.

ArtNet.com
(www.artnet.com)
Estimate the value of an artwork by comparing it to similar auctioned works.

Candlemaking.org.uk
(www.candlemaking.org.uk)
Waxing lyrical on candles of every shape and size.

Craft Site Directory
(www.craftsitedirectory.com)
Get a helping hand with your beadwork, quilting or even gourd art.

Porcelain Painters International
(www.porcelainpainters.com)
Two free on-line lessons introduce you to porcelain or china painting.

Rittners School of Floral Design
(www.tiac.net/users/stevrt)
Wildly enthusiastic about floral design with scores of possible arrangements.

SoapTeacher
(www.soapteacher.com)
How to make soap that looks and smells like a slice of apple pie.

Fine art
Art History Search
(www.arthistorysearch.com) 172

Artserve – The Australian National University
(http://rubens.anu.edu.au) 173

The Mother of all Art History Links
(www.umich.edu/~hartspc/histart/mother) 173

The Getty Provenance Index
(http://piedi.getty.edu)
Multiple databases of books and CD-ROMs for tracing the past ownership of works of art.

Galleries
Art Gallery Online
(www.art-gallery-online.org) 173

The Louvre
(www.louvre.fr) 146

Museum of Modern Art
(www.moma.org) 146

The Getty
(www.getty.edu)
View the museum's huge collection of costumes, photographs and sculptures.

National Gallery
(www.nationalgallery.org.uk)
Guide to the collection and news of current exhibitions.

Royal Academy of Arts
(www.royalacademy.org.uk)
Find out about the popular Summer Exhibition in which talented newcomers can get their work viewed and sold.

Tate Gallery
(www.tate.org.uk)
Explore the four UK Tate galleries, with 50,000 images from the collection, from Turner to Tracey Emin.

Van Gogh Museum
(www.vangoghmuseum.nl)
Includes a virtual tour and Van Gogh's life and times.

B

Bizarre

Books

MISSION BRIEFING   AGENT ZONE

E
Education

Ask Dr. Math
(http://mathforum.com/dr.
math)
*Browse the maths questions and
answers or ask Dr. Math a
question of your own.*

Microsoft Encarta
(http://encarta.msn.com)
*Integrated learning resource
offering help, advice and an
extensive reference source for
students, teachers and parents.*

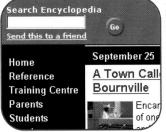

21stNetwork.com
(www.21stnetwork.com)
*Offers courses on using various
software with demos to try
before you buy.*

4Courses.com
(http://4 courses.4anything.
com)
*Advice on how to study as well
as what.*

Academy of Web Specialists
(www.academyofweb
specialists.com)
*Make your site stand out from
the crowd with the help of this
on-line course.*

Globewide Network Academy
(www.gnacademy.org)
*List of more than 17,000 courses
from all over the world.*

**The International Distance
Learning Course Finder**
(www.dlcoursefinder.com)
*Information on more than
50,000 distance learning courses
in over 100 different countries.*

A-levels.co.uk
(www.a-levels.co.uk)
*Surf your way to A-level success
with this large collection of
useful links.*

AngliaCampus
(www.angliacampus.com)
*Subscription service for teachers
and pupils, offering support for
all National Curriculum subjects.*

DiscoverySchool.com
(http://school.discovery.com)
*US site offering homework help
for students and advice, and
related features for teachers
and parents.*

Heriot-Watt University
(www.hw.ac.uk)
*Particularly strong on technical
and engineering subjects.*

National Union of Students
(www.nus.org.uk)
*Keeping students informed with
advice, entertainment, jobs,
news and discount offers, both
nationally and locally.*

Food and Drink

The Good Beer Guide

Fancy a decent pint? It l pubs and breweries are bewildering speed that valued friend to take you guarantee good beer in surroundings. That's wh Beer Guide with its unri dating back more than 2 no paid inspectors and for entries. It's research the Campaign for Real A pubs and breweries on once-a-year spot check

Mental

Mind
(www.mind.org.uk)
The Web site for the UK's largest mental health charity, with details of their local groups and factsheets on government policy.

The Mental Health Foundation
(www.mhf.org.uk)
Useful information on where to get help and news of the latest research developments.

UK Mental Health
(www.uk-mentalhealth. co.uk)
Friendly site with useful advice on what it means to be 'sectioned' and what to expect from a mental health institution.

Pharmacies

Allcures.com
(www.allcures.com)
NHS or private prescriptions can be ordered and delivered free of charge within the UK.

Pharmacies2u
(www.pharmacies2u.co.uk)
On-line chemist offering prescription drugs, and health and beauty products.

Support groups

AltaVista
(www.altavista.com) 123
Lycos
(www.lycos.co.uk) 125

Samaritans
(www.samaritans.org.uk)
Provides a background to the work of the Samaritans and suggests ways to get in touch.

History
Ancient

American Expedition to Petra
(http://todacosa.com/ petra/aep.htm) 231

About.com's Ancient/Classical History page
(http://ancienthistory.about. com)
Articles and links relating to the ancient world and classical figureheads, such as Homer and Alexander the Great.

Celtic Art and Cultures
(www.unc.edu/courses/ art111/celtic)
Illustrated introduction to the design and origin of Celtic art and artefacts.

De Imperatoribus Romani
(www.roman-emperors.org)
Biographies of every Roman emperor, with historical contexts, an atlas and Roman history links.

Exploring Ancient World Cultures
(http://eawc.evansville.edu)
Richly woven account of eight ancient cultures and literary traditions.

General

History Today
(www.historytoday.com)
On-line edition of the leading history magazine, with extra news stories and features.

BBC Online History
(www.bbc.co.uk/history)
Visit London Bridge in the 1500s or find yourself in a WW1 trench, via detailed 3D models.

Medieval and Renaissance

The Crusades
(http://crusades.boisestate. edu/contents.html)
The stories of each of the seven Crusades retold and placed in context.

Life in a Medieval Castle
(www.castlewales.com/life. html)
Page describing daily life inside a medieval castle.

Palladio's Italian Villas
(www.boglewood.com/ palladio)
Analysis of the work of architect Andrea Palladio, with illustrations and biography.

The Vikings
(http://viking.no/e/)
Introduction to the Viking world with ideas for school projects.

Modern

AP 20th Century Timeline
(http://wire.ap.org/APpack ages/20thcentury/timeline. html)
Stories from every year of the 20th century, in the words and pictures of the Associated Press.

BBC Online World War II
(www.bbc.co.uk/history/war/ wwtwo)
Discover the stories behind key moments of the Second World War through news clips and personal accounts.

Internet Modern History Sourcebook
(www.fordham.edu/halsall/ mod/modsbook.html)
From the discovery of America through to today's Pop Culture. Aimed at US college students and teachers.

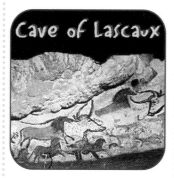

Pre-history

The Cave of Lascaux
(www.culture.fr/culture/ arcnat/lascaux/fr)
Virtual tour of the famous palaeolithic rock paintings of Lascaux in France.

Neanderthals: A Cyber Perspective
(http://sapphire.indstate.edu/ ~ramanank)
Could Neanderthals converse and are their art objects the earliest ever made? Plenty of questions raised and discussed.

Stone Pages
(www.stonepages.com)
A guide to European megaliths, including British sites, Stonehenge and Avebury.

UK

The Domesday Book
(www.domesdaybook.co.uk)
Check to see if your home town had an entry in the Domesday Book, and find out what life was like in the 11th century.

Britannia History page
(http://britannia.com/history)
Articles on every aspect of English history, from the myths of King Arthur to the study of Sussex churches.

The Victorian Web
(www.victorianweb.com)
So much of Victorian science, technology and art had a far-reaching effect on British society - find out what, why and how.

World

Any day in history
(www.anydayinhistory.com)
Enter a day and month to see who was born or died on that day in history and what major events happened that day.

HistoryWiz
(www.historywiz.com)
Photographs and images tell of significant moments in history, from ancient civilisations to current affairs.

History World
(www.historyworld.net)
Choose an era and a topic to explore (such as religion in the 19th century) to see a timeline of relevant events.

Home and garden
Design and furnishing

BathWeb
(www.bathweb.com) 184

BBC Online Homes page
(www.bbc.co.uk/homes) 185

Google
(www.google.com) 184

Home Arts
(www.homearts.com) 184

Homebase
(www.homebase.co.uk) 184

**The Kitchen Specialists
Association**
(www.ksa.co.uk) 184

Quote Checkers
(www.quotecheckers.
co.uk) 183

Habitat
(www.habitat.net)
Browse the catalogue and
design your personal look by
experimenting with colour-
matched products.

Ikea
(www.ikea.com)
Room-by-room design guide
and shop. Unlike the store, you
don't have to trawl the whole
site to find a particular item.

Interior Internet
(www.interiorinternet.com)
Stylish furniture site. Move each
of your chosen items to a mood
board to see the overall effect.

DIY

Fred's Shed
(www.fredshed.co.uk) 184

Homebase
(www.homebase.co.uk) 184

This to That
(www.thistothat.com) 183

Build It UK
(www.buildituk.com)
Instructions for most common
DIY tasks, plus a free on-line
quote for jobs where you need
a contractor.

DIY Fix It
(www.diyfixit.co.uk)
Browse under room type or
click on a task such as plumbing
or wallpapering for a step-by-
step guide.

Do It Yourself.com
(www.doityourself.com)
American site covering home
improvements, building,
appliance repair and car
maintenance.

The Natural Handyman
(www.naturalhandy
man.com)
Select a home repair project
from the menu to get instant
expert advice.

Gardening

British Trees
(www.british-trees.com) 157

Crocus
(www.crocus.co.uk) 185

Garden UK
(www.garden-uk.org.uk/
reference.htm) 184

Greenfingers.com
(www.greenfingers.com) 184

grogro.com
(www.grogro.com) 184

HomeCentral.com
(www.sierrahome.com) 184

The Postcode Plants Database
(www.nhm.ac.uk/science/
projects/fff) 184

BBC Gardener's World
(www.gardenersworld.
beeb.com)
Learn how to create a perfect
garden, through landscaping
and picking the right plants.

BHG.com
(www.bhg.com)
On-line edition of Better Homes
and Gardens magazine. Includes
how to renovate and decorate
your windows.

Garden Composer
(www.gardencomposer.com)
Design software that lets you
'walk through' your virtual
garden and view it at different
times of year.

Gardening in the UK
(www.uk.gardenweb.com/
forums/ukgard)
Join the discussion on subjects
such as which sort of compost is
the best.

Kids Gardening
(www.kidsgardening.com)
Inspire children to learn about
gardening through planning
and designing their own garden.

Natural Gardens
(www.natural-gardens.
zetnet.co.uk)
Information on the principles of
natural gardening, for example,
encouraging wildlife.

Plants for a Future
(www.scs.leeds.ac.uk/pfaf)
Directory of 7000 'useful' plants
– all edible or with medicinal or
other uses.

RHS Plant Finder
(www.rhs.org.uk/rhsplant
finder/plantfinder.asp)
Enter a plant's name into the
Royal Horticultural Society's
Plant Finder to learn about its
growing requirements and find
a local supplier.

The Telegarden
(http://telegarden.aec.at)
A 'tele-robotic installation' that
allows Web users to remotely
view, water and monitor a
living garden.

House buying

Charcol Online
(www.charcolonline.
co.uk) 205

FTyourmoney
(www.ftyourmoney.com) 205

Good Homes
(www.goodhomes.
beeb.com) 185

Moneynet
(www.moneynet.co.uk) 205

Up My Street
(www.upmystreet.com) 205

Yahoo!
(www.yahoo.co.uk) 205

Your Mortgage
(www.yourmortgage.
co.uk) 205

Alliance and Leicester
(www.alliance-leicester.co.uk)
Calculate the cost of your
mortgage and apply for it.
Click **Moving and Improving**
for useful ideas and advice.

International Real Estate Digest
(www.ired.com)
If you're planning to buy a
house abroad, consult this
international house buying and
finance directory.

Winkworth
(www.winkworth.co.uk)
London-based estate agent with
plans, photographs and 360-
degree virtual tours of many of
the properties for sale.

Humour
Cartoons

Doonesbury Electronic Townhall
(www.doonesbury.com)
Today's strip, an archive going
back 30 years and complete
character biographies.

Looney Tunes
(http://looneytunes.warner
bros.co.uk)
Official site, with new cartoons,
games, history and advice on
how to draw the characters.

South Park Studios
(www.southpark
studios.com)
Find out why Kenny always
dies and help Cartman defeat
Evil Cartman.

Comedians and shows

Harry Enfield
(www.powerage.demon.
co.uk/enfield/home.htm)
One fan's guide to the Harry
Enfield and Chums scripts, with
a breakdown of the sketches
and complete character listings.

Jongleurs

(www.jongleurs.com)

Details of shows at Jongleurs comedy clubs around the UK, plus sound clips and a handy joke archive.

MontyPython.net

(www.montypython.net)

Huge Python archive, with more than 1000 sound files and 500 complete scripts.

Petercook.net

(www.petercook.net)

Tribute to the life and comedy of the infamous Peter Cook, including articles by Clive Anderson, Jonathan Miller and Ian Hislop.

Jokes

Comedy Zone

(www.comedy-zone.net)

Jokes, quotes, trivia, TV comedy and links.

Funny.co.uk

(www.funny.co.uk)

Comedy portal with directory, links and listings of comedy performances in the UK.

Humor Database

(www.humordatabase.com)

Vote for the funniest joke or cheer up a friend with a comedy card.

Joke Post

(www.jokepost.com)

Post your favourite jokes, select

a funny screensaver or browse the silly pictures.

Satire

The Onion

(www.theonion.com)

Hilarious and satirical take on the latest news stories.

Private Eye

(www.private-eye.co.uk)

Laugh at jokes and cartoons from the current issue.

I
Internet
Advice

CNET's Help.com

(www.help.com)

Find help with selecting the right ISP or finding on-line Internet courses.

How Stuff Works

(www.howstuffworks.com)

Find out how absolutely everything works at this site – car engines, mobile phones, the Internet and more.

The Internet Help Desk

(http://w3.one.net/~alward)

Internet troubleshooting, with links to help pages on all topics.

The Internet Society

(www.isoc.org/internet)

A guide to the Internet from the people who should know – the industry's movers and shakers.

Chatrooms and communication

Audio-tips

(www.audio-tips.com) 91

BTinternet

(www.btinternet.com) 93

Chatter's Jargon Dictionary

(www.stevegrossman.com/jargpge.htm#Jargon) 101

CNN

(www.cnn.com) 96

The Core Rules of Netiquette

(www.albion.com/netiquette/corerules) 101

Deja News

(www.dejanews.com) 92

The Directory

(www.thedirectory.org) 96

Download.com

(www.download.com) 96

Eyeball

(www.eyeball.com) 91

Google

(www.google.com) 92

Infoseek

(www.infoseek.com) 92

Internet Relay Chat (IRC)

(www.irchelp.org) 169

Jumbo

(www.jumbo.com) 93

Microsoft NetMeeting

(www.microsoft.com/windows/netmeeting) 91

mIRC Web site

(www.mirc.com) 100

PalTalk

(www.paltalk.com) 91

PhoneFree

(www.phonefree.com) 91

Topica

(www.topica.com) 93, 170

Yahoo!

(www.yahoo.com) 97

Yahoo! Chat

(http://chat.yahoo.com) 99

ZDNet

(www.zdnet.com) 95

MedChat

(http://community.medchat.com/commun_v3/scripts/directory.pl)

Message boards and chatrooms on health issues, such as

women's health, psychiatry and dental care.

NewzBot

(www.newzbot.com)

Database of free public access newsgroup servers worldwide.

Connection

ADSL Guide

(www.adslguide.org.uk) 85

BT Openworld

(www.btopenworld.com/broadband) 85

Nokia

(www.nokia.com/phones/9210/index.html)

Find out about the Nokia Communicator which is compatible with Windows software and has a keyboard for sending e-mails.

Internet Service Providers

AOL

(www.aol.com) 16

CompuServe

(www.compuserve.co.uk) 16

Demon

(www.demon.net) 16

Hotmail

(www.hotmail.com) 17

Internet Magazine Resource

(www.Internet-magazine.com/resource/isp) 17

ISP Review

(www.ispreview.com) 17

The List

(http://thelist.internet.com) 17

Net4Nowt

(www.net4nowt.com) 17

Netscape

(www.netscape.com) 16

Tiscali

(www.tiscali.co.uk) 16

X-Stream

(www.x-stream.co.uk) 16

News

InternetNews.com

(www.internetnews.com)

The latest technology and Internet business stories, updated daily.

News.com

(http://news.com)

Tech news portal from CNET, covering personal computing and hi-tech business information.

The Standard

(www.thestandard.com)

On-line edition of the leading Internet business weekly, not to be confused with London's evening newspaper.

VNUNet.com

(www.vnunet.com)

All the latest computer products and developments reviewed from a UK perspective.

Search Engines

AltaVista UK

(http://uk.altavista.com) 61

AOL

(http://search.aol.com) 62

Ask Jeeves

(www.ask.com) 62

Ask Jeeves Kids

(www.ajkids.com) 67

Babelfish

(http://babelfish.altavista.com) 77

Diggit

(www.diggit.com) 68

Web Searching Tips
Learn how to search better and how the major search engines work from a searcher's perspective. Also see how people search and other fun stuff.

Search Engine Listings
Find all the major search engines; popular meta search engines; MP3 search engines; kid-safe services and much more.

Searching tips and help on registering your site with all of the major search engines.

Enter your search term to use five search engines or directories at once.

Enter your preferences and the site will monitor the Internet and alert you whenever a new reference is made to your topic of interest.

Security

Free encrypted anonymous e-mail service.

Web design

Web Pages That Suck
Learn Good Design by Looking at Bad Design

About.com's Web Design page
(www.webdesign.about.
com)
*Advice on designing,
maintaining and tracking your
Web site, with a Getting Started
page and a Site of the Week.*

GIF Animator
(www.ulead.com/ga/
runme.htm)
*Downloadable software for
creating animations.*

MyComputer.com
(www.mycomputer.com)
*Company that monitors site
traffic to help you to judge the
success of your Web site.*

PageResource.com
(www.pageresource.com)
*Tutorials, graphics, tools and
articles on creating your own
Web pages.*

2Cool Animations
(www.gifanimations.com)
*20,000 animations, ClipArt and
backgrounds.*

Webmonkey
(www.webmonkey.com)
*Web design help at all levels,
with tutorials on HTML, Flash
and more.*

Web design – business
Bigstep.com
(www.bigstep.com)   301

Bizhosting.com
(www.bizhosting.com)   301
Boo.com
(www.boo.com)   299
FreeMerchant.com
(www.freemerchant.com) 301
InternetMall.com
(www.internetmall.com) 301
NewBusiness Magazine
(www.newbusiness.
co.uk)   300

Web hosting
The Directory
(www.thedirectory.org) 111
FortuneCity
(www.fortunecity.com) 289

Internetters
(www.internetters.co.uk)
*Offer a range of Web hosting
packages and the chance to
register a unique Web address.*

The Web Site Hosting Company
(www.websitehost.co.uk)
*Web hosting and site design.
There's a free UK Web address
with every site.*

L
Leisure
Betting
AltaVista
(www.altavista.com)   159
Ananova Sport
(www.ananova.com/
sport)   159
Casino On Net
(www.casino-on-net.com)159
Flutter
(www.flutter.com)   159
Gamblers Anonymous
(www.gamblers
anonymous.org.uk)   158
The Gambler's Edge
(www.thegamblers
edge.com)   158

Ladbrokes.com
(www.ladbrokes.com)   160
Sportsbook
(www.sportsbook.com)   158
VIP Casino
(www.vipcasino.com)   158
William Hill
(www.willhill.com)   159

All Sports Casino
(www.allsportscasino.com)
*Bet on your favourite sport, and
try yourt hand on a variety of
on-line casino games.*

The Big Book
(www.thebigbook.com)
*Have a flutter on all major
sports and on special events
such as the Oscars.*

Bingo.com
(www.bingo.com)
*On-line bingo, poker and arcade
games, with prizes. Chat to the
other competitors as you play.*

Gambling.net
(www.gambling.net)
*Dozens of sports and casino
games to bet on, plus news, links
and gambling tips.*

Collectibles
Auction Watch
(www.auctionwatch.com) 165
Celebrity Merchandise
(www.celebrity
merch.com)   165

Collectiques
(www.collectiques.co.uk)
*Directory of Web sites for
collectors of every persuasion.*

Starsigned
(www.starsigned.com)
*Locate and buy the autographs
of famous actors, politicians,
musicians and models.*

Genealogy
The Commonwealth War
Graves Commission
(www.cwgc.org)   162
Cyndi's List
(www.cyndilist.com)   162
Family Origins
(www.genealogy.com)   161
Family Search Web site
(www.familysearch.org) 163
FamilyTreeMaker.com
(www.familytreemaker.
genealogy.com)   161
The Genealogical Software
Report Card
(www.mumford.ab.ca/
reportcard)   161
Generations
(http://shop.sierra.com) 161
GENUKI
(www.genuki.org.uk)   162
Louis Kessler's Genealogical
Program Links
(www.lkessler.com/
gplinks.shtml)   162
The Society of Genealogists
(www.sog.org.uk)   161

A Gilkison Family Tree
(http://w3.one.net/
~gilkison/genealogy)
*A good example of how far
personal family research can go.*

Genealogy.com
(http://genforum.
genealogy.com)
*Site with surname search and
tutorials on how to get started.*

Genealogy Online
(www.genealogy.org)
*One of the oldest genealogy
sites on the Web, packed with
tips and worldwide links.*

Genealogy Online's chatroom
(http://chat.genealogy.org)
*Chat to other family researchers
for tried and tested tips.*

PeopleSite
(www.peoplesite.com)
*Use the message boards to
make contact with other people
researching your surname.*

Museums
MuseumNetwork.com
(www.museum
network.com)   173

Museum of Modern Art
(www.moma.org)   146
Museums Around the World
(www.icom.org/vimp/
world.html)   173

24 Hour Museum
(www.24hourmuseum.
org.uk)
*Charity dedicated to increase
visitor numbers at UK museums,
galleries and heritage centres,
and to direct surfers to their
Web sites.*

MuseumNet
(www.museums.co.uk)
*Search for information on
hundreds of UK museums.*

MuseumStuff
(www.museumstuff.com)
*Thousands of links for museums
around the world, plus a 'virtual
exhibit' section featuring on-line
interactive exhibits.*

M
Motoring

Auctions

Classic Motor Auction
**(www.classicmotor
auction.com)**
*One of the few UK car auction
sites that allows you to bid
on-line. Includes some specialist
lots such as Mary Pickford's
1926 Rolls-Royce Phantom 1.*

Automobiles

The AA
(www.theaa.com)
*Buying advice, on-line valuations
and insurance quotes, traffic
news and a route planner
covering the whole of Europe.*

Auto Express
(www.autoexpress.co.uk)
*On-line edition of the UK car
magazine, with road tests and
accessory reviews.*

BBC Top Gear Shopping Guide
(www.topgear.beeb.com)
*Prices and estimated running
costs for hundreds of new and
used cars.*

BumpStop
(www.BumpStop.com)
*Lively site for lowriders, custom
cars and classic trucks.*

New Reg
(www.newreg.co.uk)
*Search the database of over
11 million 'old' registration
numbers, such as JON 321, and
make a purchase on-line.*

Vanishing Point Car
**(www.vanishingpoint
car.com)**
*Enthusiasts' homepage about
the 1970 Dodge Challenger, as*

featured in the cult car chase
film Vanishing Point.

Yahoo! Automotive page
**(http://dir.yahoo.com/
recreation/automotive)**
*A good place to start for car
enthusiasts or anyone looking
for parts and maintenance tips.*

Brands

BMW
(www.bmw.co.uk)
*Compare models, select and
configure your ideal car, locate
a dealer and book a test drive.*

Citroen
(www.citroen.co.uk)
*Information on current models,
options, local dealers, insurance
and special offers, plus a used
car search.*

Lamborghini
(www.lamborghini.com)
*Dream on … get close to the
Lamborghini driving experience
with these stylish graphics and
exciting sounds.*

Mini.co.uk
(www.mini.co.uk)
*Good graphics, games and lots
of photographs and
information about the new-
generation Minis and their
classic forebears.*

Volvo
(www.volvocars.volvo.co.uk)
*Packed with performance and
safety information. Includes a
Selected Used Cars locator.*

Buying and selling

Fish 4 Cars
(www.fish4cars.co.uk)
*Search for a new or used car or
register to be notified by e-mail
when a suitable ad is placed on
the site.*

Classic

Classic Car Directory
**(www.classic-car-
directory.com)**
*UK directory of parts, services
and dealers, with classified ads
and a classic car price guide.*

Classic Cars
(www.1inamillion.com)
*American site with classic US
and foreign cars for sale. If
you're not in the US, you can
still look – and drool.*

Scions of Lucas
(www.team.net/sol)
*Entertaining site devoted to
classic British cars. Parts,
maintenance and clubs.*

Importing

Broadspeed.com
(www.broadspeed.com)
*Compare European imports by
make, model or price.*

Oneswoop
(www.oneswoop.com)
*Buy new and imported cars
on-line, and find out about
specialist finance packages.*

Eurekar.com
(www.eurekar.com)
*European imports delivered to
your door.*

Maintenance

About.com's Auto Repair
(http://autorepair.about.com)
*Think you could be a professional
mechanic? Enter the quiz and
see if you can pass the test.*

Ehow.com
(www.ehow.com)
*Under 'Automotive' there are
guides to all the essential tasks
of car care.*

MOT UK
(www.motuk.co.uk)
*Make sure your car passes first
time. Technical guide to the
MOT, including the Tester's
Manual and a directory of
test centres.*

Under the Hood
**(http://library.thinkquest.
org/19199)**
Troubleshooting diagnosis tool,

repair guides and lessons in the
basics of motor mechanics.

Motorcycles

BikeWeb
(www.bikeweb.com)
*Motorcycle portal with
discussion boards on topics such
as new bike designs.*

Metal Horse
(www.metalhorse.co.uk)
*Hire a Harley Davidson by the
day from this Sevenoaks-based
company and cruise the mean
streets of south-east England.*

Old Bike Mart
(www.oldbikemart.co.uk)
*The place to buy and sell
vintage bikes and parts on-line.*

ScooterStop
(www.scooterstop.co.uk)
*All the advice you need to buy
into the scooter lifestyle or get
your Lambretta Vega back on
the road.*

Triumph Motorcycles
(www.triumph.co.uk)
*Details of every model, a dealer
directory, maintenance advice,
accessories and clothing.*

Clothing   Dealers

MUSIC

Blues

The Blues Archive

(www.bluesarchive.com) 24

Big Road Blues

(www.bigroadblues.com)

Blues portal with Internet radio links and slide guitar lessons.

Blue Flame Café

(www.blueflamecafe.com)

Interactive biographical encyclopedia of the greats of blues, with sound clips.

Classical

Andante

(www.andante.com)

Record company site and portal. News, profiles, concert calendar, reference section and exclusive Web-casts.

Classical Music UK

(www.classicalmusic.co.uk)

Site for classical musicians as well as fans. You can find out about job vacancies and buy scores on-line.

OrchestraNet

(www.orchestranet.co.uk)

Gateway to orchestras, with Webcasts, scores, CDs and MP3s.

Country

Country.com

(www.country.com)

Recording and concert news, artist profiles, Internet radio, MP3s and video files.

Country Western Song Generator

(www.outofservice.com/country)

Computer-generated country- and-western song lyrics. Opening

lines include *"I met her at a truck stop wrestlin' gators"*

IFCO

(www.ifco.org)

Web site of the International Fan Club Organization. Has links to over 300 country artists.

Netradio.com's Country page

(www.netradio.com/learn/country)

Introduction to country music, with a historical outline and links to biographical information and sound files.

Downloads

Excite

(www.excite.com) 277

Partners in Rhyme

(www.partnersinrhyme.com) 277

Real.com

(www.real.com) 115

Sounddogs.com

(www.sounddogs.com) 277

Sound Effects

(www.stonewashed.net/sfx.html) 277

Ultimate Sound & Music Archive

(www.ultimatesoundarchive.com) 277

Folk

Folderol

(www.piper-kj.demon.co.uk)

English, Irish, Scottish and Welsh folk music recordings, performers and national events.

Folk & Acoustic Music Exchange

(www.acousticmusic.com/fame/famehome.htm)

Reviews of new releases in contemporary and traditional folk, Celtic and bluegrass.

Troubadours

(http://geocities.com/frabaxter)

Guide to British folk-rock musicians such as Richard Thompson, Sandy Denny and Nick Drake.

Jazz

A Passion for Jazz

(www.apassion4jazz.net)

History and commentary, MIDI files, music theory and the Virtual Piano Chord tutor for budding musicians.

Jazze.com

(www.jazze.com)

New releases, artist profiles, a jazz jukebox and a global jazz performance calendar.

What is Jazz?

(http://town.hall.org/Archives/radio/Kennedy/Taylor)

Listen to a lecture on the history and development of jazz, with links by artist and genre.

WNUR-FM JazzWeb

(www.wnur.org/jazz)

US radio station site offering 24-hour Webcast, information on jazz artists and styles and a jazz links page.

MP3

Epitonic.com

(www.epitonic.com)

Free MP3 source, specialising in cutting-edge rock, electronica, hip-hop, experimental and contemporary.

MP3.com

(http://mp3.com)

Thousands of MP3s. Musicians can register to submit their own songs to the site.

News

All Music Guide

(www.allmusicguide.com) 202

Global Electronic Music Market

(http://gemm.com) 202

Musicfans.com

(www.musicfans.com) 165

Online Price Guide

(www.onlinepriceguide.co.uk) 202

Popstazz.co.uk

(www.popstazz.co.uk/fanclubs.htm) 165

Q magazine

(www.q4music.com) 171

Billboard

(www.billboard-online.com)

On-line edition of the record industry's trade magazine. Test your trivia knowledge with the interactive music crossword each day.

Dotmusic

(www.dotmusic.co.uk)

Catch up on the latest music gossip and buy CDs on-line.

MTV

(www.mtv.com)

Concert Webcasts and exclusive music videos from the people who made the pop video as important as the song.

Sonicnet

(www.sonicnet.com)

Browse by artist or genre for biographies and links, and register to receive e-mail news of your favourite artists.

Pop

AndPop.com

(www.andpop.com)

US portal for Top 40 news and artists, with photo galleries and video interviews.

BBC Eurovision Song Contest page

(www.bbc.co.uk/eurovision)

More than you ever wanted to know about Eurovision. Includes trivia and classic clips.

HISTORY
From Bucks Fizz to [Boyle, get some fac impress your friend from our Eurovision history file.

BBC Top of the Pops

(www.bbc.co.uk/totp)

Look up an artist, album or track in the Encyclopaedia Poptastica for an instant pop gratification.

The Girl Groups Fan Club

(http://members.tripod.com/~ggfc)

Site devoted to pop and soul girl groups from the 60s and 70s.

Netradio.com's Pop page

(www.netradio.com/learn/pop/index.html)

History of pop music from the 50s to today, with links to other sites on 60s soul or electronica.

Rock

Elvis.com

(www.elvis.com)

Sadly, no word of the King's whereabouts but you can take a virtual tour of Gracelands at this official site.

The adult l[...]
Africa, are [...]
The lions in [...]
16:00. The [...]
chickens - [...]

livecam   sc[...]

The Daily Telegraph
(www.telegraph.co.uk)
Find the latest news and articles under useful category headings.

Falkirk Herald
(www.falkirkherald.co.uk)
Falkirk's local newspaper is on-line for the world to see.

The Independent
(www.independent.co.uk)
On-line edition of the UK daily broadsheet with lots of extras.

M2
(www.m2.com)
An electronic newsletter service sent straight to your inbox.

Moreover
(www.moreover.com)
Brings you news headlines from hundreds of sources such as the BBC, New York Times and Middle East Newsline.

NewsNow.co.uk
(www.newsnow.co.uk)
News updates every five minutes for headline addicts.

Newsweek
(www.newsweek.com)
Breaking news and informative in-depth analysis.

Reuters
(www.reuters.com)
The news agency that all the other media rely on.

UK Environment
(www.ukenvironment.org)
The latest environmental news stories, updated daily.

Washington Post
(www.washingtonpost.com)
The renowned US broadsheet, good on politics and world news.

World Health News
(www.worldhealthnews. harvard.edu)
Focusing mainly on American health news with plenty of opinions and articles.

Tickers

MyYahoo! Ticker
(http://my.yahoo.com/ ticker.html) 113

AOL.co.uk
(http://aol.co.uk/aim)
Stay on top of UK stories and monitor your stocks and shares.

BBC Online
(www.bbc.co.uk/inform)
Easy to install and customise to display headlines in the news categories of your choice.

infogate
(www.entrypoint.com)
Get the headlines from a variety of industries at this US-based news source.

WorldFlash
(www.scroller.com)
Colourful news ticker that can display headlines relating to the topics of your choice.

World

CNN Europe
(http://europe.cnn.com) 113

Sydney Morning Herald
(www.smh.com.au) 114

Drudge Report
(www.drudgereport.com)
A world-shattering scandal may be about to break – read about it first here.

Foreignwire.com
(www.foreignwire.com)
An intelligent and different angle on world current affairs.

Institute for war and peace reporting
(www.iwpr.net)
Unbiased analysis of wars across the globe.

World News
(www.worldnews.com)
News directory with international stories and a range of tickers, including environment and education updates.

R
Reference
Children's

Ask Jeeves Kids
(www.ajkids.com) 67

HERO
(www.hero.ac.uk) 137

Kids AOL NetFind
(www.aol.co.uk/ channels/kids/netfind) 67

KidsClick
(http://sunsite.berkeley. edu/kidsclick) 67

Learn.co.uk
(www.learn.co.uk) 137

Monster
(www.monster.co.uk) 136

S-Cool!
(www.s-cool.co.uk) 139

Yahooligans!
(www.yahooligans.com) 67

Fact Monster
(www.factmonster.com)
Dictionary, encyclopedia, atlas and almanac – plus fun facts on every subject.

Dictionaries and grammar

The Blue Book of Grammar and Punctuation
(www.grammar book.com) 137

Chatter's Jargon Dictionary
(www.stevegrossman. com/jargpge.htm#Jargon) 101

GrammarNow
(www.grammar now.com) 137

The Grove Dictionary of Art
(www.groveart.com) 173

Merriam-Webster OnLine
(www.m-w.com) 71

The Chicago Manual of Style FAQ
(www.press.uchicago.edu/ Misc/Chicago/cmosfaq.html)
The editors of a leading style manual answer your questions about grammar.

Dictionary.com
(www.dictionary.com)
Dictionary and language site, including foreign language dictionaries and word games.

Lang to Lang
(www.langtolang.com)
Multi-lingual dictionary translating between any combination of English, Turkish, French, Spanish, German, Russian and Italian.

YourDictionary.com
(www.yourdictionary.com)
Dictionary and thesaurus, plus links for learning a language.

Encyclopedias

ArtCyclopedia
(www.artcyclopedia. com) 173

Britannica.com
(www.britannica.com)
Enter a subject to see related entries, magazine articles and Web links.

The Encyclopedia Mythica
(www.pantheon.org/ mythica.html)
Documenting myths of cultures around the world from the Australian Aborigines to the ancient Egyptians.

Heroes

Refdesk.com
(www.refdesk.com)
Search out facts from medical and law dictionaries.

Wikipedia
(www.wikipedia.com)
Help build this encyclopedia by writing entries of your own or editing other people's.

Xrefer
(http://w1.xrefer.com)
Look up 50 reference books at once, including the Oxford Dictionary of Medicines and the Penguin Dictionary of Women.

Maps

Mapmaker
(www.mapmaker.co.uk) 70

Ordnance Survey
(www.ordnance survey.co.uk) 227

Getmapping.com
(www2.getmapping.com/ index.asp)
Aerial photos of every square foot of Britain. Type in your

postcode or address to see your own house.

Mapquest
(www.mapquest.com)
Find road maps of anywhere in the world.

National Geographic Map Machine
(http://plasma.nationalgeogr aphic.com/mapmachine/)
Political, historical, physical and other maps all available to download and print out at a range of scales.

Russian Subway, Railway and Tram Maps
(http://parovoz.com/maps/ind ex-e.html)
Fascinating tips on navigating your way around Russia.

Miscellaneous

British Government
(www.open.gov.uk) 109

The Newspaper Society
(www.newspaper soc.org) 109

Royal Mail
(www.royalmail.com) 69

United States Postal Service
(www.usps.gov/ncsc) 69

Biography.com
(www.biography.com)
25,000 biographies of people past and present, from Napoleon to Mary Tyler Moore.

Teldir.com
(www.teldir.com)
Links to phone books covering the entire world. You can also find someone's address if you know their number.

People-finders

100hot.com
(www.100hot.com/chat) 170

Anywho
(www.anywho.com) 170

The Commonwealth War Graves Commission site
(www.cwgc.org) 162

Cupidnet
(www.cupidnet.com) 170

Cyndi's List
(www.cyndilist.com) 162

Dateline
(www.dateline.co.uk) 170

Excite Personals
(http://personals. excite.com) 170

Family Origins
(www.genealogy.com) 161

FamilyTreeMaker.com
(www.familytreemaker. genealogy.com) 161

Forum One Communications
(www.forumone.com) 170

Friends Reunited
(www.friendsreunited. co.uk) 170

The Genealogical Software Report Card
(www.mumford.ab.ca/ reportcard) 161

Genealogy Software Springboard
(www.gensoftsb.com) 162

Generations
(www.sierra.com) 161

GENUKI
(www.genuki.org.uk) 162

Louis Kessler's Genealogical Program Links
(www.lkessler.com/gp links.shtml) 162

SingleSites
(www.singlesites.com) 170

The Society of Genealogists
(www.sog.org.uk) 161

Yahoo! Clubs
(http://clubs.yahoo.com) 170

WorldPages.com
(www.worldpages.com) 171

IPCH
(www.ipch.com)
This site provides links to a variety of ways to meet people through the Internet, such as chatrooms or profile sites.

Kiss.com
(www.kiss.com)
Use the Romance Wizard to help you find your ideal mate.

Thesauruses

Merriam-Webster OnLine
(www.m-w.com) 71

Thesaurus.com
(www.thesaurus.com) 137

The Phrase Finder
(www.shu.ac.uk/web- admin/phrases/)
Enter a word to find related phrases and sayings – handy for generating ideas for headlines, song lyrics or advertising copy.

S
Science
Discovery

AltaVista
(www.altavista.com) 143

Apollo Project Archive
(www.apolloarchive.com) 142

British National Space Centre
(www.bnsc.gov.uk) 142

Detailed Chronology of Events Surrounding the Apollo 13 Accident
(www.hq.nasa.gov/office/ pao/History/Timeline/ apollo13chron.html) 144

European Space Agency
(www.esa.int) 142

National Aeronautics & Space Administration
(www.nasa.gov) 142/143

Russian Space Agency
(http://liftoff.msfc.nasa. gov/rsa/rsa.html) 143

SETI@home
(http://setiathome.ssl. berkeley.edu) 144

SETI Institute
(www.seti-inst.edu) 143

Spaceflight Now
(www.spaceflight now.com) 143

SpaceKids
(www.spacekids.com) 143

Astronaut Connection
(www.nauts.com)
Biographies of the world's astronauts, with a space exploration timeline and guide to space vehicles.

CERN (Conseil Européen pour le Récherche Nucleaire)
(http://public.web.cern. ch/Public)
Everything you ever wanted to know about anti-matter. The people at CERN just happen to have invented the World Wide Web too.

Space Exploration Merit Badge
(www.execpc.com/~culp/ space/space.html)
Win a merit badge by completing the range of on-line tasks.

News

Discovery Channel
(http://dsc.discovery.com/ cams/cams.html) 149

Discover
(www.discover.com)
Keep up to date with topical issues such as allergies or genetic research.

Institute of Biology
(www.iob.org)
News on recent advances in biological research.

New Scientist
(www.newscientist.co.uk)
Subscribe to this on-line magazine and gain access to a huge archive of scientific articles.

Popular Science
(www.popsci.com)
Follow the search for life on Mars and discover the world of virtual sport.

Scientists

Albert Einstein Online
(www.westegg.com/ einstein)
List of links to other Web sites with Einstein related material.

Darwin and Evolution Overview
(http://landow.stg.brown. edu/victorian/darwin/ darwinov.html)
Text-based site which avoids academic jargon.

Art deco pieces, c. 1927-

Shopping
Antiques

Auctions

Books

CDs and records

DVDs

purchase. You can also get the BlackStar team to track down deleted videos.

E-commerce

ZDNet E-Business
*(www.zdnet.com/
enterprise/e-business)* 296

**About.com's Electronic
Commerce page**
*(http://ecommerce.
about.com)*
*Directory of links and resources,
including the 'Beginner's Guide
to E-Commerce'.*

Florists

Interflora
(www.interflora.com) 211

Internet Flowers
*(www.internetflowers.
co.uk)* 221

Flowergram
(www.flowergram.co.uk)
*For every floral order a £1
donation is made to Macmillan
Cancer Relief.*

Flowers2send
(www.flowers2send.com)
*Bouquets for every budget –
from £10 to elaborate £50
floral creations.*

Teleflorist
(www.teleflorist.co.uk)
*Click an arrangement to send it –
same day, next day or abroad.*

Furniture and houseware

BathWeb
(www.bathweb.com) 184

Google
(www.google.com) 184

Homebase
(www.homebase.co.uk) 184

**The Kitchen Specialists
Association**
(www.ksa.co.uk) 184

BLUEdeco.com
(www.bluedeco.com)
Contemporary products for the

home, such as storage jars or
kitchen chairs.

Empire Direct
(www.empiredirect.co.uk)
*Save up to 40% on the High
Street cost of domestic
appliances, audio-visual
equipment and cameras.*

Furniture 123
(www.furniture123.co.uk)
*On-line furniture at discount
prices. If you can't decide on a
colour for your sofa, send off
for free fabric swatches.*

Liberty
*(www.liberty-of-london.
com/shopping)*
*Fabulous furniture and unusual
gifts from the famous store.*

MFI Homeworks
*(www.mfi.co.uk/mfihome
works)*
*Order furniture on-line, with
free delivery anywhere on the
UK mainland.*

General shopping sites

eBay
(www.ebay.co.uk)
*The world's biggest flea market.
Sell and buy items, from
computers to travel tickets.*

Excite Outlet Center
*(http://outletcenter.
excite.com)*
Name brands at discount prices.

Kelkoo
(www.kelkoo.co.uk)
*Compare prices from hundreds
of different on-line retailers
before you buy.*

Raven Dancer Gallery
*(www.ravendancer
gallery.com)*
*Purchase Native American art,
crafts and clothing on-line.*

Top of the Shops
(www.topoftheshops.co.uk)
*Shopping portal with access to
over 1000 UK stores.*

Gifts

Blue Mountain
*(www.bluemountain.
com)* 220

The Chocolate Lover's Page
*(http://chocolate.
scream.org)* 221

Hard2Buy4
(www.hard2buy4.co.uk) 310

London Zoo
*(www.zsl.org/london
zoo/adopt.html)* 219

Madopolis
(www.madopolis.com) 221

Sayitwith
(www.sayitwith.co.uk) 219

Star Registry
(www.starregistry.com) 219

Toys "R" Us
(www.toysrus.co.uk) 179

Allpresent.com
(www.allpresent.com)
*Send distinctive gifts to your
loved ones; chocolates, biscuits
or champagne.*

Out of the hat
(www.out-of-the-hat.co.uk)
*Generates gift ideas to help you
find something for the person
who has everything.*

Voucher Express
(www.voucherexpress.co.uk)
*Send gift vouchers to anyone in
the UK.*

Greetings

Cards4You
*(www.cards4you.co.uk/
ecards.html)* 219

CardStore
(www.cardstore.com) 221

Clinton Cards
*(www.clintoncards.
co.uk)* 219

Greetsomeone.com
*(www.greetsome
one.com)* 221

Posty City
(http://postycity.net) 221

American Greetings
*(www.American
greetings.com)*
*Check out the largest selection
of free greetings cards on the
World Wide Web.*

Egreetings
(www.egreetings.com)
*On-line cards in categories such
as weddings, kids and family or
movies and TV.*

Hallmark
(www.hallmark.com)
*Includes useful links to other
sites so you can send gifts with
your e-card.*

123 Greetings
*(www.123greetings.com/
general/getwell)*
*Great selection of free e-cards.
Particularly strong in the 'get
well' section.*

High street

Asda
(www.asda.co.uk) 192

Currys
(www.currys.co.uk) 249

Dixons
(www.dixons.co.uk) 249

Homebase
(www.homebase.co.uk) 184

PC World
(www.pcworld.co.uk) 249

Sainsbury's
(www.sainsburys.co.uk) 192

Tesco
(www.tesco.com) 192

Argos
(www.argos.co.uk)
*The full Argos catalogue range,
including everything from
breadmakers to ceiling lights.*

The Body Shop
(www.thebodyshop.co.uk)
*Health and well-being pages,
plus a virtual makeover, in
which you try out looks on a
model of your choice.*

Marks and Spencer
*(www.marksandspencer.
co.uk)*
*Knickers and socks, naturally,
but you can also apply for a
loan on-line.*

Next
(www.next.co.uk)
*Click a picture to see details and
prices and buy the item. You
can also order an old-fashioned
printed catalogue.*

Society
Charity

Government

Law

Gravitydex
(www.gravitydex.com)
Adventure sports portal with news, links to participants, retailers and manufacturers.

Trails.com
(www.trails.com)
Resources for planning, booking, and equipping your next adventure.

Boxing

Boxing.net
(www.boxing.net)
Boxing news headlines as they happen, 24 hours a day.

Boxing Records Archive
(www.boxrec.com)
A comprehensive record of more than 60,000 boxers and their bouts, updated daily by a dedicated group of enthusiasts from around the world.

SecondsOut.com
(www.secondsout.com)
Explanation of the Queensbury rules and a look at great fighters of the past.

Cricket

Cricket 4
(www.cricket4.com)
Guide to every Test match, plus a fascinating stats archive, which you can use to compare the records of players from every era.

England's Barmy Army.com
(http://englandcricketfans. rivals.net)
A riot of fun and nonsense about the die-hard fans who follow England.

The Official Home of English Cricket on the Internet
(www.ecb.co.uk)
News service to keep you up to date with the latest events.

Wisden
(www.wisden.com)
Well-written feature articles, oodles of stats and a busy bulletin board.

Cycling

Bikemagic
(www.bikemagic.com)
UK site encouraging mountain bikers to get the most out of their sport.

Bikezone
(www.bikezone.com)
Cycling equipment is reviewed, compared and rated in the 'GearZone'.

Cannondale
(www.cannondale.com)
News of the Volvo/Cannondale race team, tools to help you choose your ideal bike, plus clothing, accessories and links.

Marin
(www.marinbikes.com)
Technical support plus the chance to share experiences with other mountain bike enthusiasts.

Trek
(www.trekbikes.com)
Includes a bike finder section where you can find the exact model you want.

Fishing

AnglersNet
(www.anglersnet.co.uk)
Plenty of stories, hints and tips from professional anglers and pictures of fish to help you identify the one that got away.

Fish & Fly
(www.fishandfly.co.uk/ contents.html)
The art of fly fishing explained with advice on how to tie unusual lures such as the 'Hot Spot Epoxy Buster'.

Fishing.co.uk
(www.fishing.co.uk)
Competitions, e-shopping and news of the latest tournaments from around the UK.

Go-Fishing.co.uk
(www.go-fishing.co.uk)
Advice on your next fishing trip – from hiring a boat to booking a guest house.

Football

Arsenal World
(www.arsenal-world.net)
Send an Arsenal e-card to a fellow gooner, or search the archives for evidence of Lee Dixon's last goal.

Association of Football Statisticians
(www.the-afs.com)
Includes upcoming match previews and a gallery of football's memorable matches and stars.

Celticfc.net
(www.celticfc.co.uk)
Trade your memorabilia and visit the Glasgow club's hall of fame.

Chelsea
(www.chelseafc.com)
Follow the match day action live and have a rant with other fans at the same time.

ESPN.com
(http://espn.go.com/soccer)
Latest scores, statistics and schedules in Britain and Europe.

FA-Premier.com
(www.fa-premier.com)
Detailed look at action in the premier division.

FIFA.com
(www.fifa.com)
A look at the history and work of football's governing body.

Football 365
(www.football365.co.uk)
Knowledgeable writers take a witty and irreverent look at contentious football issues.

Fromtheterrace.co.uk
(www.fromtheterrace.co.uk)
Book reviews, a daily quiz, the chance to place bets and a weekly newsletter.

Kop Talk
(www.koptalk.co.uk)
Dedicated to Liverpool FC, this is one of the best unofficial fans' sites on the Web, with columns by greats such as Jan Molby and Tommy Smith.

Leeds United Football Club
(www.lufc.co.uk)
Bet on the team, watch the games and get all the behind-the-scenes info on the club.

MUFC
(www.m-u-f-c.co.uk)
Song lyrics, chat and banter from the Old Trafford terraces.

Rangers.co.uk
(www.rangers.co.uk)
Exclusive player interviews and pre-match build-up for the blue half of the Old Firm.

Scottish football.com
(www.scottishfootball.co.uk)
The latest news and fixtures in Scottish football, plus live match updates.

Soccer-fanzine.co.uk
(www.soccer-fanzine.co.uk)
A collection of on-line fanzines from clubs around the world.

Sunday Football League Directory
(www.sunday-football.co.uk)
Find yourself a Sunday League team to play for.

Teamtalk.com
(www.teamtalk.com)
Live football commentary.

UEFA.com
(www.uefa.com)
Join the legendary UEFA Champions League Fantasy Football game.

ZoomSoccer.com
(www.zoomsoccer.com)
All the European football gossip and news.

Golf

The Open golf championship
(www.opengolf.com) **146**

19thHole.com
(www.19thhole.com)
A light hearted look at the game of golf.

Golfcourses.org
(www.golfcourses.org)
Find a course anywhere in the UK and read reviews by fellow hackers and slicers.

Golf today
(www.golftoday.co.uk)
For both armchair golf fans and those looking for a course.

The Royal & Ancient Golf Club of St. Andrews
(www.randa.org)
Video clips, plus a discussion of how global warming might affect golf.

Horse racing

Ladbrokes.com
(www.ladbrokes.com) **160**

William Hill
(www.willhill.com) **159**

Racecourse holdings trust
(www.aintree.co.uk)
Delve into the history of The Grand National.

Race-horses.com
(www.race-horses.com)
A good starting point if you're thinking about buying a share in a racehorse.

Racing Chronicle
(www.racing-chronicle. co.uk)
Some of the best racing photography on the Web – plus attendant reports and results.

Racingpost.co.uk
(www.racingpost.co.uk)
Live commentary and the latest news from the racing world.

Martial arts

Black Belt
(www.blackbeltmag.com)
Self defence tips for the serious martial arts enthusiast.

Martialinfo.com
(www.martialinfo.com)
Covers all aspects of martial arts, from finding instructors to magazine subscriptions.

TaeKwon-Do
(www.itatkd.com)
Innovative use of animation and a large archive of step patterns and articles.

News

BBC Sport
(www.bbc.co.uk/sport) **239**
Fanzone
(www.fanzone.co.uk) **239**
Google
(www.google.com) **239**
Icons.com
(www.icons.com) **239**
Yahoo!
(www.yahoo.co.uk) **239**
TalkSport.net
(www.talksport.net)
Listen to the latest sports news on this Internet radio station.

Racquet sports

The Wimbledon Championships
(www.wimbledon.org) **240**

International Badminton Federation
(www.intbadfed.org)
Offers a regular badminton news bulletin by e-mail.

Tennis.com
(www.tennis.com)
Tennis tips and news from around the world.

World Squash
(www.squash.org)
Coaching tips and a friendly guide for beginners.

Rugby

Planet-Rugby
(www.planet-rugby.com)
An impressive line-up of lookalikes, competitions and downloadable screensavers.

The Rugby Football League
(www.rfl.uk.com)
Check out the hall of fame in this official rugby site.

Scrum.com
(www.scrum.com)
Argue the toss with fans from both hemispheres and read regular columns by stars such as Wallaby lock David Giffin.

Sports issues

Ananova Sport
(www.ananova. com/sport) **159**
League Lineup
(www.leaguelineup.com) **238**
Scottish Sports Council
(www.sportscotland. org.uk) **239**

Chat Sports
(www.chatsports.com)
Chat to people about your favourite sport.

Sports Coach UK
(www.sportscoachuk.org)
Find out how to become a coach in your chosen sport.

Sports Council for Northern Ireland
(www.sportni.org)
News, events, useful contacts and youth sport are covered.

Sports Council for Wales
(www.sports-council-wales.co.uk)
Promoting sports in Wales at a local level.

Sports Medicine
(http://sportsmedicine. about.com)
Excellent database on the subject of good health in sport.

Sportsmatch
(www.sportsmatch.co.uk)
A good starting point for information on sponsorship deals at grass-roots level.

Water sports

Scottish Canoe Association
(www.scot-canoe.org) **239**

Aquaskier.com
(www.aquaskier.com)
Photo contests, interviews with champions and information on courses around the country.

Boards Online
(www.boards.co.uk)
An interactive map gives details of windsurfing shops and schools all over the country.

Coldswell.com
(www.coldswell.com)
Site for surfers that includes a beach guide, weather information, a surf check and the chance to view waves around the world via Web-cams.

Excite Water Sports
(www.excite.com/sports/ water_sports)
Links to watersport sites, such as diving clubs.

National Water Sports Centre
(www.nationalwatersports. co.uk)
Site for the UK national watersports centre. There is a page of activities for children.

Overtons.com
(www.overtons.com)
Equipment site mainly for powerboat-related gear.

Sub-Aqua Association
(www.saa.org.uk)
Information on courses, conservation, archaeology – and links to other useful sites.

UK Diving
(www.ukdiving.co.uk/ ukdiving.htm)
Information and advice on every aspect of diving.

Winter sports

Boardtheworld
(www.boardtheworld.com)
A snowboarding site with equipment and resort reviews.

GoSki
(www.goski.com)
Read other skiers' accounts of resorts and package holidays to help you plan your trip.

Ski Central
(www.skicentral.com)
Links to hundreds of Web sites covering everything from snowboarding equipment to helicopter skiing trips.

Skidirectory.com
(www.skidirectory.com)
Find out the latest weather reports from resorts around the world, plus links to clothing, chat and competition sites.

Snowlink.com
(www.snowlink.com)
Filled with tips for beginners on how to ski, what equipment you need, the rules of the slopes and much more.

Yahoo!
(www.yahoo.com/ recreation/sports)
News, articles, weather reports and links to other sites.

T
Television
Broadcasters

BBC
(www.bbc.co.uk) 149
BBC1
(www.bbc1.co.uk) 149
BBC2
(www.bbc2.co.uk) 149

Carlton
(www.carlton.co.uk)
In-depth coverage of all Carlton channels, plus current affairs and TV listings.

Channel4
(www.channel4.com)
Programme guide, and information on how to join the audience of a Channel 4 show.

> **Site Picks**
> News & Weather
> Get Involved
> Soap Fans Forum
> Channel5 Archives

Channel5
(www.channel5.co.uk)
Has a flashback section for trips down memory lane.

Food Network
(www.foodtv.com)
Includes a range of video teaching guides and recipes – great for any would-be chef.

ITV
(www.itv.co.uk)
Includes the opportunity to play 'Who Wants To Be A Millionaire' on-line.

Children's

Blue Peter
(www.bbc.co.uk/bluepeter)
Read about past and present presenters and watch video clips of the famous sticky-back plastic creations.

Disney Channel
(www.disneychannel.co.uk)
Games and the opportunity to explore different parts of a make-believe Disney studio.

Live & Kicking
(www.bbc.co.uk/kicking)
Worth visiting for the wallpapers and games alone.

SausageNet
(www.sausagenet.co.uk)
For fans of cult children's TV programmes. Background information, links to other dedicated sites and sound clips to download.

The Simpsons
(www.thesimpsons.com)
Find out Chief Wiggum's first name and learn about Moe's murky past as a child actor.

Classic

LikeTelevision
(www.liketelevision. com) 151
TV Cream
(http://TV.cream.org) 149
Yesterdayland
(www.yesterday land.com) 149

Starfleet
(www.sfi.org)
International Star Trek Fan Association site, with fan club and convention listings and contact information worldwide.

TV Guide Online
(www.tvguide.com)
TV listings and nostalgia with episode guides for classic shows such as M*A*S*H.

Listings

Ananova
(www.ananova.co.uk) 113
Radio Times
(www.radiotimes.co.uk) 149

EuroTV
(www.eurotv.com)
European TV schedules. Search by country or theme.

Gist TV LISTINGS
(www.gist.com)
American site with soap opera updates, juicy gossip and funny video clips.

UK TV Guide
(www.uk-tv-guide.com)
Every TV and radio programme listed for the days ahead.

Programmes

Discovery Channel
(http://dsc.discovery. com/cams/cams.html) 149
TVEyes
(www.tveyes.com) 149

Brookside
(www.brookie.com)
Get potted histories of all the characters and houses in this eventful suburban cul-de-sac.

Changing rooms
(www.bbc.co.uk/ changingrooms)
Everything from feng shui to Handy Andy's biography.

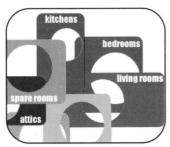

Coronation Street
(www.coronationstreet. co.uk/content.html)
News, articles, competitions, games and video highlights.

Voice an opinion on the message board or join a scheduled chat with one of the actors.

Dawson's Creek
(www.dawsonscreek.com)
A picture-led companion to the self-obsessed US soap.

EastEnders
(www.bbc.co.uk/eastenders)
Take a virtual tour of Walford and look up profiles of all the characters including those who have fallen foul to the scriptwriter's thirst for blood.

Epguides.com
(http://epguides.com)
Episode guides for over 1700 TV shows, ranging from The A-Team to Whose Line is it Anyway?

Jerry Springer
(www.jerryspringer.com)
More from the king of bad taste, plus tickets for the show.

Neighbours.com
(www.neighbours.com)
Behind-the-scenes features, cast photos and contact with the stars via e-mail.

Wish You Were Here
(www.wishyouwerehere. co.uk)
This site gives quick summaries of lots of locations you might want to visit.

Yahoo! TV
(http://TV.yahoo.com)
Catch up on your favourite soap and read interviews with actors.

Web-cams

EarthCam
(www.earthcam.com) 146

On-Line Photographic
SEAR

Cool Places

Health

Foreign and Commonwealth office Web site
(www.fco.gov.uk)   231

Healthy Flying
(www.flyana.com)
Information on everything from pressurised air to fear of flying.

MedicinePlanet
(www.medicineplanet.com)
Advice for travellers on health risks and good practice.

Travel Health Online
(www.tripprep.com)
Everything from altitude sickness to yellow fever.

TravelHealth
(www.travelhealth.com)
Includes a mobile phone medical network where you can get instant professional advice.

Holidays

African walking safaris
(www.zambezi.co.uk/
walking)   226

About.com's Archaeology page
(http://archaeology.
about.com)   231

Campsites in Europe
(www.interhike.com)   226

Cheapflights.com
(www.cheapflights.com) 229

Earthwatch Institute
(www.earthwatch.org)   231

ebookers.com
(www.ebookers.com)   230

Excite
(www.excite.co.uk)   229

Greyhound
(www.greyhound.com)   230

Lastminute.com
(www.lastminute.com)   229

Lycos.co.uk
(www.lycos.co.uk)   235

Thomas Cook
(www.thomascook.com) 228

Airtours
(www.airtours.co.uk)
Order free brochures to save you a trip to the travel agents.

Bargainholidays.com
(www.bargainholidays.com)
Search a database of over 75,000 holiday bargains.

British Airways
(www.british-airways.com)
Book on-line and check out special offers.

Buzz
(www.buzzaway.com)
Low cost airline with discounts for on-line booking.

Deckchair
(www.deckchair.com)
Comprehensive database of cheap flights.

Disneyland Paris
(www.disneylandparis.com)
Explore the magic of Disneyland with this easy-to-use site.

EasyJet.com
(www.easyjet.com)
All you need to book flights and rent cars on-line.

Expedia.co.uk
(www.expedia.co.uk)
Maps, packages, flight details, news, features and everything you need to plan a holiday.

Fodors.com
(www.fodors.com)
Information on world destinations with news, family, business and hotels sections.

Go
(www.go-fly.com)
Get discounted air travel if you book on-line.

GORP
(www.gorp.com)
Wide-ranging site full of ideas for outdoor recreation.

Kuoni Travel
(www.kuoni.co.uk)
Swiss longhaul tour operator with wedding and honeymoon destinations.

Let's Go
(www.letsgo.com)
Budget travel – especially good for students.

Lunn Poly
(www.lunn-poly.com)
Clearing shop for all the company's last minute deals.

Teletext Holidays
(www.teletext.co.uk/
holidays)
A easy way to browse through thousands of offers available only on-line.

Thomson
(www.thomson-holidays.
com)
Lavish holidays – from skiing breaks to cruises.

Travel Travel
(www.travel-travel.co.uk)
The database of holidays is updated every 20 minutes.

Travellers Web
(www.travellersweb.co.uk)
Build your own package holiday or choose from the special offers available.

Travelmag.co.uk
(www.travelmag.co.uk)
Search travel articles for information on your chosen holiday destination.

Yahoo! Travel
(http://travel.yahoo.com)
Great starting point for those planning a holiday. Links to specialist holiday companies, destination guides, luggage shops and much more.

Maps

Mapmaker
(www.mapmaker.co.uk)   70

Ordnance Survey
(www.ordnancesurvey.
co.uk)   227

Multimap
(www.multimap.com)
Street maps and aerial photos of cities in the UK.

Stanfords
(www.stanfords.co.uk)
Well-stocked travel bookstore, specialising in maps from all over the world.

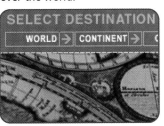

Streetmap.co.uk
(www.streetmap.co.uk)
Search by street, postcode or telephone codes for the location you need.

Terraserver.com
(www.terraserver.com)
Library of aerial shots of famous landmarks and streets all over the world.

travelling with an animal to the weather in foreign destinations.

Britannia.com
(http://britannia.com)
Specialised portal for Americans travelling to the UK. Includes virtual tours and city guides.

CenterParcs
(www.centerparcs.com)
Book a holiday on-line at CenterParcs around the world.

The RAC
(www.rac.co.uk)
Key in your departure and destination points and the RAC will find the fastest route.

W
Weather
Forecasts

BBC Weather
(www.bbc.co.uk/weather)
World-wide weather information, including regional 5 day forecasts, ski reports, travel destination reports and weather facts.

National Climatic Data Center
(www.ncdc.noaa.gov)
The world's largest archive of weather data. Pages on climate change, weather extremes and El Niño.

Weather.com
(www.weather.com)
Weather reports for all the American states.

World Climate
(www.worldclimate.com)
Search by city or town for details of weather around the world.

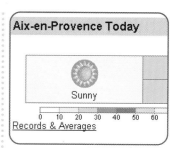

Yahoo! Weather
(http://weather.yahoo.com)
Five day forecasts and weather records for towns and cities around the world, plus features on weather phenomena.

YBW.com Weather
(www.ybw.com/weather)
Yachting & Boating World's weather and tides service. Look up the weather in numerous ports and marinas, plus complete UK inshore and shipping forecasts.

PLANET THREE PUBLISHING NETWORK

Edited, designed and produced by
Planet Three Publishing Network
Northburgh House, 10 Northburgh Street, London EC1V 0AT

EDITOR Jon Asbury • **DEPUTY EDITOR** Stephen Fall
SUB-EDITORS Louise Aikman Laurence Henderson Lewis Lyons
Amie McKee Laura Ward
ART DIRECTOR Paul Mitchell • **ART EDITOR** Harj Ghundale
DESIGNERS Nancy Dunkerley Heather Dunleavy Kate Painter
ILLUSTRATOR Nancy Dunkerley

FOR READER'S DIGEST
EDITOR Jonathan Bastable • **ART EDITOR** Julie Bennett
EDITORIAL ASSISTANTS Liz Edwards Rachel Weaver
PROOFREADER Barry Gage

READER'S DIGEST GENERAL BOOKS
EDITORIAL DIRECTOR Cortina Butler • **ART DIRECTOR** Nick Clark
EXECUTIVE EDITOR Julian Browne • **DEVELOPMENT EDITOR** Ruth Binney
PUBLISHING PROJECTS MANAGER Alastair Holmes • **STYLE EDITOR** Ron Pankhurst

CONTRIBUTORS
Paul Bradshaw • Stephen Dunthorne • Lewis Lyons • Lisa Magloff • Sandra Vogel • Kevin Wiltshire

CONSULTANT Barry Plows
INDEXER Laura Hicks

How to do *just about* ANYTHING ON THE **INTERNET**

was edited and designed by The Reader's Digest Association Limited, London.
First edition Copyright © 2002 The Reader's Digest Association Limited,
11 Westferry Circus, Canary Wharf, London E14 4HE.

We are committed to both the quality of our products and the service we provide
to our customers. We value your comments, so please feel free to contact us on 08705 113366,
or via our Web site at www.readersdigest.co.uk

If you have any comments about the content of our books, you can contact us at:
gbeditorial@readersdigest.co.uk

Copyright © 2002 Reader's Digest Association Far East Limited.
Philippines Copyright © 2002 Reader's Digest Association Far East Limited.

Origination: Colour Systems Limited, London

Printing and Binding: Brepols Graphic Industries, NV, Turnhout, Belgium

ISBN 0 276 42560 X
Book Code 400-066-01
Concept Code UK 1426/G